Consciousness

Studies in Phenomenology and Existential Philosophy

Consciousness

A PHENOMENOLOGICAL STUDY
OF BEING CONSCIOUS AND
BECOMING CONSCIOUS

Henri Ey

TRANSLATED FROM THE FRENCH BY JOHN H. FLODSTROM

INDIANA UNIVERSITY PRESS

Bloomington and London

Library of Congress Cataloging in Publication Data

Ey, Henri.
Consciousness.

(Studies in phenomenology and existential philosophy)
Translation of La conscience.
Bibliography.
Includes index.   1. Consciousness.   I. Title.
BF311.E913   1977   153   76-26429
ISBN 0-253-31408-9   1 2 3 4 5 82 81 80 79 78

Acknowledgments

I wish to express my appreciation to the following persons whose invaluable suggestions have made the completion of this translation possible.

Charles F. Breslin, Philosophy Department, University of Louisville, and William Hood, Oberlin College, have each read several chapters of this work and have given many hours of their time helping with some of the more difficult passages.

Allen J. Wutzdorff, Psychology Department, Alverno College, has worked with me on many of the psychological sections. He has been most generous with both his time and his knowledge.

In the chapter on the neurobiology of the field of consciousness, Dr. Robert L. Bornschein, Kettering Institute, University of Cincinnati, has provided innumerable answers and deciphered some technical passages which demanded an intensive and broad knowledge of this whole area. Dr. Kenneth H. Reid, Physiology and Biophysics Department, University of Louisville Medical School, has read major portions of this chapter and provided many useful suggestions.

William M. Schuyler, Jr., Philosophy Department, University of Louisville, has offered several very happy solutions to problems of long standing.

Very special thanks are due to Belinda Broughton, Jean Lawson, Kathryn Flodstrom, and Mildred Creager for their help in preparing the manuscript, especially in its final stages, and to John R. Walsh for redrawing several of the illustrations.

I cannot express my thanks strongly enough to all the above for their encouragement and help.

I also wish to thank the University of Louisville for granting me sabbatical leave to work on this translation.

JOHN H. FLODSTROM

CONTENTS

Part Four: The Unconscious

Part Five: Conscious Becoming

Consciousness

Henri Ey
1900–1977

Preface to the English Translation

After the publication of the third volume of my *Études*
(1954), which was devoted to the topic of the erosion of structure (*déstructuration*) of the field of consciousness in acute
psychoses, the Presses Universitaires de France commissioned
me to write a work on "Consciousness" for its collection "Le
Psychologue." This work has now been translated into German,
Spanish, and Japanese, and its second edition, much enlarged,
was published in 1968. It is the second edition which is today
offered to the English-speaking reader.

I am pleased that the translation of the work's title and its
subtitle captures the spirit of the work rather than being simply a literal translation of the original title. I have not, in fact,
written a book on "consciousness" considered as a substantive
(which betrays rather than expresses the process of becoming
conscious). What I have wished to set forth are the configurations of the order that the subject introduces into mental life by
commanding a personal model of his world. As far as I am
concerned, it is not a question of describing "consciousness" as
an object or a machine. Nor is consciousness to be described as
a function, for this would be the same thing as to deny it. Conscious being and becoming constitute the form, the legality, of
lived experience and of possible existence. This fact allows us
to understand to what metaphysical discussions concerning the
immanence or transcendence of the Ego and concerning subjective and objective knowledge this living dialectic of the system of values and reality proper to each person has given rise.
I am well aware of the contradiction by which Cartesian dualism has divided the act of consciousness by separating the body
from the mind which it unites. But I am also well aware that
in the "Anglo-Saxon" countries, in the tradition of thought
which derives from Hume's empiricism, from behaviorism

(even though it be molar, or oriented by motivation), from the Freudian psychodynamic conception of the Unconscious (though it be oriented in the sense of Ego-psychology), and from the cybernetic models of nervous activity (though they be more modulated or flexible), there has existed since William James a very strong tendency to deny "consciousness." In other words, a work of this sort that undertakes to describe the dynamic of conscious acts is in serious danger of running up against a systematic misreading of a "mental reality" which is rejected as being only an "epiphenomenon."

Nevertheless, I invite the reader to proceed in the very direction of a phenomenology of the real structures of conscious activity, to seize this reality that is itself constitutive of reality: the movement of conscious becoming insofar as it is a phenomenon of *emergence* within the open system of the ontological organization of the *psychical body.*

In order to shed some light on this exposition of the structures of conscious being and becoming, I should like to present several observations. The first concerns the definition and description of the different modes of conscious being, starting from a consideration of psychopathology. The second deals with the connection between conscious being and the integrating activity of the central nervous system. The third is a discussion of the reasons which make of the affirmation or denial of conscious being the stakes of the value system that is implicit in any anthropology.

1) It seemed to me that the most sure way to approach the problem of the definition of consciousness was to start from the evidence of the Unconscious. There is no doubt but that the common experience of sleep-dreaming directs us to the very reality of an unconscious life peopled with images. The phenomenon of sleep-dreaming is thus the paradigm of unconscious psychical life. Now, in the eyes of the clinical psychiatrist who knows how to break away from artificial nosographic barriers, psychopathology appears to be organized in relation to unconscious being and becoming. In the first place, all "crises," "acute psychoses," "twilight states," "confuso-oneiric states," etc., appear as levels of the structural disintegration of the field of consciousness (I include here those states which are called manic and depressive).[1] In the second place, the psychopathology of the field of experience is connected to the psychopathology of another mode of unconsciousness, un-

conscious being and becoming, insofar as these are the pathology of the person (*alienatio,* schizophrenic psychosis, chronic delirium, and neuroses) and are characterized at different levels by the unconsciousness of the unity and identity of the "Self." It is thus that, by way of psychopathology, conscious being (the reverse image of unconscious being) appears both as a *synchronistic* structure of the organization in the field of consciousness of presently lived experience and as a *diachronistic* structure of being someone (another reverse image of unconscious being). Such are, in a few words, the investigations I have pursued for the last forty years concerning the phenomenology of the psychopathological forms of existence that have allowed me to bring to light the very reality of the structures of conscious being and becoming. It seems evident to me that this "phenomenological reduction" of the essence, of the description, and of the classification of the various psychopathological modalities makes it possible to produce in the field of psychiatry the order which it lacks, which is not and cannot be other than the very order of the structures of conscious being. For it is not the Unconscious which is pathogenic, but the dissolution of conscious being which brings with it the psychopathological forms of experience and existence. This explains why I have given so much prestige to the fundamental intuition of Hughlings Jackson.

2) It is obvious to common sense, as it is to the most certain neuro-bio-psychological knowledge, that there is a relation between "consciousness" and the "brain." This, however, does not prevent certain thinkers from remaining closed off from this evidence, either by considering that "consciousness" does not exist (that it is a question of a superfluous concept or word) or by considering it to be a simple "function" (such as memory, intelligence, etc.). These negations of consciousness lead either to excluding it from the brain or to localizing it in one of its parts (the notion of "centers" of wakefulness). In both cases the problem of the relations between the brain and consciousness is distorted by the dualism that radically separates the brain and the mind or that juxtaposes in the cerebral space a function of consciousness as well as other functions having their seat in one or another part of the brain. The genial intuition of Hughlings Jackson, who conceived of the activity of the central nervous system as a hierarchical system that evolves in time, this conception, *on the condition* that it be disencumbered of

the dualist or parallelist principle of concomitance (to which the great English neurologist held strongly!), makes it possible to arrive at a model that is closer to contemporary conceptions of general systems theory. It is from this "neo-Jacksonian" perspective that I have undertaken in Chapter 3 of the second part of this work—and more recently in my book *Des Idées de Hughlings Jackson à un modèle organo-dynamique en Psychiatrie*[2]— to deal with the problem of the isomorphism of the central nervous system and conscious being. Of course it is not possible that there be a spatial identity between thought and the brain. But if the brain ceases to be considered as a simple mechanical apparatus, if its cyberneticostochastic model allows that it itself moves itself in and through its negentropic organization as if it were an "arrow of time," and if, all things considered, it appears to be what it effectively is, the very organ of freedom, then we truly cannot see in the name of what metaphysical principle the science of man would be prevented from understanding the relations of the brain and consciousness as being those of the very dialectic of the production of the model of the world, which is constructed at the same time as the existence proper to each person emerges and becomes organized. It is more appropriate to affirm the isomorphism of nervous activity and the very organization (synchronistic and diachronistic) of conscious being, but only on the express condition that we examine the movement and order of subordination that integrate *at each level* the means to the ends and assign its sense to their production.

In order further to clarify this viewpoint which seems to me to coincide with the very notions of *emergence* and of *autonomy* ("boundary conditions") in the general theory of open systems (K. E. Boulding, L. Von Bertalanffy, A. Koestler, K. Menninger, etc.) and of "self-organizing systems" (H. Von Foerster, M. C. Yovits, H. R. Maturana, etc.), it would have been necessary for me to have completed this work with a critical exposition of important works. The numerous works of the Soviet school especially come to mind (Ustnatze, Zourbachvilli, Wanschenk, Bassine, the 1960 Congress of the R.D.A., etc.). There is, in fact, no doubt that since the time of the important discussions on the relations between consciousness and the brain in the perspective of and with regard to the ideas of Jackson (F. M. Walshe, W. Riese, Lord R. Brain, Max Levin, and the Symposium of Sainte-Marguerite) there has been much progress on this fundamental idea.

I would also have liked to have laid open and to have turned to account the more recent notions concerning the problem of the relations between sleep and dreaming,[3] a problem whose terms have changed somewhat since the earlier works of Kleitman, Dement, and Jouvet which I have examined in this work. However, I do not believe that these new acquisitions have profoundly changed the basic sense of the problem which is of primary interest to psychiatrists: that of the relations of the negativity of sleep to the positivity of dreaming, with reference to the negative disorders of the formal structures of conscious being, and the positive sense of the symptoms which manifest them in mental illnesses in general. Such has been, in effect, the theme of my own reflections upon my theory of the generalized relativity of the relations of sleep-dreaming (disorders of consciousness and manifestation of the unconscious) in psychopathology.[4]

3) The fundamental idea that I defend in this work is this: to be conscious and to be unconscious are two complementary modes of the ontological structure of perhaps every living being, but certainly of every human being. One cannot, of course, imagine a human psychology or an anthropology that could reduce all psychical activity to consciousness. But it is also obvious that man cannot be reduced to his unconscious. Now, it is of this extrapolation from psychoanalytic doctrine (the hegemony of the Unconscious) that Freud himself—and to how much greater an extent his epigones—has made himself guilty. What most often and most profoundly characterizes the psychoanalytic conception of man (of his neuroses and his psychoses, as of his dreams) is that everything would happen as if the activity and the structures of conscious being were superfluous (if not pathogenic), as if behavior, ideas, feelings, and the relational system of man were entirely governed by the Unconscious and that we would be riveted to the "inferiora" of our primitive being.

It is in order to rise up against this ideology of the leveling, that is to say, of the annihilation, of values and of the system of reality that this book was written. How could we not find in the reader who is himself conscious of a system of values, of the seat of indeterminism represented by the individual consciousness, a certain echo of the veritable malaise of civilization? How could we not feel, in fact, the necessity to put a certain order back into the ontological organization of Man, of the Ego, by very naturally subordinating his Unconscious to the forms and legislation of the system of reality that assure his "self-organization," that is, his modes of being and becoming conscious? Could we continue, we psychiatrists, psychotherapists, anthropologists, or psychoanalysts, to consider the self to be a "poor thing" ("ein armes ding," said Freud) of "consciousness," as a petty porthole scarcely half-open onto the world? Perhaps by thus asking these essential questions this little book will be able to contribute to bringing it about that, for want of restoring order into the very constitution of man, into the organization of his psychical body,[5] the perception of the world in its reality and its values should not itself be overturned. Let us simply say that the order of consciousness and the forces of the instincts are complementary but that the sense of existence (like that of the awakening of the sleeping person) consists in subordinating the unconscious to the negentropic order, to the modes of conscious becoming.

Paris, December 1976   HENRY EY

Preface to the First Edition

The problem of consciousness is formidable. I have had the audacity to tackle this problem only because psychiatry has something to say, which it has not yet said, concerning conscious being, the disorders of which form the subject matter of its special field of knowledge.

In the course of my clinical work, the essence of which is contained in my *Études psychiatriques,*[1] I became aware that a very complete examination of this fundamental problem was needed. This is the object of the present work.

Having studied the structure of the field of consciousness during the process of its loss of structure (Volume III of my *Études,* 1954), and before undertaking the study of the structure, distortions, and alienation of personality, I found it necessary to distinguish between what had already been established and what I had still to bring to light. To be more precise: 1) What is the correlate of the duality of conscious being considered as both living the actuality of one's experience and being the person at the center of one's world; 2) Since *conscious being* is always a *conscious becoming,* what unity might conscious being possess which can be grounded upon the distinction of these two manners of existing. This work is an attempt to satisfy this dual exigency. Its goal is to insert a middle ground between the transcendence of the self and the brain: the possibility which the subject has to emerge from his body so as to "fall" into his history, forming at each moment the field of lived actuality.

There is, however, a third exigency which is no less urgent. This is the question of the *relationships between conscious being and the unconscious* as they are set down and, in a certain sense, become evident in psychopathology. If the range of psychiatry is the realm of the appearing of the unconscious in human existence, the psychiatrist then has good grounds for saying something concerning the order to which disorder refers him, for it is the psychiatrist's task to understand and to cure this disorder. The solution to this third question should thus help us to solve the problem raised by the first two. For in the last analysis it is through its unconscious reverse side that the being of consciousness receives as it were the proof of its strength and of its structure.

At least in its project, this is the dialectic of this little book. We would be obliged to ask the indulgence of philosophers for our work being too psychiatric and of psychiatrists for its being too philosophical, if its object, *conscious being,* did not imply, in its ontology and its functional problematic, both the sense of reason and its opposite madness.

H. E.

Preface to the Second Edition

CONSCIOUS BEING, PSYCHOANALYSIS, "STRUCTURALISM," AND NEUROBIOLOGY

The success of the first edition of this work and its excellent translations into German by Karl Peter Kisker (Berlin: Gruyter), Spanish by Dr. Garces (Madrid: Gredos), and Japanese (Misuzu Shobo, Tokyo) have given me some justification to enlarge this edition. I beg the reader's forgiveness for thereby increasing its difficulty. But the reader must himself be strict in the demands he places upon an author who asks his indulgence for having made so few concessions to facility when concerned with the most difficult of problems.

With his "revised and enlarged" edition, we feel even more strongly the need to revise the title of this work (which title conforms more to the demands of the collection in which it takes its modest place than to the sense which we intended to give it). This book is not concerned with the substantive *consciousness,* which implies a sort of mythical and fetishist hypostatization. We are instead interested in the development of psychical being which, by being and becoming conscious, gains possession of itself by *commanding* a personal model of its world.* For a human being, *to be conscious* is to cease *to be* unconscious, but it is also *to have* an Unconscious, to be a subject who can establish his autonomy only by conceding it to an unconscious *part* of himself. To be conscious as a human being, it is not enough that the subject have a body which he takes as his own special object. He must also have a psychical corpus which is just as much an "object" for him, an object in itself of which he, the subject, knows only the opaque objec-

---

*Ey uses the term *"disposer"* in a strong sense of free choice and liberty, in the sense that one has his property at his command.—Trans.

tivity without knowing its characteristics—which characteristics are, moreover, his own. This mysterious object which exists for the subject causes him to raise the question of his being. However, when another person interprets it, it ceases (or can cease) to be an object which is separate from the subject. It is reunited with his subjectivity. Since the time of Freud we have become well aware that the most usual way for the subject to become aware of that object which is his Unconscious in such a way that it can be admitted into his conscious being is by being refracted in the consciousness of another. In this manner the subject causes the unconscious object to appear by causing it to disappear as an object. In other words, conscious being is constituted only by containing an immanent object, the id, outside of the transcendental subject: this is the theme which is constantly being developed throughout this work, especially in its new and final sections. The whole organization of psychical life is nothing other than the living dialectic in which conscious being and its Unconscious are opposed to one another and reconciled. Nothing, then, is further from our conception of the structures and processes of conscious being than the idea of a consciousness considered as a state, a simple function or a pontifically sovereign system.

Since its first edition, the urgency of the theses enunciated in the dialectical exposition of this work has been heightened by the tumult of ideas[1] which in our time has brought conscious being to trial. This demand that an account be given threatens both consciousness and the Unconscious (which are consubstantially linked) with being jointly condemned to death.

When we read certain of the formalist interpretations of the Unconscious, we could wonder, once conscious being has been reduced to nothing, what might be the significance of an Unconscious without a person, of a system of meaningless signs for representing only an impersonal grouping of elements which are detached from the signified *par excellence:* the subject. For to speak of consciousness, of the Unconscious, or of the subject is to decline the modes of psychical being.

The reestablishment of conscious being might be challenged by certain fanatical advocates of the Unconscious as being a derisive, outdated, or harmless "anti-Freudian" enterprise. However, we see it instead as a *return to Freud's primary and fundamental thought,* which discovered the reality of the

Unconscious only by a thorough penetration, which is in effect a hallowing, of the reality of the structures of consciousness. By enveloping the Unconscious within the organization of psychical being, these structures free it from elementarist interpretations and make of it the object of a science of man. Not, however, a science of man considered simply in his culture and as viewed from outside, but a science which grasps man in his body, in and through precisely that which prescribes to the psychical organism its meaning, the limits of its possibilities, and the hierarchy of its forms.

Such is the general sense of this study of "consciousness" which culminates in the *Freudian* idea of a natural *subordination* of the sphere of the Unconscious to the structures of conscious being which inhibit or frame it. For it is obviously true that psychical being's organization can appear only in the hierarchical structure of what Freud called the "psychical apparatus." For this reason we have thought and stated that, far from opposing Freud's doctrines, the ontogenesis and the ontology of conscious being guarantee its validity and bring to it that complement which it lacks when mental being has been submerged by its Unconscious, causing the Unconscious to lose the autonomy which it derives from its repression.

Having shown that the vivifying return to the structures of conscious being is at the same time a return to the origins of that Unconscious to which they give rise in accordance with the first theory of repression, that is, a return to the foundations of Freud's theory, we feel that in this new Preface we should clarify our positions, and our oppositions, regarding three important topics of great interest in scientific and philosophic milieus and which have been very widely propagated through the *mass media!* First there is the problem of the interconnection of conscious being and its Unconscious in the formation of the mental organism. Then there is the problem of the assimilation of psychical structures to impersonal logical-linguistic systems. And finally, there is the question of the relationship of the psychical architectonic to the organization of the brain.

This new Preface should, then, help the reader to see clearly that the exposition and all the explications of conscious being which are set forth in this work define a distinct position with regard to *psychoanalysis, structuralism,* and *neurobiology.*

1. THE STRUCTURES OF CONSCIOUS BEING AS THE FOUNDATION OF THE FREUDIAN THEORY OF THE UNCONSCIOUS

The Unconscious is the repressed. This is Freud's fundamental principle, his *"Urtheorie."* The discovery of the Unconscious, no longer considered merely in its negativity (*un*conscious) but in the positivity of its organization, constitutes it as a substantive (the Unconscious). If this is an accurate account of this fundamental postulate of the whole psychoanalytic theory, it is and should be obvious that this substantiveness belonging to the Unconscious is the primordial product of the constitution of conscious being. If there is no development of conscious being, there is no Unconscious. Without this constitution, man would remain a "simply" unconscious being, like the infant or newborn child (to the extent that they are deprived of consciousness!). Only when the development of the structures of conscious being furnishes an opposite —when the desire which strikes against the surface of the worldly mirror produces the image of consciousness—only then, after the first awakening of the conscious awareness of the world, is the Unconscious constituted as such. The genesis of the Unconscious is its generation, its filiation by conscious becoming, for such is its so to speak genealogical subordination as regards this absolute paternity, which, naturally, returns constantly not merely as the simple fantasy of the father but as the primary filiation of the Unconscious itself, the "id par excellence" insofar as it is the cursed and disowned son of the first relationship of the Subject with the Law.[2]

The constitution of the Unconscious is the reverse of the constitution of the conscious in that nothing is prohibited it in the formation of fantasies, that is, in the organization of the desires which imply the dialectic of pleasure and pain and still more profoundly the dialectic of life and death. It is its reverse also in that these *inferiora* of the system of vital relations,* since they obey only the impulsive forces which animate them, hollow out within the subject a vertiginously attractive chasm which represents the entropy of an unbound system, as Freud has explained. On the other hand, conscious being is always

---

*Ey uses the phrase *"vie de relation"* in the traditional sense of Bichat and Claude Bernard. It is a functional system of vital relations. The term includes the nervous system as the apparatus of this "life of relation." The phrase expresses, in Ey's words, "the ensemble of relations between a living being and his environment."—Trans.

constituted in accordance with the organizing legislation of reality, that is, of agreement with others and with the world, in its negentropic opening to freedom. Repression results from the conflict between these two systems. Freud's doctrine of the constitution of the whole of psychical being demands a dynamic, economic, and topographical insight into *this internal conflict, this bipolarity which forms the dynamic structure of human being.* The meaning and the finality of conscious being and of conscious becoming appear at one and the same time as a "liberation" with respect to unconscious determinism, an exoneration from the weight of the unconscious and an opposite direction to the Unconscious's contrary sense. All in all, this is a difficult conquest of that which, as a part of the model of the world over which the subject has no control, resides in the subject as a body which is foreign to what he should be. But he is this Unconscious which he has (and not which has him). He is it, as the shadow of his own body (as Venus attached to her prey), consubstantial with his own being. Conscious being can never treat it otherwise than as the exigency of what it should bear without ever being able to rid itself of it in order to form itself. Conscious being and becoming do repress the Unconscious. But the Unconscious in turn unceasingly makes felt its demands which—if they are to be satisfied, from this point onwards—must be transformed. At the end of this work we shall explain that the instincts of the Unconscious, if they are to direct the conscious being, must undergo a mutation. They must undergo a metamorphosis in order to be sublimated. As thus formulated, we find the completion of Freud's thesis (in the very sense of the hope which he had often expressed[3]): *the importance of the structure of conscious being in the theory of the Unconscious.*[4]

2. THE ARCHITECTONIC STRUCTURING OF THE PSYCHICAL ORGANISM IS INCOMPATIBLE WITH THE "STRUCTURALIST" THEORY OF IMPERSONAL SYSTEMS

At this point we must discuss the authoritative place which Jacques Lacan holds in "French structuralism." We must show clearly that this form or this formalism is opposed point for point to German structuralism, which leans more towards Krüger, Dilthey, Brentano, and Husserl than towards Heidegger. Moreover, the debate[5] which has arisen on the subject of the work and conceptions of Claude Lévi-Strauss, of Michel Fou-

cault, of Louis Althusser, of Roland Barthes, etc., recalls the
internal quarrels which rent Gestalt psychology apart between
the schools of Graz and of Berlin. This is because the words
"structure" and "structuralism" are used in two different
senses. In reaction against "psychologism," they sometimes refer to the interchangeable elements of a combinative system
whose arrangement constitutes a form. On the other hand, in
reaction against the associationist atomism of the nineteenth
century, they sometimes refer to the operations and the phases
of psychical life in the totality of their sense. In this way structuralism in general constantly oscillates between these two
poles or these two levels. In a spirit of intellectual dauntless-
ness (which has even been called an intellectual terrorism),
French structuralism, directly inspired by logical positivism,
has taken shape as a radical contestation of all the "values"
which, it asserts, create mystification in the pure objectivity of
closed systems that order the forms of thought, of language,
and of the institutions which overwhelm the individual and
destroy his intentions to be someone.

It has been precisely on the level of the Unconscious that
French structuralism has discovered the path along which its
chains of meanings move.

The Unconscious can be imagined as an agglutination of
images; or it can be thought of as something which cannot be
thought of. It can also be made to speak. We could even say that
it can be perceived only in synchronous chains of signs, or more
exactly, in the intervals in which the meaning appears between them, in the combinations and permutations which con-
vey relations from sign to sign. Lacan is noteworthy for having
taught this truth, that in the facticity of its appearing, the Unconscious must be the object of a structural-linguistic analysis
which gives its full sense to Freudian psychoanalysis to the
extent that it is applied to what speaks without saying everything, if not without meaning to say anything, that is, as a
fragmentary text. The *symbolism* of the Unconscious consists
in that game of hide-and-seek which demands of the psychoanalyst a technique which is preliminary to and analogous
to linguistic interpretation, a *Sprachendeutung,* a rule which
ordains that it weave its way through this labyrinth without
hope of encountering the least Minotaur, other than one which
is a myth formed by the couplings between words. When considering this "trial" by reflections, it reflects only the images of

the instincts, their representatives, or even the representatives of these representatives which, alone, pass through its expression. In order to cause the Unconscious to speak and to speak *ex nihilo,* it must be caught as it emerges, at that preconscious level to which Freud relegated the verbal function of the Unconscious. It must be caught at precisely the point where the object signified is systematically lost in the maze of signs,[6] at the point where it is cut off from its significant relation to the signified ("from what it means"). Here we touch upon the symbolic artificiality of the "trial" of signs, which is truly the form in which the Unconscious appears. From this point onward, the Unconscious could be said to be extracted, floating, and as if necessarily abandoned to a sort of absolute negativity, the avid and empty gaping of a desire whose essential negativity delivers all the primary and secondary processes (the Unconscious as the Conscious, and *vice versa*) over to a purely abstract formalization. By "sticking" to the object of his analysis, the psychoanalyst risks being caught in the trap of the Unconscious: carried along in his vertigo, seized by this level of the psychical apparatus which is privileged by its search, he runs the danger of losing himself in the game of the signs, the combinative structures of language, when he forgets that "that which speaks" means something, that is, that the subject is present in speech. In other words, he risks missing the sense of infralinguistic meaning of this subject who in his speech articulates the law of his own constitution.[7]

Why is it, however, that these games of metonymy and random syllables and these parrotings cannot exist apart from the realm of that which is signified, that is, from the intentionality of the instincts? How is it that they cannot have the same structure as language, which naturally accompanies conscious being? These are the two major criticisms which have been directed against the formalism of signs. The first was raised by the "orthodox" psychoanalysts. The second by Paul Ricoeur.

If we follow Ricoeur's critique, it would seem that the objectification of language as a closed system of signs (following the Saussurian model as it was expressed by Louis Hjelmsler) very naturally finds its limit in the production (Humboldt, and more recently the school of Chomsky) of speech, which is the creation of the events which engage the subject—not the "I" whose diffuse and tenuous character has been emphasized by Edouard Pichon, but the "full-bodied" self, asserted as a person.

We thus find that if the psychoanalytical-linguistic interpretation of the Unconscious is grounded as a technical means, it runs the risk of covering up the very essence of the relationship between the sign and the signified. In this work we are insistent upon the mediating function of language which appears to be the region where the Unconscious becomes conscious. It is not the Unconscious which is structured as a language. It is conscious becoming which is language to the extent that the subject speaks in it, while leaving in the depth of himself a remainder, an opaqueness which enters only metaphorically into the speech which he engages in with himself.

However, by extending logical models and impersonal stereotypes beyond the verbal games of the Unconscious to the point of overwhelming and destroying personal being (and consequently by denying personal being), structuralism has very naturally given rise to some lively reactions. In spite of the diversity of their points of view, we should note the common elements running through the ideas of Raymond Ruyer, Henri Lefebvre, and Mikel Dufrenne. Unless one has a taste for subversion or paradox, one can scarcely reduce man to being only a combinative mechanism with a borrowed language, to being only a machine, and then bestow upon this machine the power to construct man without taking into account his peculiar organization as a living being according to the strictly human model. Now this model is necessarily architectonic. In simplest terms, we could say that it is organic, in order for it to be precisely organized. The structures of conscious being, which we describe in its constant relations with the Unconscious, include certain infrastructures and superstructures. The structure of conscious being as it is envisioned by structuralism is therefore only a level, a phase of its organization. The object of the science of man is not an object but rather the subject incarnated in his body, in that living body which must think and speak in order to emerge from his unconscious being to take control of his world.

We now see what might be considered to be structuralism's "vice" insofar as its common root is an abstract formalization, a mathematization, a sort of new-style rationalism which sets aside as basal and elementary processes certain *specific* models of sociological, linguistic, or psychoanalytic forms. In the final part of his monumental work, Paul Ricoeur has profoundly investigated the trial against the anthropological loss of values which represents the burial of values (the teleology of human existence) in its archeological strata. Our own study of the organization of psychical being could only win us over to this position. It is true that this "analysis" of man and this reduction of man to a sequence of words or of things compromise his existence and kill man. But this Nietzschean murder could be only the murder of an image or, as Jacques Lacan puts it, of a fetish. Michel Foucault is carried along by the movement which leads so many scientists and humanists to denounce an "outmoded humanism." At the end of his penetrating and fascinating study of the archeology of the knowledge of man and of its development through its separation from things or their representation,[8] Foucault sees man as a contingent object that has only recently appeared in the history of science and of philosophy. He does not hesitate to declare that psychoanalysis, like sociology, both of which are restored to their epistemological pedestal, dissolves man in order to adapt itself to its "object." But if the disappearance of man in Foucault's eyes inevitably indicates the mutation of the fundamental dispositions of knowledge, it still remains to be determined whether, in spite of the "sophists" of our "modern times," this object does not remain just as much the subject, that "being for itself" which has its own organization. In any case we are concerned with this organization. We shall attempt to grasp it in its reality, in the existence of a conscious being which has gone beyond its objectivity, the corporeality of closed systems, in order to open up to the world and finally to speak its own speech: to be at the same time both object and subject of its knowledge. This knowledge is the object of the knowledge of the human sciences. It is this knowledge which coincides with the construction of conscious being. A science without consciousness (*conscience*) is here only illusion!

3. THE ORGANIZATION OF THE BRAIN AND THE CONNECTION
BETWEEN CONSCIOUS BEING AND THE UNCONSCIOUS

A certain number of those who read the first edition of this work were surprised that a book on Consciousness should devote so much space to neurobiological problems. There was a time when matter and memory, mind and brain were separated by a metaphysical abyss, even though (and especially in this case) they might be related to one another according to a certain parallel concomitance which theoretically laid down that their encounter was purely random. Our present view of the brain is far removed from the nineteenth-century picture of cerebral localizations where psychical functions which had been artificially isolated by atomistic psychophysiology were traced upon the parts of the brain's surface. The conception of the brain we now have had been furnished by our superior knowledge of the living brain's organization insofar as it is the nervous system of the organization of the system of vital relations and of the architectonic integration of the planes which compose it. Our knowledge of the brain's function not merely of reproducing but of producing, not merely of mechanical transmission but of creation of the milieu in which the constructions of experience and of the person develop and are built up, has helped form this new view, as has the importance given to the functional *patterning* which belongs to the systems of sleep and of waking and the relations between sleeping and waking. Because the brain's organization is seen to be dynamic on the structural level, the hierarchy of the functions implied in the relationships between the unconscious and the conscious must be shown to be both parallel to the brain's organization and naturally bound to it. Merleau-Ponty, who was obsessed by the problem of the incarnation of experience and of existence, would have been even better able than Bergson to have joined his reflections with our conception of the organization of psychical being which is rooted in the organization of the brain. In order to avoid being reduced to an untenable elementarist materialism, such an embodiment can be validated only by having recourse to the principle of a complementary isomorphism (to use Ruyer's expression) between the activity of the cerebral organism and those organic structures of conscious being which regulate its relations with the external world and the interior world of unconscious images. Insofar as it is embodied—even if this be on a different level from the rootedness of the unconscious in the sphere of the instincts and bodily motives, complexes of desire, pleasure, and anguish—conscious being cannot be held to be a pure transcendence or a simple juxtaposition with regard to the body and the brain (which constitutes the center of the body). This type of hypothesis entails a complication and increase of the problems which concern "consciousness" and the "highest level" of superior nervous activity; but it is implanted in the very reality of the different manners in which conscious being can break down:

the realm of psychopathology.[9] As a consequence of this it is rooted in the very reality of the structures of conscious being which psychopathology reveals. An anencephalous theory of the Unconscious is more to be feared in this regard than is a cerebral mythology of conscious being. It is indeed too easy to assert that the problem of the relationships between the brain and conscious being, and the problem of its connection with the unconscious, do not arise. These problems do arise. And their appearance should warn us against that abstract "metapsychology" which, in spite of the brilliance of its stylistic exercises or its manipulation of ideas, can in effect lead only to the annihilation of the object of its investigation, to the point of murdering man. Such a metapsychology could only attempt to be cleared of this, because man's involvement in his living complexity rebels against being only a reflection or a mirage. For man's *reality* consists neither in the molecular structuralism of his brain (which denies man by asserting the outdated materialist thesis), nor in the abstract structuralism of his language (which denies man by asserting the newly revived nominalist thesis), but in the very organization of this organism which man himself forms by tying together through his body and through his language what he had been, what he is, or what he has to be.

The ideas which we have set forth here by way of preface to this second edition have naturally been reconsidered and deepened in the revision and enlargement of this volume.

We have developed them still more in Part Five, which has been added to this edition. In this final reflection upon "Conscious Becoming," we have attempted to reconsider the whole problem of the intersystematic relationships between the conscious and the unconscious, in order to show that the Unconscious[10] could neither originate nor be in man before he had risen to a certain level of organization of his conscious being or before the relationship between unconscious being (to the extent that it represents the *positivity* of the desire for being) and conscious being (to the extent that it *imposes* the negativity of Law upon desire) form the organic order of psychical being. The psychiatrist, better than anyone else, can get a hold on this order, in the disorder of the psychical organism's disorganization. For if it were not for madness—and dreaming—it is conceivable that the ideology of a purely cultural anthropology or

the systems of structuralist antianthropology could imagine
that man as a conscious and organized being did not exist. But
they are called to order by the undeniable facts which appear
as what is lacking in the dreamer (as in the psychotic or neurotic person) and which attest to the organization, that is, the
pluridimensional reality, of conscious being.

H. F.

PART ONE

Conscious Being

I The Problem of the Definition of Consciousness

To be conscious is to *live* the uniqueness of one's experience while transforming it into the universality of one's *knowledge*. Consciousness is a complex structure; it is the organization of the system of vital relations which binds the subject to others and to the world.

Consciousness arises out of such antinomies as immanence and transcendence, the immediate given and reflection. The reality of conscious being lies in this interweaving of lived experience and judgment (Husserl).

The attempt to define consciousness leads not only to the problem of this particular reality, but to the problem of reality in general. The defining of consciousness oscillates between two theses: one which attributes to consciousness the being of a thing (which it is not); another which holds it to be a nothingness (which also is not its nature).

In the course of this work we shall often find it preferable to use the expression "conscious being" rather than "consciousness," since the former phrase better expresses the essential ambiguity implied in the word "consciousness." "Conscious being" can be understood either as a mode of being which is predicated of a subject (being conscious) or as a substantive category of the objectively definite existent (a conscious being). The distinction which is made in German between the two expressions *Bewusstsein* (being conscious) and *bewusstes Wesen* (a conscious being) is more precisely expressed by the single term "conscious being" than by the substantive "consciousness." The expression "conscious being" more strongly indicates that "consciousness" is not a simple "function" of

3

being but is instead its organization insofar as it is constituted at the same time as both *object* and *subject.* Conscious being, which is the appropriate mode of being in the world, can exist neither as a pure subject nor as a simple object. The ambiguity of its *constitution* (to be enclosed within its organization and open to its world), of its *status* (to be for itself and for others), and of its *problematic* (to be, to appear, and to become) makes of conscious being an entity which is condemned to the infinite diaspora of its migrations, one which posits itself "in raising the question of its being" (Sartre). It is understandable why so many writers prefer to deny consciousness so as not to have to define it.[1]

1. THE DENIAL OF "CONSCIOUSNESS"

One manner of denying consciousness is to consider it as a purely subjective phenomenon which as such cannot be an object of knowledge.

A second way to deny it is to make of it an "epiphenomenon," a contingent reflection or an abstraction which can be substracted from psychical life just as it can be added to the "electronic tortoises" of Grey Walter.

A third form of negating consciousness consists in reducing it to a "simple" property or function called wakefulness.[2]

On the other hand, there is a fourth form of negating consciousness which inflates it to such a degree that it becomes lost in the generality or the supremacy of psychical life by being assimilated exclusively into the "highest level" (reflective and creative thought), whether one defines it by the self and personality or confuses it with *praxis* and the ethics of will (moral consciousness).

A fifth and final form of this negation dissolves consciousness into a network of existential relationships (Heidegger, Sartre) or impersonal structures (Structuralism). By default or by excess none of these negations takes into account the very nature of the structure of conscious being which constitutes its reality. In this work we shall attempt to "discover" what this nature is.

To that end, it is appropriate to begin by trying to discover those "aspects," "phenomena," and "modalities" of psychical being in which everyone (even those who deny *consciousness*) recognizes the quality of being *conscious,* in order to establish that these "functions," these "qualities," these "states," or these "givens" have a meaning only in the framework of an architectonic of conscious being, which implies consciousness to the extent that it excludes the Unconscious, or that, at the very least, it sets itself up in opposition to the Unconscious.

2. THE REALITY OF CONSCIOUSNESS

It is impossible to examine consciousness—one's own or that of others—without referring to *"sensing,"* to a *"lived,"* to an irrefutable experience of the subject which lives it. But *subjectivity* is not a simple and absolute attribute of consciousness. Certainly it involves a subject, but it is always—as has been unceasingly repeated since Brentano[3]—*consciousness of something,* that is, it is invincibly bound to the laws of the objectivity by virtue of which its being is constituted. This is so firmly established that the idea that only "objective" phenomena exist or are objects of science is at the origin of that distrust which is often inspired by the notion of a "subject" which reflects only the world of objects. But in order to reexamine *objectivity* and to reintegrate consciousness into it, objectivity must be grasped as a phenomenal reality which is not and cannot be purely subjective; it is exposed to the view and knowledge of all for the simple reason that it brings about the convergence of *esse* and *percipi.* This double procedure has given rise to Husserlian phenomenology, which consists in an interplay between idealism and realism,[4] as if it is trying to make them coalesce in the most intimate structure of reality. Gestalt psychology, too, had established that the subject and the object are constituted by being connected and combined in the very construction of the "forms" which link the subject to his world in and through the appearance of the *meaning* which confers existence and coherence upon objects. In the articulation of the positions and intentions of the existent no one has surpassed Husserl's grasp of the emergence and "formation" of lived reality as such. Since then, the distinction between a *subject* cut off from objective reality and a world of *objects* subjected to the "hypothesis of objective constancy" has been continually questioned. Consciousness cannot be separated from the objective world; it is caught up in this world at the very moment that it takes possession of it. Thus, *nothing is more foreign to the phenomenological attitude than the radical "subjectivity" of consciousness*. Consciousness has its objective status. This bilateral subjective-objective reality, this essential ambiguity forms the ontological structure of conscious phenomena: they are neither completely objective nor exclusively subjective. And it is precisely to this reality, as the hinge of all reality, that the reality of consciousness corresponds.

In their transitive movements, their emerging, appearing, and disappearing, their articulation and implications, the phenomena which constitute consciousness are presented in their essence as "intentional or significant wholes," as "radical configurations" (Husserl) which comprise lived phenomena in their order of existence; it is in this that they are *structures* of "pure consciousness." Before describing them, therefore, we can and must say that the aim of those phenomena which are revealed as psychical reality's lived experience opens up to us their diversity, not as faculties or functions but as *structures*. It is in this sense that we currently speak of the structure of perception, of the person, of memory, of behavior, of intelligence, etc. This conceptual "model" of the psychological object can be applied to those forms of being such as operations, intentional systems, and groupings as *Gestaltqualitäten*. These form an organized system which we recognize as having the character of *being* conscious or unconscious, depending upon whether they do or do not enter into the lived experience which the subject who is open to his world is able to communicate. "Structure" is the term which best applies to this reality of psychical life, since it denotes that manner of being in which the dynamic organization of psychical life comes into being. For of course we are not simply referring this notion of structure to a mechanical or even a cybernetic model.[5] "Psychical structure" refers to forms of organization, to dynamic schemes to be envisaged in the manner of Bergsonian intuition, to a space within duration. As Merleau-Ponty has so excellently written, these "dynamic structures are likely melody, they are nothing but a certain mode of enduring."[6] This notion has been developed by Krüger and Dilthey as well as by James and Bergson. It has been a sort of leitmotif of contemporary psychology since the works of the Wurzberg school and especially since the school of Graz.[7] Lying between the idea of a pure constitutive intentionality (Ehrenfeld, Meinong, Husserl) and that of a contextured "form" of perception (Wertheimer), psychical structure expresses an internal and active organization of being, especially insofar as each one of them can be presented in a particular phenomenal organization. We shall return constantly to this notion: the reality of psychical structures belongs to the order of lived time and to the order of the space which is contained within its actuality. Sense, lived space, and lived time are a single function of the will *(désir)* in a being's relations with the experience and the construction of the world. As psychical structures reveal themselves to us in a hierarchical order, which is the order of the development of freedom, it is understandable why certain writers somewhat arbitrarily use the words "structure" or "form" *(Gestalt)* with a meaning which supposes a more or less fixed determinateness or organizational stability.[8] According to Merleau-Ponty, however, "this notion of structure, which implies the notion of organization, can be conceived and understood only in its rootedness in the body," in its "latent being."

Having made these preliminary reflections we find ourselves somewhat more confident concerning the *real structures* of psychical being. In any case, each of them must be defined not only by the totality of its organization, but by its genesis, its movement, and its finality. Each of these structures must be defined by what it has been and by what it is going to be, since the reality of every structure implies a hierarchy of levels of being which constitute the order of its temporality and of its internal implications. It is from this perspective that we must now ascertain which structures are generally accepted, so as to have them "enter into consciousness" either as "formal invariants" or as "aleatory syntheses."

3. THE MODES OF CONSCIOUS BEING

In order to approximate a logical analysis of the concept of conscious being, let us examine the "intuitions" or "facts" to which the "natural or naive attitude" (as Husserl calls it) refers us.

A. From Bioconsciousness to Human Consciousness

There are certain *qualities* or *functions* attributed to living beings which are prerequisites for granting them some form or degree of consciousness.

Conscious being is "naturally" refused to *inanimate beings.* Consciousness thus appears in its initial recognizability as a vital phenomenon. (As Bergson has said, consciousness is coextensive with life.)

Among living beings, plants seem to be deprived of consciousness since they do not have a system of vital relations. Those who do attribute consciousness to plants do so only by attributing to them a certain *sensibility* which is correlative to the specific thrust of their growth, perseverance, or reproduction, a sensibility which remains enigmatic since it is not communicated and can only be inferred.

Sensibility is more widely attributed to animals, since their movements express it and communicate it to us. Consciousness can be denied to them only by demanding that their behavior be understood as "mechanical," which it is not. They respond to stimuli by "reactions" in which they are capable not only of moving themselves under the influence of tropisms or instincts but also of being able to postpone the object of their desires, overcome obstacles, and dispel dangers to such an extent that even in the lowest species this possibility of self-determination, of choice, of adaptation, or of motivation (to use the term employed by objective ethology) appears. This is why it seems to be a logical impossibility to speak of the "consciousness" of automata or machines, even if they be self-governing. Be that as it may, this model of zooconsciousness or neurobiological consciousness[9] attributed to lower species necessitates the presence of at least sensibility, memory, and an organization which causes a certain indeterminateness, a certain non-being to appear in their being. For it is only when the insect does not mathematically follow his "instinct" or his "prescience" and when his behavior remains as if subject to the accident of its perceptions, his memory, and his present and individual dispositions that we judge it "conscious." On this point, modern ethology, no matter how "objective" it may be, very "naturally" attributes to many different species this changeable structure of consciousness at this first degree of its indeterminateness, that is, of its individualization, perhaps from the time of the very first "imprinting."

In the case of those higher animals whose system of vital relations is organized precisely like our own by a central nervous system, we attribute "consciousness" to them and make them "co-conscious" with our own consciousness to the degree that "by themselves" they show themselves like us, when there are instituted between them and us communications which bring us together and give rise to similarities among us by making us "understand" each other. It is to the degree of this "identification," to the degree that we speak about them as if we could speak to them (Buytendijk), that we attribute to them a consciousness analogous to our own. When we consider their "learning," the elaboration of their perceptive or mnemonic schemas, their "conditioned reflexes," their emotions, their feelings, and their motives, we project into them our own states of consciousness, the affective and cognitive rudiments of psychical life. In short, they lack only language!

Language is at once the condition and the undeniable manifestation of the reality of our consciousness. This is as true for its expressive as for its concealing function. For if through language one man can know another and know himself through the other, this knowledge of oneself and of others carries with it an element of the unknown, a mystery which is like a shadow which consciousness casts upon itself. Language establishes the possibilities for consciousness both to open itself to relationships with others and to close upon itself. But if speaking being is the most authentic form of consciousness, the being of consciousness appears through the dialectic of the indeterminateness of expression, on this side of and anterior to verbal formulation, which reaches its highest point in human consciousness alone.

This first glance at the phylogenesis of consciousness and its uncertainties shows consciousness to be the organization of the subject, not following a purely subjective model but as the very reality (which our cogito does not place in doubt) of its constitution as a "milieu" which is shared by the "objects" of its own knowledge, objects which make up its internal and external world.

Once it has been established that consciousness appears to us as the most fundamental reality of the organization of psychical being, insofar as this organization constitutes the autonomy of its system of vital relations, we must try to find out what is the "distinctive characteristic" of this organization, so as not to extend it abusively both to the "life" of all beings and to the "whole psychical life" of a single individual. In order to do this, we must determine what it is that distinguishes conscious from unconscious structures, so that we might form an idea of what is essential in the structure of conscious being.

B. The Characteristic Aspects of Conscious Being

Psychologists have all attempted either to investigate or to dismiss this "conscious" quality, directing their attention more especially toward certain psychical phenomena. No doubt all mental operations and processes can be or have been endowed with a "coefficient of consciousness." Whether I walk in my garden or think about what I shall do tomorrow, whether I remember some event or anticipate the next, whether I concentrate, meditate, or calculate, whether I rejoice in good news or am anxious about something, all my thoughts and plans, the *"Sorge"* and *"Vorsorge"* of my existence, all my worries, actions, and feelings can be considered as rising out of or having necessarily arisen from my consciousness, insofar as they are experiences recognized and retained as such by my own power of reflection. As will become clear when we examine the Unconscious, it is in this sense that many psychologists have identified consciousness with psychical being, consciousness with self, without being aware that the analysis of the "conscious state" implies the existence of the Unconscious for the reason that no reflection of consciousness upon its object is possible without some relation to the unconscious stratum from which it emerges, as we shall see in each case. Thus, in order to understand the various modalities proper to conscious being, we must compare them in all these "phenomenal" aspects with that which is not conscious.

In the most characteristic of these "phenomenal" aspects, conscious being presents itself sometimes as *undergoing* lived experiences which *affect* its being, sometimes as capable of *adapting itself to reality,* sometimes as having the power of creative *reflection,* sometimes as a *personal system,* and sometimes as *free to determine itself* through the knowledge of its own goals. The meanings which are sought in the analysis of conscous being as it is manifested in the consciousness of the self and of the world converge upon or imply the following five attributes: affectivity, experience of the real, reflection, personality, and will.

1. CONSCIOUSNESS AND AFFECTIVE LIFE (SENSIBILITY, AFFECTIVE STATES)

When it experiences the diverse modes of its sensibility and, more generally, of its affectivity, conscious being is a subject affected by a sensible experience. This conscious sensible experience, however, emerges in part from the Unconscious and is never simply sensible. The modalities of pleasure and pain are always lived as complex "feelings" into which are mixed overtones of the fundamental affective states which are always and everywhere the correlatives of appetitive and conative tendencies (desires, tendencies, needs). Thus, our feelings, moods, and all the infinitely diversified varieties of lived experiences always appear as emotional "expressions" of underlying strata, of that "endothymic" stratum which, according to Klages, Palagyi, Lersch, etc., would be the preeminent given of lived experience, the vital stratum which is necessary to any experience *(Erlebnis)*. This is because pleasures and pains emerge from an opaque background; they arise out of unconscious tendencies. These affective states, then, possess a certain blind spontaneity owing to their rootedness in the body and have a depth which, to a very great extent, escapes consciousness.

The implicit depth of these affective states is precisely what Freud has shown us. Feelings are never simple but are *complex,* or ambivalent, in that they are always at least partially unconscious. But in spite of the fact that they are unconscious, feelings are part of lived experience. Though they enter our experience only to polarize it, they appear in it indirectly and symbolically. Every lived experience is impulsive and therefore escapes in part from the factors which determine it; the affective states that animate it are not all present within it in their entirety.

Our first examination of lived affective experience has shown us a stratified and articulated phenomenon which directs us towards an organization possessed by conscious being upon which affective experience depends. Far from defining consciousness, the affective state presupposes consciousness as the very condition of experience, of sense data, and of felt intentionality. We have here touched upon a sensitive point of consciousness; but we have done so at the point where this point is not a point, where the phenomenon is revealed in its structural complexity.

It is very true that this modality of affective being is a fundamental modality of consciousness, that of a pathic structure (Weizsäcker), that of the sensible experience which is so much a part of conscious being that no mode of consciousness can arise without being actually lived, without being endowed with a quality of sense or of feeling. Condillac well understood this when he had his statue's consciousness develop from the odor of a rose. And in fact all valid criticisms of "sensationalism" and of empiricism, when reproaching them for resorting to a psychological atom, inevitably collide with this quality which is required for every "state of consciousness": the quality of being the affective state of a sensible being. In this way Husserl causes the eidetic structure of consciousness to flow from a bestowal of sense *(Sinngebung)* in which the lived experience is immanent and absolute. A lived affective state is not given in rough sketches.[10] Any analysis of reflective thought which adds its atmosphere of ideal being to the radical phenomenon does and can take nothing away from this sense datum which is more or less directly a datum of the senses. To be conscious, whether it be called by this name or some other, is to have sensations, all of which affect the body or set off reactions within it when they play upon the body; it is to cause sensations or to receive them, to remember them or to imagine them, but it is always to be actually "affected" by them. To be conscious is to feel; this supposes not a state of consciousness but a *structure* of consciousness across which experience as *lived* appears with its overtones and its implications within the range of the sensible.

2. CONSCIOUSNESS AND THE EXPERIENCE OF REALITY

In *adapting itself to reality,* a conscious being unfolds a complex operational capacity which institutes the categories of reality as lived in sensible experience. The "functions" of memory, perception, and verbal communication are generally considered to be acts which are constitutive of reality and to be so fundamental that each has been used to define the essential activity of consciousness. All of them refer back to conscious being's capacity to *posit reality,* that is, to the "thetic" or "noetic" function of knowledge.

We shall see that each of them implies unconscious psychical infrastructures and a structuring of lived actuality which is never reduced to simple conscious thought, since this latter excludes or implies precisely "something" which is not itself.

a) Memory and Consciousness

Memory obviously is attuned to the demands of temporality (with the particular "properties" and "functions" which this presupposes and implies: fixation, engram, retention, storing and temporal ordering of memories, recall, recognition, etc.). Memory consists in setting out the order of time, in making present or representing the past or the future, both of which are necessary for the unfolding of present experience. It is an essentially *selective* operation which chooses to remember that which *ought* to enter into the actuality of the thematic field. Thus we are concerned with a structure of consciousness which is characterized by a multiplicity of angles and perspectives, of "views" which can be taken upon time and of uses to which time can be put in order to adapt itself to the thematic of the moment, to the phase or the portion of life actually lived. Memory thus appears as a conscious act which implies and explains the Unconscious.

Not only is memory's infrastructure immersed in forgetfulness and the Unconscious, but memory's very activity presupposes a sort of duality between the automatism of its reproductions *(motor memory)* and the effort which pulls the possibility of *pure memory* out of interconnected past events which have been forgotten or absorbed in habits. These two "memories," which Bergson intuitively opposed, point even more profoundly to the two fundamental dimensions of psychical beings: as actuality of what is lived, memory furnishes to this actuality what it still requires from that which is past; as a system of personality, it takes up and continues the history of the self. But under both these modalities, which are too often confused, memory always appears as synonymous either with what is unconsciously "contained" as potential (whether excluded or implied) in the momentary selection of lived experience, or with what is "contained" as repressed by the forces of the self in order to ensure its own progress.

b) Perception and Consciousness

In perception we find once more, and in a special way, this stratified and conflicting structure, which is implied by every phenomenon of consciousness as it brings us back to the unconscious. We need only notice the manner in which we grasp what presents itself to us as "the 'things' which are in *the reality of my experience*," in order to bring forth the problematic of being and appearance, of the objective and the subjective, of the real and the imaginary. All the familiar analyses of the philosophies of perception (Aristotle's matter and act; the opposition in the psycho-physiological assemblages of intuitive,

sensory, and noetic "factors" in the analyses of Bergson, of Gestalt psychology, or of Husserl) point to a structural ambiguity
which reflects the connection of the body and the mind, of the
natural world and the subjective world, of empirical experience and the ideality of the understanding.[11] This is because, as
has been said so often, to perceive is to surround the object with
the existential operations of choosing, showing interest, projecting, admitting, expecting, desiring, grasping, naming, judging, contemplating. All these, however, must be expressly
referred back to the "givens" of our senses.

As perceiving is an act which envelops external perceptions
without ever being able to be completely sure of them or to
restrict itself to them, the images or representations which
appear as reflections of, anticipations of, or substitutes for our
sensations can also be, and always are, "objects of perception."
If perception is an "exception" (*Das Erfassen ist ein Heraus-
fassen,* says Husserl), notably insofar as it is perception of an
external object, this is because it constantly includes the lived
experience of the body itself, of subjective experience, of representation and intuition, all of which form a configuration of
meanings of which the perception of external objects is a particular and quasi-theoretical case: the field of perception is always simultaneously internal and external.

The problematic of perception, which no perception can
completely resolve (ambiguity, affective projection, intentional
context of the perceptive field, interaction of the real and the
imaginary, etc.), points necessarily to an unconscious infrastructure because the "given" or "intended" object can be
grasped only across a stratum *(hyle)* of memories, tendencies,
and images which are like the *Vorgestalten* (Klaus Conrad) or
the "readiness" of what Bruner and Postman call the "hypothesis" of perceived forms.

To the degree that it is neither exclusively external nor exclusively conscious but rather is the order of the distribution of
the coefficients of the reality and identity of the objects which
make up the realm of lived experience, perception is not a
simple phenomenon even if it does imply, if only by reference
to the absolute of sensing, the grasping of the thing "in the
flesh" *(leibhaft),* as Husserl puts it. To the extent that the coherence of a perception is the result of its "development" or
motivation, as Merleau-Ponty has so admirably shown, it implies a global intentional structure (that of the thematic of the

future state of which objects are only figures), a "thetic" differentiation of the values of reality and the orders of existence (objective space, body, subjective representation) and an orientation through which the coordinates of objective space and time enclose or distribute the field of perception. Because of this, the perceptive act is formed as a phenomenal field, as a "structure" which sends us back to the matrix structure of consciousness (insofar as it is a structure which is prior to all actual experience), that is to say, to an architectonic of lived experiences.

Husserl took great care in the course of his "reduction"[12] that perceiving considered "purely" as consciousness (and in abstraction from the body and bodily organs) should appear as a thing without essence *(wesenloses)*. This is because first qualities, the "data" of sensation, exercise a figurative function which reveals itself only sketchily, whereas lived experience is not given in a sketchy manner, though the "lived" is nonetheless never completely perceived. Lived experience is thus the absolute of experience, whether it be perceived or not.

Consciousness thus envelops perception, rather than being reduced to it. But it can also be said that the phenomenology of perception brings to light a sort of infrastructure, an incarnation of consciousness more profound than itself. For at this level of sensing, we find ourselves in the structure of consciousness which constitutes, as it were, the atmosphere of experiencing the body, in which the relations of consciousness bind themselves together. We find ourselves in a sort of *Urempfindung.*[13]

Thus we see that perception points toward one of the fundamental attributes of consciousness, which is to give to itself lived experience, to grasp itself therein, to present it to itself in its objectivity. This shows us that though the structure of consciousness does not coincide with external perception, this latter enters as a privileged model into the very constitution of consciousness in a manner that includes affective states and memory.

c) Language and Consciousness

The same is true for language. It is common knowledge (psychologists have all noted—and it is not an original discovery to repeat it) that to be conscious is to know one's own experience, and that all experience insofar as it is "known" by the subject is discursive. William James[14] has written on this subject: "The part of truth to which the word consciousness refers is formed by the susceptibility to be related and to be known which is possessed by the parts of experience." Consciousness's proper manner-of-being-in-being-said, its proper language, lies in the verbalization of the phenomena which unfold in consciousness. The comprehensive psychology of conscious being, that of *homo sapiens,* teaches us that to be conscious is to be capable of grasping one's own knowledge in the categories of verbal communication. Such, in effect, is the conversational structure of speech through which all the phenomena which enter into the structuring of consciousness are grasped. As Janet has insisted, to be conscious is to recount one's experience; language is thus a structural quality of consciousness through which precisely this consciousness can arise in men. Speech is here the locus at which experiences are mediated and placed at the disposition of the subject (cf. below, especially pp. 106 and 366–373).

However, these vague generalities obviously do not suffice; we must penetrate further into the relations which unite the conscious being and the speaking being, while at the same time bringing ourselves into relationship with the two extremes of this bilateral structure: language as experience (the object or actual content of consciousness) and language as a *mode of the self's existence.*

To enter into a linguistic system, to understand and speak a language, is in a certain sense to use a symbolic apparatus as an instrument for conquering reality. All the above mentioned operations of adapting to reality must therefore necessarily pass through the verbalizing power of consciousness. To name objects, to express desires, to formulate one's thoughts, to communicate with others, etc., are so many manipulations of language which unfold in the specificity of the verbal act. Without this verbal act ever ceasing to be mine, it adjusts the presence and absence of the self and the other. I can say nothing which is not revealed first of all to myself, which does not unfold myself (sometimes in spite of myself, sometimes with my complicity, sometimes at my command), and which does not remain a part of myself in spite of having been the result of random chains of events. Language is just as much undergone as it is executed. "Things are said and thought as if by a Word or Thought, not one which we have, but one which has us."[15]

Language is a part of the *pathos* of consciousness, that is, of its "given" or "imposed" stratum. It is essentially an *interior language,* an automatic germination and growth, as has been shown by the most penetrating studies of aphasia. It is possible only to the extent that I can "dream of acting," as Hughlings Jackson says, when I allow to arise in myself words and phrases which are for me both reflections and anticipations of things. This significant spiritual material, "this second system of signals," which is both a cultural heritage (collective subordination or communication) and an invention or personal stylistic creation, is-there-in-us as the letter of our remarks, compliant or rebellious, representing semi-objectivity, the atmosphere of sense, the "milieu" in which our own thoughts are elaborated, formulated, expressed, and interpreted. Whatever the trans-conceptual relations which unite words to images or representations might be, it is indeed by this world of signs that consciousness is perpetually solicited and captivated; consciousness lives through the significant world just as much as it does through external perceptions, even if "perceiving" objects should be ultimately only a logical-noematic decoding executed by our senses. To the extent that it implies speaking being,[16] conscious being is the mode of being which through speech binds the subject to his world, and is that through which the subject offers or presents his world to himself. Language is made possible through this ability to "affix the world to oneself" (Lersch), for it is only through language that the subject can seize the world, grasp himself in it, and arrest the infinite (because nonverbal) flux of his "animal" experience. Thus the word which dwells in consciousness is a discourse, an oratorical art and not a simple transmission of signals. In other words, the structure of consciousness can be constituted only in and through the dialectic of a being constituting its language. In this respect language is not a contingent superstructure, nor an anonymous structure of consciousness, but is the structure of consciousness in debate with itself. This is to say that in constituting itself, language (more a decoding than expression) implies that what it says leaves in the shadows what it does not say, what does not and cannot enter into the clarity of consciousness, which is also a discursive elucidation and an assumption of meanings by means of those explanations and reflections which unfold the original undeveloped expression. Again, in constituting the structure of consciousness, the structure of language implies that the Unconscious is manifested in the gaps of a discourse which is never entirely conscious.

We are thus approaching the reflexive structure of consciousness to which language adds its power by constituting itself. Of course, language can be only what the *subject* says, this "subject" of experience which we here encounter for the first time in the "first person," precisely because he names himself. In assuming the function of speech, even before being able to say "I," the subject stands up before the world, for in identifying this world, in designating it, he confronts it and he comes to see himself. Man does not linger at this first stage of subjective emergence, for *the other* does not exist only outside of himself but exists in him from the moment that he is penetrated by and inhabited by language. Ever since Hegel, the theme of this otherness which is constitutive of one's identity has become a sort of leitmotif. It has been developed in all its senses and in all its modalities by Marx, Freud, Heidegger, and it could be said by all existential phenomenologists and all psychoanalysts (Sartre, Lacan, Hesnard, Merleau-Ponty, etc), who have again and again taken up the glimmering reflection of the "mirror games" of that self-consciousness which is implied in the verbal relation of the subject with his world, particularly in the relation of the subject with the other. Such is the verbal *nexus* of this identification which can, in effect, be explained only through the declension and conjugation of grammatical relationships, through the logical articulation of discourse and the syntactical forms which are syntheses of consciousness, the noetic-noematic stratum of the logos (Husserl).

For the time being it is enough to have noted that conscious being, as a subject of his world and of the discourse which produces this subject by binding him to others, in this way is divided by the generative movement of his manner of "speaking to himself" which is "for him" and also that manner of speaking to others, of speaking of him and of others, by taking with regard to himself the distance implied in the positions (the "theses") which, in speaking, he assigns himself or assumes.

Thus language, interwoven with the intersubjective ties which are its vehicle, forms within itself a heterogeneous space which is the lived and verbally articulated space of the field of consciousness, but which is also the *logos* of the self insofar as the person is formed only in uttering itself. But in and through this double function which incorporates it into lived experiences and into the formation of the self, *it enters into consciousness only by positing the Unconscious as a dimension of its own discourse.*

3. THE SUPERSTRUCTURES OF THE OPERATIONAL FIELD OF CONSCIOUSNESS

To be conscious is to sense; it is to be able to perceive and to speak. This "functional footing" constitutes the very foundation of the consciousness of being. By giving the term "structure" the sense of "infrastructure," that is, of a buried structure, this structuring of consciousness corresponds to its formal constitution, which appears only as it is implied in all the configurations of conscious being. At this point we see that this conscious being, or rather this conscious becoming, must be grasped through structures which are in fact facultative superstructures which extend to their furthest powers the functional potentialities of the formal infrastructures of which we have just become aware. Because of their reflexive and protean transcendence, those structures, being the "most conscious," are sometimes considered to be the prerogatives of human consciousness; this is true only so long as they are not separated from the footing which supports them.

We are thus led to examine the dynamic aspects of attention and reflection.

a) Attention and Consciousness

Attention is that force or effort through which Maine de Biran, William James, Bergson, Janet, etc., have defined psychical energy and dynamism. Attention to life, interest, concentration, intentional orientation, motivation, etc., all express the tension toward a desired goal, proposed or prescribed, which constitutes the "intentional kernel" or "seat" of a "state of consciousness" (William James's "stream of consciousness"). This state is not merely a "state" or a simple stream of consciousness, for as we shall see, the present field of experience is neither a passive "given" which comes from or reflects the world of objects, nor a continuous and internal flux, nor a quantity of energy. We have had the occasion to study the notion of psychological tension in the psychology of Janet,[17] where we showed that there, too, the concept of structure should replace these concepts of energy. Attention is constituted only on a thematic field which implies a hierarchy of levels. The succession of thematic fields is essentially discontinuous, the transitions which connect these fields in the unfolding of a particular experience being subordinated to the meaning of that experience, that is, to the power of the actual significations which arise from the world, from relations with others, or from autochthonous interests. The "degrees" of attention which we have in view when we consider the phenomena of conscious being are not simple "quanta" of a single function, but are rather a hierarchy of forms, from involuntary functions to free and creative acts, which are organized according to the existential categories of the experience in progress. These degrees of attention or of wakefulness are the most advanced forms in which consciousness can analyze its contents into "clear and distinct ideas." Alertness and attention are not simple functions which illuminate or awaken consciousness so as to raise it to the highest degree of clarity; they are rather the result of a functional composition (or "dynamic structure") which arrives at lucidity (that is, at the optimal power of differentiation) only by acquainting itself with the infrastructures from which they emerge.

b) Reflective Consciousness

Reflection, the process through which thought returns upon itself and duplicates the acts which it directs, is carried to its furthest power by attention. It is important to understand correctly this movement from the spontaneous to the unreflected; we must reflect upon reflection. Reflection or phenomenal conjugation (I look at myself, I feel myself, I resolve myself to . . . , etc.) of the relation of a "content" of consciousness to the conscious subject is an autochthonous quality of consciousness, which we have already seen when we referred to the "I feel" which is an "I feel myself," the "I perceive" which is an "I perceive myself," the memory which is an "I remind myself," the attention which is an "I concentrate myself upon," the language which is an "I express myself." We shall benefit from the analysis of this natural opening of consciousness, of this schizogenesis of conscious being, when we deal with the phenomenology of the field of consciousness, which introduces a doubling back, an interval or a space in its "re-presentation."

However, as regards reflective thought, this reflecting structure of consciousness is not a radically different sort of thing (since the former implies the latter); it is another structural level. Thus far we have used the usual psychological descriptions and analyses in order to describe these spectacular or specular activities of conscious being which observe the subject as it emerges from unconsciousness and "becomes conscious" (as, for example, in the case of the nursing infant or the moment of awakening), at which time, through its memory, perception, attention, and language, the subject opens itself to the system of fundamental relationships involved in its presence to the world. We have discerned consciousness to be the fundamental mode of experience, a reflection which is completely closed up within itself and coalescent with its eidetic and intuitive givens. Having generalized this concept by applying it to the higher levels of psychical activity, we must now deal with a region of psychical being which goes beyond *the conscious being in the actuality of his lived experience* to become *the conscious being in the act of his intelligence.* If we admit that a man might be highly "conscious" without being highly "intelligent," or that a man might display "degrees of consciousness" which do not necessarily imply cognitive operations or discursive thought, we are only saying that in reflecting, in reasoning, in calculating, etc., one elaborates contents of consciousness *by adding* to his conscious being certain discursive or logical exercises which define his *Reason.* The superior forms of conscious being which we are now about to describe (the operational field of thought, the system of the personality, moral consciousness) are thus, in a certain sense, its most highly conscious forms. But we will not commit the error of which many philosophers and psychiatrists are guilty and define consciousness by its "highest level," for the contingency of its intellectual and moral superstructures indicates that they are so little constitutive of consciousness that they instead depend upon its constitution. There is a difference both of structure and of level between these two modes of conscious being. Let us remain aware of this distinction, knowing that we will naturally be led back to this difference which separates constituted consciousness from the consciousness which constitutes, the infrastructure from the consciousness of its superstructures.

When we arrive at this level we enter the operational field

of thought. It is self-evident that this is a dimension of reflective consciousness, for all discursive thought is an exercise in elaboration and construction which presupposes a differentiation of the contents of consciousness.[18] These operations develop and make explicit the implications of the sense *(Bewusstheiten)* which orient the thematic (topic) of the actual occupation or preoccupation of reflective thought. They are like a spectacle of acts which treat the "contents" of thought as a balancing act or a prestidigitation of the things in the world: they grasp them, move them, turn them over, make them appear and disappear in the infinity of temporal perspectives which constitute the dynamic schemata, the performances of intelligence.

Consciousness should be defined by the framework which it brings to its ideas, rather than by the ideas which it contains. It appears to be reducible to its intentional vector only when consciousness develops through discursive thought. However, in order that these operations conceal their infrastructure, the apparatus of consciousness *(Bewusstsein)* must permit the development and elaboration of its vectors of signification *(Bewusstheiten)*. In other words, if we renounce any perspective which considers consciousness to be only a flux of intentional lived experience (a succession of significant contents all of which are alike in their presentation), and if we attempt to discover the precise description of the formal structure of conscious being with its intentionality, we ought to say that this formal structure *regulates the presentation* of the lived phenomena and that this finishing touch is the necessary but not sufficient condition of its discursive development. The most highly developed operations of consciousness will then no longer appear to be the essential element in consciousness. They will be "merely" its higher level. Since we cannot make up our mind whether or not to place on the same plane all the activities of consciousness, its formal apparatus, and its contents, we must seek to determine what is the hierarchy of the structures of consciousness and what is their order of subordination. If we should follow Husserl[19] and superimpose the noematic-logical contents of judgment on the constitution of the real moments of the lived experience, it would be obvious that all the operations of discursive thought (intellectual and logistic schematization, reasoning, inductive and deductive processes, etc.), the whole process of the mind working upon itself in creative reflection, is consciousness constituting itself rather than constituted consciousness.

4. CONSCIOUSNESS AND PERSONALITY

To say that someone is someone is to affirm that he is conscious of himself, for the self-revelation of this someone can occur only through an intersubjective communication which inaugurates or implies intrasubjective communication. The word "personality" refers to the individual who ceases to be merely any individual whatever and becomes a "person" in whom "to be" and "to have" are conjugated in a manner which is characteristically his own. This physiognomy of the person, this distinctiveness of the personality, supposes a hierarchy of interwoven forms and structures between the body and the person, between the person of the self and that of others. Certain theories of personality tend to simplify it by solidifying the multiplicity and complexity of the individual psychical being into a monolithic whole. Such a simplification gives unity to the originality of the conscious being and becomes a synonym for consciousness, if consciousness is identified with the self. For this reason many psychologists, psychiatrists, and psychoanalysts use the terms "self" and "consciousness" synonymously. The fact is, however, that the self is not simple but complex. It is not the foundation of conscious being but rather its structural and historical result. In order that personality be properly situated in conscious being, it should be placed not at its base but at its summit, so that both its development and its interactions with the fundamental structure of consciousness might appear.

It is true that all experience demands a subject which is the referential center for all relations with objects (both the objects which fill the geography of its existence and the human "objects" with which it coexists). But this subject, this subjectivity *(Selbstlichkeit)* which is scarcely differentiated when the pronoun "I" is used, is constituted as a person (myself) only during its development, at which time its temporality coincides with the movement of its transcendence:[20] the self is constituted only when it differentiates itself from its body and is "thrown" into historical existence.

As we shall see, personality cannot be reduced to what belongs to the body; a study of character must be a study of the person. The constitutional "biophysiological" given is merely a basis to which the construction of the self constantly refers, without ever merging with it.

The personality is a history. It is constructed as a biography which links together all the self's modes of being into a series of events. This historicity of the self nonetheless implies precisely a self in a state of reciprocal genesis (Pradines) which causes it to engender by itself the very events which constitute it.

In this manner the system of the person is developed as a creation of its own world, and the self is the author of its own person, which is at one and the same time both borrowed from and opposed to others.

Now, if self-consciousness involves founding one's own person, and if conscious being here appears as belonging to the very nature of the person (being not simply one of its dispositions but a dispositional right, a theme which we shall develop in the third part of this work), neither the totality nor the basic structure of the person can be reduced to this manner of being conscious or to this ideal of consciousness. For the very notion of a self which controls itself implies that its person is dealing with experiences which at each moment make up the coin of its historical capital. The personality and the self thus represent the transcendental aspect of *being someone* with respect to its *having consciousness of some thing.* It is true that the self is the supreme form of conscious being, but it is "only" this supreme form, which is in a way "secondary" to its development, taking into account both its contingency and its liberty.

5. MORAL CONSCIOUSNESS

Only at the level of the highest organization of the self, which we have just described, do moral and "psychological" consciousness coincide. The various discursive operations, the structures and levels of personality, can be considered as stages which reason (theoretical or practical) passes through or presupposes. Since it is a reasonable being, the self which emerges from these stages must be grasped "in its situation" or in its world, in the problematic of its existence, which is openness to others in the world of values. Contemporary "anthropology" (whether it be derived from phenomenology, cultural social psychology, or psychoanalysis) admittedly has disengaged the political and "moral" dimension, the "axiological" being, from the structure of human being. Let us simply recall that Heidegger has made of this openness of consciousness to the world of values the very being of consciousness. From this point of view, which has been so richly developed, the meaning of the word "consciousness" *(Bewusstsein)* is reflected in its other meaning: that of moral consciousness *(Gewisse)*. The ethical excursion of Sartre's philosophy is most interesting. As early as *The Transcendence of the Ego* (1936), Sartre attempted to ground his ethics and politics upon the absolute objectivity of consciousness, as if consciousness was only as acknowledged by others. From this developed his doctrine of involvement. Consciousness is obsession with this freedom of action, for if, as Sartre says, we are condemned to be free, this freedom weighs upon human consciousness as its proper manner of problematic being.

In the *Philosophy of the Will,* Ricoeur states that consciousness becomes moral consciousness when it evaluates and reflects upon its values. The themes of the immanence of responsibility and of openness to the world of values bring us back again to the phenomenology of will.

We can find a kind of common "style" in all these contemporary studies (Lavelle, Mounier, Marcel, etc.). They all attempt to show that the transcendence of moral values emerges from the structure of consciousness, from the ambiguity of the choices and hesitations which form the problematic of its operations.

"Moral consciousness" cannot be radically separated from "psychological consciousness." Far from being a sort of principle of absolute self-determination, as prescribed by Kant, morality is caught up in that "sea of reflections" called consciousness. To be fully conscious is indeed to be in an alert state, not just in Pavlov's "reflex" attitude, but in a state of perplexity and calling into question, a theme frequently taken up by Heidegger.

What we have already said about the self can also be said of values' "manner-of-being-in-the-world"; this can be thought of as the most human form of human consciousness (that which opens directly upon the projects and accomplishments of *praxis*); this form of ethical consciousness is truly consciousness, but it is consciousness which has attained its most extreme degree of differentiation. To demand as a part of its definition that it be and remain at this supreme, if not exceptional and ideal, level is one way of denying the structure of consciousness.

In this ultimate aspect of "the-most-conscious-possible-being," we understand still better that it is a part of the very being of consciousness for its being to be in question: the structure of consciousness necessarily implies a conflicting and ambiguous constitution, that of a being for itself which is torn by its intestinal strife (Maurice Blondel).

Thus the modalities of the self's existence, thought, or constitution all lead us back to "consciousness," which we find to be the structural reality upon which each one of these aspects depend, and not to a juxtaposition of functions whose sum could arbitrarily add up to or exclude the being of consciousness. We also see that *conscious being* presents itself to us as a *conscious becoming* which appears as a structural hierarchy which cannot be defined by reducing it either to its formal instances or to its operational and motile field. For "conscious being" is not condemned to the automatism of its infrastructures, in spite of the fact that these are necessary to the free movement of its facultative superstructures.

4. THE DEFINITION OF CONSCIOUSNESS

All these hierarchical modes of conscious being, these "operations," "functions," and "structures," naturally impress us as being "conscious" phenomena. It can be said that *memory, attention, reflection, language, knowledge, intelligence, sensibility, perception, the self, moral consciousness, self-consciousness* are in part or in whole conscious modes of psychical life. "Conscious being" is thus seen to be an attribute belonging either to some particular aspects of psychical activity or to its whole. In this sense consciousness has been described as being either thought in general or only a quality which may or may not be added to all psychical phenomena; but this, we insist, refuses to consciousness its own structural hierarchy.

Would it be possible either to accept a functional psychology which cuts psychical life into pieces and consciousness into the partial mechanisms of memory, perception, intellectual or verbal schemas, etc., as if consciousness were only a collection of heterogeneous phenomena, or to accept a phenomenology of mind which gives a general description not only of the intentional flux, the presentations, the developments and complications of "lived experiences," but also of all the manners-of-being-in-the-world, the conjugation of the self, the interlacings and reboundings of the self and the other, the historical and ethical problematic of man, as if consciousness were absorbed by the generality of man's *Dasein,* "Reason," and *praxis?* The merits and validity of the first of these points of view are based upon the possibility of an operational analysis; the second has the advantage of being a more comprehensive grasp of the sense of existence. However, both are in principle opposed to the idea of an organization of psychical being, the first remaining indifferent to the interconnections of the parts which it has distinguished (consciousness is an abstract totality), the second opposing any rooting of consciousness in the body (consciousness is not a natural phenomenon).

Must we, then, necessarily accept an idealism which admits only meanings or essences for the object of a true phenomenology, as if we were pure spirits? Are we necessarily condemned to an empirical realism which claims that it is concerned only with a mosaic of independent functions or of functions which depend only upon the experience which is inscribed upon the brain which "associates" them?

We can attack the problem of the definition of consciousness only if we abandon these presuppositions or substitute another for them. Our starting point must be the modes of conscious being which we have described above, insofar as they show us both the unity and the heterogeneity of conscious phenomena. We must arrive at both a general definition of conscious being and a particular definition of the fundamental structures which compose it. We must discover in the first place whether conscious being can be reduced to a fundamental structure, then what this structure might be, and finally whether it is possible to enumerate fully and distinguish between the different modes of conscious being. It will thus be necessary for us to set out resolutely from a point of view which has escaped or been systematically denied to most writers and schools: that of a hypothesis concerning the *organization of psychical being.*

1. CONSCIOUS BEING IN GENERAL

We shall first examine the dynamic structure of conscious being which is exhibited throughout the first approximations of a definition and the successive definitions which we have already given.

1) *Conscious being implies an autochthonous organization.* The different ways in which phenomena appear in conscious-

ness give us the idea and the empirical content which defines the being of consciousness. Conscious phenomena appear as conscious only given the condition that they constitute a "milieu" which interposes an autochthonous organization between the vegetative life of the organism and the world with which it is in relation: this milieu being the relation of the milieu of psychical life and of the intramundane milieu, the relation of a center and a horizon of existence which constantly affect one another. This "milieu" is not interior; nor, more generally, is it in space. It is in the movement (dynamism, intentionality, will, etc.) which envelops the objectivity of the world in the representation of the subject. It is that autonomy which is represented by consciousness bound to its own mode of function (Bergson, Weizsäcker, Merleau-Ponty).

2) *Conscious being objectifies itself and reflects itself in a model of its world.* This autonomy cannot be confused with subjective interiority, for consciousness is not constituted as the product of the ego; the ego rather presupposes its constitution. In other words, consciousness constitutes itself as an object. In this sense we can say (along with Husserl, Sartre, etc.) that consciousness is in the world because the world, especially the world of others, enters into its constitution. From this point onward, consciousness for a living and specifically human individual is the possibility for a subject to constitute itself as an object for itself and for others. It is the construction of a *model* of the world which is not only its task but its being. Consciousness is divided within itself by this essential objectification of consciousness, through which it presents itself with its proper object (knowledge) and through which it recovers its knowledge (reflection).

3) *Conscious being organizes itself in the order of its temporality.* This "partition" refers us not to space but to the *temporality* of the conscious being (Heidegger), for the ordering of one part of the self by another part of the self is essentially the faculty of subordinating the one to the other in duration, of seizing hold of it either in the actuality of an experience which is organized according to the order of simultaneity (synchronism), or in a project which conforms to its history (diachronism). The law of the temporal constitution of conscious being is, in effect, the *order* which it makes prevalent by extending the ideal within which it becomes a person to the movements of its body and of its world.

4) *Conscious being is structured as a reverberation of the self upon its experience.* Finally, conscious being appears not as identical to the self, but as a being which demands that its self transcend its lived experience.[21]

This defines a conscious being as a being which is organized so as to *have* an experience at each moment of its history and to *be* the person which emerges through this history. If lived experience does in fact enter into consciousness as a *property of the self* (entering into the self's domain, the *Eigenheitsphäre* which constitutes its core), it is only by becoming conscious of itself that it becomes master of its experience through the objectification of its being in its own self.

Thus, as a result of these successive approximations (autochthonous milieu, construction of a model of the reflection of the world in the subject, temporal order of its constitution, creation of its own person), we can now define conscious being in the generality of its being as the possibility for an individual to incorporate within himself a model of the world in which his own experiences are organized and which is ordered by his person. We can condense the structural complexity of consciousness into a schematic formula by saying that *to be conscious is to command a personal model of the world.* In emphasizing the *ordering* of this *personal model,* we intend to define conscious being as a mode of being, the structures of which are ordered by relation to the subject which they constitute, but which also constitutes them. We do not revert either to the thesis of psychological subjectivism or to that of a structuralism "without a person."

2. THE TWO MODES OF CONSCIOUS BEING

Conscious being's command of the model of its world can be understood only as a manner of arranging time. It rests upon a fundamental dimension of the structure of being: that of temporality, whose demands constitute *memory.* A being's memory is obviously not merely the mechanical conservation of remembrances; it is rather the *possibility of willfully commanding time,* in order to focus it into the actuality of the *present* and to polarize it in the *project* of existence. In this way the mnemic or temporal structure of psychical being coincides with the structure of conscious being. We find here a "bilateral" or "articulated" structure which cannot be made to correspond to any simple or linear model; it corresponds rather to a functional cycle *(Gestaltkreis)* whose two complementary hemicycles engender each other reciprocally. Because of the organization of its temporal structure, consciousness is the connection of these two ways in which the subject can arrange his experiences and can survive them. Conscious being takes form along this double coordinate in such a way that the temporality of the conscious being, his memory, and this double constitution are one and the same thing.

The two fundamental levels of conscious being correspond to this double exigency of the constitution of consciousness as organization of its domain: *the consciousness which comes to a stop in the actualization of lived experience and the consciousness which develops in the system of its personality.*

All too often one commits the error of confusing these two structures of conscious being. Once this is done, the only way to clear up this confusion is by abusively defining consciousness either by its basic structure, or (more frequently) by its peak, or still more frequently by noting its heterogeneity and thereby deny its reality.

We must do our best with a difficult situation: consciousness is both real and complex. This complexity constitutes the organization of the psychical being which contains the Unconscious, but which also contains two modes of being conscious: the *consciousness of lived experience* and *self-consciousness.* These are present not as two distinct parts of the conscious being but rather as two articulated systems which, as complements, stabilize the objectification which the subject introduces into his own being in order to know himself and to direct himself toward his goals.

3. THE STRUCTURING OF CONSCIOUS BEING

If we wish to anticipate the dialectical movement of this work in its search for the dynamic structuring of conscious being, we might indicate at this point as an hypothesis,[22] or as a corollary of this first examination of the problem, how these two modes of conscious being and their interconnections present themselves to us.

a) The Actualization of Lived Experience as Basal Structure of Consciousness

Consciousness appears in this central region of the psychical being as the *field* where experience comes to be or-

ganized according to the structure which constitutes its autochthonous organization (Gurwitsch). "The lived" necessarily
must pass through the constitution of this field of presence.
"Das Bewusstsein ist dass augenblicklicher Ganze ... Das
Ganze der momentanen Seelenleben nennen wir das Bewusstsein," writes Karl Jaspers, who assigns the ephemeral structure
of a moment of time to our viewing of the intentionality of "the
consciousness of something." Consciousness cannot live its experience without presenting it in the present which it constitutes as an interval and a "space" of time (between the
retention of the past and the protension of the future) which is
placed between that which has been and that which is to be.
*Consciousness introduces the space of the representation into
the actualization of its lived time.*[23]

This "lived" is referred to the corporality of experience, to
its sensible givens (whether of perception or of imagination);
at the same time, it requires that the structure of consciousness
assure that there be a legislative or thetic function (posing the
category of the real) which assigns the exact values of subjective and objective to that which is presented in its field. The
structure of consciousness here appears as a legislation (noematic) of the lived (noetic), which implies its structuring (or
its constitution). This organization of the field of present lived
experience supposes a formal structure which is a sort of formal invariable (Gurwitsch), the object of a Husserlian type of
phenomenology of consciousness.

b) The Transactuality of Conscious Being as Structure of
the Self

Corresponding to the field of consciousness's structure of
actuality is conscious being's structure of potentiality and of
implication: the structure of the self which has been constituted into a person by the autoconstruction of its own system of
values and in its historical development. It emerges from the
field of experience as a differentiation of its subject, which
passes from a confused subjectivity to that of a self. The self
shows itself here as the reflexive form of self-consciousness in
the consciousness of the other. As basal consciousness has a
field structure, the self plunges into the past or aims at the
future following an unceasing trajectory (axiological) which
binds one's existence to its beginning and to its end as its own
destiny. For this reason, all that can and should be said about

this transcendence of the self-conscious being can be enunciated only in the style of the existentialist analyses or of Heideggerian *Dasein*.

c) The Relations of the Field of Consciousness and the Self

It is no more possible to place Husserl and Heidegger in radical opposition than it is to separate radically the field of consciousness from the trajectory of the personality, the being of its immanence from that of its transcendence, and its mode of actualization from its mode of implication, without feeling obligated to articulate these two complementary forms of conscious being. As we shall later insist, to *have* consciousness of something, that is, to incorporate the experiencing of something into oneself, constitutes the functional substratum of self-conscious being. In this dialectic between *being* and *having* we find the relations of both reciprocity and subordination between "consciousness" in the strict sense (the organization of lived experience into a field of actuality) and the self (the auto-construction of the personality in self-consciousness). For this last is "superior" or "transcendental" to the other, not because it commands absolutely but because it represents the system of integrating values which all lived experience obeys.

In the full exercise to which it is brought by its highest degree of attention, of reflection, and of liberty, this double structure of conscious being cannot be discerned. Even less are the infrastructures of the field of consciousness revealed in this state.

It is precisely because mental pathology brings to light what is not apparent from the fact of the integration of the conscious being and of its relations with the unconscious, that this perspective (which has been hidden both to philosophers and to common sense) should now be disclosed so as to indicate to us the order in which we ought to expose the organization of conscious being, that is, a full enumeration, from the field of *present lived experience* to the historical configuration of the *construction of the self* and then their relation with the *Unconscious*. Such, in effect, will be the plan of this work.

Before we undertake this task, let us investigate the views of some philosophers on these subjects. For if the psychiatrist has something of import to say—as his goal—concerning the inner face of conscious being, the existentialist anthropologists, philosophers, and psychologists have said many profound things on the subject of its outer face.

II Philosophy and the Problem of Consciousness

We are not able here to give a full exposition of the notion of "consciousness" as it developed throughout history, for the philosophical problem of consciousness is that of the relationship of being to consciousness; it is the problem of philosophy itself.

We have pointed out the structure of consciousness by emphasizing the ambiguity, the bilateralness, and the multiplicity of its constitution. We could perhaps say that the structure of present experience, the field of consciousness, constitutes its lived experience at the limit of a conflict between that which presents itself and that which *I* grasp, in a positive appearance which implies a negation: the negation of the moments of time which are excluded by the presentness of the lived experience. We can also assert that the "me" appears as a construction of the self through the successive negations of the other in a person's history. With regard to the temporal structure of the field of consciousness, we shall see that James and Bergson have made this a central element of their analyses. Heidegger, on the other hand, has more particularly developed the excursion of the self into its world. Husserl can be said to be situated at the juncture of these two dialectics of the constitution of conscious being.

We shall discuss only the fundamental views of the philosophy of consciousness as they have been developed by these four philosophers. We shall not consider the "mechanistic" psychologies and philosophies of nature, for these are essentially negations of consciousness and are limited to unilateral graspings of an epiphenomenal "conscious" quality which leaves out

33

of account its dynamic structure of involvement. This is notably the case with the atomist or associationist psychologies
which are heirs to (or encroachers upon) Cartesianism—*sensationist empiricism* and its developments in the *behaviorists*
(Watson), reflexologists (Bechterew, Pavlov), or the *Gestalt psychologists* (at least in the sense of Watson, Wertheimer, Köhler,
Koffka). It may be true that when "behaviorism" becomes "molar" (Kantor, Tolman), and when Gestalt psychology returns to
its original inspirations (Krüger, Meinong), this "empiri-
cal-sensationist" movement approaches structural psychology;
however, it then becomes more or less confused with those
fundamental aspects of phenomenology which have their roots
in the intentional psychology of Brentano or the Gestalt theory
of the school of Graz.[1] Without denying their considerable interest for other studies, we can thus leave out of consideration
these currents of contemporary philosophical and psychological thought.

The genealogy of contemporary studies on consciousness
naturally goes back to Hegel. This is especially true of their
phenomenological direction. We must remember, however,
that in the *Phenomenology of Mind* Hegel prescribed an absolute ideality to the dialectic of the figures of human consciousness (an ideality which brings about the unification of mind
and of self-consciousness). It is, however, important to bear in
mind that Hegel starts from the basis of a phenomenology
which he himself calls the "science of the experience of consciousness" and moves from there to the generation of the
forms of self-consciousness; this dialectic constitutes the spirit
of our own exposition of conscious being.[2]

The Hegelian frontispiece of the philosophies of consciousness which we shall now discuss is nonetheless an "idealis-
tically" oriented system which attracts toward itself all specu-
lation about or analysis of consciousness insofar as consciousness is imposed upon or extracted from its nature. One of the
two currents derived from Hegelian idealism has remained
more rooted in the "immediate givens" of the subject's lived
experience (James and Bergson); the other, having set the constitution of consciousness higher as the statute of knowledge
(Husserl) or as the unfolding of existence (Heidegger), has remained more resolutely idealist. Nonetheless, it is the problem
of the immanence or the transcendence of the act or the struc-

ture of consciousness which naturally lies at the center of any philosophy of consciousness.

1. "IMMEDIATE GIVENS" AND THE STRUCTURE OF CONSCIOUSNESS IN JAMES AND BERGSON

The view of William James, who at one point defined "consciousness" as a "stream of lived experience" but then did not reintroduce this definition into his "pragmatic" perspective, and the view of Henri Bergson, who, on the contrary, attempted to endow "the immediate givens of consciousness" with an intentional and temporal structure, are discussed together at this point as being two movements based upon a purely intuitive grasping of experience and which pose the problem of its organization.

1. WILLIAM JAMES

William James's "pluralism" is the point of view of *pure experience* or of *radical empiricism*, holding that reality appears neither as finite nor as infinite but simply as indefinite: "It flows in such a way that we cannot say whether or not it has a single direction."[3]

In response to this characterization which Bergson made of his *philosophy of experience*, James, in his famous Oxford lectures *(A Pluralistic Universe)*, acknowledged all that he owed to Bergsonian intuition. James's views concerning the "contents" of consciousness underwent certain variations after his 1884 article[4] on "The Stream of Consciousness": what is richest, most concrete, and most really lived *in* consciousness is a flux composed of facts of consciousness. These complex and heterogeneous facts, all of which are constantly affected with a subjective factor, unfold themselves in consciousness in such a manner that consciousness appears to introspection as a content without form, the object only of a radically empirical and intuitive cognition.

These states do form a part of a *personal consciousness;* this, however, means only that they are "bound" to the activity and existence of a personal self, that they are a property of this self and are on the whole juxtaposed with it. *The flux of this stream* is irreversible and never ceases its flow. *The continuity of consciousness* implies two things: first, the consciousness which follows a "time-gap" feels as if it belonged together with the state of consciousness which preceded it and in which it recognizes another part of its self; and secondly, its qualitative changes are never abrupt. The words "chain" or "train" inadequately express this reality. It is rather a perpetual transition and flowing.

However, this perpetually changing movement contains different stages within it. James called those states in which thought came to rest "substantive parts" and those in which it moved forward "transitive parts." These givens are only mobile intermediaries leading from one substantive conclusion to another and always excluding any problem concerning their constitution in favor of a pure sensible intuition of "contents" or "givens."

There is a "fringe" surrounding every thought object, which allows its "psychic overtones," its "halos," to intermingle with those surrounding it and introduce into the field of consciousness a plurality of simultaneous contents. This order is nonetheless thematic (a "topic"), that is, it is centered around a theme which serves as focal point or center of gravitation for the ideas presently entertained by consciousness. In this manner the facts of consciousness combine among themselves as the result of a *selection*.

There is a double set of relationships between this "stream of consciousness" and the self. (James had considered using the term "sciousness" in order to avoid the traditional corruptions of the term "consciousness.") They affect the *self* (the empirical and corporeal subject that is affected by the affective changes in consciousness, which reflect all the subjective modes of the facts of consciousness which are recognized as "mine") and the *I* (or transcendental *Ego*) which constitute the principle of the continuity and the unity of psychical life. However, these relations authorize a division of being more than they bind together empirical elements into an organization of consciousness. In this manner, these "concrete states of consciousness" or these "fields of consciousness"[5] appear in a kaleidoscopic heterogeneity which is incompatible with the constancy of a structure.

In 1906 William James formally stopped considering consciousness as other than "the quality of being conscious," a tautological formula indefinitely taken up by the "shameful deniers" of consciousness. "After long years of hesitation," he told the Fifth International Congress of Psychology, in Rome, in 1905,

> I very decidedly ended up taking sides. I believe that consciousness as it is commonly represented either as an entity or as a pure activity, but in any case as fluid, non-extended, diaphanous, spiritual, void of any content of its own but capable of knowing itself directly—I believe that this consciousness is a pure chimera and that the total concrete reality that the word "consciousness" denotes should be given a totally different description.[6]

It should, that is, refer only to concrete phenomena, to *pure experiences*. Here are the conclusions (somewhat surprising and contradictory) of this renowned communication:

> Consciousness, as it is ordinarily understood, does not exist any more than does matter, to which Berkeley has given the coup de grâce. What does exist and form the element of truth contained in the word "consciousness" is the susceptibility which the parts of experience have for being related and known.

As concerns this susceptibility, which summarizes and presents the whole problem, it would reside only in the relations of the contents of consciousness toward one another. Some of these contents, then, are found to play the role of things known, others the role of knowing subjects. James continues:

> These two roles can be perfectly defined without going outside the fabric of experience and without having to invoke anything transcendental. The attributions subject and object, represented and representative, thing and thought, thus signify a practical distinction which is of the utmost importance but which is only of a *functional* order and is not of an ontological order as classical dualism presents it. In the final analysis things and thoughts are not fundamentally heterogeneous. They are instead made of the same stuff, a stuff which cannot be defined as such, but can only be experienced and which can be called, if one so desires, the stuff of experience in general.[7]

But though it is dogmatically excluded, the reality of the constitution of consciousness is no less affirmed. The constitution of experience, "insofar as" (an expression which James did not like) it is "centered" by a theme (a "topic"), is described in wholly spatial terms. This description has been revived by Aron Gurwitsch[8] from a point of view which on the whole considers "Jamesian" consciousness as a structure. "Fringes" are transitive states, evanescent atmospheres which have an affinity with the object and are considered to be attributes of the "substantive part" of the object intended by consciousness. All in all the object is grasped in a "topic" of significations which arrange a shadow around it. The structure of consciousness appears here as being propositional. But it is a proposition which emerges and develops as an experience, a text which has a "context" (the noematic context of which Husserl will speak). It is, then, truly a question of an organization, presence, and simultaneity in conformity with a signification which appears and develops. Such a "Gestaltization" of experience, as it is given or as a stream of consciousness, was, moreover, already indicated in James's early writings—in his *Principles of Psychology,* when he refused to consider the stream of experience as being a discontinuity or an aggregate. He then wrote that a state of consciousness was a unity, "a single pulse of subjectivity, a single psychosis, feeling or state of mind."[9] Moreover, James's thought constantly oscillated between the idea of a primordial chaos of immediate givens, a surging forth or intuitive expansion of lived experience, and the idea of an order which selected these "sensible totalities." Precisely because he was more attentive to the formation of experience in his early works and more sensible to its meaning in the later works, James's theory of consciousness is formulated and even formulatable only in his earlier writings. It is therefore to these works that Aron Gurwitsch refers when he attempts to relate James's theory of the field of consciousness to that of Gestalt psychology (or at least the early form of James's theory to the earliest form of the theory of the organization of *Gestaltquälitäten*) and even to Husserl's noetic-noematic structure (figural factors). This is as much as to say that the "Jamesian" grasp of the pure lived experience of consciousness does not eliminate but rather necessitates the problem of its constitution.

2. HENRI BERGSON

Maurice Merleau-Ponty[10] has written, with regard to the "stunning description" of being as perceived by Bergson (in the first chapters of *Matter and Memory*): "This circuit between being and the self, which brings it about that being is 'for me,' the spectator, and also that the spectator is 'for being,' has not yet been adequately examined. Consciousness springs from this rebounding of the world on the self, from this shock of life upon cognition."[11] Jeanne Delhomme has shown that being, which is in counter-current and is constituted only in relation to a necessary negativity, is for Bergson the object of the "temporal *cogito*" that grasps consciousness as an *interval of actuality* and, in the last analysis, of *action*. The *temporal cogito*, which is at the heart of Bergson's philosophy of consciousness, makes of life itself the being of consciousness. It does this to the extent that consciousness "can gather itself up, be reflected, and catch hold of itself in a *duration* whose memory, action, interest, and freedom are dynamic structures and processes which pass through the body and its brain, and which go beyond them in and through that temporality which is the self's disposition and state of being disponible."

If it is coextensive with life, consciousness is not a purely vital and instinctive phenomenon, as we have already noted. Indeed, consciousness is born of the variance which separates instinct from intelligence. Because it is too organically determined, instinct is a consciousness which has been annihilated by its own predestination: it is an operation without representation. Representation occurs only when instinct collides with reality. The living being's consciousness is defined as an arithmetical difference between virtual activity and real activity. It measures the interval between representation and action.[12] For this reason, consciousness ceases to be fundamentally a pure vital phenomenon and is constructed according to a spatial model of intelligence. In Bergson's philosophy, consciousness appears as the juncture between duration and space, as a construction of "the attention to life," of which the brain is the organ.[13]

In the contingency of possible orders, consciousness appears as a reality which forms itself across the reality which is left behind. It is in the process of "forming itself."[14] In our opinion, this is, in all its breadth and depth, the most important position held by Bergson, who was himself in the process of "forming himself" (Merleau-Ponty).

Consciousness is thus that "form" of life which is precisely not a "point," but the structure in which body and mind meet. It is an indeterminate zone in which the movements which engage action are described. It is a need of creation.[15]

Consciousness withdraws when the action of free choice ceases. This freedom belonging to consciousness is its *temporality,* the possibility of rendering time *facultative,* of anticipating the future and turning back to the past. It is *memory* which constitutes this *faculty.* This is the sense in which Bergson assimilates consciousness to the possiblity of constituting pure memory. Consciousness, he states, signifies first of all memory[16] because all consciousness is *attention* and *expectation.* Conscious being is characterized by its unfolding in time; for, to use Leibniz's expression, matter is only a "momentary mind." The essence of consciousness resides in this movement that pulls being out of this succession of instants following one another in time and makes of it an unfolding *in duration.* Consciousness "retains the past, unrolling it upon itself in a simultaneous progression with the unfolding of time." At least this is the case for the consciousness which ceases to be rudimentary, as in the case of instinct and of animals, and becomes, in the course of creative evolution, one which excavates the act of consciousness within its own duration. This act is itself an actualization and in some manner a duplication, for it implies the doubling of the present.[17]

However, once Bergson had seen consciousness as an actualization of the experience which was the object of attention, he then assimilated it to the self. In fact what he says about the self he could just as well say about consciousness—especially in *Time and Free Will,*[18] or when he writes[19] that the self is something which mistakenly or correctly appears to overflow all the parts of the body joined to it, to go beyond it both in time and in space.

Thus, despite his first and fundamental intuition, in Bergson's philosophy consciousness embraces the self's life, memory, perception, and intelligence.

In his discussion of perception, in *Time and Free Will,*[20] we find the most profound descriptions of the symbolic constitution of space and time, that is, of *simultaneity.* In *Matter and Memory* Bergson presents his famous analyses of the perceived movement which is involved in the *real duration* of the *profound* self, in which the multiplicities of being are grounded in the unity of its free act. In chapter three of the same work, when discussing perceived movement in space, he causes us to make a transition (which is the "high tension" transition of a duration which cannot adapt itself to a homogeneous space) from the play of memory to the imaginative activity of the mind. Moreover, Bergson's works describe the operations of a consciousness whose function is an "explication," a "distend-ing," which can unfold only in a finite order, the order of an "integral experience" (Delhomme) in which an experience is *integrated* into the exigencies of free action and which from its side *integrates* the intuitions of the vital urge.

If William James renounced the notion of a structure of consciousness which appeared to him to be incompatible with the fluidity of its lived content, Henri Bergson has felt, on the level of the connection of instinct and intelligence, the neces-sity for conscious being to organize this encounter. In this he saw the foundation of the reality which belongs to the *field of the present* or the *field of consciousness,* the reality upon which his whole philosophy has been grounded. This philoso-phy may have appeared to be one which separates matter from memory, mind from the brain—which it did at certain stages of its development. But after having passed through creative evolution, it arrived at a spiritual energy which fuses body and thought together to a much greater extent than it separates them. The brain is then no longer an organ of movement in space but an organ of attention and, in the last analysis, of freedom. Bergson might well be reproached for this biological dynamism, by those who cannot uphold the idea that con-sciousness is also in Nature and not merely in History. But if consciousness is "of the body," no one has done as much as Bergson to place it there, to cause it to emerge from it, and, in short, to define it by this movement.

2. PHENOMENOLOGY

Phenomenology has taken on the task of going to the things themselves, to that constitution of a being which validates it by stratifying and interlacing the stages which cause that being to appear as a nucleus of meaning. The foundation of this seizure of being—and here it is very much a question of existing, that is, of human being—implies an intuition of essences (eidetic), a reflection upon the acts which constitute the being in its reciprocal relation of objectivity and subjectivity. Phenome-nology attempts to grasp consciousness in its intentionality; but this is manifested only in the reciprocal reflection of the object and the subject. Since it is neither "naturalistic" or "empiricist" on the one hand, nor "logical" or "psychological" on the other, phenomenology may be defined as a specifically mental procedure, about which there is unceasing discussion as to whether or not it is purely idealistic, whether or not it is "rationalistic." It obviously does more closely approach a philosophy of transcendence through its method of "reduction" of the natural attitude, from which it always starts but in which it never remains.

1. EDMUND HUSSERL

Husserl's phenomenology attacks "psychologism" and does not allow us to confuse psychical life with its intentional object. In this respect it implies the thesis of transcendence; but for Husserl the movement by which consciousness is directed towards its object hides another movement which could be called subjective, except that instead of being a simple turning back of the psychical mass it remains intentional and is concerned with that sphere which is *other* than the subject's selfhood, in which Husserl in the last analysis situates the object. It is delineated as the horizon of objects or as their "background."

These lines from an important article by Emmanuel Linas[21] greatly clarify the debate over the fundamental positions and ambiguities of Husserlian concepts.

a) Goal and Method of Phenomenology

The "reduction," which has its beginnings in the fundamental phenomenological "meditation," first of all goes beyond the natural attitude; then, in the course of grasping "hyletic" moments, it goes beyond the material and noetic "stratum" *(Schicht)* of the flux of the phenomenological being[22] to arrive finally at the other side of the eidetic configuration: the noematic structures of transcendental consciousness. If we limit ourselves to these phases of phenomenological asceticism, we can well ask whether phenomenology is a philosophy of transcendence or of immanence, whether it is an idealism or a realism. Here we are dealing with ambiguities which often have been questioned in depth.[23] It is by its own procedure that phenomenology responds to these questions. For in its fundamental design phenomenology aims at "detaching the totality of the natural world from the domain of consciousness" as if to turn "pure consciousness" into that region of being where objects, "data," lived experiences, and the meanings of each constituted reality intermingle *(verflechten)*. Consciousness is this intermingling.

The reduction *(epoche)* is a conversion of the subject itself, which breaks free from the limitations of the natural attitude. It is a step in the "purification" which, by placing them "within brackets" *(Einklammerung)*, sheds all the empirical determinations which hide the subject from itself because they make it a "party," a "thing" in the world, whereas it is their "ground." What this reduction ought to show us is that the world is a correlate of consciousness—but of absolute consciousness, which is at the summit of this asceticism which aims at that supreme transcendence wherein intentionality is *creative* both of the Self and of the World.

The phases of this "phenomenological reduction" constantly go further into the transcendence of a more and more pure consciousness which is constantly separating itself more and more from the natural attitude and which idealizes the world of things to the point of turning them into an absolute of reason. We must understand that the phases of this reduction nonetheless suppress neither the reality of lived experience, nor the reality of things, nor of nature. In order to ground this "asceticism" it must first be shown that it is possible to build a science which is not empirical but "eidetic" (*eidos* is used in the sense of "essence"). The region "consciousness" is the region of essences. It is not a coordinate of the region "nature," which is rather included within it. Consciousness thus does not exclude nature. It goes beyond nature. The "given" of eidetic intuition is a pure essence; this intuition necessarily implies something which comes from the subject *(Sichtigkeit)*. The empiricist thesis which identifies experience with "the primordial dator acts" (that is, those acts which limit intuition to sensible experience), and the idealist thesis which ignores the fact that pure intuition implies a "given" as well, both these theses are equally untenable and, as Husserl has said, absurd. Phenomenology is like consciousness itself: both give meaning to the world by drawing it out of their own constitution. Without being so pretentious as to become involved in metaphysical reflections about reflection, we shall content ourselves with saying that this problem of the immanence or the transcendence of consciousness cannot be unilaterally resolved. The meaning of Husserl's phenomenology demands that this ambiguity in the constitution of being be maintained.

We must examine the question of what benefit the social sciences (psychology, psychiatry, etc.) might derive from phenomenology, in the light of Husserl's statement that he "definitively abandoned the terrain of psychology, even if it be descriptive,"[24] and that his phenomenology was instituted above all empirical knowledge which arose from the natural attitude. This does not, however, prevent phenomenology, at the end of its *excursus,* from reflecting upon this knowledge. As Merleau-Ponty emphasizes, "There is also a truth to the natural attitude."[25] In order to understand the meaning of this problem, which is fundamental for us, we shall first of all attempt to sketch the main topics of Husserl's phenomenology as they occur in the course of the laborious exercise of its exposition.[26]

b) The Constitution of Transcendental Consciousness

Having examined the initial goal and the method of phenomenology, we must now determine what it is that is given and what it is that is taken in intuition. This is the reason that one must perform those phenomenological exercises which aim at grasping the articulation of the structural levels which constitute that reflection which, at the heart of being, bestows meaning and which, across its connections and different levels, engenders the configurations of consciousness. The phenomenological reduction thus embraces the actual and virtual changes, the virtuosities, the multiplicity of acts which are performed and left behind in the process of forming the fabric of lived experience. By briefly recalling how *Ideen* progresses through the various levels of this constitution, we shall bring to light the order and connection of these essential hierarchical constructions.

The reduction of the "thesis of the natural attitude" should serve as the springboard of our ascent. It is thus that the fundamental phenomenological considerations are initiated.[27] The being of consciousness is an immediate intuition ("I have the experience of") which includes its present "objects" in a field of intuition as being copresent *(mitbewusst).* But this present field is penetrated and surrounded by a dimly conscious horizon of indeterminate reality. This is true for both the spatiality and the temporality of experience. The result is that I can construct a series of present experiences whose occurrences, variations, and differentiations are evidence of my waking consciousness. The being of consciousness is thus a being which both implies and is implied. It is not the being of things; it is a world of its own bonds and values. (The temporal horizons of the present are much more richly described, notably in §82.) All these "apparitions," *data,* and acts, and each of these multiform states of affectivity and will can be included in the object of the *cogito* insofar as it is the *fundamental form of all waking life.* The *cogito* takes cognizance of *that* which from "its side" (as *cogitatum*) is unreflecting and of that which from "my side" (insofar as *I* live it) does not have the quality of an object. In this way a plane of cleavage and of relation is established between the *natural world* (or "the world" in the ordinary sense of the word) and *consciousness.*

Instead of remaining in the natural attitude which can only record this bilateralness, we must subject the natural attitude to a radical transformation. What position can we take, what can we judge about the existence of that which we have just described? The Cartesian "doubt" does not reach the being of consciousness. It does not shed any light upon the being which it allows to subsist. We must therefore essentially suspend natural reality without destroying it by placing it "within brackets"; by so doing we set the general thesis of the natural attitude "out of action." It is not, however, a question of denying the world, as did the sophists, or of doubting its actual existence, as did the skeptics, but rather of restraining ourselves from making any judgment concerning its spatiotemporal existence. We have received this world into our experience; we must now recognize it without contesting it.[28]

What, then, remains when we put the whole world, ourselves included, out of action? Certainly not the *solus ipse,* says Merleau-Ponty,[29] but the copresence of my consciousness and my body as original constitution *(Urempfindung).* In the analysis of perception, when "I perceive" (in the sense "I perceive that ... "), what I perceive carries with it an area of intuitions forming a background, but this background is found again in all other lived experiences (memories, imagination, etc.); it accompanies, precedes, and follows each lived experience as such, for the flux of lived experience could never be constituted out of pure actualities. The present lived experience implies a halo of nonactivity. Eidetic analysis brings it about that the *cogitatio* addresses itself to an intentional object towards which the "mental gaze" reflexively turns and makes of it an object of inner perception.[30] This flux of lived experience

which is intermingled (we have not yet left the natural attitude) with the natural world, insofar as it is linked to the material world and is lived by a man or by an animate being in
general *(animalia)*, has the eidetic status of *sensible experience* (that of a corporeal individual), which supports the general thesis of a bound totality. The analysis at this point will
profit by bracketing this identification. A lived experience is
not given in bits and pieces; it is, as lived, directly "perceived,"
whereas the object of perception can be given only a bit at a
time, since perception focuses only upon the phenomenal being of a thing. The immanent being of a thing is absolute, but
this can be grasped, can be perceived, only through the mode
of reflection. We are here following an outline of the process of
the detachment *(Ablösbarkeit)* of consciousness from the natural world which is the goal of a phenomenology whose object
is the region and structure of pure consciousness.[31]

The structures of pure consciousness, its "constitution" (its
Urkonstitution), are the correlation between the "characteristics of the object focused upon" (noema) and the "characteristics of the focusing" of consciousness (noesis). The noema is the
object-side of consciousness and the noesis the subject-side, as
Ricoeur emphasizes.[32] Intentionality is constitutive of this constitution; but this is a reciprocal and reverberating intentionality which is not only that of the subject towards the object but
also of the object towards the subject.[33] *It is not a question of
starting from a "psychologically" envisaged lived experience
but rather from that reflection which grounds lived experience.* Reflection itself is a double-faced sphere of pure givens:
one face is oriented towards the subject, the other towards the
object. All lived experiences, the flux of lived experiences
which constitute the unity of consciousness, involve sensory
lived experiences whose intentionality depends upon a sense-
bestowing stratum *(Sinngebung)*, for the sensible *hyle* is lived
as an intentional *morphe.* Such is the noetic phase *(noetische
Moment)* or more briefly, the noesis.[34] Husserl establishes that
the hyletic and noetic phases are real phases of lived experience.[35] The constitution of the transcendences of consciousness
(the Self, temporality, and the *hyle*—"a sort of trilogy," writes
Ricoeur, "which calls forth a protoconstitution only acclaimed
from afar in the *Ideas*")[36] orients us primarily towards the
"noema." Because of its noetic phase every intentional experience [37] harbors *(berget)* within itself some element of meaning.

A *noematic content,* or noema, is constituted by a multiplicity of "data" which are susceptible of manifestation in a truly pure intuition and which correspond to the multiplicity of "data" which constitute the noetic content. Perception has its noema as lived experience which is perceived as such; but this is true of all species of intentional experience. In memory we find, after the reduction, memory *per se.* In each of these lived experiences is contained a noematic meaning (notably the "doxic" characters, the theses of "positionality" involved in judgments and beliefs). When it is a question of "doxic" modifications, these noetic-noematic structures form theses of actual or potential "positionality" which form the stratum of the "logos," of its meanings and expressions.[38]

Finally, in the fourth and last section, Husserl tackles a problem which had not yet been touched upon in this work: the reference of the noema both to the object (Fink), that is, the problematic of reason, and to rational consciousness insofar as it fills the void of signs with the fullness of presences (Ricoeur) and is capable of endowing its signs with a coefficient of presence, as if with a capstone of reality.

Thus, by the method of "reduction," which has always been for itself an "enigmatic possibility" as Merleau-Ponty reminds us, Husserl has extracted from consciousness the relationships of sense and of essence which constitute it. But reduced and pure consciousness cannot reduce the world, which it can ground only by incorporating it within itself, unless it both pose and propose it (Ricoeur). "Donor" intuition and its "seizure," this action of consciousness upon itself in the process of its own essential constitution, do not reduce the world to the situation of depending only upon a legislation which is formal (in the Kantian sense); they cause the world to surge forth from a presence whose reality is that of the lived experiences of consciousness, which at the same time both refers to this and creates it. By expressing the metaphysical sense of *Ideas* in these terms (which are otherwise questionable), we gain a fuller understanding of the controversies over idealism and realism to which Husserl's phenomenology has given rise. We have been most concerned with grasping that profound rhythm of thought which oscillates between lived experience and reason, as if this movement was the very pulsating of being, specifically that of conscious being.

What is "real," what corresponds to the constitution of consciousness, is neither the thing nor some aspect of cognitions which could be said to be extrinsic to consciousness. The *cogito* focuses upon the immanent composition, either the inclusion of nonintentional matter in the cogito, or the inclusion of the *cogitatio* in the flux of lived experience.[39] Husserlian phenomenology focuses upon this "real" to the extent that it is sensible and manifest. Having made a definitive break with Cartesian dualism, Husserl was obliged to refuse choosing between external and internal, between external perception and idea. He had necessarily to substitute the heterogeneity of the constitutive process of consciousness for these two dichotomies. If we have understood Ludwig Landgrebe correctly, the constitution of consciousness[40] is that composition which incessantly makes and unmakes itself by moving from that which it "gives itself" to that which it "takes." In the last analysis Husserlian idealism returns upon itself in order to grasp "the things themselves" which are what constitute consciousness. This incarnate ground of consciousness is the fundamental intuition which comes to mind when we think of Husserl.[41]

c) The Problem of Psychological Consciousness

Rather than remaining on this insecure metaphysical ground, we shall now move to the examination of two questions which are essential to our study of consciousness: When it reduces psychological consciousness to a pure consciousness, does transcendental phenomenology annihilate the possibility of any "psychology of consciousness"? and, What interest can the phenomenology of "pure consciousness" have as far as the psychological problem of the structure of consciousness is concerned?

As regards the first point, we have already emphasized the fact that when the *epoche* "annihilates" the world it only brackets it; passing beyond the natural attitude does not exclude its object. As regards the relationship of psychology to phenomenology, things are not so simple. On the one hand Husserl states that, "as concerns the eidetic material spheres there is one which distinguishes itself to such a degree that there can be absolutely no question of putting it out of action: this is the eidetic sphere of consciousness itself after its phenomenological purification."[42] It thus seems that a phenomenological psychology (a term which is often used in contemporary works) can be validated. In our exposition, which followed the "reduction" through the different levels of being, we have shown the importance of recognizing the good reasons for not losing sight of the fact that there are "regions" of being, a sort of ontological hierarchy. The regional indices of the natural sphere, including the category of body, correspond to the eidetic level.[43] For this structure of being there should be, if not an empirical psychology, at least a psychology which will profit from being treated in its phenomenological perspectives. We join with many commentators more authoritative than ourself in emphasizing that the placing out of action of the objects of natural cognition or of the empirical and natural sciences does not thereby suppress the level of their validity, even if the *epoche* attempts and ought to go beyond it. In §§53 and 54, concerning psychological consciousness, we find the clearest expression of Husserl's position. As a real *(reales)* event, consciousness is subordinated to the interior of this world; only through its empirical relation to the body does consciousness become a real human or animal consciousness. This *incorporation of consciousness,* is the condition of mutual understanding. But if pure consciousness does not lose anything to this interweaving on the level of awareness or in this psychophysical relationship on the corporeal level, this consciousness is not *essentially* corporeal. Many have commented upon Husserl's statement that "An incorporeal and, paradoxical as it may seem, inanimate and impersonal consciousness can certainly be conceived of."[44] Thus, to the extent that it is a grasping of the essential structure of pure consciousness, phenomenology necessarily goes beyond the phenomena of consciousness as long as they are integrated "only" with the real in nature. Even when the object of empirical psychology and the object of the intentional psychology of the first steps of eidetic analysis are fused together, phenomenology still remains possible, as is indicated in §76. This seems to us to be of capital importance, for, as can be seen from what we have said concerning the first steps of the reduction and the analysis of lived experience, Husserl's "descriptions" and even his first "transcendental intuitions" form a style of structural analysis of consciousness which, before attaining the pure essence of consciousness, not only permits but forces us to seize its organization, its fundamental constitution as reality (cf. below, pp. 99–100).

In his earliest writings Husserl insisted precisely upon this fundamental *reality*, especially in the fifth of the *Logical Investigations*.

The second question is that of determining in what way a transcendental phenomenology or a pure structure of consciousness can be useful to an eidetic science which approaches a psychological science of nature,[45] that is, a structural and intentional psychology of consciousness. Husserl responds to this question each time that he points out [46] that the disconnecting *(Ausschaltung)* of natural realities and of their own proper sciences implies not that they are nothing but that they receive their method (or that their objects receive their status) from the preliminary phenomenological reductions. As far as the object of phenomenology itself is concerned, phenomenology is in effect the only means of attaining the real structure of consciousness, not because consciousness is an artifice or an abstraction, but for the very reason that it is enveloped and as it were guaranteed by an ideal form of existence. "Consciousness appears first in itself as absolute consciousness and then in its correlate as psychological consciousness, which from this point onwards is immersed in the natural world."[47] We thus understand how it is that all the exercises of reflection and reduction which are operative within consciousness and which cause the modalities of its constitution to appear, are and ought to be an indispensable preface to the study of a structural analysis of consciousness directed towards its phenomenal reality. Far from excluding a psychology of consciousness, phenomenology seems rather to demand such a psychology; for the whole process of grasping the transcendental structures of consciousness, no matter how absolutely idealist it may be at this level, uncovers the stratum, *hyle*, the unconscious groundwork of its constitution, the *Urempfindung*, which corresponds to that which is beyond it: the absolute of the body and of the sensible thing.

The profound impression produced upon the reader of *Ideas* is fruitful to the extent that it places him within an architectonic of presentations, within a multiplicity which both compromises and composes the unity of consciousness. As regards the conscious being which is constituted into the self of lived experience, the *Cartesian Meditations*[48] give the clearest presentation of the phenomenological foundation of the domain of the self *(Eigenheitsphäre)* which our examination of the definition of conscious being showed to be the very essence of conscious being's autonomy. This is what ensures it its being (self) and its having (experience). The totality of the relations of the self, such as it is, with all its having, constitutes *habitus* with its two aspects of proprietorship and possession.[49]

Husserl's phenomenology is thus a guarantor and indispensable guide for the study which we are about to undertake. It is most illuminating and vivifying to examine this "reflection" of the movement of consciousness towards its own foundation. This movement provides Husserlian phenomenology with the rhythm at which its pulsations alternate between the "turnings into ourselves" and the "goings out of the self," between ideality and reality, between the "given" and the "taken" of existence. This is especially true since, in spite of the claims of certain exegeses and interpretations, this reflection appears to plunge into the infrastructure of being just as much as it surges forward towards its ideality. Whatever some may say, Husserl is not so very different from Bergson, if we look at the men themselves rather than listening to their zealots and commentators. We have been encouraged to make known our own reflections on this intricate subject by Merleau-Ponty's description of this aspiration of phenomenology as it is borne towards the shadows by its own light, which he expressed so felicitously shortly before his death in the chapter of *Signs* devoted to "The Philosopher and His Shadow." The fact is that "what resists phenomenology within us—natural being," states Merleau-Ponty, "cannot remain outside phenomenology and should—as Husserl understood it—have its place within it."[50]

Merleau-Ponty believed that it was necessary to descend to the level of our "archeology," for there is "incontestably something between transcendental nature, the being-in-itself of naturalism and the immanence of the mind." This something "must be the body, that *vinculum* of the self and things, that copresence which links my consciousness to the other." For this reason "the whole problem of empathy *(Einfühlung)*, like that of my incarnation, opens on the meditation of the sensible."[51] In this way Merleau-Ponty, by going beyond his previous analyses of behavior and of perception, emphasized his concern to set the body at the center of experience as a nonrelative for all relativities, for its sensing, its affections, and its actions; he has made it the point of reference and attraction for all the constitutive and constituted acts which bind consciousness to its

world. This is the living significance of Husserlian phenomenology as the *incarnation* of the spirituality of conscious being.

2. MARTIN HEIDEGGER

On the whole, Heidegger's analysis of *Dasein* develops another style of phenomenology which moves in a different direction, that of the ec-centricity and the ec-stasy of ex-istence. If
Husserl plunges us into a profound abyss, it would take an
infinity of books and even of libraries to examine the "horizontal" infinity of relationships open to a being in and through its
Dasein. We must therefore resign ourselves to a rudimentary
"abridgment" of the Heideggerian style of analysis of being.

The distinction which Dilthey introduced among "beings"
between "being as a thing" and "being as subject, being, or
soul," this principle of a heterogeneity between consciousness
(or life) and things, is a leading idea of contemporary thought.
In *Being and Time*, Heidegger made the attempt to think of
mind in a manner which is "radically different" from the manner of thinking of things, as Alphonse de Waelhens writes.[52]
According to Dilthey the inadequacy of causality as regards
Dasein (the being of the existing subject) is opposed to its application to the being of a thing *(Vorhandischkeit)*. This opposition must be taken as the starting point if all *"Jenseitigkeit"*
(all "othersidedness") is to be excluded from life (from consciousness). This point is of capital importance if we are to
understand from the outset that "consciousness" cannot be an
object of analysis in Heidegger's phenomenology; for being,
appearing, and sense constitute a sort of indivisible unity behind which there can be nothing else.[53] From this point onwards it will never be a question of *"Bewusstsein"* but always
of *"Dasein"* when he wishes to designate the being of an existent. Because Heidegger sees man as submerged by his being,
he might be considered a precursor and pioneer of structuralist
neopositivism (Mikel Dufrenne). The *"Jemeinigkeit"* of a being (the status of selfhood) may in fact appear to be volatilized
in the generality of the being of all existents, as we shall see
later.

The existential analytic shows that *Dasein* (in opposition to
the thing, which is "blocked up in its being") is characterized
by its uncertitude; it is the modes of its existence which constitute its essence. This is the central idea of existential anthropology. This *Dasein* always presents itself as a self, that is,

as a certain manner of taking sides for or against certain possibilities. Thus, to be a self necessarily involves a possibility of being against the self. From this arise the two fundamental perspectives of authentic being and inauthentic being, of which ordinary existence *(Alltäglichkeit)* is the usual mode.

Being-in-the-world is the first "existential" which Heidegger's analytic encounters. This is not a question of the relationship of a content to that which contains it. It is the expression of a transcendental relationship of *in-der-Welt-sein*. It enunciates a relationship to a non-self. "Being in" is not some attribute or characteristic which a person would possess along with other attributes; it is the very being of existence. This first mode of being entails "preoccupation" *(Besorge)*; for to exist is to be preoccupied with, to be bound to the world, to that world which *is there*, as the *being-there* of the existent. This world is composed of things which are more or less tools or utensils *(pragmata)*, manners of being at hand and of being able to be grasped and utilized by *Dasein* insofar as he is the source of possibilities. Intramundane beings are organized in relation to a spatial inherence which is not proximity in space but is rather the order of an anthropological space (direction, dimension, places, points, routes, lines, horizon, regions, distances, etc.). This "space" of *Dasein* implies the possibility of surmounting, approaching, and organizing the surrounding world.

What is the subject of this "existence in the world"? Ipseity belongs to *Dasein*. But there is no pure consciousness detached from the world. The Self is being with another *(Das Ich-sein ist Mitsein, mit Anderen)*, for its existence excludes solitude. This dependence could be that of "one" *(man)* who fundamentally is not anyone *(man nicht)* and who produces only an inauthentic existence through his "coexistence." The vicissitudes of *Dasein* who has been cast into the world and abandoned *(Geworfenheit* expresses the fact of having been thrown or flung into the world) constitute the vicissitudes of the human condition which are taken up by Heidegger (sentiments, fear, the theme of death, care). Selfhood *(Selbstheit)* is born of care *(Sorge)*. As seen from the "beyond" of the first existential analytic, human being is viewed by Heidegger as temporalizing, happening, and historical being; man is open through his relation to "the space of history" (Fink). This constitutes the historicity of *Dasein*, "the fact of being by prolonging oneself," of unfolding. Since *Dasein* is not entirely master of itself, it "is to be," it must become; but to the extent that it remains finite it is the place at which being can break through, the seat of the clearing through which it receives its light.

We are not able here to develop the extraordinary richness of these explications of being in its world and in its history. We have, however, perhaps said enough (following the account of de Waelhens) to be fully aware that it is here that the problem of consciousness has emerged and that it meets much the same fate as a *Geworfenheit* which throws conscious being off-center *(ex-centre)* in the infinite ec-stasies of these modalities of being, and in some way expands it to the point where it coincides with its World. Though this is true, we sometimes find perplexing this "ontology" which dissipates the being of consciousness by opening it up to the infinity of its progress and possibilities.

3. GESTALT PSYCHOLOGY AND STRUCTURALISM

In order to point out the essential points and the diversity of Gestalt psychology, we shall make special reference to the fundamental work of Aron Gurwitsch (cf. below, pp. 91–95). The notion of form or structure is not the same for the schools of Graz, of Berlin, or for the Anglo-Saxon schools; nor is it the same for von Ehrenfels and Meinong or for Köhler and the behaviorist or operationalist Gestaltists. "Structuralism of Form" might focus either upon an order which is composed only of environmental variables (Skinner, Ryle) while contesting all internal organization, or upon this organization itself to the extent that it is animated by the intentionality of the subject. Since Gestalt psychology has moved more and more towards logical-mathematical "formalized" models, it cannot be utilized to accomplish the goal of this work, a goal which it systematically rejects: a description of the organized structures of conscious being, which Gestalt psychology considers to be mythical. It is difficult to understand how something or rather *someone* would be able to survive the rigorously and methodically artificial treatment of a strictly mathematical psychology ("with no presuppositions") which is constructed on the level of paradigms, following the rules of a formalization which abstracts any value and meaning from the signs it employs at the point at which the formalistic models[54] and impersonal structures converge.

What might be called "French structuralism,"[55] which is paradoxically enough allied to, but defiant of, "depth psychology," is not very different from that Gestalt psychology which posits a world of abstract forms. It is understandable that this philosophical-cultural movement should have been designated a neo-logical positivism for which the notion of a psychical structure of the subject in general, and of a structure of its conscious being in particular, could have no meaning.

In its fundamental sense, the notion of "structure" is here utilized as a logical or abstract form, as an extra-human "system," a verbal, cultural, institutional milieu into which man is thrown and with which he must deal. This system of relations or of meanings exists, is maintained, and is transformed without the intervention of man, who is at most its illusory effect and not its cause or agent. Humanity is laid hold of from the underneath and the outside of these word-things which constitute the aleatory structures of its plural being. In other words, what was already implicit in Heidegger's "phenomenology" or Sartre's existentialism has become the leitmotif of contemporary structuralist antianthropology, of "French structuralism," which assumes "the death of the subject" and of the "fetish-self," as if structuralism reunited the forms of Gestalt psychology "*ohne Gestalter*" with the "poor creature" *(ein armes Ding)* which is the Freudian ego. This "analysis" of man reduces his humanity to systems of signs forming a verbal strategy which is immobile in its specific or archeological constancy ("the one and immobile world" of these modern Eleatics, as Henri Lefebvre expresses it). It reduces man's humanity to a mere skeleton, rigorously deprived of life. The representatives of this "analysis" (Foucault, Lacan, Barthes, etc.), all of them subtle, bold, and often genial, believe that they have been able to draw out of linguistics (the taxonomic and combinative aspect of language) the model of the automatic construction of man—a model borrowed from the logicism of the Vienna Circle. Everything is, in fact, possible and in certain respects useful in the domain of ideas. In dealing with the problem—which we do not dare to call peculiar—of conscious being, it seems obvious that "structuralism" has been a salutary reaction against the subjectivism of pure lived experience; as Domenach has written, the time was ripe for the impersonal to appear as a structural element of the personal universe. This is certainly true, but only on the condition that the impersonal should *become* personal. For the impersonal is a reference to reality, reality being that over against which the subject is constituted as subject. The whole dialectic of conscious being (which has been systematically denied by the conceptual system of this neopositivism), which creates man across the various structures of his consciousness and his history, opposes the destruction of its own work, the annihilation of the subject, its speech, and its consciousness (Ricoeur, Dufrenne, Lefebvre, etc.).

The metaphysical goals of "consciousness" have been set in order in terms of this notion of "structure." Were "structure" to imply a "model," an "assemblage" which is regulated physico-mathematically, there would be no reason for describing the "aleatory structures" or "open structuring" of mental and especially conscious being, which becomes lost in the mechanisms of "associations" or "conglomerates."

Our reason for emphasizing the *biological* concept of organization in our discussion of psychical structures and the structures of conscious being is to be able to restore to structure its hierarchical structuring, the infrastructures and superstructures which compose structure in such a way that by no longer being closed to its Unconscious it might be opened to the freedom of choice and action which this makes possible.

The whole series of tenses and moods of verbalized thought (the conjugation of verbs represents these diverse configurations of conscious being) hides, in the opacity and pauses of speech, that which speech cannot say. From this perspective we shall examine both the structures of conscious being and its relations with its Unconscious. We shall examine the modes by which the subject passes, as Freud has said, from the nonbound energy of the primary processes to the energy which is bound to acts through which the subject disentangles himself by becoming conscious of himself, by becoming that second himself who is the self when his psychical organization goes beyond its nature by means of its culture.

PART TWO

The Field of Consciousness or the Actuality of Lived Experience

I The Destructuration of the Field of Consciousness

(Sketch of a Phenomenological Psychopathology of the Field of Consciousness)

Classical psychiatry, which is directly inspired by "associationist" and "functionalist" psychology, has divided the object of its study into a number of "functions" (memory, affectivity, perception, imagination, intelligence, consciousness, etc.). We place ourself in a radically different perspective, not in order to describe a contingent variety of mental disorders, but so that starting from these disorders we might come to understand the hierarchy of the levels of the destructuration* of consciousness, of "crises," or of those "states" of mental disorders which effectively constitute "experiences" (*Erlebnisse*) of pathological modes of actualizing lived experience.

This "hierarchy" consists of a series of "structures" which traditional psychiatry has artificially dissociated. It appears as the natural ordering of the levels of consciousness, whose architectonic structure is discovered by examining the process of its destructuration. Through the spectral analysis of its pathology we find the "field of consciousness" to be the product of those activities which control the actualization of lived experience and which comprise the spatiotemporal organization of the immediate experience of being in the world here and now —in short, of the "field of presence." This is the general sense of the structural analyses which we have developed at length in other works and which provide us with the essentials of the

---

*Ey uses the term *"déstructuration"* (verb form: *se déstructurer*) to indicate "a disorganization of an organically unified whole." In order to retain the root "structure," we have most often simply used his term. In some cases, however, for the sake of clarity, we have substituted variations of the following: erosion (or breakdown) of structure, structural disintegration, loss of structure, disorganized.—Trans., in collaboration with the author.

position developed in this chapter. We refer the reader to our *Études*[1] for a more detailed and complete exposition of the facts and reflections which have provided us with a basis in rigorous clinical observation from which to approach this problem. A phenomenological description, which alone can lead us to the essential or constitutional structures of consciousness, must be grounded in this kind of "clinical observation"; for these structures appear only to the degree that their destructuration reveals them. They are revealed through their negation, when this annihilation "frees" the positivity of lived experience, when it "frees" that which it is still possible or even necessary for it to reveal.

To our eyes, this clinical observation, this "knowledge" such as we have grounded it, is irrefutable. It establishes *facts* which no clinical psychiatrist can place in doubt:

1) the fact that the mental disorders which all clinical psychiatrists admit, encompass numerous "other disorders," including all those possible disorders which can be observed in the "crises" of which the epileptic crisis is the model;

2) the fact that clinical observation (and especially that of "periodical psychoses") presents us with confusional states, oneiric states, delirious* or hallucinatory experiences, states of excitation or depression, in a *continuum* which can be broken up only artificially;

3) the fact that all these psychopathological structures are presented in an irreversible and constant order, in such a way that they can be described as a hierarchy of structural levels whose superior levels of loss of structure are implied by the inferior levels, but not vice versa;

4) the fact that the same process of dissolution brought on by causes which are toxic (psychotomimetic substances)

---

*The French word *"délire"* is used for two different phenomena: 1) delirium, considered as a delirious experience or state and which is more or less analogous to dreaming, and 2) the delusional idea, which is characterized by lucidity of consciousness.

German rather systematically uses two terms: *"Delirium"* (*"deliriöse Zustand"*) and *"Wahn."*

The difference between these two terms is very important in this work; for in it the author shows how these two modes are distinct, one (delirious experience) corresponding to the destructuration of consciousness, the other to the disorganization of personality.—Trans., in collaboration with the author.

or infectious (encephalitis) or more generally cerebral (epilepsy, tumors, traumatism), whether this process is exogenous (acquired) or endogenous (constitutional), is manifested clinically in all states of the structural disintegration of consciousness. (The highest levels correspond to the beginning or restorative stages.)

Since the details of this clinical demonstration have been established elsewhere, we shall here refer only to its most essential points.

1. SLEEP AND DREAMING

Before we describe the phenomenological structure of these levels of the destructuration of consciousness, let us simply state that they derive their crucial importance from a "primordial fact," as Moreau de Tours calls it: the fact of sleeping and dreaming[2] to the extent that this both exhibits and demonstrates that consciousness "contains" the imaginary as a lived "content" of its unconscious levels.

The vital phenomenon of the "closed nature" of consciousness contrasts so greatly with its "wakeful activity" that "consciousness" and "unconsciousness" are often taken as synonyms for *waking* and *sleeping.* Sleep even appears to be a zero of wakefulness or of consciousness. Dreaming seems to deny this negation, for the consciousness of dreaming is not a nothingness. Dreaming is a "lived experience" of sleeping consciousness. Other than through the memory of a dream, this "lived experience" manifests itself to others only through conjectural, but nonetheless significant, indices (the psychomotor manifestations of dreaming). This fact shows us that the relationship of sleeping and waking cannot be reduced to the alternative of all or none. Consciousness cannot be defined "purely and simply" by wakefulness, for it contains different levels of lived experiences within its destructuration. But what is this lived experience "for oneself" which is lived by the dreamer? It is nothing but a lived experience which can scarcely be lived; it is an experience which is so instantaneous and rapidly decaying that it can be lived only as "having been," or at most as "having just occurred." The essence of the thinking which occurs during sleep or of the imaginative consciousness of dreaming is to be bogged down in sleep. It is enough to awaken the sleeping person, or that he wake by himself, and he will feel that he has "interrupted a lived experience" which it is impossible to grasp again, but of which the experience insofar as lived could only have appeared by disappearing into unreality. This lived experience would have only a dimly felt and vague being if it were incapable of becoming a "dream," when it goes beyond the limits of sleep and takes on the form of a memory, a narrative, or even of a radically original experience (as we shall see in the chapter "The Neurobiology of the Field of Consciousness"). At this point we arrive at the extreme point of that which is "lived,"[3] this past participle which is the only mode in which we can conjugate immediate experience, since immediate experience can be only if it lasts long enough to survive itself. The "lived" aspect of sleep can become a "dream" only by entering into the fabric of existence in such a way that it can pull itself out of this fabric. For this trickling of dreaming into waking consciousness, this entering of sleeping consciousness into the alert state of consciousness is "recalled" as the memory of a lived experience which was "really" lived during sleep, but which could introduce itself into the open world of the dreamer only by remaining outside this world. It is through the narration of what has occurred during the dream that this dream is formed as a dream which has been drawn out from a certain depth of sleep[4] and which is incompatible with the clarity of the waking state. Such are the conditions for the appearing or the presentation of the lived experience of sleep. These conditions guarantee that it will be a "really unreal" lived experience, since the images during a dream are neither nothing nor something. They are precisely what so many analyses of oneiric consciousness have "laid bare" as being its irreducible core: the projection of intentionality into its imaginary objects (Sartre), an appearing in response to a call, but an appearing which arises with no other context than that of its own presentation. Such and such a scene, an image, a face, an object arise and develop against a background of nothingness, against the background of the night of sleep. The thematic development of the rapid changes within a dream is only the making explicit in images of meanings which are implied much more than they are expressed (imagery unfolding in its symbolic metaphors)—assuming that waking or its secondary elaboration does not introduce as an afterthought more than was contained in the experience itself.

The "lived experience" of dreaming can appear as endowed with a purely "noetic" structure (in Husserl's sense of the term) and as responding only to a "sense datum" (which emerges from the depths of the body of the dreamer, who is indifferent to or absent from his world as if it were only that immanence and in some way that passivity of a "given" of consciousness). This is because the dream, as Sartre has so admirably described it,[5] is an "imaginary event" without worldliness, a purely imagining consciousness, for "this consciousness lacks the thetic function," the faculty of positing and of positing itself in the categories of objective and worldly reality. In this respect dreaming is in a fundamentally ambiguous position. It is absolutely lived in its immediacy, but is lived independently of any problematic of reality. In Freud's terms, it obeys the absolute of the "pleasure principle," and not that of the "reality principle." It is in the same category as that absolute lived experience which shows only a bit of itself at a time (Husserl) and which arises in the brilliance of an object which is there before us. All this is certainly true, for insofar as it is a presentation and actualization without any system of references, a dream is a lived experience which takes possession of the sleeper to the point of fascinating him. The coalescing of the experience (of which the dream is the narration) and the dreamer (who, having lived it, recounts it) is such that the sleeping person and his sleep are in effect suspended during his dream.[6] What Emmanuel Mounier has said concerning consciousness in general—that it is "grasping" and grasped in the necessity of its own choice, that it is the captive of its own capturing—is especially true with respect to this "imaginary consciousness."

If this "noesis" is a "germinating" of the sense contained in the oneiric lived experience, which seems to be formless and only the appearing of a flux which slips away, it is nonetheless characteristic of thought during sleep in general, even of that which does not come to be formed into a scenic dream. In order that such dreams can be organized and can survive themselves later on in their recounting, it must be presented in a form, an "analogue" of reality, that is, in a symbolic context. To say that a dream can be expressed only through hieroglyphics which at this level are the basic source of the dialectic of the Unconscious and the conscious (cf. Part Four of this work) is to understand dreams as if they were structured by "rules"—whether by rules of syntax or merely those of rhetoric—which indirectly impose upon them or remind them of the law of reality, of objectivity. Even at this level the noematic structure of lived experience is apparent, as if to assure us that in order for the experience of the sleeping person to be a dream, this experience is never simply given, for it is taken up again by him in the exigencies (which might be more or less demanding) of the legislation of lived experience. The intentionality of the lived experience must obey this legislation if it is to be able to be symbolic of something, if it is to appear as an event. Thus, even when experience, which here appears in the first possible stage of its formation, is presented as being simply a sort of virtual experience, this virtuality can be actualized only by making itself objective, or at the very least in the necessary apparition of an objectification. Such is the sleeping person's experience. It is an experience which obviously depends more or less directly upon the sleep state, sleep being a kind of formal incapacity which reduces consciousness to a state in which it is not able to unfold itself, in which it cannot open up, cannot confront the world. This state suppresses the opposition of a "for itself" which is fated to remain only an "in itself" when the sleeping person's rigid and agglutinate consciousness congeals. We take this process of sleeping-dreaming to be the very model of the destructuration of consciousness. If sleep takes place in the "third person" (and in neuter gender), it also takes place in the "first person," for we can just as easily say that "we were overcome by sleep" as that "we abandoned ourselves" to it. When "we go to sleep," either sleep seizes us or we give in to it.[7]

2. ONEIRIC-CONFUSIONAL STATES

In clinical psychiatry there are a great number of "syndromes" or "confusional states," the study of which has won deserved renown for French psychiatry (Delasiauve, Régis, Chaslin, etc.). We shall not concern ourselves here with their pathogenesis, which is usually held to be toxinfectious since these states are typical of encephalitis or of the action of toxins. They disturb consciousness on the model of "intoxications" which are brought on by neurotropic poisons (alcohol in particular). These states of oneiric delirium are "pathological dreaming," as Lasègue stated over a hundred years ago. The person suffering from a confusional state is not sleeping. Even in its stuporous forms his "wakefulness" only allies him but does not identify him with sleep state, and to an even lesser degree with coma. The confusional state is a "ground" lacking structure in which the negative modes of "not being conscious" make their most obvious appearance in the clinical and critical analysis of this disorder. Much more than is the case with dreaming, its "unconsciousness" is still a "consciousness," whose mode of existence allows the possibility of developing into delirium.[8]

In the confusional state one does not sleep in his motility; but he is asleep in his consciousness. The sleeping person lives (as he breathes) his dream in the quasi-immobility of his body without expressing anything to anyone else unless it be through his movements, especially through his ocular movements, so as to allow himself to speak of his dream only as a story which he could recount to himself or to others. A person in the confusional state, on the other hand, lives an experience which unfolds as if outside of himself. He lives this experience through his psychomotor expressions (attitudes, movements, turbulence, pantomime, agitation, etc.) and through his verbal expressions (often enough he will say what is happening as he lives it; it is almost always possible to enter into his experience through the "communication" of clinical examination). Oneiric delirium is thus even more distinct from the ipseity of dreaming. It nevertheless retains close and profound links with this experience.

This oneiric confusion, which is more or less open to others, does not in fact suppress the *absence* of the subject. The subject himself is there without being there, as if fascinated by the kaleidoscopic imagery. This "lived experience" is for him like that of dreams. It is a lived experience which will not be retained, or will be only poorly retained. It is an experience which cannot be relived (the amnesic character of confusional experience), or can be relived only with great difficulty. The "world" of confusional states does not have any more existence than that of dream states. It is merely an "analogon," a delirious semblance and, in the last analysis, an imagined fiction, "without worldliness," which unfolds without having the horizon of the world. This lived experience arises and develops only under pressure from certain chaotic "givens" which are its appearances. Their scenic sequence resembles a panting of impulsive significations which is animated by often intense feelings (anxiety, euphoria, terror). The "aesthetic," "ecstatic," or "erotic" character of this lived experience expresses the profound relation of oneiric delirium to the pleasure or pain principle, or, more generally, to the sources of eagerness or of fear. The confused person's enchantment (even when it is a case of the frightening bewitchment of a nightmare) is the experience of this intentionality which binds images to desire, to its substitutes, its stirrings, or its aftereffects. The person in a confusional state thus lives a "spectacle" to the very degree that he is transformed into a "spectator." Indeed, because of the annihilation of any other possibility of interest or freedom, the "film" which occupies his attention suppresses his participation as author, and he himself becomes what he "sees" and what he "lives." Oneirism is therefore almost always an experience of visualization of experience to the extent that the experience demands its absorption in the gaze which observes it. The subject is reduced to being a mere object, the object of his desire or of his anguish such as they appear to him in an imaginary experience, which, to the extent that some consciousness remains in it, is itself the prisoner of its condemnation to being only symbolic.

What attracts him so much—an attraction exercised over him and in him by the power of the imaginary—is the *absence* of the subject in the dream which he constructs, this abyss which has grown in him because of the intoxicating urge to be a thing, to cease being someone, to keep leaning until he falls outside himself. Nothing more, then, exists for him but these fantasies of ecstasy, of love and of death, which exclude the self from their representation. Nothing, unless it be a thin horizon of virtuality, a vague presence of real objects and persons. Even these become deformed (false recognitions, illusions); they appear only so as to be represented in his phantasmagoria. Like the rush of a totality of events without history, without space or time, whatever appears in this unstructured consciousness explodes there with violence and is detached from the outlines, nuances, and contingencies of reality. This "worldless world," this spectacle which has replaced reality, is now there in such a manner that there is no possibility of its being neutralized by those distances, perspectives, and noematic categories which could free the subject from the vertiginous grips of a radically subjective experience. For in confusional states, as in sleep, the subject whose consciousness has lost its structure finds himself alone with himself, and with a "himself" which has itself disappeared because it has lost its faculty of transcendence. Since

he has become identified with the intentional or noetic movement which carries him along, the person in the confusional
state has lost all possibility of *being present to the world,* of
being for others and of being for himself, of being able to constitute that "face-to-face" contact between himself and another
person which is the first generative movement through which
consciousness becomes open and opening. He is "absent." He
has lost his access to the world, his ability to create it—as might
happen to us when, at the moment of waking, we no longer
know who or where we are, and for an instant stand aghast
before this gaping abyss of nothingness. In confusional states,
however, this abyss is not a pure nothingness. It is peopled, but
only with "lived experiences" which rise up in this gulf without being able to fill it: one is captivated, or, more accurately,
captured, by his "images." Oneiric confusion is thus seen to be
that deep degree of unconsciousness in which consciousness
has lost the possibility of opening itself to the world, of constituting its first constitutive movement, that of an *orientation* or
direction towards its world. It has lost the ability to situate itself
within those dimensions which are precisely the primary
groundwork of the "field of his freedom."

3. TWILIGHT STATES AND "ONEIROID" STATES

The modes of consciousness which clinical psychiatry
(Mayer-Gross) describes by these terms are so close to oneiric
confusional states that it is often difficult and sometimes practically useless to try to distinguish them. From the phenomenological point of view, these forms of transition from oneiric
experience towards hallucinatory experience are, however, of
very great interest. If, in fact, the state of confusion, which we
have just discussed, is a sort of hypnotic sleep which is more
open to the world than the sleep of the sleeping person, it is no
less characterized by the smallness of this "opening" and condemned to be constituted only as a "private" experience. That
is to say, it is drawn by the subjective pole of the bilateralness
of the self's relation to its world, which is the foundation of the
category of reality itself.

On the other hand, at the level of the ongoing experiencing
of imaginary events, which constitutes the essence of these
twilight states (also called "hypnoid," "oneiroid," etc.), the
world is not annihilated, but transformed. In these states the

"lived" is lived in an atmosphere, an environment, of menacing opaqueness, a sort of existential landscape which is broadened to its horizon by the immensity of the tragedy or the ecstasy of which the subject is both the center and the spectator. Events slide by or are condensed in muddled perspectives, across confused and moving backgrounds. At this level, the world appears so transformed that it is composed of images, of ideas, and of perceptions whose "locus" in the lived space of the representation of the world is that of a magical interval which has been hollowed out between the self and its world. The delirious event does not take place by submerging all experience, as in dreaming; nor does it unfold by breaking experience up into sensory regions, as in hallucinations. Instead it unfolds as a flow of the fantastic which thwarts the logic of space by introducing a third world into it: the twilight-state world, disrupted in its spatial structure. Indefinite spatial divisions refract and reflect an infinite multiplicity of mirrors, of ricochets, and of echoes. In this telescoping of sizes and perspectives, all its symbolic metaphors, allegories, and images advance, withdraw, merge together, fade, weave, hide, rise or fall in the unreality of their unprecedented modality. This strange "worldliness" is subject to the prestidigitation and the magic of a still self-conscious fantasy—as if it were suspended at the horizon of existence between heaven and earth in the twilight of their reality. This strange "worldliness" appears as a miraculous or monstrous encounter of the self with its other world.

At this level of disorganization, representation,[9] which is implied in any structure of consciousness as a fundamental dimension, remains an *apparition:* that of a face, a scene, an event which ceases to be merely represented for itself and becomes presented and made present. But this presentation in this twilight-state atmosphere of reality is an unprecedented presentation. If re-presentation were entirely abolished from the consciousness of the dreamer, who has himself been eclipsed as the author of his dream (and even, in a certain sense, as the spectator insofar as he is watching what he watches), in this case, to the extent that it is "represented," the lived slips into the constitution of experience as an "other world," a "beyond the world." A normal subject, without going beyond the mirror of his own subjectivity, has the discretionary power to cause any "lived experience" whatever (even if it were imaginary) to appear, on the condition that he adapt himself to it by regulating the distance which separates him from it. The subject of this "oneiroid" experience, by ceasing to keep this experience under the control of the law of a reciprocal exclusion of the objective and the subjective, now admits the ambiguousness of their blending. This is the reason for the artificial character of his representation, which he accepts both as being (lived) and as not being (unreal), that is, as "surreality." The "twilight-state" experience thus is constituted as an event only by bracketing its reality. The "thetic" positions or forms of this experience are ambiguous. They are necessarily ambiguous: this is the ambiguity which is found at that degree of destructuration by a consciousness which is no longer able to constitute itself as a reality, though it has not entirely lost the ability to form a world for itself, provided that this be the world of the artificiality of the artificial. The "mystery," the *numinosus,* of lived experience is a primordial character of this unprecedented "representation." The lived experience of this level of destructuration is thus inevitably chained to certain modalities of its constitution (dramatization, artifice, mystery) in such a way that the thematic of the twilight state (the "twilight of the gods") symbolizes the shock of its disorganization as an event which represents its wretched distress or orgiastic intoxication.

To the extent that it is a disorganization or an unorganized state of the lived space of representations, as we have just described it, this experience is typically the experience of the invasion of a world of fantasy into the field of consciousness. This "invasion" is an irruption of "this" which "happens" as a fabulous event in a vacillating world, a "supernatural," "cosmic," and apocalyptic event.[10] Every sort of archetype, all the figures and fables of mythology, all the fantasies of ancient tragedy, all the dramas of human existence rush headlong into the abyss of this profound and radical loss of structure. The atmosphere of the twilight state is, in fact, essentially lyric and metaphysical. The experience which arises during it has its source in the problematic of reality and existence, in the primordial status of the human condition at the juncture of desire and being, of life and death, in the most profound thematic of the existential drama.

It is important to note that this "half-openness" to the world of oneiroid or twilight-state consciousness allows lived experience to be both "grasped" by the observer and "retained" by the subject's memory.[11] These experiences of the fantastic are not (as so often happens in the case of oneiric confusional states) separated radically from the web of existence. Their survival and the emotion which results from them are sometimes very lively. Patients subject to them remain perplexed and dizzy when they come out (sometimes with great difficulty) from under their fascinating hold.

4. DELIRIOUS EXPERIENCES OF DISSOCIATION OF PERSONALITY

The visualization of lived experience as a "spectacle" or "apparition" is a structural quality of both oneiric and "oneiroid" consciousness.[12] Because of this, the structure of the imagining consciousness is seen to be essentially a "gaze." Later (p. 103) we shall return to the topic of why this gaze, by exploring the lived experience which is grasped as the spectacle of its intentional object, has so often caused the structure of consciousness to be assimilated to an "optical apparatus." We here arrive at the level of hallucinatory consciousness, which we must now describe. This *experience of voices* is a mode of experience which is not compressed in the *figuration* of an event, but rather in the sense of a sense (Erwin Straus)—that of hearing. It is, in fact, a question of the form of verbalization of lived experience which, once again, sends us back to *a disordering of the lived space of the representation.* The analyses of Eugène Minkowski and Erwin Straus are fundamentally in accord with this statement of Merleau-Ponty, which is so pregnant with meaning: "What protects the sane person against delirium or hallucination is not his critical faculty, it is the structure of his space. . . . Like myth, hallucination is brought about by the shrinking of lived space."[13]

Only when reinserted into its "mythic space" does hallucination appear as it is: that "imposture" which suppresses the destructuration of consciousness by making the hallucination possible for the subject and impossible for the other. Up to this point we have described delirious experience as a correlate of the structure of lived space, in the sense that the imaginary was no longer "in its place" in the world's order, either because there was no room for anything other than itself or else because it was permitted to occupy an unwonted dimension within it. As we move up the hierarchical series of levels of the destructuration of consciousness, to the degree that consciousness accordingly appears to be less profound and more "normal," to the extent that it is more "lucid," more "open," and admits more "differentiation" and more "perspectives" within the diffused, comprehensive, and seemingly ineffable character of these oneiric or oneiroid agglutinations or telescopings, more cohesiveness and organization within the field of actualization appear. We have already seen how a consciousness which is swallowed up and submerged, as if reduced to slavery and darkness, can struggle vainly to organize itself in a chaotic worldliness and then admit into its world a profusion and an invasion of fantasy which was juxtaposed with or superimposed upon reality. We are now concerned with a consciousness which constitutes itself above the lower level which we have just described.[14]

The world is there. It is there even in the quasi-plenitude of its perspectives and projects and, all in all, its legality. It is there as the world of perceived objects, for in this case perception is not only possible but required. "Lucidity," consciousness's ability clearly to differentiate and order its contents, exercises its control and its vigilance. But this agreement with "objective reality," with the natural world, is in striking *contrast* with the singularity of the lived experience. This latter is partitioned off and divided up by "dotted lines" of strange significations, all of which are impostures, tricks, illusions, or intolerances which have been introduced into the *experience of communication.* In order to be capable of greater clarity at this level, destructured consciousness is once more open to the fundamental experience of *coexistence.* It appears to have been freely altered at this level at which language enters into the constitution of consciousness so as to furnish it with its essential dimension.[15] This is the "dimension" of an "inner space," a kind of shadow of objects, or of their signs or chains of meanings, if you will, which not only furnish the key to reality but themselves form a reality. This "reality" is obviously not that of an object. Its language is not the language which circulates objectively in the world. If its materiality is that of the body, to the extent that the body itself can speak, this materiality demands that the body must be inhabited by the other who takes part in its interlocution. We can therefore grasp this level of the erosion of the structure of consciousness only for what it is: a lack of organization within the experience of our communications with others, that is, of the "logistics" of our relations. This necessarily involves a "milieu" (a "place" ["*lieu*"] or a "region") through which messages, calls, demands, and responses circulate and respond to one another. It is an essentially ambiguous and paradoxical milieu, because it is the space of our "thought" and because the middle (*le "milieu"*) of this "Milieu" is displaced onto others. In the full organization of the perceptual field, this milieu is lived as such only in the imaginary space of its representations, as a transparent or virtual space which can become part of our experience only through reflection. It is there as the sensible support (insofar as it is "lived" by my body) of the sense of the exchanges; but it disappears under the sense of its sense.

In order to appear, every "yes," every "no," every noun, every verb, every proposition, every preposition, even every abstraction must "play upon" the keyboard of the sense of the senses (Erwin Straus). All the facts which fill consciousness cause their harmonies to resound upon it—strange harmonies which are neither waves nor vibrations but the living investment of the sensible of the senses by its sense. Here the "noesis" is lost or is completed by the noematic structure which language adds to it as the object of an "apperceptive consciousness" of the sense, the intimacy and the propriety of the thought which takes possession of its objects by enunciating them.

This problematic of consciousness which takes as its object the experience of its own thought in its communication with others is falsified at this level of its destructuration.[16] This "virtual" space, whose "sensible givens" are moving and disappear under their "sense" (signification), falls into a spatialization in which speech is metamorphosed (through metaphor, metonymy, and all the other grammatical tropes) and "caught." That which I think becomes an object which detaches itself from me. That which I say becomes that which someone says to me. "I am speaking to myself" becomes "Something is being said within me." More generally, my thought is lived as being someone else's thought. Transmission of thought is a thing which as such is submitted to the physics of the natural world (vibrations, waves, fluid) whose acoustical properties prevail over the sense. What is lived by the hallucinating person can thus be "repeated" (or "paraphrased," as R. Mourgue put it) by a certain theory of hallucination which takes this experience literally or for its cash value (this is the illusion of the mechanical theory of the mental automatism of G. de Clérambault). If it is true that spatial metaphors (dissociation, bifurcation, echo, abstractions, intrusions) form the foundation of this experience of the mechanization of thought (this same author's prodigiously phenomenological description is exemplary of this), then, to keep ourselves from falling prey to the illusion which grounds it as *lived,* this experience must be described in the atmosphere of an illusion which grounds it as *error,* that is, in the disintegration of the structure of the lived space of thought and of language.

Estrangement, the "other," the thing which is implied in the verbal relation, these burst forth in the *voices* which are truly the subject's own voice; but they are the voice of a subject who, remaining "unconscious" of the deterioration of his experience, relates it to some place *other* than to within himself. This thought in the depths of myself flows or runs in the silence of my consciousness, in its intimacy, in its secrecy, as being that most private thing which the world has for me. This thought escapes me, possesses me, haunts me, echoes in me, embeds itself in me, invades me, and penetrates me to the depths of a self which receives it only to reject it. My speech is now directed towards myself and against myself. It is no longer directed towards others. It no longer serves me for speaking to others or to myself. It is no longer pliable as the instrument of my freedom. It returns to me like a boomerang, like a weapon aimed at me. These hallucinatory experiences involve or imply the experience of the intrusion, of the strangeness—when it is not the martyr's dread—of the torment by which these "experiences" become "experiments" of which the hallucinating person feels himself to be the *object* (persecution, influence, telepathy, suggestion, spells, etc.).

Moreover, it frequently happens in clinical cases (and always in psychoanalytic or simply psychopathological hermeneutics) that the experience of this penetration, of this cohabitation, is *erotic:* the voice which enters and leaves the body and the brain is a symbolic vehicle of all the forms of rape, for this "voice" is the very image of the power of creation and of communication, that of the phallus in which this word becomes flesh. In this way we reach the foundation of this hallucinatory experience of voices. This hallucinatory lived experience of hallucinating consciousness is indeed a "sensible" or "sensory" or "aesthetic" experience, in that the experience of voices and all the phenomena which form their retinue of events are lived in the absolute and irrevocable mode of the "sensed," the "felt," the "experienced." They are grasped in the irrevocable actuality of a form in which the space of the body and the space of time, which are the dimensions of any actually lived experience, are blended together.

But hallucinating consciousness deludes itself. It is hallucinating for itself. It performs an inversion or at least an upsetting of the values of the *sense* which language can have "for itself" insofar as it is constituted by the indefinite forms of the infinite number of possible ways in which the self can be related to others. The "having" of the subject "possessing" his thought becomes a *being*, a *being two* (dual mode of relation as object); it becomes a being divided in its "proprietorship" and pledged to a position of passivity and of subordination. This loss of self-mastery coincides with the solidification of lived space, of this personal domain which is the locus in which the self develops and reigns. This loss is at the same time the manifestation, the condition and the effect, of this shrinking; for the only essential aspect of speech which can be lived is its meaning. The phenomenology of the experience of split personality thus calls for the lived experience of an objectification (of an illusory mechanization and materialization of thought under the form of a mental automatism) and of a falsification of the relationships with others which change their sense in the "voices," or rather, of which these "voices" constitute the change of sense. For the infinity of perspectives which open upon the mediated world of the possibilities of its speech, of the duality of the dialogue which is its form of transcendence relative to its own special givens, hallucinating consciousness, having fallen into a sort of realist illusion, substitutes the immediate experience of a "voice" which has come from outside itself as if it were an object belonging to the "external world." This "external world" can be lived only as an irruption, an invasion, a penetrating to the interior of the self within the closed-off space of the representation: the object of thought enters the field of the subject's experience as a foreign body. The hallucination is a rape.

5. EXPERIENCES OF DEPERSONALIZATION

The structural disruption of the field of the experience of language and of thought thus brings us back, as if to its condition, to a bodily experience which envelops it and bestows upon it its reality as lived experience: every hallucination is first of all a hallucination of one's "personal body" (Merleau-Ponty).[17] But this "personal body" is not merely the somatic body of the organs contained within the skin; it is not merely the living body animated by its needs and sensibility. It is the body which is intimately united to the person and his world. The body is that object and that space which occupies a position which is both basal (or vital) and superior (or noetic-neomatic). The body is at the base of all that I live, for nothing can be lived which does not cross it or is not in some relation with it. All that comes from it is mine (or belongs to me); but it also becomes confused with me and my world as I become confused with it. In this way the experience of the body implies a deep-seated ambiguity: it is within the world as an object, but it belongs to me as forming me and providing my foundation.

Nothing, then, is perceived in its organs, its functions, its organs of sense, in its needs, its appetites, and its movements which is not a confused or keen experience of pleasure or pain, of well-being or discomfort, of harmony or dissonance with the order of the spatiality of sensing. The "sensing" which emanates from one's own body, or which is reflected upon it, can be only a protopathic or cenesthetic experience. It is the most fundamental experience involved in any perception. It is given all at once as something which is revealed on this side of the problematic of the objective and the subjective, as the protopathic (and even epicritic) sensibility of the body, inasmuch as it is mingled with all our sensations and all experience.

This layer of sensing is revealed just as naturally in any pathology of perceptions and of psychosensorial agnosias. This is especially true in the case of *disorders of the body image* which brain pathology has brought to our attention. Lesions of the fifth and seventh areas of the superior parietal region (which is the primary center of somatognosis, of the perceptions which give the organization of the postural model and organize the segments of bodily space) provoke bilateral disorders when they affect the dominant hemisphere (generally the left) and provoke contralateral hemisomatognosic disorders when it involves the other hemisphere. All these disorders upset the perceptions of the spatial ordering of the body insofar as this is perceived as an object which belongs to the world's space. Certain parts of it can disappear or can be confused without any deterioration to the consciousness which considers the body as the medium of the self and of its world. In this way what is confused with the level of integration of sensibility is, on the contrary, a differentiation whose perceptions can be distorted without causing the whole consciousness of sensible reality to be modified by it.[18]

In this stratum of "cenesthetic" sensing, the organization of bodily space is found to be integrated into the experience of the body itself. This is so because the body is the central object of the subject's world, the place in which the subject encounters the world of others, and the vehicle of the connection of the subjective and the objective which he constantly lives as an existential problem. When the *experience of depersonalization* occurs, the solution to this problem escapes him. When the body "wastes away," "grows empty," "begins to petrify," or when, on the contrary, it becomes evanescent, disembodied and marvelously light, these "experiences" are not merely charged with a metaphorical sense. In order that these metaphors can cause the lived experience to take on a figurative meaning, the gap separating them must be eliminated and the delirious experience must take over. In this "metaphoric" pathology of depersonalization, the body is transformed only at the price of a metamorphosis which truly constitutes an experience of fusion and of confusion of its sensory and somatic *data,* of the *Gestaltqualitäten* of the world of outer and inner objects. But this experience is above all a mutation of its own "states of mind." Whether it happens that, as we have described, the room's light softens and allows its objects to float in a heady atmosphere which is subject to the caprices of *euphoria,* and these contents become enlivened, and this animated, neat, and trim world becomes enriched to the point of strangeness because of the excess of its sumptuousness; or whether, on the contrary (as we saw in Volume III of our *Études*), "it becomes obscured and filled with shadows and gloomy chasms, with its reality disturbed and its space having lost its equilibrium and its fixity, so as to stagger in the vertiginous movement of *anguish* to the point of representing the darkness and the opaqueness of a hostile world, a strange world in which it feels itself a stranger; in both these cases the lived experiences of depersonalization constantly incorporate the body's changes into a more entire strangeness which belongs to the external world. Both these forms of distortion of the body and of bodies are

enveloped in an all-encompassing atmosphere of drama, ec-
stasy, or of terror."

Depersonalized consciousness belongs to the level of its very
constitution, where our body image is intertwined with our
person, with this locus of our encounter with our world. Depersonalization is not found there in the same way as are "simple"
disorders of the body image, lived as a part only. It is there as
a fundamental dimension of the condition which binds the
depersonalized person to a radical alteration of his dispositions
and of his projects. If "metaphor" is involved in the suffering
of tabetics as it is in the disorders of somatognosis, it nevertheless remains on this side of the delirium which suppresses it.
On the contrary, it holds sway in those "states of depersonalization" which we here perceive as a metamorphosis in which the
total state of mind, the delirious mood (*Stimmung*), radically
modifies experience, exercises over it the magic of a transmu-
tation, and ignites within it a blaze of dreaming: objects displace themselves, grimace, speak, penetrate one another, in a
word, they "cheat." The arm extends itself into the leg, the
interior of the body extravasates, or the body is reflected to
infinity in a world of mirrors; the body's anatomical figures, its
erotic props, its shameful parts, or its nerve centers are reversed or combined; solidified thought breaks like glass or is
drawn out or knotted like a string, etc.

The "depersonalized consciousness," or, to be more exact,
this "chimerical consciousness" of depersonalization, is essentially an "intoxicated consciousness." In fact it can be observed
most clearly in intoxication or *psychedelic experiences* (alcohol, hashish, opiates, cocaine, mescaline, lysergic acid, etc.).
Among the many writers, philosophers, doctors, and poets who
have described these marvelous experiences of the overturning
of consciousness, in recent times it is Henri Michaux[19] who has
most effectively expressed the magic of drugs through the
magic of words. His mescaline, cannabis, or psilocybin "sequences" follow the inner itineraries of the "paltry dance"
which causes the intoxicated person to "work" and expels him
from "his home" to plunge him into *engulfing situations* in
which he encounters precisely those incoercible, anxiety-filled,
or ecstatic lived experiences which occur in the "second states"
which Régis has shown to be essentially connected with drug-
induced oneirism. The action of drugs and the states of intoxi-

cation which they produce unleash into lived experience, like a first wisp of dreaming, the exigencies of the desires which lay sleeping in the body image.

The experience of depersonalization is bound to the body's fantasms. It is always ready to substitute the "complex" distribution of their affective "geography" for the order of represented space. At this level, the problematic of these "spatial" values of desire towards its object, of the subjective and the objective, is either blocked or resolved by vacillating in the imaginary.[20]

The psychopathologies of lived space and of temporality are inseparable. Nothing is lived as a spatial dimension without being integrated into the process which gave rise to the temporary configurations in this space. This leads us to the forms of destructuration of the highest level of organization of the field of consciousness, that level at which experience ceases to coincide in its operations with the laws of action in the field of the present.

6. MANIC-DEPRESSIVE STATES

An emotionally disturbed consciousness is a consciousness which has been upset in the dynamics of its *temporality.* As we have emphasized, "temporality" must be understood in the sense of a structure of mental life which unfolds not according to the chronological order of measurable time but according to the *movement of lived experience.* This movement is "lived time," the experience of the intentional movement and direction of consciousness. To be afraid is to flee. To be happy is to dash joyfully into the future. To be sad is to stop one's movement or even to reverse it by retrograding towards past regret or remorse. This dynamic structure of the temporal unfolding of a consciousness, which at one moment looks forward to the future and at another is nostalgic concerning the past, constitutes a *temporal-ethical* structure. We have so designated[21] this mode of the direction and movement of consciousness to point out that this is a temporality which is tied up with the problematic of desire and consequently with its control and its constraints. We are thus better able to understand that the experience lived by a consciousness at this level of destructuration is an emotional "stupefaction" or "unleashing" which disturbs consciousness to the point of compromising, if not

destroying, its present. Not only does emotion prevent consciousness from stopping in the present (whether it turns it
backwards, fettering it to what has already been lived or to
what has just been lived, or whether it pushes it forward so that
it might escape towards what is to be lived, what is to come),
but it also develops a flood of imaginary experiences and fantasies. This is the situation which Sartre so perfectly depicted
when he described emotion as an imaginary situation, an
imagining fascination. Emotion is always filled by the imagining of its object, and the object is enlarged, swelled, overvalued
by the "affected consciousness" which, Sartre tells us, resembles the "consciousness which dreams."

Such, then, is the "affective" or "emotional" level at which
this destructuration of consciousness must be described as an
experience of the overturning of its temporal-ethical structure.
The term "thymic" is often—if not always—used to designate
this disorder of mood. And this disorder of mood is often—if not
always—not included within the pathology of consciousness. It
is certainly the point at which our own studies of acute psychoses clash most strongly with the accepted opinions of a long
clinical tradition. For this reason it has been only by means of
clinical work[22] that this "routine" could be broken, by returning to another tradition—a tradition which holds that there is
a profound identity between confusional states, paranoid reactions, and manic-depressive crises.

The phenomenological psychopathology of the manic psychosis makes it obvious that the "manic consciousness" is a
leap, a whirlwind, an impulse which carries lived experience
beyond an impossible present towards a future to be born and
reborn indefinitely, a future which is swollen with the omnipotence of an unrestrained desire. This is the sense of Binswanger's phenomenological study of the "flight of ideas"
(*Ideenflucht*). The Unconscious of the manic is opened to the
infinity of the possible. His exaltation, his play, his impetuosity,
his "eccentricities," and his euphoria rush him forward as if
they were the irresistible attractive power of an impetuous,
insatiable, and endless hunger. In a "bigmouth" manner (*gross-
maulig*) he devours time and space, unable to stop himself,
without taking any obstacles into his consideration, particularly that major obstacle of the subordination of the satisfaction of desires to a temporality which necessitates that the
suspended and postponed "time" of future and always condi-

tional actions be interposed between his desire and its object. The present does not exist for this vertiginous race towards the future. From this moment on, the future is there, as if all possibilities were equally possible. The rising up of lived experience in the face of any constraint and legality is shown by the fact that the instincts and affections which rush into this experience are propelled towards the single value of pleasure.

At this point, the analyses of Freud, Abraham, and all the psychoanalysts who have taken manic psychosis as the prototype of a regression to the "oral" stage of pleasure, to the cannibalistic orgy of a libido savagely liberated from any "duty," from any obedience to the law of the superego, these analyses completely join forces with the physiognomy of this manic "being-in-the-world" whose "volatility" is nothing other than the carelessness of a radical extratemporality, of a lightness which flies above the demands of the present without the slightest concern about coming to terms with reality. Manic experience refuses to pause. It frees itself from the prison in which lived time has been locked up by the law of its constitution—a law of measure, of balance, of prudence, and of postponement. It does this in order to be liberated in the anticipated satisfaction of unrestrained desire. Manic awareness is carried along with neither truce nor rest by an "id" which carries it away, towards a "this" which is there, before me, as an absolute end, an eternity which is open to that which is to be forever and insatiably consummated.

In the face of this devouring desire whose object is *always* attained outside of the legislation of all the tenses (times, *temps*) of the present,[23] the lived experience of melancholia is the experience of a *never*. For even when the depressive regrets his past—and this is the very form of the actuality of his experience—this past has never passed as it ought to have. This past is never in fact past. The present of this returned past is endowed with a temporality which is essentially stopped. The past is a fated event. "Fated" both as a misfortune and as an inevitability. This fatedness confers an absolute and extratemporal value upon this event in which time has been arrested, as if the event had been once and for all taken hold of in the immobile form of a crucial experience which no other experience could defer or exceed. The depressive stops time in his past according to a categorical imperative that it never be gone beyond or forgotten. This past is there as an obsession in which any possibility of becoming or of change has been congealed. He draws the present impossible into a gulf of remorse and of regrets whose object is subject to an eternal reproach. For if the manic leaps into the eternity of the possible, the depressive is frozen in the eternity of the impossible. What has taken place should never have happened. It has occurred only on the condition of binding the subject to this unfortunate experience as to a fault. The depressive's guilt, his self-accusation, his feelings of unworthiness, his desire for death (the only precipitancy which is possible to him), these are only the signs of this manner of being riveted to his actions, of being condemned to nothingness for a past which is itself immortal: in other words, to be *damned*. Melancholia is both a "stopping of time" and a "stopping of destiny."[24] It is the pathetic immobility of a time which is suspended from the irreversibility of the past mistake, the syncope of a time which can no longer flow, from which any movement of hope has been abolished.

Thus manic and depressive psychoses are symmetrical (and clinical work has shown them occasionally to be interchangeable) structures of a disorder at the same level. They are the two sides of the ethical temporality of a lived time which can no longer be constituted into a present. For the present is precisely that form of time, that miracle of time which tears itself away from the past and postpones the future so as to create an interval between them: an interval which is at one's disposal. No human action is possible, or can be recorded in the real history of the person and thereby cease to belong to the realm of dreaming, if it has not passed through the *field of the present*. This field which causes the actuality of experience to become a real present can be constituted only through the movement of a consciousness which is able to describe and prescribe the figures and configurations of its agreement with the world. If this structuring should become too much "caught up" in the past, or if it should "rush forward" too rapidly into the future, the impossible present gives way to nightmares and dreams: to the nightmare of the frozen universe of *fault* or the *dream of exoneration from all duty*.

At the "highest" degree of its dissolution, then, the structure of consciousness appears as the form of the actualization of its lived experience into a present which is tempered between the necessity of an inevitable chain of events brought about by the past and the freedom of an evasion into the future. The present does not accommodate itself either to the captivity or to the emancipation of consciousness. Consciousness is in fact precisely that form of organization into a field of the present which balances this necessity and this lack of constraint. Consciousness thus appears when we consider it in its plenitude (or before it loses its structure). As we have already seen (Chapter One), it then appears as the organization of the actuality of experience insofar as this is *a field well-tempered by the present and by its presence to the world.*

Before drawing any conclusions from this study of the destructuration of the field of consciousness, which we have examined from its lowest levels to the stage where only its highest structure is altered (that is, moving in a direction opposite to that of a consciousness in the process of destructuration by losing first of all its most elevated form and losing something even more of its structure at each of its lower levels), we must return to clinical observation which *alone* justifies this description.

When going over the phases of this destructuration of consciousness, we have constantly been referring to epilepsy. This unequaled example of the dissolution of consciousness allows us to follow the process of the erosion of its structure in a quasi-experimental manner. This was well understood by Hughlings Jackson, whose conceptions concerning the stages of the evolution (or integration) or dissolution (or disintegration) of mental and nervous activity have always referred to this clinical "prototype." We ourselves have attempted to find an experimental verification of our hypothesis concerning the hierarchy of the levels of the destructuration of consciousness in the studies we devoted to the pathology of epilepsy.[25] The whole range of forms of destructuration we have just described spreads itself before us in this case. The impossibility—which we challenge any clinical psychiatrist to refute seriously—of operating in the clinical continuity of this "series" of states of consciousness or of these degrees of the unconsciousness of radical separations or distinctions, this impossibility proves the unity which underlies the diversity of the levels which it necessarily involves.

Far from restricting us to the routine idea of their radical distinction with respect to disorders of consciousness, the study of manic-depressive states, of periodical psychoses, has shown us—as it daily shows any clinical psychiatrist who does not close his eyes to this reality—that it is impossible to separate the manic-depressive structure from the structures of depersonalization, of split personality, of twilight state or oneiric-confusional states.

The obvious cogency of these facts has authorized us to undertake and pursue this "spectral analysis" of the acute psychoses which reveal themselves to us as the levels of the destructuration of consciousness.

This analysis leads us to these two important points:

1. The composite order of the structure of consciousness, which comes to light through its decomposition, and the hierarchy of the stages of this disorganization of the field of consciousness reveal the order of its temporal structure and consequently of the acts of *memory* to which the intimate experience of its unfolding corresponds. At the highest levels of manic-depressive experiences, if the integration of past and future does not allow the interval of the present to hollow itself out between them, without being abolished, this integration is either blocked and pushed back into the past or propelled into a future whose actualization it forestalls. It thus happens that if memory is falsified in the movement of its temporality, immediate memory is not falsified. When, in its lower levels, the erosion of the structure of lived spaces is added to the destructuration of consciousness's temporality, or rather when temporality falls into the actuality of lived space, delirious experiences, and even more so oneiric-confusional experiences, are annihilated or tend to be swallowed up to the extent that consciousness loses its structure. It is as if by letting go of real space, experience breaks its ties with the order of history. Each additional degree of unconsciousness thus is presented in clinical work as an increasingly profound disturbance of memory, to the point where (in epilepsy) unconsciousness and amnesia merge.

2. By following the order of its decomposition, our description of the pathological configurations of consciousness brings to light the neurobiological process of this dissolution. The importance of hereditary-genetic factors in recurring psychoses and acute confusional states, the importance of toxinfectious etiology, the central notion of epilepsy, which is, we repeat, the model of this pathology of consciousness, all this joins with the efficaciousness of "biological" therapies (shock therapy, insu-

lin, anticonvulsive and neuroleptic drugs) to constitute an irrefutable *demonstration* of the dependence of lived "experiences" upon the physiological conditions of this destructuration. We shall return to this topic later. For the time being we content ourself with pointing out that recent *psychopharmacology* has brilliantly confirmed the organodynamic concepts of Moreau de Tours.[26] Through the experimental usage of mescaline, lysergic acid diethylamide, psilocybin, etc., psychopharmacology has made it easier to penetrate the "engulfing situations" (Henry Michaux) which these drugs excavate in the depths of a consciousness whose structure has broken down.

The destructuration of the field of consciousness thus allows us to speak—in a manner other than by reference to pure reflections or meditations on the *Cogito*—of the basic structure of consciousness as it constitutes the field of present lived experience.

Its most fundamental constitution appears as *organization of present experience in its reality.* The activity, "Gestaltization," or "structure" of consciousness are terms which point to this organization of experience, whose spatiotemporal, logical, verbal, and practical order guarantee its agreement with its world. This should be obvious from the above discussion. For, each level of its destructuration (or of its unconsciousness) draws consciousness into an increasingly profound collapse into the imaginary (that is, as we shall see later, into the language and images of the unconscious). At each stage of this process of dissolution, the experience of this actualized imaginary "for itself" is a modality of thought, an objectification. The very conditions of its presentation hide its "falseness" or illusion from the subject who lives this experience. At the end of this journey into the night, oneiric consciousness is only able to live its image without worldliness, sometimes giving the dreamer the illusion of a lived event. But this is an illusion which one leaves behind only to awaken, and from which one can break away only by forgetting his dream. The structure of consciousness thus appears as the form in which every event is lived: it is real if consciousness can place it in a real world; it is imaginary, but "passes for" real, if consciousness loses the power of organizing its experience, of subordinating its "noesis," insofar as this is the absoluteness of the lived, to the noematic structure, insofar as this is the condition of possibilities.

As if in response to Zutt's question,[27] the pathology of the field of consciousness discloses its organization, that is, its constitution as a *constituted consciousness.* This organization implies infrastructures, groundwork, an ensemble of dynamic and architectonic apparatuses which are, to use Gurwitsch's terms, its "autochthonous organization": *the formal constant of the field of consciousness.*

How is it that the developments, differentiations, and elaborations of this basal structure of consciousness cause it to disappear into the normal consciousness of which it forms a sort of "unconscious stratum"? We shall examine this in the next chapter. Let us now simply say that the forms of the destructuration of consciousness which are lived as *experiences* of the imaginary make their appearance only when consciousness has lost the freedom of its movements, has lost the ability to place itself at a certain distance from its lived experience.

The loss of its liberty, of its personal autonomy, of its direction, imposes upon the destructured consciousness which we have just described a sort of obligation to fall into the level of a "common," or "generic," consciousness. The generic traits of the degradation which we have just described are simply a certain manner by which the structure of consciousness can fall from the level of personal and intersubjective experiences to that of "archetypical" common experiences. It is by falling into this gulf of poetry and mythology, into this world of image, that consciousness touches the other side of reality, in that unconscious which so many oriental, mystical, or romantic philosophers have considered to be the foyer of supranatural cognitions—and which is, in any case, the irrational to which consciousness opens when it frees itself from reality, that is, from the regulation of its reason.

Such is the lesson which we can draw from psychopathology as we now, strengthened by the knowledge of philosophers and by our clinical experience, take on the problem of the structure of consciousness as the *field of the present* which presupposes and implies these latent infrastructures which have been brought to light by the psychopathology of acute psychoses. This psychopathology has as its object—as in dreaming during sleep—the falling of consciousness into the unconscious, that is, toward the actualization of the experience of the imaginary.

II The Field of Consciousness

(Outline of a Phenomenology of Lived Experience)

It is as difficult not to use the word "field" as it is impru-
dent to use it. The "field of consciousness," Henri Delacroix has
said, is only a simple "metaphor" which sets up a hazardous
analogy with the structure of physical space. Nonetheless, in
spite of the disrepute into which it has fallen, this metaphor
appears in its turn to correspond to the reality of the fundamental structure of conscious being insofar as it constitutes the
actuality of its experience. The word "field" is employed in
order to designate the "structural totality" of this actuality, an
interconnected assemblage of "parts" which form a somehow
mathematical "totality" of the *hic et nunc,* of "that which I live
as my present experience." In this respect, the "field of consciousness" fits in well with what we have said concerning the
necessity of describing the conscious being first of all as living
a personal experience. It also accords well with what we have
just said concerning the erosion of structure of the consciousness which, as it fades, loses the faculty of actualizing itself
according to the law of its constitution. The notion of the "field
of lived experience," of the "field of the present," points precisely to this *constitution.*

1. THE NOTION OF FIELD OF CONSCIOUSNESS

A "field" is an organized and limited totality. No doubt it
would be absurd to try to assimilate the field of consciousness
to a portion of space which depends upon some property which
would define it (as we designate such and such a "field" delimited by a juridical and spatial *property*). Even in its ordinary

and agricultural sense, the concept of "field" refers not only to a certain manner of being "within boundaries" but also to a production which is contained within its limits. Moreover, the "field" has a history, a genealogy, a stratification, a subsoil; it is even capable of changing. We thus see that the meaning of the term "field" is not purely spatial and static. This explains why the "analogical" use of this term constitutes an arbitrary extrapolation only if it is applied to empirical contents which are inadequate or too strict: to a delimited portion of homogeneous extension or, what comes to the same thing, to a physical formation.

Though consciousness is not a thing, it is a *structure.* Our experience gains its "actuality" by being related to this structure. The original being of consciousness therefore can appear only in the constitution of an experience which cannot be described except as it is lived: in the form of a "field" which is circumscribed within the *temporal* dimensions which bind the self to its world. What appears within this field is not only contained, but in its very presentation depends upon its autochthonous *organization* (Gurwitsch). The being of consciousness, as we wish to describe it here in its fundamental constitution, resides in the simultaneous configuration through which present experience appears. The words "presentation," "representation," "actuality," "appearance" designate not merely the attributes of this being, but its very essence insofar as it is subordinate to the law of its constitution as a field. To say that through its *Urform* consciousness sends us back to this actual constitution and to its organization in vectorial perspectives is to say that it is an order of simultaneity in its finality. In other words, the notions of field of consciousness, field of the present, field of perception, field of attention, field of action, and field of experience are identical to the degree that they all point to the constitution of conscious phenomena as "lived" (*Erlebnis*), being ordered in relation to its "intentionality" so as to form its actuality. In still other words, the content of consciousness is essentially "framed," and it is this simultaneously significant and "thetic" framing which is referred to by the notion of a field which is "delimited" as it is "defined" by its structural properties.

At the beginning of this work we spoke of different discussions of the notion of "lived experience" (pp. 10–11). Since this term refers to a conscious experience and not merely to a vital phenomenon which could be unconscious, the distinguishing feature of this lived experience is clearly that, in order for it to be *felt* as the *impression* of the experience, it must *present itself.* This *presentation* is precisely what we could call its manner both of filling and of forming the field of consciousness —of constituting itself as a *present structure.*

The "field" structure (*structure campine*) of consciousness corresponds to the necessity which lived experience has to *circumscribe* itself within its sense, within its dimensions as a momentary, transitory, and synchronistic structure.

Once again we shall examine the views of certain philosophers and psychologists concerning the difficulties or demands of this "notion" of the field of consciousness.

When studying *concrete states of consciousness,* William James designated these states as the *field of consciousness,* [1] which he considered as a mass of heterogeneous givens. However, James emphasized that the configuration which binds all conscious phenomena to one another in and through their copresence, by distinguishing (through the effect of selective interest) the "center" or "focal object" from its "marginal" areas, its "substantive parts" from its "transitive parts," has introduced an order which is in some manner "spatial." For if the *stream of consciousness* in its pure state was truly lived as a "big blooming buzzing confusion," though it may be essentially rebellious, this very surging forth admits an organization. It is because he did not take this organization to be the essence of consciousness that in 1907 James refused to attribute any meaning to the word "consciousness." The notion of a field of consciousness is incompatible with that of the flowing of its contents, for the simple reason that it demands a momentary stability of its organization.

This *organization* has been admirably described by Henri Bergson in *Time and Free Will,* in *Creative Evolution,* and later in *Mind-Energy.* However subtle and dazzling it might be to describe the stream of that which flows and slips by as being the very duration of our psychological life—that is, its sense and its intentionality—it is always in terms of *acts,* of *actuality,* of *choice,* of *interest,* and of *attention,* that Bergson describes this retention of the past and this anticipation of the future, this rolling up and this unfolding of time, through which consciousness organizes its present by stopping in it. No one has shown better than he how the "immediate givens of consciousness" arrange themselves to *compose* the *field of the present.* But if the skeletal and mechanical schematism of intelligence is, for Bergson, added onto this actualization, it does not remain foreign to it, for any framing of lived experience is itself a part of this lived experience. His analyses of perception, of its givens, of the fusions and transitions which perception implies, do not take anything away from the intelligibility which action, in the course of being performed, imparts to them so as to constitute them.

We have already set forth the essential points of Husserl's phenomenology, but it will be worthwhile returning to it once again, for these admirable texts should serve us as a guide in our description. By endowing consciousness with its essential structure of "knowing," Husserl has given us a clearer view of the relations which unite the subject to its object as "functions" of consciousness. In his transcendental phenomenology he has focused upon the essences of pure and even, as he says, disembodied consciousness. But in its very purity consciousness sends us back to the foundation of its constitution. Far from being foreign to it, the concept of "field" is constantly implied in its constitution, as we shall see.

Consciousness is constituted as the region of being, the "milieu" through which we gain access to all that exists and in which we constitute "reality" through a process which grounds the *appearance of the phenomena* which arise from the subjective exigencies of experience (noesis) in order to attain their status of objectivity (noema). If the thing itself is given, it turns into perception only by returning to this region through doubt and inadequacy. Reflection alone is capable of grounding the indubitable character of the perceived thing. In each lived experience of perception is to be found a "noematic" meaning[2] which endows lived experience with its coefficient of reality: here the *perceived,* there *memory,* etc.—that is, all the modalities which depend upon the core (*Kernbestande*) of eidetic or noetic givens. The movements, excursions, judgments, reflections, redoublings, and positions which constitute the "configurations" of the blending of lived experience with its objective status (noetic-noematic structure) do not direct us merely to a logical structure of pure consciousness. More exactly (by following the very sense of the reduction of this "pure consciousness") they are anchored in its original constitution as the dispositional order of lived experience. The being of consciousness, which is established in the actualization and the horizons of the lived experience, appears to this subject as a figurative function (*darstellende Funktion*). Whether it refers to the "ground" (*hyle*) of experience or whether it focuses upon the "milieu" where its constituting reflection is mediated, Husserlian consciousness is a "field of production," and this production is always in the form of a structure which we can and must call "field" ("*campine*"), its organization demanding both an *intentionality* (a *Sinngebung*) and a *legality*, both of which circumscribe its activity and its actuality. Husserl very accurately designated[3] this delimitation of its essential freedom within the figures of the self's cogitations as "a field of free execution" (*ein Feld freien Vollzugs*). The lived experience gains its absolute value in the temporal structure of the repeated grasping of these primordial givens when it constitutes itself as a "living now" between this "retention" and these "protensions."

What is "actually perceived" and "more or less clearly copresent and determined" (at least from some perspective) is on the one hand permeated by, on the other hand surrounded by, an obscurely conscious *horizon* of indeterminate reality. But both the *background* and the *figure* are subject to certain "indeterminable determinations." This spatiotemporal dimension of lived experience constitutes the eidetic law of the structure of consciousness.[4] Every lived experience, in effect, is subject either to the law of succession or to the law of simultaneity. This means that every "now" which affects a lived experience has a horizon of lived experience which also has the formal originality of the now: it is the horizon of originality (*Originalitätshorizon*) of the pure self, its "now" of total and original consciousness. To this Husserl adds that we must thus have recourse to a new dimension, that of the total *field*, of phenomenological time. Such is the matrix form (*Ur-form*) of consciousness. One of the specific aspects of this spatiotemporal structure of Husserlian consciousness is its atmosphere of *inner horizon*,[5] that zone of indeterminacy and ambiguity found in lived experience. Every experience or content of consciousness is in effect surrounded by a field of "open possibilities": to perceive or to sense never constitutes a simple or immediate given but rather a mediation which is refracted in the sphere or the harmonies through which the lived experience can be grasped in its resonances.

In this way we find that we are constantly given justification for considering the structure of consciousness as a *field* by Husserl's phenomenology as it progresses through the unfoldings, implications, explications, positions, and reflections of consciousness which *actualize* the reality of its lived experience as it is constituted into a temporal structure, that is, in its problematic of succession and simultaneity. We shall later examine how Maurice Merleau-Ponty has developed this fundamental intuition in connection with the "field of presence."

As we examine the positions of Gestalt psychology, we shall see that this idea of "field," when it is extended into space, into the milieu from which it borrows its physics, risks compromising the dynamic temporality of its original structure. In spite of this reservation and this danger, the structure of consciousness has been well perceived from the perspective of Gestalt psychology. It is noteworthy that the only book with the title *The Field of Consciousness* was written by Aron Gurwitsch for the very purpose of reconciling phenomenology and Gestalt psychology.[6] We shall here give special attention to this work which examines the use which Gestalt psychology has made of the notion of structure and the tendency it sometimes has to assimilate it to a physical or mechanical spatial form, an "impersonal structure" (an anticipation of contemporary "French structuralism").

We must recall that Gestalt psychology is, or has rapidly become, a theory of the perceptual field. In order to seize and solve the problem posed by the constitution of lived experience, this theory turns towards and limits itself to perception as source of all reality; this lived experience can no longer be "sensation," a psychical atom whose extrinsic prolongations are incapable of giving us an adequate account of internal unity. Since the work of William James, Henri Bergson, Charles von Ehrenfeld, etc., psychologists of perception have been constantly preoccupied (as Aristotle was with matter and form—and in exactly the same terms) with the problem presented by "sensory givens" (which imply the "constancy hypothesis") and by the "formal structure" of the perceived object (which demands the participation of the subject). By having recourse to the term *"Gestalten"* ("Gestalts," *"formes"*) ("big cousins" of sensations, Böring has called them), by turning to theories of the perceptual field which were more "molar" than "molecular," this problem was thought to have been avoided. However, this concept of an organic unity of the functional and the psychological, this immediate synthesis, this sudden and primitive crystallization of a configuration which is required for the perception of movement, of differences, of intervals, of melodies, of optical-geometrical illusions, the alternation of figure and ground, and of the formation of good gestalts or the equilibrium of a good constitution, in *all* these authors this has encountered distortions which have arisen out of the ambiguity and bilaterality of the perceptual act. Thus we find that in the work of Ehrenfeld (as in Husserl) the "sensory givens" (William James's "stream of consciousness") have never been able to be reduced, for if they are not constitutive of reality itself they at least do constitute that point of impact with reality which is the foundation for all perception. If Gestalt psychology occasionally believes itself to have been freed from the necessity of a composition, genesis, or operative synthesis of the perceptual act, it is not Köhler and Piaget alone who bring it back to them. The very facts to which they refer accomplish this. Ehrenfeld admits that there must be a sensory *Grundlage* in order that the *Gestaltqualitäten* be constituted; and Meinong's *Gegenstalttheorie* grounds *Komplexionen* on their "infrastructures" (*inferiora*); all of which results in stratifying and complicating an act which was originally posited as *simplex in unitate*. Gestalt psychology thus finds itself divided between the two positions which it thought it had reconciled if not surpassed (the sensory *elements* and the perceptual *whole*).

In fact, the Gestalt, through its dialectical solution to the contradiction which it was thought to have overcome (subject-object, sensation-perception), at first appeared to be capable of resolving the problem of the field of experience by making it arise out of the subject or by placing it on the level of the surface of the subject's senses so that it was reflected in his motor responses. It is thus that Köhler availed himself of the fact that *"was unsere ist, ist aussere,"* in order to develop—along with so many other contemporary psychologists and psychophysiologists—a Gestalt theory which, when all is said and done, is peripheral to perception. Some have even made the attempt to reduce this structure to a mechanical model, in the sense in which Titchener or Böring have understood it.[7] Guillaume,[8] by admitting that the "field of perception" is differentiated into two parts, the external phenomenal world and the phenomenal self, is brought to reintroduce a "dualism" which is incompatible with the total field of consciousness, which field cannot be divided since it is itself the point of junction of these two poles of the act of the "*percipiens.*" There thus exists in certain Gestalt theories a fascination for making the Gestalt fall into the external milieu, whether these theories have the result of moving the Gestalt out of its center of subjectivity or whether they result in dividing it. Another deviation from the "Gestalt" theoretical model consists, as we have already pointed out, in representing the Gestalt with neither genesis nor thickness and as being radically deprived of any "front," of any "back," of any above or below; this is precisely what Kurt Lewin says on this subject in his *Dynamic Theory of Personality* and in his *Principles of Topological Psychology.* The vectorial and topological model which represents psycho-organic behavior does not for him represent the *brain field* but the *life space,* the vital space in which are represented, in the connection of the parts and the whole, the topological relations which bind the subject to its environment in its "psychological field." This latter is purely and absolutely present. In this presentness resides the *concreteness* of the situation which is lived in complete subjection to the law of a rigorous "contemporaneity." Whether it loses its center of gravity, with the "behaviorist" Gestalt model, or its antecedents and underpinnings, with the "topological" model, we shall not make use of this particular notion of field—for the reason that it falls precisely under the unified criticism of the psychology of intentionality and of depth psychology.

In effect, this collapsing of structure into the physics of space, this arrangement of parts which have neither history nor depth, is incompatible with the formation of consciousness as a field of experience. This means that we must return to the first intuitions of the school of Graz so that the perspectives of this field should be those of the senses rather than those of objective space. It is not enough to show that the segregation, the connection, the coherence of the parts, the arrangement or the configuration of the Gestalt should necessitate an intrinsic activity. It is instead much more suitable to appeal to vital or integrative processes in order to explain the *Verschmelzung* (Husserl), the fusion (James), or the copenetration of qualitative multiplicities (Bergson), that is, the necessity, in apprehending the real, that the subject should make use of an internal and foundational structure which is both temporal and noematic. But we must go even further, to the very roots of the perceptual act in the essence or the universality of perception, laying hold of the obviousness of Stern's aphorism, "There is no form without someone who forms it" ("*Es gibt keine Gestalt ohne Gestalter*") and the self-evidence of what Weizsäcker has designated as *the encounter of subject and object.* The object can no more be absent from perception (in spite of the formative activity of the subject) than the subject can be excluded from it (in spite of the sensory givens or the figural factors which are immanent in the object). As Gurwitsch has said, on this point all aspects of perception ought to be treated in the same manner. They should all be considered to be givens and facts of *authentic sensible experience.*[9]

If we wish to uncover all the lessons which Gestalt psychology has lavished upon us in its rich and profound analysis of perception, we must do so by considering as valid its thesis of a composite multiplicity, and not that of a pretended holistic unity whose only significance is that it throws off center the whole which is outside the subject in such a way that it dissolves it. The "Gestaltization" of experience necessitates not a "behavioristic" perspective of a pure description, but the notion of a *total structure of experience* which envelops both the givens of lived experience and its "Gestaltization"—which envelops them in a process of integration which is itself conceived as an operative act composed and set in hierarchical form without excluding either of the two poles involved in the encounter of the *subject* with its *world.* The fact that a being encounters the reality of *its world* implies precisely that this encounter itself should not be an object, that it cannot be reduced to being a pure objectivity.

This excursion into the realm of Gestalt psychology, of this "handmaid" of contemporary psychophysiology, has allowed us to emphasize that this latter appears to be grounded only to the extent that, by resolutely repudiating any "reflexological" or "behaviorist" or "mechanistic" interpretation and returning to its sources, it sets its sights on *an internal organization of the psychical being of which the field of consciousness, including both the external and the internal, is the environment.* This seems to be precisely the path which both Gurwitsch and Merleau-Ponty point out to us, in spite of the differences of their viewpoints.

Gurwitsch does not hesitate to tell us that *organization is the autochthonous characteristic of consciousness.* All the qualitative, typical, or dimensional differences which might exist between the conjunctions and connections of mental states depend upon this organization; in the articulation of the total field as a thematic and marginal field, he adds,[10] we become aware of *a formal invariant of all fields of consciousness.* However this "formal structure of consciousness" cannot be only "formalized" as an isomorphic property of the nervous system and of the act of consciousness of which the perceptive act would be the model. This structure of consciousness is not merely the atmosphere of meanings which would "form" only "contents" of consciousness; it is the very legality of the bonds which the modalities of its encounter with its human world impose upon the subject. The *field of consciousness* cannot be merely the object of a functional description of a "Gestalt" style in general and of a behaviorist Gestalt style in particular; it must also be the object of a phenomenology of actually lived experience, as being that which *must* now be present. This seems to us to be the sense of the work of Aron Gurwitsch, which completes the formal analysis of the constitution of the perceived field by making use of the Husserlian logic of the order or the category of existences.

Just as Husserl has joined consciousness to experience, to the extent that experience is the lived world of consciousness and that this interrelation (between the "world of Nature" as sphere of the *Urpräsentierbar* and the "world of persons," of minds) is the essence of consciousness, Merleau-Ponty has been fascinated, he tells us, by the flashing of the *Urempfindung* as anticipation of the "constitution" of consciousness in the stratum of living experience. It is this which constitutes the *phenomenal field,* the field of the *apparition* of the world to itself, which belongs to this manner of the advent of being to the world. And if, as he states,[11] "Phenomenology is the only philosophy which speaks of this field," this is precisely because by grasping itself in its grasping of the world, this grasping is disclosed as the gaze which causes the spectacle of the world to appear. This happens not merely as a pure "reflection" but as a reflection upon the nonreflected, the juncture of which is the living body (it is in the world as the heart is in the organism: it continually keeps the visible spectacle alive, it animates it and nourishes it from within). The "hyletic stratum" of experience cannot be cast out of consciousness as an "opaque being."

The natural world is the horizon of all horizons. In this interior and exterior horizon of the thing and the landscape, there is a "copresence" or a coexistence of profiles which knit themselves together across time and space.[12] This synthesis of horizons is essentially temporal: it merges with the very movement of the passage of time. The sensible protoexperience (the primordial or primary experience) is merely a nonthetic, preobjective, and preconscious experience.[13] It is within its horizons and its temporality that consciousness unfolds; but time does not flow like a river, like a "succession of nows," and consciousness cannot itself be this succession of nows.[14] Time is not a "given" of consciousness; it enters into consciousness only by forming it. Consciousness unfolds and constitutes time.[15] The *field of presence* is the dimension of consciousness that becomes rooted in being and in time by assuming its situation therein. This presence is at the same time both the *present* of experience and *the inherence of this experience in its subject.* It is through this present that we are "centered," that the freedom of our projects emerges,[16] and that their "sense" becomes anchored in the cradle of all significations, this sense of all senses. We shall move in this direction as we present our description of the "field of consciousness" as the field of experience across which experience passes from its antepredicative form (as Merleau-Ponty calls it, considering its primordial stratum) to its reflected form and to the freedom of its movements.

We thus see that the structure of the present field of experience, or of the "field of presence," gains the greatest import in the eyes of the philosophers and the schools of psychology that have most thoroughly examined the "structure of consciousness," its architectonic, and especially the structure of perception. There is no question of using the term "field" in an abusive manner which would be purely verbal or analogical. On the contrary, it is important that we fill it with precisely that rich reality which abstractionism refuses to give it. For this reason a too simple reduction to a plane surface or a flat actuality must be excluded from this notion. It should rather be considered as a dynamic, organized, and living whole.[17]

Once they have been validated in this way, the reality and the organization of the field of consciousness are revealed as being the very actuality of lived experience, that is to say, as *sensible experience* anchored in the space of the body and in that space of time which constitutes consciousness while constituting itself. By accepting Herder's formula that man is a *"sensorium commune,"* Merleau-Ponty chains us not to empiricism but rather to the very reality of that which must be presented in order to be lived. All that has been said and that can be said on the subject of the *actualization* and the *actuality* (*hic et nunc*) of psychical life, that is, the present moment (*Augenblick*) of its structure; all there is to say concerning *the scene and the horizons of lived experience* as the framework and distribution of the phenomena of consciousness in their relation with the natural world; or again on the subject of the *intentionality of consciousness* insofar as it is consciousness of something, relative to which the meaning in the configuration of lived experience is ordered: all this converges and focuses upon this *field* as a reality to be described, as a field which is engendered by the reflection of being upon its own present experience.

This "manner of being in duration," of being "a moment of duration," a "stationary equilibrium," an *unitas multiplex,* implies a fundamental bilateralness, a congenital struggle of the being of consciousness to constitute itself into a field of actuality or of presence, into a directional field, oriented or polarized against that which it does not have to be. *The phenomenal field* thus can be reduced neither to its static aspects (state), nor to its concrete aspects (contents or immediate givens), nor again to an empty form. It is neither space, nor flux, nor rigid frame; except in the case of those diverse levels of the destructuration of this field which have been revealed when it is in the state of being disorganized, actually lived experience never loses its "essential qualities."[18] But since it exists only as an effect of an autochthonous organization which is not only the condition but the very reality of such and such a presentation of lived experience, it can be considered as such (as field of presence) only in and through an *organization,* which is the true object of a phenomenology of the field of consciousness.

2. PHENOMENOLOGICAL DESCRIPTION OF THE FIELD OF CONSCIOUSNESS

There is nothing more difficult than to grasp the dimensions and structural qualities of this field. It is much easier to describe only a formal invariable which is reduced to a derisory simplicity (function of wakefulness), or to describe the infinite modalities of concrete lived experience (contents of consciousness), that is, all that forms, has formed, or will form the experience which is lived by each person at each moment of his existence! We can avoid this double danger of a formalism which oversimplifies or of an infinite thematization by grounding our description in what we have learned about the reality of the field of consciousness from its destructuration. The "pathology" of this decomposition has, in effect, furnished us with a model which is the inverse of what an "analysis" of the autochthonous traits of its organization would permit us to discover.

In order to allow ourselves to return to "the things themselves," we shall direct our attention to the field of consciousness only as it is "reduced" to its essential properties, on this side of its reflexive superstructures (cf. above, pp. 19–23).

The psychopathology of the field of consciousness has revealed to us that the structure of consciousness *is a "ground" of consciousness which is in some way unconscious* and which appears only when the field of consciousness has lost its structure. On this basis, by referring to what we have said concerning the degrees of this destructuration (first of its temporal-ethical organization, then of the organization of its perception of its lived space, and finally of its most profound level, that of its very opening to the world), it becomes possible for us to describe for the field of consciousness *an infrastructure* of *constituted consciousness* which is, in fact, the ground of its field. It is precisely the vertical movement of this constitution as it is elliptically designated by the notion of alertness or of the passage from sleeping to waking which we describe as the *Ur-form* (the primitive strata) of the field of actualization of lived experience. When constituted in this way, the "field of consciousness" is "well-constituted," "solid." It has as its property this other property: to vary. The experience of the normal, waking subject consists in his ability freely to modify this changeable field which is at his disposal. Because it is restricted to the actuality of lived experience and is animated by the subject, who injects his desires and his power into it, the field of consciousness *affects the self with relationships* which must be elucidated.

The phenomenology of the field of consciousness must successively be developed: first, as a grasping of its constitution (*consciousness constituted as field*); second, as a grasping of its facultative operations (*consciousness which is constitutive* of its operational relationships with reality); and third, as a grasping of conscious being as the subject of his experiences (presence).

1. THE INFRASTRUCTURE OF CONSCIOUSNESS CONSTITUTED AS A FIELD

As we have just repeated, the destructuration of the field of consciousness has laid bare the framework which composes it, the levels of its organization or the strata which constitute it. Such a stratification can attain its normal level, that of a well-constituted field, only through a vertical movement, through a process of building up, which, passing from sleeping to waking, causes consciousness to cross, in a single bound, all the infrastructures which had been passed through during its ontogenesis. We must now describe three structural levels or three stages of the constitution of consciousness as a field: the constitution of an experience which is oriented towards the world; the constitution of a lived space in which the relationships of the subject to its world are bound together; the constitution of a *present.*

a) The "Field" Circumscribed and Oriented by Its Sense

From its very origin, and therefore at all times, the "field" is determined by its *sense.* Brentano stated that consciousness is always consciousness of something (*auf etwas sich beziehendes*). This is so because consciousness is an *aiming,* and its field appears, as if to respond to this aiming, by representing it. Its "time" is that of a duration which carries desire towards its object, as well as being that of an interval which separates them. Its space is one wherein the figures which engender the steps towards its goal are described. The objective, the object of this first vectorial organization, is the simplest possible field in which consciousness can be constituted. This "protoexperience" of consciousness *statu nascendi* is born of the obstacle which is interposed between the desire and its object. Consciousness is posited by opposing this shock. Between the desire and the reality rises the *image* which symbolizes the reality of the desire. All the configurations of the field of consciousness can be constructed and developed on the basis of the simplest expression of this model. This intentional relation—the first and fundamental bilateralness of consciousness—opens and orients the field by presenting to itself this something which is focused upon by the subject. In this first glimmering of consciousness or of wakefulness, the subject opens up to his world as to that with which he must deal and with which he must come to terms. The world is presented along with the question of its *orientation* and of its *signification*. No matter how rudimentary or how slightly open it might be, every field of consciousness has a thematic or is a "topic" (James). It is organized in relation to this bestowal of sense (*Sinngebung*), which is the axis or the vector of experience. Nothing in its dimensions, implications, or temporal or spatial explications can be revealed in this experience which is not engendered, carried, and developed by its sense. The "field" of consciousness is thus only occasionally reducible to the quantity of phenomena which figure in it, that is, to the "span of awareness" of Wundt's psychophysiology. This is the sense which determines most particularly the beginning and the end, the concentration or the dispersion of the actuality of experience. It is the only "measure" of the *Augenblick,* of that moment which constitutes the lived *hic et nunc* in any event. By "event" we refer equally well to the arising of an image in a dream or a memory—whether sudden or sought after, as a "situation" which we provoke or which circumstances thrust upon us.

We would not dream of describing the perspectives which are opened by meaning (the subordination of the accessory to the principle, of the immediate to the distant, and, more generally, all the symmetries and reciprocities of relations which are established among the infinity of possibles); but it is possible for us to describe the conditions of the appearance and development of this theme. That which appears, that which interests or captivates (that "end" of the present moment which is lived as the experience of this emotion, of this search, or of this contemplation), appears in two rather different conditions. Either the appearance *arises* from the depths of the being as an affective exigency (need, feelings) or a noetic exigency (intuition, idea): the "sense" bursts forth as a need for orientation, a desire, a demand; or the appearance is that of an external event or object, and the sense is then found to be not imposed but assigned by the external world as an urgency or interest. The oscillations of the field of consciousness are thus suspended from a sort of inner *panting* and outer *harassment.* The impossibility of avoiding this double bestowal of sense prevents consciousness from ever being able to cease "giving itself" the field of its desire, of its knowledge, of its perception, and from ever being able to go beyond the preoccupations and cares which maintain its alertness.

However, the appearance of the lived experience, with the sense which animates it (by arising as the urgency, the necessity, or the wish of being there), is not constitutive of the field of consciousness except as its goal. The means of this polarization—the forms of its expressivity and of its facticity—depend upon the possibility of the development of the experience which has arisen and is sighted. To the extent that this intentionality constitutes the opening of consciousness to an object, that is, to the possibility of a bilateral relationship of the self to its world, this intentional dimension of the field of consciousness is truly its original being; but since it persists throughout its development, it necessitates an unceasing metamorphosis of this pure intention. We can find this intentionality in the rudimentary forms of these lower levels, even in the destructuration of sleep, but only through the fulguration or the anacolutha of images on the background of the annihilation of an impossible world (cf. above, pp. 61ff.). In the earliest stages of its organization, this forms only the meager, concrete, and undeveloped field of an experience which is lived as a prisoner of the desired thing or of the perceived thing. In the higher degrees of its unfolding, this embryonic form of meaningful figuration comes to be orchestrated in a multitude of reflexive possibilities which form the composed, but indefinitely open, multiplicity of its experience. This latter, then, becomes the experience of a situation, of a problem whose sense is not entirely "given" but only shows itself in order to demand that it be taken and retaken in a cascade and series of profiles and sketches. These outlines are nothing other than the forms of discourse which make it possible to decipher and execute the projection of its sense into a language used by the subject to discover its implicit figures. It thus becomes evident that if its sense is the *Urform* of the field of consciousness, its matrix form, this form cannot be reduced to intentionality, *for intentionality itself is subordinated to a structure of possibilities or of the instrumentality of signs.*

Whether "sense" creates a "field" of consciousness which is immediate and closed up in its ipseity, or a field of consciousness which is mediated to the point of extending to its whole world, these "fields," all these "fields," are for the subject its manner of grasping an experience which fills a moment of its existence. In effect, the "lived" of experience is always an historical lived which emblazons each moment of our time. The more concrete and full of imagery the meaning remains, the less it lends itself to discursive development and the more it then remains secret and poetic, as if its ineffability consecrated it for consciousness. It fascinates consciousness as an aesthetic object, rather than as an event for its history. Inversely, every reflection and every retrospection upon these intimate experiences, upon this pure duration, in this "poetic" field of meaning in which Bergson and Proust meet, each of these is a bestower of aesthetic sense.

Later on we shall see how this "interesting spectacle" comes into bloom, how the "suspense" of experience unfolds when it comes to be constituted "scenically." For the moment it will suffice for us to show that the *originative dimension of the field of consciousness is its sense;* it opens up only in response to a question ("Who am I?" "Where am I?" "How can I satisfy my desire?" "What ought I to do?"). To the extent that the experience which enters into consciousness is consciousness of some object, it is a *lived event* which is ordered in relation to its *orientation.* What we have just seen to be the semantic essence of the field is that which all fields of consciousness have in common. It is consequently unable to account for the category of reality of any of these appearances. It cannot explain the autochthonous relationships of the meaning with its field. By reducing the field of consciousness to its intentionality, we have touched upon its origin, but only at the point of its germination.

b) "Field" as the "Scene of Lived and Spoken Actuality"

If, then, it is true that the meaning, the "idea," of each experience furnishes the experience with its text or its scenario, it could either be confined within the image or the object as an immediate relationship—as is a flashing of desire—or, on the contrary, it could grow and become more complicated in proportion to the discursive development of the field of consciousness. From this point onwards, in order to allow the possibility of a "cinematographic," simultaneous representation of successive or implied planes,[19] the structuring into a field must now occur as a disponibility of the space which is necessary for the unfolding of the *representation.* The field thus appears as the place which is organized for the appearance, as the receptacle and the vehicle of its thematic shiftings. This scene,[20] in which the significant and meaningful configurations (verbalized or verbalizable) which *represent* the sequence (so rightly called "scenic") of lived experience appear, come, and go, this scene is very much "ordered" as a function of the action which unfolds within it. But at the same time it imposes upon it the order of its own construction. We may, then, call it a "scene"; but it is a scene which cannot be reduced to a homogeneous space, since it is impossible for it ever to be empty. Nor can it be detached from the personages and episodes which enter into it. These arise from the very modalities of the space and time which form with its sense the architechtonically bound totality of the scene and of the spectacle. This amounts to saying that this scene is no more in space than it is in time or in the scenario.

From this point of view the "field of consciousness" is very different from the "visual field" (to which one cannot help but compare it at every turn because of the "spectacular" phenomena of experience which unfold for one within it and as if before the subject's very eyes). The field of vision[21] causes a spatial extension along with its objects to enter into our experience; but if this extension does not coincide with space, if it is only a reflection of it, this is because, far from enveloping the field of consciousness, the visual field is included within it, as we have emphasized above, (pp. 15 and 65–66). Even more generally, the field of consciousness is not merely the perceptual field; at least it becomes this only on the condition that it has transformed this field of the perception of external or corporeal objects into a field of present experience which both goes beyond and includes perception. The field of consciousness, such as it here reveals itself as being a "scene" or a "location-of-lived-spaces-within-present-experience," is thus not an object which belongs to space but an analogical structure which combines time and space as the *medium* of its "representation."

Moreover, to say that the field of consciousness is a scene and that within it unfolds a *re*-presentation is—because of the doubling implied in the prefix of this last word—to lay hold of the scenic lived aspect ("theme," topic) of experience as a correlative arrangement of the bilateralness of the intentionality of the subject and its object. We are here attempting to describe not only the *presentation* of the lived aspect of the consciousness of the subject who lives it, but also a referential order of the spatialization in which this lived experience is distributed, extended, and unfolds in this *medium.* It is indeed a question of a *representation,* since experience is constituted as an action which unfolds with the subject. It is this "within" which constitutes lived space and which can be only that of the body which grants and assigns to it its sensible properties, not as a support but as a symbol of its representation. Thus, even when the scene of consciousness is filled (as an "exception") with the perception of external objects, these are themselves incorporated within this field, which, moreover, is set within the self only to go out of it, as if it was its essence never to be able to coincide with a given space, never to be able to be settled.

All the "spatial determinations" of this field, its perspectives, its dimensions, its parameters, its partitioning, all that involves the "here" or "there" of lived experience, all this is never anything but a referential "space" which is symbolic of movement. The space of the phenomenal field is a copresence, a simultaneity of the things which make up the order of actuality. In other words, this "space" is within time.[22] It is in movement; it is nothing but movement. The representation which plays upon the scene or the field of consciousness can borrow its space only from the kaleidoscope of a succession which has been cinematized in time. These manners of appearing or disappearing, of coming or going, of approaching and withdrawing, of being superimposed or blending together, all these constitute the spatiotemporal modes which are proper to the field of consciousness.[23] It is not and cannot be a question of the time and the space of mathematics, for the field of consciousness is not the geometrical place of a juxtaposition of objects in space or of their modification in objective time. The natural world, the world of objects is certainly not outside of consciousness as the "constancy hypothesis" (or the "hypothesis of objectivity") supposes. Nor is it within consciousness; at least it can enter into it only by being limited by the permanent horizon of a world which is necessary to the historicity of existence. We shall return to this horizon of the world when discussing the constitution of the self. But here, on the level of lived experience, if lived experience indeed does happen to admit the data of the senses—that is, its encounter with an exteriority which cannot be reduced to its own subjectivity (Weizsäcker, Buytendijk, Prince Albert Auersperg, etc.)—perception can nonetheless never enter into the field of consciousness without becoming a lived experience which is grasped in the self-moving nature of its constitution.

In this perpetual movement, the center and the periphery, the figure and the ground, the perspectives of up and down, of in and out, of front and back, of near and far, of container and contained, in every case these are only contractions or expansions, progressions or retreats, anticipations or retrogressions, protensions or retentions, which by their interlacing form "as it were" a space, an analogue of space, the "only" milieu in which "lived" worldliness can continue to live, as it is given or as it is taken, that is, suspended in this milieu which consciousness holds as a net between the subject and its world.

To say of this field of consciousness which is organized as a momentary space that it is a manner of enduring is to say in addition that the field of consciousness unfolds only as a memory which envelops experience with a halo of the past; for, in effect, nothing which enters into it, not even that which enters through the boomeranging of perception, is ever purely instantaneous. The "cognition" of experience is always a "recognition," just as its presentation is always a representation; they demand a pause in time during which the simultaneity of things (*cogitata*) is brought together. The field of actuality appears only in this mnemic continuity, in such a manner that we must refer back to Bergson (consciousness signifies first of all memory) and to his profound analyses of the structure of consciousness insofar as it is the composition and copenetration of a multiplicity (the very heterogeneity of duration) of time—which Paul Valéry called "the mind's body."

The structure of this "lived space" is very well that of a living body[24] which "retains" the sensibility of its body for and in its experience. Whatever the "sense data" and the form of representation might be, all experience leads back to perception. This latter crosses the body through the organs of sense, which bestow their *Gestaltqualitäten* upon it. No matter how purely affective or abstract or imaginary it might be, an experience can be constituted as a "field" only by connecting this field to its own manner of feeling. In order to be lived, the field must be organized as a "coherence" (Weizsäcker) of the feeling and the movements of the body through which it lives. But even here it is not the objective space of the body which gives experience its fundamental dimensions; the body is a bestower of space and qualities only by incorporating lived experience into the temporality of its self-movement[25] by living it in its representation.

This "space," which is lived as a scenic field of representation engendered by the exigencies of time, and which presents the virtual movements of the sensible body, this "medium" in which experience unfolds, is "occupied," "filled," and structured as a system of relations between communications, information, and messages, which make of human experience an experience which is open to others. Speech is the possibility of signifying, of declaring, and, by actualizing verbal chains, of enunciating not the materiality of signs—although the body's movements do figure into this "inner language"—but their functional connections: intervals, ellipses, scansions, figures, "tropes." All these modes of speech, of discourse with oneself and with others, make use of a space which is subtle but yet rebels against submitting to these exercises. It is precisely through these resistances, the obscurity of words, the gaps in speech, its innuendos, its silences, its ability to overwhelm, that language both determines and rejects a space, or rather a system which refers to space, with its gaps, its reliefs, its gulfs, its luminous expanses where it can flow, slip away, rebound, stumble. In this way the field of consciousness appears as a *field of language.* This field is a "context" of all the communications which unite the subject to others and to himself; it is the context of the experience of the "bodily presence" (Merleau-Ponty) of the self in words. Whatever can be said about language presupposes this organization which refers to a space or an interval which is the location of its relations, an operational and semantic field in which are bound together those two aspects of speech which Cassirer has distinguished (discursive logic and creative fantasy), or again those two modes (metonymy and metaphor) which Roman Jakobson and Halle have assigned to the structure of language, to the degree that it is constructed or, more exactly, is carried on in the criss-crossing of its coordinates of contiguity and similarity.

We too have arrived at this "surrealistic conjugality" of words, which couple amongst themselves and create a symbolic and mythical world, without, however, ceasing to be joined to the world of reality, whether this world reflects or rejects it. The field of consciousness is the raising up, the creation of a finite world whose very necessity, like that of a painting or of a melodic or poetic form, through its intimacy, expresses the aesthetic fascination of the order of its architecture. We have already pointed this out when discussing the enchantment brought about by the senses. The gasping caused by the surprise at our foresight and by the foresight of our surprise is the seizing of consciousness by its own lust. In the language of psychoanalysis this is called erotization of thought. The field of consciousness acts like a magnetic field, a magnet (*"aimant"*) which attracts, aroused by desire. The "tendencies to create spectacles," which have been so thoroughly analyzed by Maurice Navratil,[26] are not exceptional, peculiar, or purely representative tendencies; they are implied in the organization of lived experience into a field, in such a way that the poet—and with him the phenomenologist—can always reduce it to this aesthetic radical (that of a radical originality, of a radical intimacy) of a bewitching or ecstatic experience, or to that of an anecdotal "subject" of an art object (for example an Epinal image). We well understand how speaking of consciousness as a representation, a scene, inevitably involves us in a sort of theatricality or drama of its spectacular experience.

The figurative aspects (temporality, movement, corporality, verbalization, sensibility, aesthetic) of this field of *scenic representation* are directed by their inward and outward *orientation*. By "orientation" is meant the *here and now* seizure of the centripetal and centrifugal movement of lived experience. For experience is never constituted as the scene of an absolute theatricality. It is always a scene which is born, develops, and ends "for itself." It is a "reality which is problematical" in its representative effect. The *thetic function* of consciousness is the ability to discern in each of its conscious functions, and for each of its modes, what belongs to it, what originates within itself, what escapes it, what it clashes against. It is a sort of arbitration, which is all the more severe since the judge who passes this judgment of reality might himself be guilty of or tricked into infraction: because of its own ambiguity, the very structure of consciousness as a field of representation sets forth its own enigma. The field in which unfold the changing events which take place simultaneously both within myself and outside of myself never ceases to be animated by a back and forth movement which causes perceived objects to advance and imagined objects to fade into the background. In each lived experience, in each thematic or scenic development, we can always discover that which is outside myself in the objective legality of the external world, that which comes from myself through the subjective faculty of my desire or of my fantasy, that which emerges from the depths of myself as from an interior world which is as impersonal as the world of nature, and that which comes from others in the messages they send me and which I am able to receive only by returning them, etc. In Part Five we shall examine the importance of this structural necessity, which is a sort of obligation of lived experience to appear only when it is hidden in the analogical or symbolic formation of a world which it must create in its own image and which it can apprehend only by repressing it: *the stage of consciousness is closely connected with the wings and backstage of the Unconscious.*

c) "Field" as "Field of the Present and Field of Presence"

It is obvious that to the degree that it is lived, every field of consciousness is the *actuality of lived experience.* But the instantaneous lived experience of the dream or the deformed experience of the states of the destructuration of consciousness do not constitute a "field of presence" in the sense of an orientation of consciousness which is capable of being directed towards a present and of being absorbed in it. The "field of the present" is an opening of consciousness which remains impossible precisely to the extent that lived experience can appear only in an instantaneous or precarious actualization which is caught in a space which is merely presented or represented. We therefore must now describe this opening to the present as a higher level which normalizes the field of consciousness. To be present to one's world is in fact to organize the present as a situation in which an action is undertaken. Up to this point the process of the construction of the field of consciousness has passed through a series of experiences which have been undergone, if they have not been completely passive; that dynamism which makes of actuality an act is precisely what has been missing from them. Action, which was prefigured in the structures of the field of consciousness which we have just described, was contained in these only as a potential content, only as an experience which was more or less dramatic or significant, and which unfolded in a virtual space and in a time which is scattered through the chaotic or fragmentary movements of its episodes. This squandered and disorganized time could not be constituted into a present or be stilled so that it might allow itself to open up and to hollow out a truly present field of consciousness in the free interval of the suspended past and the coming future. We have already discussed the miraculous character of this present which, all things considered, is impossible, since it is in such a hurry to pass, and is already past in its passing. This flux of time, which is the order of an urgent need for succession—each of its instants chasing the others—without there ever being any possibility of reversibility, this urgency which carries consciousness along like the current of a river, is very truly a quality of lived time. It is indeed an inexorable march towards death, since it consumes and consummates life, that is, the possibility for being to traverse the experiences of its existence. To the extent that it is not a homogeneous, chronological, and mathematical time, time— as the duration of being—is a disposition and a state of being disponible. This faculty of holding onto time, of retaining it, of being able, against the clock, to cheat on its movement, is *the possibility of living a present which is organized as a field of presence.* Thus, the field of consciousness, which at first opened up to us as a projection of intentionality, then as a "stage" upon which something took place, now shows itself to be a now (*un maintenant*) which is able to maintain time. It is no longer merely an aiming or a location; it is invested with its own proper quality of duration, that of a necessary pause, of a resting which accords with the demands of action. It no longer is thought of merely as a polarized field or the field of a spectacle; it is a field which is constituted at the same time against both instantaneousness and speed, as if a *space of time.* It implies an unfolding which ensures a certain magnitude to its dimensions, a certain order to its perspectives. This "space of time," which in fact is sustained and animated by the meaning which constitutes it, and is unfolded in the scene which contains it, can and must endure until the very extinction of the clarity which animates it, of the meaning which specifies its limits and its end.

In such a higher structuring of consciousness as a field, its *ethical temporality* as the integration of impulses, of emotions, of the demands of instinctual motivations, constitutes the functional achievement of the actualization of lived experience into a present. This is a present which is not only presented or represented, but a present which is the manner of being really in my presence to what I do; it is a manner of attaining the lucidity and control of my field of action.

Lucidity or *clarity* of consciousness is precisely that capability of differentiation which develops its parts in the luminosity of its field while preserving between them shadows of space and intervals of time. Bergson has said that experience illuminates the space of its representation by opening itself to time. The field of consciousness can arrive at the summit of its vertical organizational movement only when it withdraws from matter (momentary mind, Leibniz has called it) to be a structure which commands enough time to gain its freedom.

The order which is thus introduced into the constitution of the field demands not only the clarity of its contours but the control of *action,* that is, the creative structure of the differentiated field of consciousness. It demands not simply the action of "automatic" behavior which is either outside of (that is, below) clear consciousness or implied in its organization as the mechanism of the act, but action whose development demands a duration of the present which is inhabited by the presence of the subject.

We thus pass from the *field of the present* to the *field of presence,* which defines experience as an experience animated by a *project* which is both explicit and *in the process* of being realized.

If we are to describe the field of experience which is constituted as present, it is not enough to appeal to the *interest of life* (Bergson) or to attention, or, with Heidegger, to preoccupation (*Besorge*) as the foundation for *existing.* For this concentration and this motivation meet in the infrastructure of consciousness which we have described. In order to ground the constitution of a present which is bound to the real presence of the subject, it is necessary to carry this curiosity, this design, or this effort to a degree of differentiation or of complexity which is such that they cease to be a simple movement or a simple impulse and become an operational form of reflection. Only controlled action can fill this present of the *presence* of the person who engenders it by willing it, sustaining it, and persevering in its duration; in order to become the execution of its project, action demands the *presence of the subject.*

The construction of the present is indeed a condition of the temporalization of experience and adds something to its rudimentary actuality, to the synchronization and the copresence of the elements which enter into its field. It is also the order of the subordination of the simultaneous nature of the present to the motion of *presence.* We can observe the appearance of this *temporal-ethical structure* of the field of consciousness, to the degree that it is "oriented" in the direction of what it must do in order to stop or to accelerate time, by submitting it to the law of present action, that is, *to the ordinance of the being which manifests its presence in it.*

It thus becomes clear that the "field of presence" and the "field of presentation" can admit lived experience only as an *act* and not merely as an actuality—an act which, in order to unfold its project of being, demands a newness of willing by which its project can tear itself away from the domination of the completed past without too strongly anticipating a future which is only indefinitely possible. It is an act which is constructed between the inevitability of a sequence of events and the infinity of an unleashing of activity, an act which recovers its balance through its own *ec-stasy* in the order of possibilities. It is no longer an actuality which is merely the form taken on by every experience as it appears, if not "without law or religion," at least without any explicit reference to an accepted present and an assumed presence.

Because it is constituted at this level of well-pondered and remembered action, the field of consciousness rises to the level of a "well-constituted" consciousness; it gains a degree of organization which allows the structure of consciousness to emerge from the state of unconsciousness and from all the infrastructures which form its "degrees." From this point onwards, since it is constituted as a field of the present which is open to presence, consciousness has gained an adequate degree of "wakefulness."

This path, which consciousness crosses in a few seconds when it passes from sleep to waking, is the same path which the ontogenesis of consciousness has crossed from its heights to its depths and which consciousness follows in the vertical movement, the dynamic structures of which we have just described as we followed, in reverse order, the progress of its loss of structure.

2. THE FACULTATIVE STRUCTURE AND DISPONIBLE NATURE OF THE FIELD OF CONSCIOUSNESS*

We have just described the constitutive and ontogenetic modes of lived experience as it exists in the form of a field (intentionality, scene of representation, organization of the present). We must now examine this structure no longer in the stages of its development but in its full activity, as this is accomplished when it passes from the unconsciousness of the newborn child to the consciousness of the adult, from the unconsciousness of sleep to the alertness of waking. This examination will reveal a new structural form of the field of waking which is characterized by the fundamental character of *varying* at the will of the subject. This is so true that the field can no longer vary (or does so much less freely) as soon as it begins to lose its structure. On the contrary, once consciousness has accomplished this vertical movement which we have just discussed and has attained its normal level of "wakefulness,"[27] it continues to vary ceaselessly, as if its *facultative* activity was a fundamental property of its field. This is because, once it has been organized as a field of action, it is not constituted as a plane surface or a static order: the action which unfolds the vicissitudes of its lived experience in this field carves out in the present a multiplicity of perspectives which resemble the angles from which the pictures of a film are taken. Without becoming separated from the unity of the thematic "Gestalization" of the field, the phases of this unfolding can arise, disappear, and follow one another, juxtapose themselves among or interfere with the others. The present is not the sum but the functional unity of this multiplicity. All the figures which the subject describes around its object appear as dimensions of this present, whether these movements be centripetal or centrifugal, whether they focus upon some detail or encompass the whole, whether they scan the surface or plunge to the depths: these are all elastic and fluctuating dimensions whose thematic meaning alone gives them the facultative ability to mark out within the reality of lived experience the configuration of

*Ey uses the terms "facultative" (*facultatif*) and "facultativity" (*facultativité*) to imply "the idea of a certain contingency or a freedom of choice." These terms express "the very opposite of obligatory."

The terms "disponibility" or "disponible nature" (*disponibilité*) refer to the "idea of being able to make use 'ad libitum' or 'at will' of something or of someone, in this case, of oneself." Ey points out that this is "the very idea of the Self."—Trans., in collaboration with the author.

its operational field. This is so true that the miraculous reality of the present presupposes an indefinite variety of manners in which it can appear throughout the simultaneous and successive movements that compose the multiplicity of the experience which is taking place, insofar as this experience is under the control of the subject who generates it. At the level at which it becomes truly *constituting,* the field of consciousness represents a sort of obligation perpetually to change its perspectives, a sort of obligation to diversity, so that it might remain within the constancy of its meaning, and therefore of its unity. The kaleidoscopic unfolding of experience thus ought not to be taken as a "flux of pure lived experience." It is, in fact, an architectonic entanglement of forms. These forms are not merely immediate givens that are heterogeneous to the structure of consciousness; on the contrary, they are seized in the direction of the movement of the field to which they are bound. The *operational structure* of consciousness, its variations and the free movements which bring about the metamorphosis of each aspect of the present without, however, compromising its unity, these can appear in their full freedom only with the consent, if not the attention, of the subject who arouses them.

Because it requires the presence of the subject, the organization of the field into a "present" is precisely what established its disponible nature. In the case of a person who creates an object, or dreams of some happening, or recalls some memory, or imagines an encounter, or prepares a speech, or analyzes a feeling, or attempts to understand his own motivation or to interpret the conduct of someone else, etc., that is, any person who is in a situation of "presence," who is in the midst of a present action, we are not at all surprised to find that these persons constantly vary their field of consciousness, not simply as they speak or breathe, but as they "think proper." This constitution of consciousness as a field guarantees and necessitates this facultativity. What does seem surprising is that this interlacing of perceptions, images, memories, ideas, abstractions, information, and words does not jeopardize the order and the category of the realities of lived experience. If the field of consciousness were to include only these thematic variations and the contingency of its "contents," the very process which created it would confirm this "concrete" heterogeneity; through the mobility of its facultative activities it could suggest that it did not exist as an organized structure. The field of consciousness would then be only an abstract metaphor whose sole purpose would be to give a fixed but fictitious framework to this moving unreality. All those who, since William James, have not succeeded in grasping consciousness in its structural organization have given in to this illusion. If this organization is essentially that of a field, this is because it is always structured and ordered by the *subject* who constructs it and who, once it has been constructed, controls its configurations, limits, and positions.

It is of the very essence of consciousness to be constituted as a field in accordance with a radically bilateral perspective. When describing the constitution of consciousness, the substructure of the field of consciousness, we have already seen lived experience in its immanence and in the spontaneity of its appearing; but even on this level of summary proprietorship (*Eigenheitsphäre*), we have emphasized that the "given" dimension of consciousness at each stage of its constitution implies the transcendental dimension of a *focusing of consciousness by the experiencing subject.*

Selbstlichkeit, subjectivity, far from separating consciousness from its world, is the dimension of consciousness which integrates consciousness into its world. Nonetheless, a consciousness that is open to the present in its lucidity is revealed in its facultativity only when its being has achieved a certain degree of fullness. This occurs when the subject is allowed the freedom to describe an infinite number of movements which are guaranteed by the formal invariability of its constitution. Our description of the operational structure of consciousness has shown us that its configurations appear as the different stages of the ontogenesis of lived experience which have been brought about by the subject of this experience. As the *I* of *what* is lived by the self, this subject is not merely the center of this egocentric arrangement of the field of experience, with relation to which experience is ordered; it is also the generator of its own appearances. We are therefore justified in adding that the "facultativity" of the field is the *property* of its subject. The "I" who speaks, who thinks, who acts, who has projects, who gives free reign to his imagination, or who takes an interest in the objects presented to him, this "I" is the self which does not consent to being possessed by experience but instead intends to possess it. When we study the Unconscious, we shall see that this proprietorship is less absolute than any subject would believe or than was believed before Freud; with respect to its origin it is unceasingly called into question.

On the other hand, the subject who is present and master of his field never ceases to exercise his legislative power: judging reality.[28] The movements which the subject describes relative to his lived experience, his facultativity, include a *thetic function,* a reality function, to use Janet's terminology. Whether a person abandons himself to his reveries or to his memories, whether he throws himself into the perception of the objects which the organs of sense present and is immersed in analyzing them, whether he is thinking, reflecting, or ordering the hierarchical composition of his action, whether engaged in dialogue or monologue, whether passively experiencing bodily affections or actively adapting his behavior, whether allowing his affections to erupt into his experience or wrapped up in the spectacle which arises or which he provokes within himself, or whether he causes certain parts of his body, of his needs, or of his ideas to come to his attention, in every case the person himself bestows some category of reality upon all his operations, intentions, and resolutions, no matter on what level they might establish lived experience. Thus, in that it is a lived experience, and insofar as it is placed in or returned to its place among the categories of reality, even the purely imaginary is always held to be real—it is an imaginary *reality.* The distinctive feature of this thetic function is that the self can transcend the immanence of lived experience by assigning to it its category of reality: "This is what I believe," "This is my own speech," "This is an inner event," "This is an external event," "This is probable," "This is an idea," "This is what I desire," "This is a reality," etc.

The structure of the field of consciousness makes all this possible *only on the condition that lived experience not only pass through the lens of its intentionality, of the scene of its representation—that is, that it be organized as a field—*but also that it *conform to the laws of its field,* to the very order of its indefinitely open and really constitutive constitution. When it becomes constitutive, the structure of consciousness as field of the present, governed by the facultativity of its categories of reality, gains autonomy in its organization. At this point it gains control of its field to the extent that it is able to fluctuate between the imaginary and the real—provided that these lived experiences be "taken" for what they are.

3. THE CONNECTION OF THE SELF TO ITS FIELD OF EXPERIENCE

The field structure of the experience which is being lived in the present moment constantly imposes the restrictions, the limits, in a word, the order of the subject upon lived experience. The subject is there in the *I* of all feeling, of all perception, and of all thought. He is the author of whatever meaning is drawn out of his unconscious. He is the spectator of the scene of his representation. He is the actor of his presentation. By giving order to the lived element of his experience, the subject stipulates changes in the field of consciousness which conform to his law. For this reason, the field of consciousness now appears as a specifically human field, as an order which is subordinated to the legislation of the self (cf. below, pp. 119 and 267 ff.).

If we are thoroughly to understand this element of "control," of alertness, of the integration of a "field" whose ultimate structure is that of the organic law of its properties, of a "Constitution" (the legal sense of all these terms should be kept in mind), we must first of all situate this order of sensible or lived experience in the architectonic of conscious being; then we must examine in what manner this order necessitates the intervention of the "legislator" in its production.

a) Levels of Consciousness and the Organization of Conscious Being: The Relationships of the Field of Consciousness to the Presence and the Historicity of the Self

What we have just described as the levels of the vertical structuring of consciousness are the stages and the infrastructures of the constitution of its field. These come into view only in the pathology of mental disorders, at which time they appear necessarily. This genesis of consciousness follows the dialectic of a progressive and hierarchical formation of experience in the noetic-noematic structures of its organizing of lived experience into the field of the present.

This level of constituted consciousness—that of a "matrix" structure existing as a field—characterizes the structuring of consciousness as it appears in the waking adult. Only to phenomenological analysis do the infrastructures which are revealed by psychopathology any longer appear as essential properties, as "autochthonous" characteristics of the field of consciousness. As soon as it has been constituted in its normal and "normative" essential form, this structure disappears beneath the superstructures which it has as its sole purpose to make possible. Since it represents a sort of *formal invariable* of its organization, this constituted consciousness is precisely that structural arrangement which makes possible the *free movements* (the disponibility and facultativity) of the field of consciousness. We insist upon this fact since it is of capital importance if we are to understand that when speaking of the mobility and variations of the levels of consciousness (which everyone considers to be a specific attribute of consciousness), there is a great danger of confusing two structural modes of the movement of consciousness.

The first of these modes is the vertical progression of its constitution, which brings about the passage from unconsciousness to consciousness (the stages of which are perhaps not too apparent when they are so rapidly crossed in the passage from sleeping to waking, whereas they become more visible in the different degrees of psychopathological loss of structure). We have called this the "verticality" of the organization of the field of consciousness in proportion as it becomes established as a well-constituted consciousness.

The other of these modes is represented by the free movements of that consciousness whose facultativity describes upon its "ground," which has already been stabilized, all the figures of reality and of speech, of its operational progressions and its thetic stipulations.

We can already see the need of examining the place of the Unconscious with respect to this constitution of consciousness; we shall consider this problem in detail at the end of this work. In anticipation we can say that this place is everywhere and nowhere. It is everywhere, if we consider that all the forms of lived experience are formed in relation to unconscious "sense data." In the generation of all the figures which are developed in its field, the structure of lived experience is a repression of the unconscious. Every destructuration of consciousness, to the extent that it is a lapse into the imaginary, is an experience of the unconscious at various levels of unconsciousness. It is nowhere, if we understand by this term a separation, within the organization of being, of a region of being which would be the dwelling place of the unconscious, "beneath" that of consciousness. We shall see that the structure of psychical being cannot be solidified in such a way that it could be conceived of as an interlocking, on the model of a nest of stack-tables. The unconscious and consciousness necessarily refer each to the other, the one being the legality which integrates the other. The levels of this integration can themselves be unconscious, as the "formal invariable" of constituted consciousness. For this reason the Freudian topography of the id, the superego, and the ego (as we shall see later) is inconceivable except through vague intuitions, incoherent schemata or representations which better exhibit the confusion than the autonomy of these "systems." The id and the superego are inevitably considered to be modes of being which are correlatives of the infrastructures of consciousness, buried in its thickness (cf. below, pp. 243–257).

If we ask what is the place of the self in the system or the ontological structure of psychical being (we shall deal with this problem in Part Three), we can say that it is truly the subject of experience and is therefore included in every field of consciousness; it is, however, without basis until it begins developing or until it becomes a subject able to detach itself from experience in order to become constituted as the "proprietor" of this experience and thus gain autonomous existence. Just as consciousness is a *field* within which the imaginary unconscious and reality meet face to face, so the self is the history of the person who is rooted in the experience of lived events but goes beyond this experience. On the one hand, the "field of consciousness" and the actuality of lived experience are caught up in the spatiotemporal structure of the corporality of experience, since—as Bergson has said—my *present* consists in the consciousness which I have of my body. On the other hand, the *historicity* of the self is constituted only outside this corporality; it enters or blossoms into the Milieu of History, where it creates and occupies its place when it forms its identity and affirms the mastery of its proprietorship.

It is clear that these two psychical "systems" are not parallel; instead they are profoundly connected and subordinate to the level of the field of consciousness.

b) The Self and the Production of the Field: The Rational Being and the Operational Development of the Field of Consciousness

We have already (Part One, Chapter One) insisted upon the reflexive structure of consciousness, upon its "dual" mode of being *that* which *I* live (lived experience can as well be the experience of a perception as of a representation, of an idea, etc.). This reflection, this specular power of the presentation of the self to the self, can indefinitely develop its reverberations in such a way that when it becomes constitutive it might bring about all the conjugations of "to be" and "to have," in all active and passive modes, in all the various tenses. All the other persons of the pronoun always refer us back to the first person as to the passive and active subject of its discursive actions. In all the extreme forms of the abstract schematism of thought, when, in the operational field, thought begins to be differentiated from its proceedings, it becomes detached from the subject so that it might develop in the formulation, or the formalizations, of communication and intellectual information, that is, in its logical and objective form. But even in this case the rootedness of its operations in the operational field demands both the action and the consent of the subject. At this point the function of the self appears in all its power, not simply as a spectator or a passive or receptive subject, but as a subject who is first of all a "bestower of meaning" and then a "director of his consciousness." In the discursive unfolding of reflective thought, the self is the guide, and assumes the function of guardian and of guarantor of the value of its operations. Through this axiological function, the self makes possible and controls the different phases of reasoning, calculating, or of conjecture; and through this function, the self guarantees the possibility of an accord with others.

The self shows itself clearly in the diverse phases of the verticality of *constituted consciousness;* but it is constructed only in the developments of constitutive consciousness, without ever ceasing to incorporate its relation with others into the formation of its own system of values. The self is therefore the self only when speaking, when speaking to itself or to others, when it is telling itself what others say, and when, through speech, it constitutes itself as the author of its history and of its world. This is so true that the articulation of the self's transcendence and of the immanence of its experience takes place necessarily within the field of experience. Nothing can be "thought" which is not lived. It is this relation of *subordination* which makes it possible to have a lived experience with a minimum of thought, but impossible to have a thought without a minimum of lived experience. This relationship is the radical index of the relationships of the self of experience, the self which is unceasingly present as the integrator of the field of experience, which is itself integrated during the historic unfolding of the self.

This *indefinite opening of the field of consciousness* through its own movement transforms it into the reflections, operations, ideas, verbal expressions, and judgments which make up the network of the meanings of the chains of meaningful expressions and intercommunications which are found in human existence.

We thus see that the reflexive grasping of the philosophers' *Cogito* takes hold of consciousness at a level of height and of virtuosity which tends either to "scotomize" the formal infrastructure of its constitution or to confuse it with the mind's logic in general. The most common analyses of consciousness describe it as "extracampine," as unstructured, since it itself is that which imparts structure. Others, as we have seen, describe the forms of its destructuration as being the essential properties of consciousness. By maintaining its constitution as a dynamic field in its place within the *milieu* of psychical being, we have been able to assign to the basal structure of consciousness constituted as a field of actuality a region of being which is superior to the stratification of the "unconscious modes of experience" which it implies, and inferior to the discursive reflection and the rational operations of the self which it makes possible.

Such are the fundamental structures of the field of consciousness insofar as the subject organizes his own actual experience within it. Consciousness exists between the life of the organism and that system of reality which man must construct in order to adapt himself to reality. Between the demands of the instincts, the desires which stir in the depths of his being, and the reality which enjoins the law of reason, there must exist within the space of time which constitutes each of the experiences which follow one another in his history, a configuration in which experience and judgment are linked together. This "space of time," or this "actuality of experience" which is constrained by its inexorable circumscription, constitutes the *field of consciousness,* the milieu in which the original reality of each of its instants is lived. Because it is established within the spatiotemporal dimensions of lived experience, this reality, which is the correlative of the assemblages which regulate it, obeys the laws of its constitution. This constitution is established, in effect, as a legislative order in which is prepared an axiological space (Raymond Ruyer) which obeys a direction (*Richtung*) and a sense (meaning), a space which is tied to the development of the self, of its values, and of its judgment. For if consciousness is constituted as experience, it still depends upon the subject which generates it. Its actuality and its inactuality—or its transactuality—are the complementary dimensions of the temporal structure of conscious being.

This study of the "field of consciousness," of consciousness which is *constituted* as a field of the present, which *constitutes* the free movements of this field and which *legislates* the order of this field, has allowed us to distinguish three fundamental characteristics of that manner of enduring which bestows upon experience its autochthonous organization and permits it to develop in its discursive movement.

The first of these characteristics is the "constitution of consciousness," the *vertical* process through which consciousness crosses the constitutive stages (which can be seen in its pathological destructuration) until it reaches the level of organization of a field of presence.

The second is the possibility, which its constitution opens up to the field of consciousness, of implying a multiplicity of variations which depend upon the disposition and the thetic position of the subject (facultativity).

The third of these characteristics is inherent in the structure of the field insofar as it is always, and on all these levels, an order, a form of organization (*legality*).

The verticality of the field of consciousness gives rise to the problem of wakefulness and to that problem of the spatiotemporal organization of lived experience in relation to the structure and dynamism of the brain. We shall examine this in the next chapter. The facultativity of the field of consciousness brings up the problem of its connection with the self. This will be examined in Part Three. The legality of the field of consciousness poses the problem of its relations with the Unconscious. This will be the subject of Part Four.

III The Neurobiology of the Field of Consciousness

At the Symposium of Sainte-Marguerite (1954), on the theme "Brain and Consciousness," A.-E. Fessard defined consciousness as the integration of experience (E.I.) to the extent that it can be both one and multiple *in each of its instants*. By refusing to assimilate it purely and simply to the totality of psychical life or to the self, he correctly presented the structure of the field of presently lived experience. This is the point of view from which we shall consider the conditions and the neurobiological dynamism of this organization of experience.

If our analyses have been exact, we can say that: 1) the presentness of the field of consciousness is constituted by restricting time to the space which is circumscribed by the sense of lived experience; 2) this fundamental structure of conscious being presupposes the verticality of an autochthonous and formal organization, which is the correlate of any experience; it consequently implies different structural levels; 3) the subject's operational facultativity, his power of reflection and differentiation, depends upon this constitution, but goes beyond it.

What neurophysiologists refer to by the single term "wakefulness" thus seems to correspond not to a simple "function" but to a structural hierarchy, which implies an organization which is closer to the order of time than to that of space. Because they lack an adequate concrete analysis, neurological theories of "consciousness," especially when dealing with the problem of the "localization" of consciousness, run headlong against the impossibility of making a thing and a faculty, a "higher level mental state" and a "higher cerebral center," coincide with one another. This problem of the "highest level"

122

has been argued ever since the works of Hughlings Jackson. More recent controversies (F. M. R. Walshe, 1957; Magoun, 1958; Max Levin, 1960), which had already been adumbrated in our own studies since 1936 and in the work of W. Riese (1954), testify to the considerable interest which is attached to this difficult problem. There can be no question of placing the "Holy See" of consciousness at the summit of the pyramid of the nervous system and in the supreme instance of a "pontifical cell."[1] As Magoun has remarked, this image, which had disturbed both Sherrington and Jackson, is an anachronism in contemporary neurobiological thought. We are no longer in the days of "Victorian" neurophysiology. The brain as we know it today is not the brain of the nineteenth century. We can no longer consider the brain to be a mere superposition of anatomical centers, the "highest" of which commands all the "lower" centers. If this were the case, the "highest level" would itself be only a reflex control center which differed from the others only by being more elevated or complicated, and the "physical" character of this anatomical center, because of its spatial materiality, would seem to contradict its psychical nature. By going to the highest level of the hierarchy of the superior psychical center, its nature is considered to be different in kind. One is then condemned to remain, with Jackson, within the parallelist hypothesis of concomitance.[2] In reality the psyche and the nervous system are interconnected from the very lowest levels of the nervous system's organization. If the most elevated levels depend upon cerebral structures, they are open, rather than being closed up within them. It is in this manner that the "highest level" constituted by the cortex depends upon its infrastructures. Far from being seated in some particular part of the cortex, it represents a dynamic system which is indefinitely open to what is outside its spatial conditions.

We must now show that the organization of the brain corresponds neither to a reflex chain (not even a vertical one), nor to a mosaic of centers, nor to a homogeneous mass without localization. This is precisely because the brain itself is a dynamically structured organism. Rooted in the needs of its body, it *never ceases to construct its own world at each moment of its time.* Since it is not a mechanism but, as Bergson foresaw, is the organ of indeterminacy, the complementary isomorphism of the field of consciousness and the organization of the brain (Ruyer) ceases to be a logical and moral problem.[3] Far from reinforcing the mechanistic prejudice of its "automation," this image of the living, waking, creative brain instead establishes its function of personal "autonomy." So great a revolution has taken place in our conception of the nervous "system" that the very term "system," which implies rigidity and fixed order, may itself even appear inadequate. A more dialectical conception of the dynamics of the "subsystems" which make up its "self-regulated growth of complexity" (Laborit) and which at each moment compromise its equilibrium and unity, such a conception places the opposition of sleeping and waking, the problem of the constitution of the field of consciousness, at the very center of its organization. The different forms of integration and of selective differentiations of cerebral activity have been described and interpreted more and more in terms of "transanatomical wholes," "anatomical-functional configurations," "patterns of connection" and other conceptions which are closer to a logical-mathematical formalization than to the older morphological models (D. A. Sholl).

The central idea of this exposition of the development of neurophysiology, of which we are here giving only the briefest overview,[4] is the notion of the power of choice and of the creation of nervous structures. Nervous phenomena are not restricted by reflex chains. Through their own selectivity and plasticity they create the continual possibility of autoconstruction and adaptation. Dynamic neurophysiology, the heir of Jackson's doctrine (but purged of its parallelism), as it is found in such basic works as those of Goldstein, Monakow, Weizsäcker, and even, in a certain sense, in the works of Freud, is not incompatible with the subject. On the contrary, it places the subject at the very center of intentionality and of the motivation of all nervous processes. It can no longer be a question of describing a "personless" nervous system. For once it has been emptied of all presence of the subject, we would find it impossible to describe its processes "in the third person," within the vicissitudes of either normal or pathological human existence.

In this respect, the following four fundamental aspects of neurophysiology deserve emphasis:

1) *The microphysiology of the neuron and its synapses* can no longer be conceived apart from the plasticity, selectivity, and inventive ability of which "soma" would constitute a "decision point" (Ralph Waldo Gerard). In spite of his fidelity to the

principle of concomitance, Eccles has described the "nodal" structure of the nerve circuits which form the fields of influence assuring the possibility of "modulation" for graduated responses.

2) In the case of *cerebral localizations,* the supremacy of subcortical formations has replaced the supremacy of the cortex. This reaction had long been outlined (Camus, M. Reichardt, Küppers, P. Guiraud, K. Kleist, etc.). Its clinical and experimental groundwork is to be found in the works of Magoun and Penfield. When these writers attribute the function of the "highest level" to the ascending reticular activating system, to the brainstem, or to the "centrencephalic" system, they naturally commit an error which is the inverse of, but equally as grave as, that which they are attempting to combat. For even if, as we shall see later, mesencephalic-diencephalic activation is necessary to the arousal of consciousness, that is, to its appearing as a field, this necessary condition is not sufficient to assimilate it to a "regulative center" of mental life to the point of assuring its highest differentiations. We shall return to this point at the end of this chapter. As of now we can assert that when the supreme power of a sort of *deus ex machina* has been taken away from the cerebral cortex (provided that it is not attributed to the reticular formation or to the centrencephalic system), an antagonism or reverberative effect is introduced into the cerebral dynamism which modifies its whole organization and allows the problem of the field of consciousness, the problem of sleep and waking, to be more correctly formulated.

3) Equally as important as the regulations or modulations ensured by the reticular area of the brainstem and by the rhinencephalon is the fact that an *instinctive-affective dynamism* has been introduced at the very basis of behavior, of learning, of "conditioning," and of subcortical activations (my teacher Guiraud always defended this idea, basing his defense upon both his clinical experience and his neurobiological theories). The appearance of this hippocampal-limbic "old brain" in the foreground of neurophysiology thus brings about a revolution in our image of the functional organization of the brain. It seems to represent a system of coordinating and elaborating the emotional and instinctive-affective motivations which constitute a point of convergence between neurophysiology and ethology.

4) Of no less importance is the fact that electrophysiological techniques (particularly those using microelectrodes, con-

trolled by stereotaxic techniques in "chronic preparations"), single cell recording, etc., have set down and sometimes renewed all the problems concerning the propagation of messages (recorded by evoked potentials) across all the specific or nonspecific afferent and effector systems in the diverse structures of the nervous system. In spite of the dangers of certain simplistic explanations (against which even the most serious and conscientious investigators are not always on their guard), the accumulation and interpretation of facts make it possible, in this case also, to avoid mechanistic models. The recourse to functional mosaics and the abuse of notions such as irritation, discharge, and excitation are self-correcting because of the necessity of constantly admitting "regulators," "modulations," and "selections" which are welded to the subject's affective motivation.

Having thus taken a very cavalier but indispensable glimpse at the tendencies of contemporary neurophysiology, and having sketched some of the problems which arise concerning the relations of consciousness and the brain, we shall successively examine the problems of the cerebral cortex (which will appear as the organ of the facultative operations of the field of consciousness) and the problems of the centrencephalic system (which will appear as the part of the brain supporting the verticality of the field of consciousness). This will lead us to envisage the brain's normal forms of organization (waking) and of disorganization (sleep), according as it is or is not capable of functioning at a higher level patterning whose focal point is in the cortex, or at a lower level patterning whose focal point is in the centrencephalic system. We shall then examine how, on the model of epilepsy, the loss of structure by the field of consciousness coincides with the pathological impossibility of attaining the higher forms of cerebral organization. Finally we shall attempt to reconcile what we learn concerning the organization of the brain with the phenomenology of the field of consciousness.

1. THE CEREBRAL CORTEX

One fact stands out above all others: both phylogenetically and ontogenetically, the development of the cortex is the index of the greatest growth of mental complexity. The role of "supreme" agency is granted to it because of its enormous neuronal mass (10^{10} neurons, which, according to C. J. Herrick's calculations, could give $10^{2783000}$ functional combinations). Contemporary neurophysiology (Lorente de No, von Bonin, McCulloch and Pitts, Sholl, etc.) interprets the cortex as a transanatomical totality; this is also the view of the cortex found in the theory of cortical patterning, which is derived from the logical-mathematical conceptions of cybernetics and information theory (Norbert Wiener, Claude E. Shannon, von Neumann, etc.). The neurobiology of the cortex is now moving away from morphological and spatial points of view: not merely from the notion of the "schemata" of aphasia (Wernicke, Dejerine) but also from the notion of the cytoarchitectonic maps drawn up by Brodmann, Vogt and Vogt, Economo, etc. However well-grounded this orientation, which is more dynamic than functional, might be, the cortex nevertheless has a cytoarchitectonic structure (which S. T. Bok has compared to the structure of crystals) and a spatial heterogeneity (Sholl). This creates the problem of functional "localizations" at the cortical level.

Since the time of Flechsig, it has become traditional to recognize zones or *centers of projection* and *centers of association* within the cerebral mantle. Certain portions of the cortex are nothing other than clusters of neurons interspersed among the six cortical layers: some connect with the subcortical sensory and somesthetic relay neurons; others are the cortical neurons of the effector pathways.

Three primary sensory areas can be distinguished. These are the cortical projections of the visual, auditory, and somesthetic systems:

The visual projection area, on the superior and inferior lips of the calcarine sulcus, contains a primary or striate visual area (area 17), which is granular or koniocortical (heterotypical cortex, characterized by the richness of the fourth layer), where the retina is projected, or more exactly, where is projected a part of the information or messages it takes in from half of the opposite visual field. Next to this striate area is the parastriate area (area 18), which has a "suppressor" function. It is bordered by the preoccipital area (area 19). These two secondary centers have a "homotypical" cortex (the typical six-layered cerebral cortex).

The auditory region is located in the temporal cortex. Its primary area consists of area 41 (transverse gyrus of Heschl). This auditory koniocortex is surrounded by a para-auditory area (area 42) and in the posterior part of the superior temporal gyrus by area 22 with its colonies of cells (compared by Economo to a sheet of rain).

The *somesthetic areas* are the postcentral area I, the somes-thetic area II, and the precentral area III. In man, the somato-sensory area I receives impulses coming from the somatic sensors after relays in the posteroventral nucleus of the thala-mus. It corresponds to Brodmann's areas 1, 2, and 3 in the as-cending parietal gyrus.

These "specific centers" have been examined as much from the cytoarchitectonic as from the connectionist point of view. It is noteworthy that the afferents which come from the recep-tors and proceed to the cortex are strictly systematized. The work of Le Gros Clark, von Bonin, McCulloch (1942), W. Ross Ashby (1952), etc., has brought much to this new mathematical analysis of visual information. The somatotopic representation of somesthetic messages in the case of ungulate animals, as has been established by Adrian, is a good example of this rigorous method. Electrical excitation of specific areas (Krause, Foer-ster, Penfield) produces more or less complex perceptions, which are experienced as images or memories.

The organs of sense can be said to be prolonged by means of a succession of relays to the cerebral cortex, in such a manner that the perceptual analyzer forms a totality which reaches from the periphery to the center. As is shown by the studies of perception to which we have already made reference, this functional unity of the psychophysics of perception is not in-compatible with the conscious and unconscious component of intentionality and motivation. Instead, the structure of sensory centers and organs forms the supreme formal law of all percep-tual formation of gestalts.

The same is true of the *centers of movement:* the motor cortex, located in the precentral gyrus (Brodmann's area 4). It is characterized by giant pyramidal Betz cells, whose axons form a large part of the pyramidal tracts (40 percent, according to some, on the basis of Lassek's studies). Its axons, however, exert their influence upon the extrapyramidal system (collater-

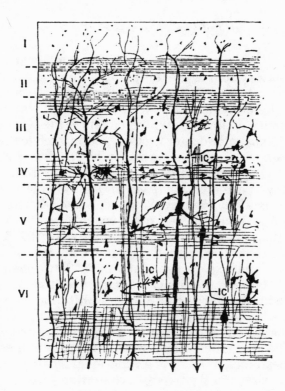

Figure 1. The six layers of the cortex (homotypical isocortex)
  I. Plexiform layer (molecular layer)
 II. Layer of small pyramids (outer granular layer)
III. Layer of larger pyramids (pyramidal cell layer)
 IV. Layer of granule cells and star pyramids (inner granular layer)
  V. Layer of large pyramids (ganglionic layer)
 VI. Spindle cell or fusiform layer (multiform cell layer)

In this diagram, certain elements (cell bodies, dendrites, and axons) have been enlarged in order to show more clearly their synaptic connections and the manner in which they cross different layers. Since Lorente de No, it has been generally agreed that there is an *afferent system* of fibers coming from the thalamus and projecting to the superior layers, an *efferent system* which is formed by the axons of the pyramidal cells, and a system of intracortical circuits (IC) which is extremely complicated with interneurons. Cellulipetal excitations of the dendrites, which are truly the modulators of the neuron, very probably occur on an electronic model. The ramification of the dendrites, which forms this "neuropil" (a vast accumulation of neurons into a network), is very much simplified in this sketch, whose purpose is primarily to give an impression of the lateral and longitudinal connections of cortical neurons.

als to the globus pallidus and the pontine nuclei, the cor-
ticocerebellar system of the temporopontine tract, and the cor-
ticorubral system). This motor portion is formed by an
agranular, heterotypical cortex. The motor area is surrounded
by a secondary motor area which envelops the secondary sensory area. This motor center is closely connected to the somato-
sensory area with which it forms, on both sides of the central
fissure, a motor-sensitive center. Somatotopic representation
(the sensory and motor *homunculus*) is systematic there (cf.
the diagrams after Woolsey, Settlage, Meyer, Seuter, Hamuy,
and Travis, in Ajuriaguerra and Hécaen's *Le cortex cérébral,*
p. 64, and Penfield and Rasmussen's diagram, p. 66). In front of
this motor area is the premotor area (area 6) which "controls"
or "activates" the extrapyramidal system. This motor cortex is
intimately bound to the somesthetic cortex. It also has a "double function" of motor excitation and inhibition (superior portion), following a schema which is to be found at all levels of
the nervous system under the form of inhibitory and excitatory
centers. The anatomical "localization" in space of these centers
is often questioned in favor of a functional localization in time
and of processes of selective differentiation.

These specific sensorimotor centers obviously cannot be
thought of as they were in the time of Ferrier and Hitzig. They
are not centers of images or of engrams. The notion of a *functional verticality* has been substituted for that of a static
"receptor" or "effector" center. Their activity does not reside
only in their local "seat." It extends into or prepares itself in the
subjacent levels. The perceptual analysis carried out by these
afferents at the cortical level presupposes their integration into
the ideoverbal schemata in which perception is formed and is
completed. In this way, all the levels and structures of the nervous system which are responsible for the development of the
spatiotemporal qualities and parameters of perception necessitate, precede, and follow the activity of these centers. Each of
them is spatially contiguous and functionally connected with
the "secondary" areas in which lived experience is elaborated.
    However, next to these areas of specific projection, there are
vast regions of the cortex which correspond to Flechsig's *association centers.* These are cytoarchitectonic structures whose
functional patterning forms a system of interconnections on
the stochastic model of an information which is distributed

according to the rules of a statistical assemblage which is constructed so as to respond, by adaptive behavior, to the probabilities involved in the "encoded" program. This depositary codification of information depends upon the marking of the RNA molecules (H. Hyden and P. Lange, 1960; F. Morell, 1961). Such is the cybernetic theory (Grey Walter, Ashby, etc.) of cortical activity, the operational matrix which contemporary neurophysiology (Sholl) tends to "release" from the processes it engenders. But if, as von Bonin states, this system of logical connections always superimposes the physicist's electromagnetic fields upon the material order of the cortical architectonic, it does not suppress it. There is indeed a cortico-cortical order which forms the physiological substratum of this connective apparatus (cortico-cortical and intracortical fibers, U-fibers). Thus, organically, these associative centers are in some way *bound* to the specific centers which they "associate," while remaining *open* to transanatomical constructions.

Between these two types of centers, one in some way profoundly bound to anatomical structures and the other indefinitely open to a probabilistic arrangement, there are "intermediary" associative centers. *Speech centers* hold an important anatomical and functional place among these. They "have their seat" in the dominant hemisphere, in and around Wernicke's area, including the insula, the angular gyrus, the posterior and medial portion of the superior temporal gyrus. This is a zone of parieto-temporo-occipital convergence. It begins to develop during the second half of foetal life (the inferior frontal gyrus whose inferior portion exhibits a rapid development and is differentiated at about the sixth month). The development of myelinated axons (Aranovitch) begins at birth through Rolando's operculum, then continues through the remaining portion of the inferior frontal gyrus and the superior portion of the superior temporal gyrus. The "sensory" zone continues to evolve until adulthood (A. Kappers). The anterior frontal zone presents a granular type structure (area 47), whereas the posterior zone (area 22), the angular gyrus (area 39), and the supramarginal gyrus (area 40) have an agranular structure.

For the past hundred years there has been much discussion of the problem of the precise localization of specific types of aphasia, the analysis of these disorders and of symbolic functions on a sensorimotor or noetic model, and the problem of the unity and the diversity of aphasia and the centers of language; but no one has seriously questioned the morphological and functional reality of these cortical centers which are necessary to the establishing and functioning of the "second signal system" (Pavlov), not even those who, from Hughlings Jackson to Head, P. Marie, and Goldstein, have objected to mechanistic interpretations of symbolic activity and of its cerebral basis. It is enough that we should simply point out that this instrument which is necessary for the execution of ideoverbal thought is itself closely bound up with the field of consciousness, which it helps to form. The systems of signs which it forms cannot be devoid of bonds with the sense of the subject's profound intentionality. This examination sends us back to what we have developed in the earliest chapters of this work. Its only aim is, from the viewpoint of a psychological analysis of language, to set forth its place as a "medium," communicating with the intermediary levels which these language centers occupy in the organization of the brain, especially between cortical areas responsible for the formation of ideas and sense data or motivational impulses coming from the centrencephalic region.

There are also other centers of symbolic activity (praxic and gnosic constructions) which we must at least mention here.

All these functions and associative centers present a curious problem which is common to them all: that of hemispheric dominance. Language centers and certain gnosopraxic functions are indisputably "localized" within the dominant hemisphere (ideational or ideomotor apraxia, Gertsmann's syndrome, pain asymbolia, object and color agnosia, etc.); certain others are "localized" in the nondominant hemisphere (dressing apraxia, anosognosia, denial-visual hallucination syndrome, prosopagnosia). Under certain conditions, however, they can migrate or change place. Split-brain preparations (Myers, Sperry) will perhaps allow us better to study the subordinations, functional substitutions, and transference of information between the hemispheres.

These centers of gnosophasopraxic association can thus be said to be incontestably localized, sometimes in a unilateral fashion. Their "asymmetrical" character, their internal correlation, and their common functional denominator, the symbolic ideoverbal schematism which forms the instrument through which thought necessitates a freedom in its own movements, all this clearly indicates that it is a question of functional centers which are morphologically inscribed within the cortical structures. 1) These structures function only in strict dependence upon subcortical formations. 2) They constitute the operational fields of the intellectual activity of thought and of action. They are essentially centers of elaboration and of differentiation which extend the field of the "perceptual analyzers."

The attempt has been made to assimilate a *center of intelligence* to these instruments. And Spearman's "*g*-factor" has been localized more particularly in the *prefrontal lobe.* We have already discussed this problem[5] and we hope to return to it in much more detail in our future *Études.* For the present, we shall limit ourself to a few brief remarks.

The anterior part of the three frontal gyri (Brodmann's areas 6 and 8) and the anterior part of the orbital gyri form the *prefrontal lobe.* Following von Bonin, these areas are covered by a homotypical cortex whose internal granular layer becomes thicker as it nears the frontal pole. Whereas the "frontal syndrome" (premotor area) involves disorders of ocular-motor tone and equilibration, and psychical disorders (moria, jocularity, lack of initiative), a considerable role has been ascribed to the anterior functions of this lobe in the functioning of intelligence and personality. G. de Morsier (1929) emphasized the triad "amnesia of fixation, apathy, instability." Intellectual disorders[6] have been brought to light either through experimentation upon animals (Bianchi, Kalischer, Marlowe and Settlage, Smith, Ward, Gleis, etc.) or through pathological observation and neurosurgery performed upon man (Goldstein, Rylander, etc.). In the case of monkeys (twelve animals watched over a period of five years, four of whom were not operated upon and served as controls), Harlow observed that among the subjects with unilateral lesions, problems and tests (immediate recall, discriminative learning, object choice task) were disturbed during the first two months, but after two years the disturbances had almost completely disappeared. In the group which had bilateral lesions, he noted a marked deficiency of delayed responses and little or no deficiency in tests of discrimination. On the other hand, more posterior lesions brought about predominantly visual disorders. Following unilateral lobectomies performed upon humans, Dandy O'Brien, Jefferson, Claude Vincent, Hebb, etc., noticed no major disorders, whereas Rylander (32 cases) observed emotional disorders, disorders of motor activity, and high level intellectual disorders (reasoning and symbolic thinking were impaired). Following bilateral lobectomies, Brickner observed euphoria, loss of incentive, lack of attention, and Nichols and Hunt have also observed disorders in categorial thinking. Hebb and Penfield, on the basis of psychological and psychometric examinations, have insisted upon the absence of any observable disorders. This is the focus of all the discussions concerning the insoluble problem of what is to be attributed to the surgical "remedy" and what to the "ailment" which led to the lobotomy. Most writers adopt Rylander's conclusions (despite the facts reported by the Greystone Research group, directed by Mettler, and the reservations of Walther Buel concerning the localization of these disorders). In all these cases we are concerned with experimental or surgical lesions of higher functions, and especially with Goldstein's categorial thought. In other words, it is a question of the least constructive differentiation of intellectual schemata. On this subject, Halstead speaks of disorders of the higher functions of wakefulness, in Head's sense.

But then a twofold question arises: How should these "disorders of consciousness" be interpreted? And is this higher level localizable?

On the first point, we touch upon a fundamental aspect of our own analysis of conscious being. For us, the processes of differentiation and of construction, this "operative field" of intelligence, obviously make up the *facultative* superstructure of the field of consciousness and not the fundamental structure of its conscious experience. This is so because not all lived experiences make use of this operational dialectic. If it is true that disturbances of the cortex upset its facultative processes, they bring about only a decapitation, so to speak, of consciousness, which does not reach the conscious being to the extent that he realizes his experience, that is, at a level which is not necessarily the level of reflexive thought.

As concerns the second point, without reverting to Lashley's thesis on the functional *equipotentiality* of the cortex and the import of its aggregate effects, it seems that we could consider the "telencephalon" to be heterogeneous and to involve three structural levels: 1) the level of the integration of specific centers, especially of the perceptual analyzers and the effector centers; 2) the level of the "associative" centers, which modulate ideomotor syntheses and gnosic and praxic verbal ideorepresentative syntheses; and 3) the level of a synthesizing activity (which activity alone corresponds to the "unifying or synthesizing centers," of which Hughlings Jackson spoke).

We have been considering the cerebral cortex no longer merely as the "level of alertness," but as a "milieu," a totality in which are unfolded and formed the anticipations, choices, and deferred actions which are needed in order to have the serial order of behavior (Lashley).

The cytoarchitectonic of the cerebral cortex shows that, with its gradients of horizontal and vertical potentials for polarization (Bremer), the cortex forms a vast polysynaptic network (Sherrington spoke of the "magic loom" which is ever weaving). Since the work of Lorente de No, the hypothesis of statistical contacts between neurons by means of their end feet has come to be accepted. The structure in closed paths (McCulloch and Pitts, 1943) has since then been subjected to statistical interpretations and probabilistic models[7] which more and more frequently make use of comparisons with stochastic models and information theory (Rosenblith; Wiener; Bigelow, 1943; Bartlett, 1955). For this reason, Sholl (1956) and other specialists in the neuronal electrophysiology and histology of the cortex think of the neuronal structure (especially the axodendritic synapses) as being analogous with the cyberneticians' "wiring diagrams." In the report on psychiatric theories which we presented to the Congrès de Montréal (1961), we emphasized that a logical-mathematical interpretation of the relationships between consciousness and the brain is possible only if their "isomorphism" be admitted. However, inventive and creative activity (which is the activity not of electronic robots and computers but of the brain which constructed them) cannot be reduced to a servomechanism. In the last analysis, we find ourselves confronted with the problem of the origin and goal of information (Ruyer). Whatever the case may be, if the cortex functions in certain respects as a machine which "encodes" and processes information, at this higher level it does not appear to be closed up, as a reflex circuit, within the stimuli it receives. Instead, within the functional cycle *(Gestaltkreis)* which sends it back to its own internal motivations, it appears to be indefinitely open to the construction of its world.

In this respect the cortex can well be said to form the highest level of psychical activity, insofar as it is the "milieu" of its constructions; but it cannot be thought of as the "center of consciousness" and the basis of lived experience.

Two fundamental manners of functioning have been attributed to the "cortical centers." We should mention the fact that, since they have been identified with the associative activities of empirical psychology, they appear either to be inferior activities or to be activities which, in order to be raised up to the level of inventiveness that is attributed to them, would have to be animated by the energy which is invested in the field of consciousness and in the unconscious and which is integrated into the truly creative operations of reflection. Neither *conditioned reflexes* nor *learning* is either purely cortical or purely associative. They are both the effect and the signs of a dynamogenesis which they imply more than determine, at least in its origins.

Pavlov's conditioned reflexes are *temporal* (or "diachronistic," to use Jouvet's term) connections between an absolute stimulus with ontological signification (appetite, pain) and a stimulus which becomes its "signal." This substitution, then, incorporates a new condition in the circuit. This *dynamic stereotype,* which Pavlov's school studied in such great detail, has allowed the principles of this conditioning to be established and has made it possible to derive from it the laws which govern the development and maintenance of the conditioned response: the necessary repetition of the signal, the inactivation of the signal by means of *external inhibition* produced by another stimulus from which it is differentiated through the discrimination of the perceptual properties of the signal *(differential inhibition),* its *negative induction* when the signal reverses its excitatory power, and finally its disappearance by means of the repetitive extinction of the excitation or of the differentiation *(supra maximal inhibition).* We thus have an experimental dynamics of the production, propagation, and functioning of these segments of behavior. On the whole, the nervous system's responses to conditioning show implicitly the plasticity of groups of cortical neurons.

In effect, Pavlov traced the analysis of the conditioned response upon a mosaic of cortical centers. Since the number of drops of saliva produced in response to a light (conditioned stimulus) and by a secretory reflex (absolute reflex) can vary according to differences in the signals, their variety in time, their sensory or nociceptive interactions or associations, they hypothetically measure the localization, the irradiation, the concentration, the internal and reciprocal inhibition of the diverse processes which appear in the experience. Zeliony's experiments allowed Pavlov to consider the cortex to be the seat of the conditioned response, since conditioned responses cannot be produced in decorticate animals. But since then, certain experimenters (J. ten Cate, 1940) have shown the possibility of conditioning in animals which have extended neopallial lesions. The destruction of the conditional analyzer does not prevent the creation of a connection whose signal arises from this sensory center. Concerning the *auditory areas,* Ades and Raab (1946) have confirmed Kalischer's experiments (1909) by showing that the ablation of the primary and secondary auditory cortex does not make it impossible to establish a conditioned response of flexion to a sound, in spite of the perceptual impairments which it brings about. The same is true for the experiments performed upon the *visual areas* (Kluver, 1936; Marquis and Hilgard, 1937; Lashley, 1939; Sperry, 1954). "Associative centers" or specific centers, therefore, do not appear to be absolutely necessary to establish conditioned responses. That is to say, the plasticity and creativity of the cortex do not have their "seat" merely in these specific areas (whether they be "secondary" or "associative"). This is the criticism which has been directed against Pavlov by all those (Lidell, Lashley) who have accused him of making use of a too mechanistic and localized schema of temporary and significant connections. The conditioned response is made possible only by an act of differentiation and a functional organization which are incompatible with superficial and contingent associations. Its facultative element, then, seems to arise from a broader dynamic functioning of the cortex. On the other hand, its "ontological" or absolute element naturally demands the lived experience of the affective impression (or an elementary automatic connection, in the case of conditioned responses grafted upon unconscious absolute reflexes). A psychophysiology which intends to interpret the givens of reflexology must do so from the *vertical* perspective of functional dynamism, as Fessard, Gastaut, Jouvet, etc., have seen to be necessary.

If the cortex does play an important part in establishing these connections, they in turn depend upon subcortical conditions. It has thus been shown (Dusser de Barennes, 1919; Culler and Mettler, 1934; Zeliony and Kadykov, 1938) not only that local decortication does not prevent the experimental production of conditioned responses (which are always, however, rudimentary in this case, as Jouvet points out), but also that subcortical formations intervene in the organization of these temporal and significant connections. In particular, lesions of the thalamus or of the mesencephalic reticular formation (Hernández-Peón, Scherrer and Jouvet, 1956) have modified conditioned responses in the cat (a fact which was not, however, confirmed by Doty, 1957). The work of G. F. Ricci, B. R. Doane and H. H. Jasper (1957), studying electrocorticograms of monkeys during conditioning, has shown that the conditional selection of a signal takes place in the auditory system, but that the conditioning appears to be "regulated" by the reticular formation. This is because the *arrest reaction* seen in electroencephalograms, that is, *attention* (or as Pavlov called it, the *orienting reflex*), is, for phenomenology, inseparable from this kind of incorporation, from a new meaning in behavioral motivation. This "wakefulness," which is renewed by "interest," is the motivating force of conditioning. More exactly, it is the only thing capable of establishing conditioned reflexes and preventing them from falling into inertia and habituation. Since conditioned responses do not develop wholly in the cortex, they cannot be reduced to such connections.[8] Conditioning both integrates reflexes and depends upon them. We here see the beginnings of that form of "reverberation," of functional cycle *(Gestaltkreis)* which moves us away from Sherrington's conception of the linear integration of reflexes and forces us to look upon the organization of the nervous system as a *circular integration* of structural levels. Conditioned responses develop in the cortex, but only as fragments which are more or less artificially isolated from the acquisition of experience. Experience alone makes it possible for the field of consciousness to become organized, which is the *very condition of conditioning.*

The similar, if not identical, problem of *learning* leads us to the same conclusion.[9] Inasmuch as the acquisition of experience presupposes some knowledge and the ability to discriminate and adapt, it can be considered to be the foundation of intelligence, if this latter can be reduced to empirical learning. This old "empirical" conception of intelligence, as taken up by the behaviorists (Watson, Tolman, etc.), has inspired the views of the Anglo-Saxon school (E. L. Thorndike, C. L. Hull, Skinner, K. W. Spence, etc.). Most of these writers give learning an essentially "connectionist" or "stimulus-response" interpretation. This is because they have limited themselves to experimentation upon mammals such as white rats, cats, and dogs. They therefore have a tendency to consider the operations of human intelligence as being only a "more complicated" form of animal intelligence. We shall not at this point go into the fundamental problem of "insight" and of discursive forms of thought. Let us simply point out that Hebb (p. 137) emphasizes that such studies consider only *primary learning,* which is characterized by its mechanicalness and by the relative speed with which it takes place, characteristics which are more likely to occur in rats than in man, and in insects than in rats. The psychophysiological problem of the nervous system's responses during the connective process, which arises in the case of conditioned reflexes, arises also in the case of the accumulation of experience stored by memory, under its "associative" form, and in the case of learning which is reduced to the possibility of establishing new connections between signals and responses by behavior which interprets them and adapts to them. The same difficulties are involved in each of these cases. *Attention* forms the functional and subcortical substratum of the processes of *expectation* and *vigilance.* These processes root the various forms of *learning* in the realm of motivations and of the organization of the field of consciousness. On the other hand, intelligence, the operational superstructures of human consciousness, cannot be reduced to a learning process which would be developed "passively" through the mechanical association of stimuli and responses stored in cortical engrams.

This problem of the cerebral cortex, like the more general problem of the central nervous system, raises the problem of *memory* (both before and after Bergson). It is inconceivable that the brain, especially the cortical neuronal mass, should retain nothing of the past that would allow it to prepare for the future and adapt itself to the present. Nor can we consider human existence to be entirely lodged in and determined by physical properties of conservation. Only if they join together can the heavy, overly mechanistic concepts which "confine" the brain within its materiality, and the spectral analysis which decomposes psychical life into its functional hierarchy, contribute towards a solution of this fundamental problem. This is not the place to examine cybernetic views of memory. But we must point out that Grey Walter considered three mnemic processes to be necessary for the establishment of a diachronic apparatus (Jouvet): extension in time, summation of the combined effects which determine a preferential claim, and retention of information. It is on these topics that some speculate, and others build machines which speculate.

Eccles (1933) "situates" the "mnemic trace" (which no psychology can do without) between the end feet of the dendrites, whereas Sarkisov (1956) makes it depend upon the *soma* of the neurons. By using the electron microscope, Couteaux has shown that these synapses form stable adhesive zones. Bock (1956) also holds that the loci of permanent change in transmission characteristics are established at the level of the dendritic apparatus. The greater "permeability" of the already existing synapses to nervous input, that is, the lasting increase of their "potentialities for transmission" (Fessard, 1959), obviously cannot form an indispensable substratum for all their temporal functional connections. Several interesting papers were presented at the 1961 Symposium on *Brain Mechanisms and Learning,* on the problem of the fixation of experience (R. W. Gerard) and the neurophysiology of recent memory (J. Konorski). We have already (p. 131) alluded to the importance of the work of Hyden, Morell, etc., on the storing of information in the "giant" molecular structures (nucleotides) which, at the level of neuroglial tissue, *reproduce* the mechanism of reproduction at the level of the chromosomes (DNA). But, as Gerard states (p. 31), this subject is still a complete mystery for us.[10]

Whatever might be the physiological or biological forms of organization of the cortex, of its *matter,* it is evident that the *memory* contained within it is not registered there passively. Self-maintained neural activity (Hebb, 1957) is an *internal disposition,* which runs counter to the conception of a conditioning (in some manner mechanistic); this is a result of the work of Weiss, Adrian, and Lorente de No.

The cerebral cortex is not simply a reservoir or storehouse. Nor is it a computer. If it is these things, it is also something more: a living organization, which does not provide for itself according to the principles of a mechanistic associationist psychology, but which is animated by all the forces and needs of the organism. The activity of the cortex does not suppress, but demands a basal functioning of the brain, to which the infrastructure of the field of actuality of lived experience corresponds. We have begun to surmise precisely that, since the centrencephalic formations are not excluded from the psychical dynamics. We shall see that if the centrencephalic formations are not the highest level (if this be taken to mean a superior and unique center) of psychical activity, they do form its fundamental structure, which allows the cortex to function as the organ of choice and of freedom, open upon its world through the subject who constructs his world while constructing himself.

2. THE CENTRENCEPHALIC SYSTEM

At the base of the hemispheres, in the axis of the brainstem, in the diencephalon and adjacent formations of the rhinencephalic old brain, are found certain structures which are entangled in an incredible complexity of neuronal masses and multisynaptic pathways. It is a totality whose morphology is fixed and strictly organized and which is very heterogeneous in its functioning (see figure 2).

For a long time neurophysiology considered these mesencephalic, diencephalic, and rhinencephalic formations to be conductors or connectors of the major sensorimotor pathways. But neurobiology, especially neuroelectrophysiology, has increasingly come to notice the synergetic and energetic importance of this subcortical integrative level which is formed by the reticular formation of the brainstem, the diencephalic-thalamic structures and the rhinencephalon.

A. The Reticular Formation of the Brainstem

The rhombencephalon[11] and the mesencephalon contain a mass of neurons (neuropil, to use Herrick's expression), the "reticular gray matter." According to van Gehuchten (1896), it is continuous with the medulla; at the level of medulla oblongata it is between the nucleus of origin of the hypoglossal nerve, the nucleus of the solitary tract, and the root of the fifth nerve. Then, at the level of the pons, it corresponds to the whole tegmentum (excluding the motor and sensory nuclei of the trigeminal nerve), and at the level of the cerebral peduncles (mesencephalon) it occupies the whole region of the tegmentum. At about the same time, Dejerine thought of this reticular formation in about the same fashion. It then becomes clear that it is extremely difficult to state the limits of the reticular formation at the level of each rhombencephalic or diencephalic section, where the nuclei are very numerous. It is just as difficult to define the upper limit of this formation, since it also extends through the hypothalamic region and into the ventral, central,

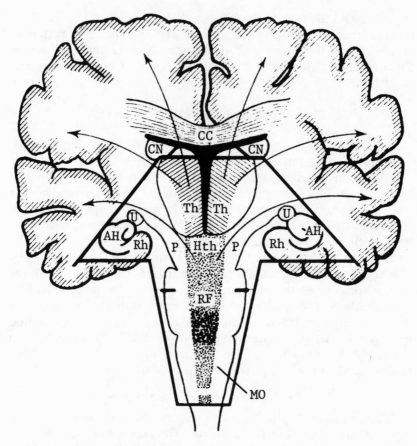

Figure 2. The centrencephalic system

Corpus callosum (CC); caudate nucleus (CN); thalamus (Th); uncus (U); Ammon's horn (AH); rhinencephalic portions (Rh); hypothalamus (Hth); pons (P); reticular formation (RF); medulla oblongata (MO)

The principal formations of the centrencephalic system are within the dark lines: the reticular formation of the medulla, pons, and thalamus; the rhinencephalic portions, including Ammon's horn and the hippocampus as far as the uncus.

and anterior portions of the thalamus. The "reticular" structure of this formation is composed of innumerable polysynaptic neurons and short (Cajal, 1909) or long axons which make up a nonspecific "neuronal field." This is generally acknowledged by neurophysiologists. They consider this gray and diffuse mass to be a functional totality (admitting, however, a certain heterogeneity in its inhibitory and excitatory functions, as we shall see later) which is connected with the major pathways and specific nuclei at the bulbopontine level, while still remaining independent of these afferent systems. On the other hand, anatomists tend to consider this brainstem gray matter to be organized more or less systematically. Olszewski (1954) thus refuses to use the term "reticular," while Cuba (1961) prefers to speak of the nonsegmentary formations of the brainstem.

From the viewpoint of functional anatomy, especially electrophysiological investigations and experiments, this *formatio reticularis* is a "crossroads" whose principal characteristic is its function of *nonspecific convergence.* Its organization as a network is a device which is favorable to the slow, "integrative" neuronal processes. The electron microscope (Roberts, 1955) has confirmed, states Jouvet (1960), the extremely dense atmosphere of nerve fibers in a network around the reticular cells. This mass is, no doubt, itself surrounded or crossed by a rich system of specific afferents; but it cannot be considered to be their simple vehicle.

What, then, is the *principal function* of this reticular formation of the brainstem, at least of that portion which corresponds to its rhombencephalic and mesencephalic portions? What are the conditions of its activity? What are its effects?

Bremer's famous mesencephalic transection (1929) forms the cornerstone of any present neurophysiological theory of the reticular formation. By isolating the anterior brain (which is why it is called the *"cerveau isolé"*), this decerebration brings about a sleep pattern electrocorticogram in animals. From this fact it followed that the activation of waking no longer reached the cortex. But this "conclusion" could not be drawn until twenty years later, when Moruzzi and Magoun (1949) showed precisely that in a lightly anesthetized and curarized animal, the repetitive stimulation of the brainstem tegmentum reproduced all the electrocortical signs that could be observed during cortical arousal. This "arousal" is generalized and self-maintained: it consists in a desynchronization of the electrocorticogram. This desynchronization, with a flattening of the brainwave pattern, forms an acceleration, a facilitation at the level of the cortex, either by neuronal recruitment, as Bremer has said (1960), or by augmentation of unitary discharges (Creutzfeld, Akimoto, and Li). Later we shall examine the neurophysiological problem of this "cortical arousal." Since 1949 there have been many important verifications by means of chronic preparations which have confirmed this fact as being one of the fundamental givens of contemporary neurophysiology. Experiments of destruction by coagulation (chronic preparations) of the reticular formation in cats and monkeys (Magoun and collaborators) have shown that the animals remained somnolent and almost comatose for the rest of their lives. These preparations have also shown (school of Magoun, 1949–1956) that *it is not the interruption of specific pathways* which brings about cortical inactivation. G. F. Rossi (1957) studied this important point with care. Thanks to his pretrigeminal mediopontine preparations, which deprive the cortex of all its sensory afferents, he has been able to show that wakefulness remained possible through reticular stimulation. The dynamogenic role of the ascending reticular activating substance is thus well established. Within this activating function can be discerned a *tonic* or continuous function and a *phasic* function which depends upon sensory stimulation (as nonspecific messages). Dell has shown that tonic afterdischarge could be maintained by an adrenergic neuronal mechanism which is aroused by a nociceptive stimulus (Bonvallet, Hugelin, Dell, 1955). The reticular formation thus represents a seat of cortical activation at the intersection of neurovegetative and sensory pathways. This is essentially true of its mediorostral portion at the level of the medial region of the medulla and of the tegmentum of the pons and mesencephalon. At the subthalamic level, the "system" seems to subdivide (Dell): the medial component extends to the posteroventral thalamic nuclei and the lateral component continues across the subthalamus and the hypothalamus towards the internal capsule. The activating action of the reticular formation of the brainstem is extended, relayed (or inhibited?) in the thalamic intralaminar substance, or else is projected directly to the cortex.

The corticoreticular projection system is twofold: thalamic (Startzl and Magoun, 1951) and extrathalamic (Nauta and Kuypers, 1957). The work of G. Macchi and F. Angeleri (1957) is of greatest importance from a connectionist point of view. The method of retrograde degeneration (Fox, 1941; Brodal and Rossi, 1955) has established the existence of a bundle of fibres ascending from the mesencephalon (from the median two-thirds of the reticular formation) to the thalamus, particularly from the reticular nucleus of the pons, which receives a major spinal-reticular bundle. Research using Nauta and Gygax's technique of silver impregnation of degenerating axons has allowed them to specify that within the brainstem there exist (1) long ascending pathways originating in the paramedial medulla and pons (reticulothalamic tract) and which end in the posterior and anterior intralaminar nuclei and in the midline nuclei; (2) a bundle of reticulothalamic specific projection fibers which joins the central thalamic group; (3) fibers which come from the tegmentum (ventral and dorsal tegmental nuclei) and which join either the intralaminar nuclei or the hypothalamus. Later we shall see that the reticular formation is very intimately connected with all the central, limbic, septal, thalamic, and hypothalamic formations (Nauta, 1958).

Having examined the activating function of the brainstem reticular formation, its projections and afferent pathways, we must now investigate the source of its energy. Bremer first considered the essential element of his famous *"cerveau isolé"* to be the process of deafferentation of sensory stimuli. It could then be thought that the reticular formation fulfilled its dynamic role only through the input pathways constituted by the excitatory impulses coming from receptors. In other words, it derives its energy only from the excitatory impulses which charged and discharged it. First of all, as we have seen, it seems to be well established that the reticular formation of the brainstem is a mass of neurons, or better, a neuronal totality which brings about vast areas of convergence (or of integration). The system of specific afferents is well known; and its centers or its projections, through which pass and are distributed the messages it receives and transmits, are perfectly known, thanks to histological or physiological techniques (evoked potentials). Their organization is homologous for all sensitive and sensory messages. It obeys a strict somatotopic distribution. In opposition to what was held some fifty years ago, the subcortical formations are not so very different in this respect from the cortical structures. For already at this level (particularly, states Dell, at the level of the complex "medial parafascicular nucleus," that is, at the level of the most medial part of the peduncular tegmentum) extremely rich spatial connections are produced between the specific afferents and the reticular formation. The proof of this is provided by the very long latency period of these propagations. Gerebtzoff was the first, in 1939–1940, to hold the idea that the collaterals leave the primary projection pathways at the level of the mesencephalon and then precipitate into multiple relays and networks. But this "despecification" of messages, that is, their integration to a nonspecific dynamogenic force, has been proven by Magoun. In certain "critical" experiments (to which we have already alluded, as well as to Rossi's experiments using rostropontine and mediopontine preparations), he has been able to show, since 1950, that the sectioning of all sensitive and sensory pathways at the level of the mesencephalon, or in the specific thalamic nuclei, does not hinder the activating function of the reticular formation. It must then be concluded that specific messages and afferents are not necessary for reticular dynamogenesis. On the contrary, their convergence has a functional significance. On this subject, Magoun states that responses from different sensory sources can be registered at one single point in the reticular formation. The study of single unit responses has even shown (Moruzzi and Magoun, 1954; Scheibel and Scheibel, Mollica, and Moruzzi, 1955) that single shocks to the sciatic nerve act upon the discharge of the isolated unit. This leads to the conclusion that if the reticular formation does not derive its "autochthonous" energy from its afferents, it instead plays a role in the integration, convergence, or controlling of messages. Where the sensationist theory was expected to win out, the dynamic theory of selection, in the sense of formation of gestalts, has come to dominate. Thus, Magoun speaks of "control of afferent messages." Reticular stimulation exerts another type of control. It has an inhibitory action, notably at the level of the first spinal relays. Hernández-Peón (1955), Granit (1955), Jouvet and Desmedt (1956) have established its depressive effects upon impulses at the level of the trigeminal, cochlear, and olfactory nuclei.

The reticular formation receives the impulses which it integrates from the neurovegetative sphere of the internal environment as well as from the sensory receptors and from bodily sensations, which are the sources of all experience. Bonvallet and Dell have shown that visceral afferents opposed the action of the other sensitive-sensory afferents. Dell's work on visceral and vagal projections and overall sympathetic control (1952) is exceptionally interesting. It forms a bridge between the work which has been done on the action of the reticular formation upon wakefulness and that which brings to light the interdependence of instinctive-affective motivation and activation.[12] This is a turning point in neurobiological studies. Its import has been shown by W. R. Hess[13] and by the whole collection of knowledge we have gained on the role of the rhinencephalon in affective, emotional, and instinctive life. Magoun has stated that the centrencephalic system has replaced the heart as the seat of affections and emotions. We shall discuss this later. The reticular formation of the brainstem, however, exerts an action upon pain (Collins and O'Leary, 1954; Livingston and collaborators, 1954), but perhaps also upon pleasure.

What, then, are the results of this dynamogenic action? We spoke above of "neocortical arousal," which is the most typical effect of the reticular formation's activity and stimulation. We have also seen its facilitative effect with respect to *conditioned reflexes* and *learning.* The experiments performed by Yoshii and collaborators (1956) have shown that the repeated conditioned response appears in the subcortical structures, notably in the mesencephalic reticular formation, long before it appears in the cortex. It is greater there, and lasts longer. The elaboration of conditioning, therefore, does not take place merely in the cortex. The process of attention (orienting reflex) seems effectively to draw its energy from the reticular area of the centrencephalic system, which we are here studying, if it does not originate there. In man, the arrest reaction or desynchronization, in which alpha rhythm gives way to a more rapid, lower voltage activity, largely depends upon sensory afferents (as Adrian showed, at the 1935 meeting of the Physiological Society, by recording electrodes placed on his own scalp), but also depends upon the phasic activity of the reticular system. In more simple terms, any cortical process which both facilitates the focusing of the senses and inhibits the opposite process (attention and distraction) depends more generally upon this "wakefulness," which is, in effect, an opening upon the world.

On this subject it is to be remarked that the reticular formation of the brainstem does not appear to research scientists to be homogeneous from a functional viewpoint. We shall not consider the most caudal segment of the reticular formation, which forms the descending inhibiting system (Magoun and Rhines, 1946). When examining the thalamus, we shall see that

Sharpless and Jasper (1951) have attempted to oppose the rostral (thalamic) reticular system, which is strictly phasic, and the "differentiated modulator" of its action upon the cortex, to the rhombencephalic-mesencephalic reticular formation, which we are now examining and which alone would be capable of a diffuse dynamogenic tonic activity. But there is more. Within this reticular column, a "zone of inhibition" has come to light. Moruzzi, C. Batini, Palestini, Rossi and Zanchetti (1958–1959) have set forth the hypothesis of a synchronizing action (inhibitory or depressive with respect to the cortex) in the caudal part of the brainstem. J.-P. Cordeau and M. Mancia (1959) have given a beautiful demonstration of this, using pretrigeminal hemisections. Unilateral lesions in cats in *encéphale isolé* preparations have provoked (excluding any baroreceptive afference which they controlled) synchronization in the controlateral hemisphere (slow waves and spindles). Bremer himself does not hesitate to state that the pontine portion of the reticular formation is a truly hypnogenic center.[14] This depressive center must naturally be in a close relationship with its "neighboring" dynamogenic function. It seems that everything happens as if their contiguity in space "expressed" a dialectic in time, in the case of a brain which has not been cut, but is living and whole, and is therefore able to regulate the effects of facilitation or of suppression and thereby can *modulate* its organization on the subject's conscious or unconscious intentionality.

We must finally point out a neurophysiological aspect of the greatest importance, which clarifies what we have said above concerning reverberatory mechanisms and forms of circular integration of the brain's organization. Not only is the activating reticular formation itself activated by the messages and stimuli which arrive directly and from "below." But it is also stimulated from "above" by the corticifugal afferents which form a vast feedback system. Bremer has shown the possibility of arousing an *encéphale isolé* by means of the appropriate sensory stimuli. Magoun, too, has emphasized the importance of corticifugal afferents upon the reticular formation (French, Hernández-Peón, and Livingston, 1955; Segundo, Naquet, and Buser, 1955). The demonstration of cortical dynamogenesis during arousal was carried out by Bremer and Stoupel and by the experiments of Dumont and Dell (1958). Hugelin and Bonvallet, on the other hand, studied a monosynaptic reflex of a masticatory muscle whose reticular facilitation was moderated by the inhibiting action of the intact cortex.

If the reticular formation today appears to be more complex in its physiological structure and its reticulocortical interdependence than it did in the past, it nonetheless remains the fundamental apparatus of waking consciousness, of the possibility for consciousness to become organized as a field of lived experience and to endow the temporal unfolding of experience with sense, interest, and energy.

B. The Thalamus and the Diffuse Thalamic Projection System

We shall now, at the level of the diencephalon, approach the structures which are responsible for the more complex integration of the affective-sensory afferents. The center of this functional whole is the thalamic system.[15] With difficulty, this system can be separated into its nonspecific portions consisting of part of the brainstem reticular formation, of the hypothalamus, and, through this, of the rhinencephalon.

We shall make only a few points concerning the organization of the *hypothalamus.* This region plays an extremely important role in metabolic functions, especially in the secretion of hypophysial hormones[16] and in organic needs (hunger, thirst, defecation, genital and urinary functions, etc.). But it has lost some of its neurobiological significance ever since it has been more clearly integrated into broader mesencephalic-diencephalic or rhinencephalic functional cycles. Its role as a parasympathetic center invested with an "endophylacticotrophotropic" property in its rostral or anterior portion, and its role as a sympathetic center in its caudal or posterior portion (possessing an "ergotropic" power), have lost some of their interest in the view of W. R. Hess. The same is true of Hess's discussions with Ranson[17] concerning the posterior or lateral localization of an active sleep center or a center of hyperwakefulness. What Hess's experiments have shown is that the stimulation, the pathology, or the neurosurgical exploration of this formation produce a diversity of behavioral disorders which are strongly instinctive or emotional.[18] In the *American Handbook of Psychiatry* (1959), Papez describes the hypothalamus as the region which controls basic biological needs. In it intersect impulses from the orbitofrontal and subcallosal region (via the medial forebrain bundle), from the amygdaloid complex (via the stria terminalis), from the hippocampus (via the fornix).[19] These descending afferent fibers start from the posterior hypothalamic nucleus, a part of the lateral nucleus (a sort of vegetative motor pathway), whereas it projects especially upon the anterior thalamus via the mammillothalamic tract.

Each of the two thalami forms half of a strictly systematized system, which is connected and unified not merely by a transverse bridge, the gray commissure, but also by the continuity of their implanting in the brainstem. Since the ovoid mass of each thalamus is divided by a lamina of white matter (internal medullary lamina) which bifurcates, a lateral nuclear mass, a medial nuclear mass, and an anterior nuclear mass have been distinguished. The posterior segment of the thalamus, which is not divided by the internal medullary lamina, forms the posterior or pulvinar nucleus. Frank H. Netter's diagram clarifies this description (cf. figure 3).

What divisions of functions exist within this heterogeneous mass, within the nuclei that can be distinguished in it?

First of all there are the *specific thalamic nuclei.* They are either sensitive-sensory relays *(posterolateral ventral nucleus* with its satellite *the arcuate or semilunar nucleus, and the lateral and medial geniculate bodies),* or nonsensory relays receiving impulses from the cerebellum *(lateral ventral nucleus),* globus pallidus *(anteroventral nucleus),* or mamillary bodies and rhinencephalon *(anterior nucleus).*

There are also *association nuclei.* These are the *dorsomedial nucleus* (receiving impulses from the hypothalamus and projecting to the prefrontal cortex); the *lateral dorsal nucleus* and the *lateral posterior nucleus* (receiving impulses from the thalamic nuclei and projecting to the parietal area); and the *pulvinar nucleus,* which is connected with the thalamic structures and projects to the occipitotemporal "association cortex."

Besides these specific or association masses, there exists an *intralaminar reticular substance* which contains the *centrum medianum* of Luys and perhaps the *reticular nuclei.* This system forms what, since Dempsey and Morison (1942), has been called the *diffuse thalamic projection system.*

Forbes and Morison (1939) and Dempsey and Morison

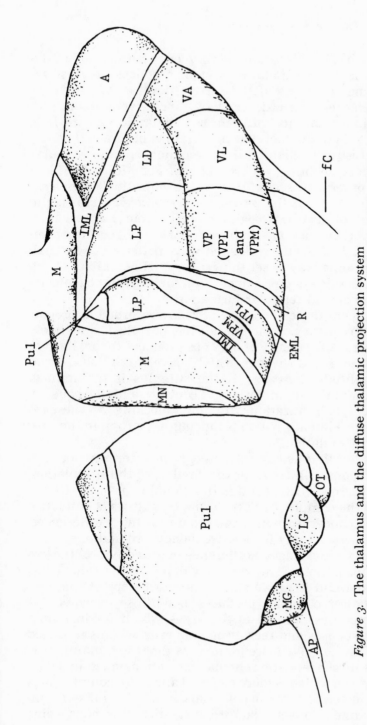

Figure 3. The thalamus and the diffuse thalamic projection system

Anterior nucleus (A); ventral anterior nucleus (VA); lateral dorsal nucleus (LD); medial nucleus (M); lateral posterior nucleus (LP); ventral lateral nucleus (VL); ventral posterior nucleus (VP); ventral posterolateral nucleus (VPL); ventral posteromedial nucleus (VPM); reticular nucleus (R); intralaminar reticular substance, or internal or external medullary lamina (IML) (EML); midline nucleus (MN); pulvinar (Pul); medial geniculate body (MG); lateral geniculate body (LG); optic tract (OT); acoustic pathway (AP); from the cerebellum (fC)

151

(1941–1942) have shown that low frequency stimulation of the nuclei of the diffuse thalamic system produces progressively increasing responses at the cortical level ("recruiting responses"). Jasper, Moruzzi, etc., have since given a more precise description of this intralaminar thalamic system. It is important to note the fact that in certain experimental conditions, the rostral portion of the meso-diencephalic reticular axis produces cortical synchronization. For McLardy (1951) and many others, the seat of this "synchronization" is the *centrum medianum* and the *parafascicular nucleus.* This is the direction which Jasper, Drooglever-Fortuyn, etc., have taken in developing their notion of the similarity of recruiting responses, spindles and the spike-and-wave patterns of petit mal, in order in some way to set the synchronizing activity of the diffuse projection system in opposition to the dynamogenic activity of the caudal reticular formation.

The fact that these opposite effects are recorded in proportion to the frequency of the stimuli has provoked some lively controversies. A frequency of 8–12 cps produces cortical waves of exactly the same rhythm, which are of high voltage and whose amplitude increases. If the stimulus is maintained, alpha-like spindles set in. By way of contrast, a high frequency produces desynchronization with alpha blocking. All these responses have a latency which is much greater than in the case of specific stimulations.

Bremer felt that he had interpreted the difference between cortical responses in terms of the rhythm of the stimulation, without running up against this functional opposition. He believes that the complexity of the synaptic pathways at the two levels he is concerned with can account for these differences, which are present only for low frequency stimulations.

Moruzzi acknowledges a difference in the activity of the two reticular formations. The research done by his school has shown that rapid iterative stimulation at 60 cps of the nonspecific thalamic nuclei produces nondiffuse "surface negative" responses, limited to the areas which produce augmenting responses and recruiting responses when stimulated at 8 cps. This has given rise to the idea that the thalamic portion of the mesencephalic reticular formation, taken in a convergent system which is more elevated and more complex, acts upon bioelectrical cortical potentials in a bilateral but nondiffuse manner. Jouvet (1960) remarks that this nonspecific activity of the thalamus cannot occur during waking because it is fluctuating and unstable. This activity is in certain respects a model of the organization of wakefulness, a structuring of the field of consciousness at a level of "psychical tone" which is less differentiated than during attention and reflection, but more nuanced than during the state of arousal for which the reticular formation is responsible. It can appear only on the condition that the overall activating action of the reticular formation has been suppressed by barbiturates or severed by a transection of the mesencephalon. This activity of cortical control is characterized by the fact that it is integrated into a functional cycle which is more differentiated and whose modulations elude the all-or-none law of the summary conditions of wakefulness.

It is even possible that the thalamic reticular formation's subordination to the reticular formation of the mesencephalon might not be unidirectional. J. Schlag (1961) thus raised the question of a thalamomesencephalocortical circuit. This allows us better to understand reciprocal thalamocortical activities, their role in waking, their comparison with specific projections and stimulations, their influence upon "isolated units" of the isocortex, and the value and identity of the recruiting/augmenting responses or "spindles," which constantly introduce differentiations (stages of braking, slowing, inhibition, or synchronization) into cortical activity.

Special note should here be made of the recent work of Nauta, Whitlock, Arduini, Moruzzi, Zanchetti, Li, Cullen and Jasper, Brookhart, etc. The apparatus through which this wave interference and these reciprocal actions take place is represented at every layer of the cortex by axodendritic synapses, whether apical dendrites (recruiting) or basal dendrites (augmenting) and spindles, in contrast to the specific thalamocortical projection system which terminates at the level of the fourth layer in axosomatic synapses.

Like histological and connectionist research, all these experiments show (as we shall see in the cases of sleep and of epilepsy) that the rhinencephalon, which is so intimately connected with the thalamic center of the centrencephalic system, also exercises its activity upon it, and through its intermediary, upon the reticular formation of the brainstem.

We could not close this brief exposition of the functions of the thalamus without making some reference to what clinical studies have revealed concerning the experience of pain. Thalamic pain is practically the only reference which can be made to subjective experience in this field. Animal neurophysiology teaches us almost nothing about it. This fact is, however, most important.[20] The opinion of Head and Holmes, Foerster, and Bremer is that influxes of painful stimuli are integrated in consciousness at the level of the thalamus. This whole question is still very obscure; neurosurgery produces more paradoxes than answers. Many writers are tempted by vertical concep-tions of subcortical and cortical reverberation. But this sheds little light on the subject. It is nonetheless true that thalamic lesions bring about hyperpathia. Clinical, or at least biblio-graphical, silence about somesthetic and somatotopagnosic disorders and about experiences of depersonalization has al-ways seemed strange to us.[21]

Be that as it may, because of its intimate relationship with the extrapyramidal system and with the rhinencephalic sys-tem, the specific and nonspecific thalamic system truly repre-sents a sensory relay, but a relay which seems to be more than a link in a chain. Its neurophysiology would indicate that it corresponds to a sort of intermediary stage between the brut-ishness of the rhombencephalic and mesencephalic reticular formation's wakefulness and the highly differentiated analyses of the cerebral cortex.[22] The formations of the thalamus seem to play a primordial role in the *embodiment* of all sensible experiences. And by embodiment we should perhaps think not merely of the bodily lived experience which is the foundation of all experience, but of the constitution of an *intracorporeal and mental* space which is lived as the milieu in which are organized the subjectivity and the objectivity of what is experi-enced. P. Guiraud is one of the first to have become aware of and demonstrated the role of this sensory integrating system in the self.

C. The Rhinencephalon (Nosebrain)

The rhinencephalon[23] was so called for the first time by Turner in 1890, for it was then thought (as it was until Brodal in 1947) that this old brain was the central olfactory organ. The limbic lobe (named the *"great limbic lobe"* by Broca, in 1878) consists of two arcs which almost completely surround the cor-pus callosum and the peduncle on the internal face of each hemisphere. This bilateral aspect does not take away the "central" and basal character of this double and symmetrical formation. The phylum of this archaic organization shows, according to Seuntjens (1959), that in its form and in its functions it has always been a singular and medial formation which is continuous, he states, with the diencephalon and the pituitary gland. Since 1954, we have described it as a part of the "centrencephalon"; since 1957, Penfield seems to have clearly incorporated it into the "centrencephalic system."

We shall see that it is neither purely nor fundamentally "olfactory." But if the archipallial paleocortex of its olfactory structures is reduced in man, the rhinencephalon as a whole possesses about a billion neurons (against a billion and a half in the largest macrosmatic, the lion). In 1935, Rose showed that the hippocampic formations reached their greatest development in man. By then much ground had been covered since the time when treatises on anatomy included the rhinencephalon only as a curiosity. (The slight degree to which it was developed in Fulton's work, even in the 1943 second edition, is striking.) Morphologically two major systems can be described: one is basal *(pars basalis)*, or the olfactory lobe; the other is *limbic* and includes the inferior portion of the *hippocampus*.

The superior-anterior portion of the olfactory lobe comprises the olfactory bulb and stalk, the olfactory gyrus and stria and the septal area *(subcallosal gyrus* and *septum)*. Its posterior portion consists of the *parahippocampal gyrus* (which in animals corresponds to the pyriform lobe), which lies between the hippocampal sulcus and the fusiform gyrus. The anterior portion bends abruptly to form the *uncus;* its inferior-anterior portion becomes lost in the *entorhinal region.* The *amygdala* is attached to this posterior olfactory system. The amygdala is a complex of nuclei. They have been thoroughly studied in man by Brockham (1938). According to Crosby and Humphrey (description in man, 1941) and Badin (description in the cat, 1951), ten nuclear complexes can be distinguished in it (including the anterior amygdaloid area).

The *limbic lobe* is much more complex. It includes two concentric arcs, surrounding the hilus of the hemisphere, which are separated in the whole extent of their semicircular form by a more or less deep and continuous sulcus. In its superior part (sulcus of the corpus callosum), this sulcus separates the *gyrus cinguli* (anterior and posterior limbic areas) from the *gyrus supracallosus* or *indusium griseum.* In its inferior temporal part, this sulcus (the hippocampal sulcus) deepens to such a degree that it produces an involution of its sides. It separates the external part (*subiculum,* continuous with the parahippocampal gyrus) from the internal juxtaventricular part. This part within the sulcus is what is properly called the *hippocampus.* The hippocampus is bordered by the posterior column of the trigone *(fornix).* Thus, each side of the deep hippocampal sulcus delimits the involutions of these structures so as to form Ammon's horn; outside of the sulcus is the *subiculum,* which is separated from the parahippocampal gyrus; inside it is the dentate gyrus (in the shape of a hippocampus); even further within is the *fimbria,* which is continuous with the *fornix.* In order to understand the descriptive and experimental complexity of work being done on the rhinencephalon, it is indispensable to know its topography and especially the double motion of the limbic lobe around the isthmus and of the involution of Ammon's horn around the hippocampal sulcus (see figure 4).

The connections of this system are also extremely complex and numerous. Here is a description of the totality of this connectionist systematic analysis, according to Gastaut and Lammers.

Above the corpus callosum, the limbic lobe *(gyrus cinguli)* includes the *cingulum,* which collects the afferents which come to the rhinencephalon from the neocortex and the thalamus. Below the corpus callosum, it includes the trigone and its posterior column, the *fornix,* which forms the major afferent pathway of the rhinencephalon, especially of Ammon's horn, but also of the inferior half of the parahippocampal gyrus.

The *hippocampal-fornix* system comprises:

(a) Afferent pathways which proceed from the retrosplenial, limbic, and parolfactory areas *(cingulum)* and from the septal, parolfactory, and limbic areas (the *dorsal fornix*). A direct temporoammonic pathway leads a large bundle of fibers from the parahippocampal area to Ammon's horn. A temporoammonic tract then crosses the endotheloid region from one side of Ammon's horn to the opposite side. Finally, electrophysiology has confirmed that there exists a septoammonic pathway.

(b) Efferent pathways are represented by the axons of the pyramidal cells of Ammon's horn. These axons follow the fornix, whose fibers number about 500,000 in the monkey and

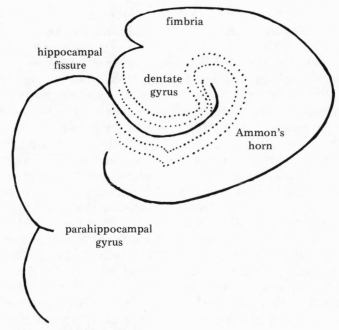

Figure 4. Ammon's horn
This diagram shows a section of the temporal lobe (fusiform gyrus) and of Ammon's horn. Ammon's horn is wrapped around the hippocampal fissure. The superior portion is formed by the dentate gyrus, which resembles a seahorse (hippocampus). Above is the fimbria, which is continuous with the posterior column of the trigonom cerebrale, or fornix.

2,000,000 in man. Within this pathway can be distinguished a precommissural group which runs into the septal and septotemporal areas, a postcommissural group (ammonomammillary and ammonohypothalamic fibers), an ammonohabenular group, and an ammonothalamic group which runs (Nauta, 1956; Guillery, 1956) to the anterior nuclei of the thalamus on both sides. These anterior nuclei of the thalamus are thus connected with the hippocampus in a double manner, first by the direct pathway of the ammonothalamic fibers, then by the indirect pathway of the ammonomammillary and mammillothalamic tracts.

A strong hippocampo-mesorhombencephalic connective system has been brought to light by Nauta and Kuypers (1958). This is the limbic midbrain circuit, which appears to terminate in the brainstem.[24]

The afferents of the amygdaloid complex are chiefly olfactory (the afferents of the corticomedial nuclei of the amygdala, the nucleus of the lateral olfactory stria of the same side and of the central nucleus project to the basomedial nucleus and to the nucleus of the stria terminalis of both sides). But above these olfactory afferents, the amygdala receives numerous sensory fibers. Certain of these afferents come from the nuclei of the hypothalamus. The efferent system is formed by the *stria terminalis,* which runs into the hypothalamus (preoptic area) and into the septum, and by the inferior longitudinal fasciculus of association fibers which effectively unites the pyriform cortex (parahippocampal cortex) to the basolateral nuclei of the amygdala. Gastaut and Lammers specify that the amygdala projects to the medial part of the stria terminalis and to the lateral part of this region by the inferior longitudinal fasciculus. The reverberatory circuits are perhaps nowhere so clearly materialized as in these rhinencephalic (in the broad sense) structures: the influence of the hippocampus extends over the hypothalamus and over the thalamus, over the orbital cortex, etc., and in their turn these send numerous efferents to the amygdaloammonic system. Papez's circuit expresses rather exactly the hypothesis (if not the fact) of these integrative cycles of intrinsic and extrinsic connection. Papez (1937) considered this circuit to be as follows: the hippocampus is its center; it projects, by way of the fornix, to the mammillary body and to the hypothalamus; the circuit continues across the mammillothalamic tract to the anterior nuclei of the thalamus; then, by way of the *cingulum* it returns to the hippocampus. Since then this fiction seems to have gained in reality.

This is thus a very complex system which forms a parallel circuit through the mesodiencephalic centrencephalic system. It is nonetheless strange that the nonspecific centers and pathways at the level of the medulla oblongata, the thalamus, or the cortex are constantly contiguous and at every level are intricately related to the nonspecific neuronal masses or centers. The rhinencephalon nonetheless remains to some extent an olfactory center, but one whose specific pathways and centers become lost in an infinitely broader nonspecific system.

Before we begin to examine the neurophysiology of the rhinencephalon in its morphology and its connections, we should say a word about another of its highly original cytoarchitectonic features: the structure of the *allocortex.*

arch which we shall now discuss lies in the experimental or
thological facts which are at the basis of the theory which
nsiders the rhinencephalon as the "affective brain" (Papez)
the visceral brain (MacLean). J. Olds and M. E. Olds (Mon-
video, 1959) have maintained that the hypothalamic-
inencephalic system is more intimately bound to condition-
g and learning than is any other part of the brain, as if it
ayed an important role in the functions which are generally
tributed to the cortex. H. Mamo (following Penfield) also at-
butes a more important place to it than to the cortex for
emory fixation (*Presse Médicale,* 1962).

A primary field of interest concerns ablations. The experi-
ents of Klüver and Bucy (1939) stand out on this subject. In
onkeys, the ablation of the temporal lobes produces a syn-
ome which is characterized by agnosia in the auditory and
ctile fields, a very strong tendency to feel, to put things in the
outh, to lick, to chew, to bite all objects; it brings about an
resistible urge to touch all objects (hypermetamorphosis), the
sence of any fear or anger reaction, even in the presence of
akes, an intense carnivorous appetite, a sexual behavior
hich manifests strong sexual urges and hetero-, homo-, and
tosexual aberrations. The tripod of this syndrome is formed
' hypersexuality, hyperphagy, and placidity.

This syndrome has been more or less clearly rediscovered
ter bilateral temporal hemispherectomy in man (H. Terzian
d G. Dalle-Ore, 1955). All the evidence thus seems to support
e view that these formations have an inhibitory effect upon
stinctive tendencies.

Since we know from the classical experiments of Goltz and
Rothman that decorticate and decerebrate animals show
ther similar behavioral disorders (Cannon and Britton, and
ter Bard, etc. have noted *sham* reactions of aggression and
persexuality), the specific character of the Klüver-Bucy syn-
ome might appear rather weak. However, the fact that de-
ruction of the amygdaloid complex (Schreimer and Kling,
53; Woods, 1956) leads to analogous disorders makes it
rthy of study. It is also worth noting that, according to Spie-
l (1940), Bard and Mountcastle (1953), ablations of the amyg-
loid nuclei provoked reactions of anger and rage. Numerous
her facts have been reported, but the sense of the affective
actions (aggression or placidity, rage or euphoria) is not
ivocal.[25]

The opposition between the hemispheri
and the "rhinencephalon" has been brough
a difference in the structure of the cortex. (
toarchitectonic considerations, the hemisph
the "isocortex"; the cortex which is engu
porohippocampal depths and the adjacent
"allocortex." This "primitive" cortex is ch
existence of only two layers (molecular layer
cells and pyramidal layer). This bistratifie
tially characteristic of the *limbic lobe,* that
pocampal formations.

From the *electrobiological* viewpoint, the
potentials has allowed many writers (Robi
1951; Dell and Olson, 1951; Green, Arduini,
Cadilhac, 1954; Matrone and Segundo, 1956,
fact that the limbic system receives afferen
cific systems after a very long latency.

Electrical stimulation of the hippocan
sponses in the septum and the hypothalamu
the amygdaloid complex over the hippocam
that the hippocampal dendritic tree "has a
and integrative function" (Gloor).

The hippocampus's spontaneous bioele
characterized by waves of great amplitude,
cps) or slow (4-8 cps), and irregularly dist
and Cadilhac). This is a *very different rhytl*
neocortex. Arousal reaction clarifies this di
level of the hippocampus a *synchronizatic*
which contrasts with the lack of synchrony

From this has arisen the conception of
physiology (MacLean) between the rhineno
the neocortical system. Passouant and Cadi
phasized the massive character of the
sponses, as compared to the differentiate
electrical and compartmental configurati
structures. But, as we have always emphasi
is complementary for all organizational lev
tems and subsystems.

However important these problems con
tional or complementary relationships be
cephalon and the neocortex might be (we
problem when dealing with sleep), the fo

Let us examine *brain stimulation studies* in an attempt to find our bearings in this labyrinth of experimentation. As far as the *hippocampus* is concerned, brain stimulation studies (taking only afterdischarges into account) provoke motor modifications (catalepsy, immobility), disorders of wakefulness (indifference and stupor), and emotional reactions (the animal seems to feel a sensation of uneasiness and inquietude) (Passouant and Cadilhac). Kaada and his collaborators (1953), on the other hand, have unleashed emotional reactions of rage, of fear, and of flight in cats by stimulating the posterior portion of the hippocampus. Delgado brought on crises of sham rage, as did MacLean. It seems that the two behaviors of displeasure and anger and of satisfaction follow one another (Passouant and Cadilhac). By depositing crystals of cholinergic drugs on a segment of the hippocampus, MacLean has provoked, in cats, very clear manifestations of pleasure, of grooming, and from time to time an erection.

Kaada, Andersen, and Jansen (1954) stimulated the basolateral portion of the amygdala of nonanesthetized cats and observed "reactions of attention and anxiety directed toward an imaginary object," along with panic reactions. After stimulating the amygdala, M. T. Liberson observed a certain indifference when its lateral portion was excited. Chemical and electrical stimulation of the amygdaloid region (Gastaut, 1952; Magoun and Lammers, 1956; Ursin and Kaada, 1960; etc.) seem, then, to release a series of fragmentary behavior patterns and of oral-emotional and oral-alimentary mechanisms. Chronic irritative lesions (Walker, Kojelov, Green, Gastaut, etc.) produce *psychomotor type crises* with automatisms and vegetative disorders. At this point, the little that experimentation has taught us can be combined with the great amount of knowledge that has come from the clinical study of epilepsy. In man, stimulation of the amygdala has provoked automatisms, confusional states, speech disorders, and memory disorders (Feindel and Penfield, 1954). Jasper and Rasmussen (1956) have provoked sensations of hunger in forty-six patients, who showed indifference, confusion, and amnesia. Heath, Monroe, and Mickle (1955) stimulated the amygdala of schizophrenic patients and provoked intense anxiety, flight impulses, and sometimes fits of anger.

By stimulations of septal-orbital areas, Olds and Milner (1954) obtained effects of "self-sustained" pleasure, which has been the subject of much neurobiological and psychoanalytic discussion.[26] Rats in whom microelectrodes were inserted could "autostimulate" this pleasure region and did so, pushing the button up to 5,000 times an hour. They were indifferent to anything other than this pleasure, until they fell asleep exhausted. Analogous findings concerning these zones have been made (Delgado, 1960; J.-C. Lilly, 1960; C. W. Sem-Jacobson, 1960) as much with respect to hunger and displeasure as to satisfaction.

All these experiments upon the rhinencephalon in large part send us back to the experiments which earlier had been performed on the hypothalamus (Hess, Ranson, etc.). All the "centrencephalic" formations, from the bulbopontine stem to the thalamic and limbic systems, which are strongly connected with the septal-orbital areas, seem to be related to organic life in the strict sense—the autonomic system (MacLean's "visceral brain"), that is, to the "motives," instinctive needs, and emotions which, at the behavioral level, express the lived experience of affective impressions.[27] Pibram and Karger (1954) insisted upon this basic relationship of emotional or affective dynamics with olfactory experience *(sentir).* The French word *"sentir"* gains its full significance here, when it expresses both the olfactory experience (to smell) and sensible experience in general (to feel, to sense).

As regards diverse emotional states and modes of expressive behavior (rage, eroticism, hunger, or, on the other hand, indifference, apathy, depression, etc.), their complexity and their essential bipolarity seem to defy any experimental stimulation or ablation which bears upon this vast and complex system. Where some observe aggression when a certain structure is stimulated, others observe it when it is suppressed. Where some provoke hyperexcitability, others observe flight or immobility. It is impossible to analyze all these "responses" by reducing them to components which would themselves be reducible to their local signs. We are better off recording what these facts and these experiments have shown: the rhinencephalic structures and their systematic mesodiencephalic circuits form a regulatory or modulatory apparatus which exerts its energetic influence (sometimes ordered, sometimes disorganized) upon the whole of the cerebral structures. The ammonic cortex, the true allocortex, seems to constitute the organizing cortex of this system (Ajuriaguerra and Blanc).

From our point of view, this "affective computer," which Wiener (following Mortimer Ostow, 1955) curiously localized in the hippocampus, is by nature not a metronome of objective time but an integrator of lived time, in the sense that the presentness of experience, its temporalization, seems to depend largely upon the processes of needs and desires which appear to be organized in its structures.

There is certainly much to say (which we shall have to omit so as not to make this chapter too long) concerning the time relationships which, in the depths of this lobe, exist between the actualization of affective motivations and memory. Penfield, with respect to temporal stimulation studies, and Gleis, Griffith, Conrad and Ule, W. Scoville, etc., with respect to Korsakovian disorders of memory, have connected the pathology of mnemic experience to these centrencephalic formations (Lhermitte, 1967).

We here touch upon a decisive aspect of the psychopathology of the field of consciousness: the connection between disorders of consciousness and "thymic" disorders (which is a sort of leitmotif of all our *Études*). What had been so artificially separated is united precisely on the level of these cerebral structures: affective life as bestower of sense and of movement to lived experience in the field of consciousness. In this respect it is very probable that this rhinencephalic portion of the centrencephalic system plays an important role in the temporal structure of lived experience.

3. PERIODIC CEREBRAL DISORGANIZATIONS: SLEEPING AND DREAMING

The phylogenesis and ontogenesis of the brain give its organization the sense of a progressive telencephalization. This is to say that the optimal organization of the brain (considered as the organ of the system of vital relations as adapted to reality) occurs when there is a maximal differentiation of activities within the cerebral cortex. Nothing can validly oppose this conception of the sense and the hierarchy of cerebral systems. It can even be said that the fullness of cortical activity is necessary for the activity of waking, reflective and wakeful thought, and for the elaborations and superstructures of the field of consciousness which characterize the attentive, discursive, and logical form of behavior or of thought which is adapted to reality. We awake, we are alert, we are in a state of attention, of speculative reflection, or of discretion because of operations which take place principally in the field of neocortical structures (the isocortex).

Inversely, when a person becomes sleepy, falls asleep, sleeps and dreams, this can only be interpreted as a weakening, a diminution, even an abolition (in any case, a negation) of this activity of wakefulness. The whole problem of sleep and dreaming thus rests upon their regressive nature. With respect to wakefulness, sleep is a dissolution, just as it had at first been a state of immaturity, being the only form of the primitive existence of the embryo and the newborn child.

What might appear to be a simple truism is not quite so obvious, for it could be possible to maintain the paradox of an active function of sleep, understanding by that not merely that sleep is not purely negative—which is true—but that the cerebral organization of sleep would have the same functional value as that of wakefulness. But to give the same value to sleep and wakefulness is the same as to give the same value to unconsciousness and consciousness. This would abolish the hierarchical sense of the organization of the brain and, more generally, of psychical being. In any case, it would be to sanction a contradiction through the notion of *active inhibition*— the suppression of precisely that which is essential to the suppression of waking activity: the incapacity, even if consented to, for wakefulness.

In this brief summary of what electroneurophysiological studies have taught us on this subject, we should not lose sight of the fact that sleep is "negative" with respect to wakefulness. What consequently must be explained is not the appearing of sleep, but the disappearance of wakefulness. This is as much as to say that the inner "mechanism" which regulates sleeping and dreaming is essentially the dynamogenic apparatus of wakefulness which must necessarily include a functional "keyboard" for the facilitation and occultation of the interneuronal passages of the various cerebral systems. It is not that the sleep center is "active," but that the waking center is made inactive. For even if the disappearance of wakefulness demands certain "dynamic" factors of active inhibition, this inhibition is no less a suppression, whatever might be the biological process which produces it. If experimentation can produce sleep, either by stimulation of the hypothalamus (Hess) or pontine area (school of Moruzzi), or by the monotony and repetition of cortical stimuli (Pavlov), this is because, however "positive" these stimulations might be or be imagined to be, their effect is essentially negative: they produce a disorganization of the field of consciousness.

The history of "sleep centers" teaches us much concerning the conceptual ambiguities to which neurophysiologists sometimes fall prey. We have long been aware (Wernicke, Economo, Demole, Marinesco, etc.) that lesions or (what comes down to about the same thing in certain experiments) electrical or chemical excitations "in the vicinity of the third ventricle" provoke sleep phenomena and disorders of consciousness or of wakefulness. After thirty years of intensive study of the hypothalamus and the thalamus, Hess bequeathed to the anterior hypothalamus (parasympathetic or trophotropic) the function of an active center of sleep. Ranson and Ingram, on the other hand, interpreted their own and Hess's experiments as bringing to light the fact that lesions of the lateral hypothalamus provoke sleep by suppressing the dynamogenic effect of these structures. This interpretation, moreover, has been confirmed as regards the activating role of the reticular formation, by Magoun, Moruzzi, etc. Thus, in place of a sleep center, considered as an active center which releases a function which is simply juxtaposed with an inverse function, there has been substituted a regulative apparatus which is capable of either activating or not activating the functional emergence of waking or, better still, the verticality of the field of consciousness. In this way the neurophysiological hypothesis has gained in realism what it has lost in simplicity. We shall not insist upon the surreptitious return to this summary theory in certain controversies over the synchronizing or recruiting role of the intralaminary reticular substance (Jasper) or the discussions concerning the cortical inhibitory centers of the pons (Moruzzi, Jouvet, etc.). Instead we shall simply note that in renouncing the spatial conception of a center which excites some function plus a center which suppresses it, the problem remains of trying to conceive a dynamic whole which is a functional contradiction, being always involved in the opposition between the objects which it brings into equilibrium (inhibition and facilitation).

Before we examine the problem of the localization of sleep and wakefulness, from the dual viewpoint defined above, and in order better to understand the great importance of *cerebral transections,* which have revolutionized our knowledge in this field since the time of Bremer, we must first consider what we know concerning the neurophysiology of wakefulness and of awakening, and concerning the neurophysiology of sleeping, of falling asleep, of dreaming, and of the neuropathology of epilepsy.

1. THE NEUROPHYSIOLOGY OF WAKEFULNESS: "CORTICAL AROUSAL"

The activity of wakefulness ("vigilance," awareness, *la veille*) upon the various modes of cerebral electrogenesis cannot be traced very accurately. This is because there exist many points of incongruity between behavior in the waking state and certain EEG characteristics of wakefulness, and because there are certain paradoxical analogies between the rapid patterns of wakefulness and the pattern of sleep, or between the rhythms of an aquatic insect and those of a Nobel prize laureate (Adrian). Most of our knowledge concerning the "waking brain" is nevertheless based upon the observational and experimental data of cerebral electrogenesis.

During waking, or better, hyperwakeful, activity, that is, during reflective problem solving activity and concentration of attention, flat patterns of rapid frequencies which admit of slight variations have been observed (Lindsley, Gastaut, Grey Walter, etc.). The wakeful activity of attention[28] is, all things considered, *aroused* by any sensory or affective event which incites an internal polarization of the field of consciousness and brings about a desynchronization of the pattern (waves of rapid frequency, between 30 and 60 cps). This *arrest reaction* is more particularly an opening to the perceptual world. The possibility of arousal by sensory messages has been the object of much study since the time of Bremer. Jouvet and Courjon (1958), for example, have studied the variations of visual responses in relation to the process of attention. Dell, Bonvallet, Hugelin (1954–1955) have studied the affect of converging signals and the phasic action exerted upon the reticular formation by abrupt sensory stimulation and variations of the inner environment. In this way, moreover, the problem of reticular wakefulness is joined to that concerning the motivations which spring from the organism's needs and emotional or neurovegetative responses (Dell and Lairy, 1958). Be that as it may, attentive wakefulness (cortical tone, to use Bremer's term) can arise when the basic rhythm which it replaces is stopped.

This morphology of cortical electrogenesis in the state of extreme wakefulness forms a contrast with the restful waking pattern, which is characterized by *alpha*. This rhythm consists of a succession of regular sinusoidal waves of about 10 cps, whose amplitude varies from 10 to 100 μV. It is primarily found in the occipital lobe (but it exists over the whole surface of the hemispheres except at the frontal pole). This specifically human rhythm seems to form a sort of "basal tone" (to which would correspond the vertical constitution of the field of consciousness considered as the functional "pedestal" of its superstructures). It corresponds to the disponible nature of the facultative processes of psychical operations. It is characteristic of nondirected attention and of automatic behavior which is effortless and undisturbed. This basic rhythm is interrupted (arrest reaction) by sensory stimuli or by difficult or reflectively performed inner processes, which brings about a characteristic desynchronization, as is true in the case of higher level operations.

As G. C. Lairy has accurately noted,[29] electrogenesis points to the existence of an organized and hierarchical structure. The ontogenesis of this functional architectonic confirms this. The work of Lindsley (1952), Grey Walter (1953), Dreyfus-Brisac and Blanc (1955), etc., has shown that a differentiation between sleep-dream rhythms can be observed by the eighth month of the fetus's life, the first spatiotemporal organization of rhythms appears at three months, and rhythmic occipital activity becomes established at five months. Up to three years of age delta rhythms predominate; from two to eight years, theta rhythms; and from eight to ten years onward, at the end of this process of maturing (which corresponds to the organizing of the field of consciousness), alpha rhythm is the indispensable condition of all higher and further elaborations.

In human beings, where this stratified organization is the clearest, thorough research is difficult or somewhat artificial. In 1953, Parker devised an apparatus for permanently recording the different modes of behavior; neurosurgeons have since been able, during their operations, to study alpha reactivity and its correlations with the process of attention.

Naturally these electrical changes in the waking brain have been studied most frequently through experimentation upon animals (acute preparations, anesthetized preparations, chronic preparations, cerebral transections, coagulations of different parts of the brain). All this research aims at determining the aspects and conditions of "cortical arousal" and its subcortical counterparts.

The process of "cortical arousal" has sometimes been defined as a mechanism of inhibition (Berger), sometimes as a phenomenon of desynchronization (Adrian). This is once again a question of whether the substitution of waking rhythms for the animal's sleep rhythms brings about a state of cortical inhibition or excitation in the wakeful brain. It has been noticed that "cortical arousal" brings about a blocking of discharges, especially in the pyramidal cells (Moruzzi and Magoun, 1949; Whitlock and Arduini, 1953). The research of Brookhart and Zanchetti (1956) has confirmed in the pyramidal animal (when the transection spares the pes pedunculi) that during arousal there is cortical blocking of the discharges which are contemporaneous with spindles and other forms of slow potentials influenced by the rostral (thalamic) portion of the reticular formation. But Bremer has shown (1960) that the processes of facilitation of cortical arousal, which seem to be very characteristic of cortical activity, are "hidden" by the "competitive convergences" which are in play at this level. It seems inconceivable that the cortex could be aroused in a general and uniform state of excitation or of inhibition. As a matter of fact, awakening, waking, and wakefulness are functional modes which are characterized not by inhibition or excitation but by their reciprocal relationships, that is, by the processes of *differentiation* and of *selection* which regulate the discharging of the neurons by integrating them into patterns determined by their sense.

Without going more into detail, let us again point out that the study of "cortical arousal," through the use of electrocorticograms and single cell recording (Clare and Bishop, 1955; Purpura and Grundfest, 1956; Brookhart, Arduini, Mancia, and Moruzzi, 1957), has been directed especially towards the cortical dendritic system and its synaptic surface-negative or surface-positive potential shifts, determined not by the law of all-or-none, but by graded potential responses. During arousal, a lessening in localized cortical responses and a blocking of responses to repeated stimulation of nonspecific thalamic nuclei are observed. The surface-negative component of the recruiting response also is suppressed during electrocortico-graphic arousal. During the *Symposium on the Nature of Sleep* (1960), Heinz Caspers showed that during cortical arousal there was a surface-negative potential shift while the animal (a rat) remained relatively motionless.

Discussion has taken place concerning generalized diffuse arousal and concerning localized arousal of specific portions of the cortex set off by means of sensory stimuli and which correspond to responses evoked in different parts of the cortex. Sensory arousal can occur during sleep, that is, when sensory signals arouse only part of the cortex without inciting the dynamogenic activity of the reticular formation (Rossi, Adrian). This leads us to an examination of the centers which regulate wakefulness.

Bremer and Terzuolo demonstrated, in 1952, that the cortex can take part in its own arousal through corticoreticular inhibitory feedback. Hugelin and Bonvallet (1957) have confirmed their discovery. And Ingvar had shown that the isolated cortex can still produce an arousal which is induced by variations in the inner environment brought about by circulation. Bremer (1960) reminds us that one fact stands out above all the others: stimulation of the cat's or the monkey's cortex always provokes electrocorticographical arousal and never drowsiness.

The role of the *mesodiencephalic reticular formation* in determining cortical arousal can no longer be doubted, since the work of Magoun, Moruzzi, Bremer, etc. (cf. above, p. 146). One problem, however, remains: the juxtaposition and interference of the inhibitory centers, especially those of the caudal (pontine) portion of the brainstem (cf. below, p. 177).

During the overall activity of wakefulness, the particular activities of the nervous subsystems are also in a state of arousal. This wakefulness naturally calls for a facilitation in the propagation or control of the various stimuli. For this reason, stimulation of the reticular formation can produce facilitatory effects in the direction of a lowering of the *thresholds of sensory response*. This has been shown, for example, by the experiments of Dumont and Dell (1958), who have provoked facilitation of transmission of visual messages at the level of the thalamus; but these facilitations are "concealed" (Bremer) by other phenomena which occur simultaneously. Equally very important are the facilitatory effects of the waking state which are maintained by the reticular formation upon motor activity. Muscle tone, and all the postural reactions involved in locomotor activity, etc., which it conditions, are naturally facilitated by the facilitatory effect of brainstem discharges on the spinal level (Rhines and Magoun, 1946; Magoun, 1950; Granit, 1955; Rossi and Zanchetti, 1957). This dynamogenic activity of the descending activating system acts directly at the level of local interneurons, whose excitation amplifies the facilitatory effect (Lloyd, 1946) through the effect of spatial and temporal summations. But here we encounter once again the problem of the relations of excitation and inhibition. For if reticulomedullary influences augment the gamma efferent bombardment of the neuromuscular spindles, they can also reduce it. There exists, in effect, a *descending reticular inhibiting system,* as if the reticular formation activated antagonistic muscles (Magoun and Rhines) or ipsilateral symmetrical groups (Sprague and Chambers, 1954). All in all, activation of these bulbomedullary levels, within the efferent system, is synonymous with regulation of gamma efferents and of neuromuscular spindles (Granit and collaborators, 1952–1955). The same inhibitory effect is active at the level of the brainstem as regards lower level sensory afferents (Hagbarth and Kerr, 1954; Hernández-Peón and Scherrer, 1955; Jouvet and Desmedt, 1956) at the thalamodiencephalic level (King, Naquet, and Magoun, 1955). As far as either generalized or particular wakefulness effects are concerned, the reticular formation has no simple and homogeneous function.

There have been just as many controversies over the role of the *intralaminar reticular substance of the thalamus* during wakefulness. We have seen that low frequency stimulation of the anteroventral nuclei of the thalamus (nonspecific projection system) provokes recruiting (Dempsey and Morison) or augmenting responses. But stimulated at a frequency of 200 cps, the thalamic intralaminar reticular substance produces a facilitatory effect in the intact animal. On this subject, Bremer (1960) emphasizes that a sort of convergence of nonspecific ascending reticular influxes and of specific sensory influxes acts upon the same neurons which are part of the subliminal fringe in responding to sensory stimuli. In other words, at the level of the thalamus, we once again find this reciprocal interaction between facilitation and inhibition which influences "specific sense data" by means of dynamogenic mechanisms which regulate or modulate wakefulness at the level of the diencephalon, but at this level with a more elevated capacity for differentiation (Jasper's thalamocortical integrating system). Jouvet (1960) points out that the diffuse thalamic system "can freely modify the excitability of the association and specific cortical areas."

The *structures of the rhinencephalon* are not excluded from the activity of wakefulness. We have seen that its structures could represent a system which regulates affective impressions and, on the whole, which regulates the motivation which gives experiential lived time its speed and its internal movement. The electrical activity of the hippocampus (Green and Arduini, 1945) is the inverse of that of the neocortex. In contrast to the rapid, low voltage activity of cortical arousal, hippocampal discharges (dorsal hippocampus) consist of a series of slow waves (3-6 cps), which are regular, synchronous, and of high amplitude. Chronic preparations have shown these to correspond, in wakeful or attentive animals, to a cortical activation pattern. Reticular stimulations which follow the pathway of the dorsal *fornix* and the *septum* provoke the same "schizophysiological" effect between the synchronization of the rhinencephalon and the desynchronization of the neocortex. Let us recall, moreover, that according to McKegney (1958), all the thalamic nuclei project to the rhinencephalon. According to Brodal, the hippocampus exercises an excitatory influence upon the mammillary bodies, whereas for Green and Arduini this action is inhibitory (the same problems recur at all these levels). Whatever the case may be, for Green and Arduini the hippocampus would set in play the affective and emotional mechanisms of "affective resonance" in the mechanisms of arousal. As far as the amygdaloid system is concerned, it appears to be a sort of relay between the activity of the reticular formation of the brainstem and the cortex (D. D. Bound, C. T. Roudt, T. G. Bioder, and V. Rowland, 1957). Its activity is analogous to that of the reticular formation (Feindel and Gloor).

The "waking brain" is thus characterized by neocortical activation. But this activation exerts its influence or, more exactly, is manifested only by a totality of processes of ordered differentiation which open towards the external world and set in action all the infrastructures which are implied in its activity. We need not insist upon this dynamic aspect in order to emphasize the "isomorphism" between this structuring of the brain and the structuring of the field of consciousness, with the vertical movement which is essential to its constitution and the "facultativity" of the figures described by its operations. We can simply state that the "waking brain," which is polarized towards reality, is organized in such a manner that its functional architectonic allows for an infinite number of possibilities and in particular for a circuit in which its higher activity continually reflects upon its basal activity and vice versa.

2. NEUROPHYSIOLOGY OF SLEEPING AND DREAMING

The examination of the problem of sleep leads us to the same conclusions. Sleep does not obey a law of all-or-none: it implies an architectonic organization (stages and levels) of its process of dissolution. It is neither a simple phenomenon nor a purely negative phenomenon. We shall see that it requires the possibility of forming oneiric experiences (dreaming) which are an original form of the destructuration of the field of consciousness.

The electrical characteristics of cerebral sleep (weak voltage and heightened synchrony) are typified by *slow rhythms* and *spindles*. On the behavioral level, these correspond to the characteristics of falling asleep or of sleeping (closing the eyes, lessening of muscle tone, elevation of the threshold of perception, change in respiratory and cardiac rate, etc.).

According to Jouvet (1962), these are the EEG sleep characteristics of the intact animal (cat). High amplitude (100-200 μV) *spindles* of 12-18 cps appear at the level of the cortex, particularly in the frontal regions, whereas on the level of specific areas (acoustic) there is rapid activity. These spindles also occur in the medial thalamic structures and in the reticular formation of the mesencephalon. Associated with these spindles are high voltage slow (2-4 cps) waves. These are produced by synchronous corticipetal discharges, and are characterized by a positive shift of dendritic potential (Heinz Caspers, 1960) in the medial thalamus, the mesencephalic tegmentum, and the periaqueductal gray matter. On the other hand, rapid activity persists at the level of the pons. There are rapid, high voltage spikes at the level of Ammon's horn.

Such is the morphology and distribution of this more or less specific synchrony which occurs during sleep. We say "more or less" specific, for atropine provokes slow rhythms without causing sleep, while ether anesthesia provokes rapid rhythms. These slow synchronous waves appear at various levels (cortex, thalamus, brainstem) of the brain (Hess and associates, 1953; Sharpless and Jasper, 1956). But according to Jouvet, who is critical of the older studies of Kennard (1943) and Morison and Bassett (1945), they occur only if the animal possesses its cortex (or at least a part of it). This fact has been confirmed by Sergio and Longo (1960). The subcortical propagation of these waves takes place through corticoreticular pathways, especially those of frontal origin.

Brief spikes on a ground of fast waves at the level of Ammon's horn (and of all the limbic structures) persist after decortication and seem to indicate that the structures of the rhinencephalon have their own inhibitory power, whose influence is exerted through the efferents of the hippocampus (fimbria-fornix, mammillary bodies, mammillothalamic tract of Vicq d'Azyr, mammillotegmental tract of Schutze) upon the reticular formation.

In man this physiological state of the sleeping brain passes through definite successive *stages* from falling asleep to awakening. The research of Loomis, Harvey and Hobart (1935), and Davis (1938) has shown the basic pattern of these bioelectrical characteristics of sleep through its varying degrees of depth to be:

A) discontinuous alpha rhythm;
B) reduction of alpha;
C) presence of spindles;
D) spindles and delta waves;
E) delta waves.

The whole neurophysiological study of sleep has developed in accordance with this fundamental schema, up until the work of Kleitman (1935–1960) and of Jouvet (1958–1962). Stage A corresponds to the stage of restful waking activity. As we have seen above, stage B is characterized by a flattening of the brainwave pattern and by the opposition between theta spindle waves, low amplitude spindles of 12–14 cps, and high spikes. Stage C is characterized by an augmenting of spindles and of theta waves. In stage D, monomorphous slow delta waves appear. In stage E, a polymorphous and areactive delta rhythm appears; that is, external stimuli no longer provoke electrical reactions.

This last point is important, for during the first four stages or levels of sleeping, sensory stimuli provoke either arousal (return of alpha) or the appearance of K complexes (non-specific responses of 8–15 cps against a background of delta rhythm after any sensory excitation whatsoever). The deeper the sleep, the greater is this reactivity. Thus, in stage C it is possible to study the effect of repeated, rhythmic stimuli, which will sometimes cause awakening (Schwob, Passouant, Cadilhac, 1954). In stage B, the reaction threshold is lower and habituation is more difficult.

For Grey Walter, dreaming would correspond to stage B. This leads us to examine the direction which contemporary neurophysiology has given to the psychophysiology of dreaming.

The direct observation of *ocular motility* (Ledd, 1892) and its electrical recording (Aserinsky and Kleitman, 1955) have shown that several times during the night there are phases of rapid eye movements (REM) accompanied by an increase in the pulse and respiratory rate. If the subject is awakened at this time, he will say that he was in the process of dreaming (Dement and Kleitman, 1957). In most cases these will be dreams involving movement (Dement and Wolpert, 1958). Kleitman's classic work *Sleep and Wakefulness* gives a detailed exposition of all the relationships of this interrupted dream activity with memory, sensory stimuli, bodily movements, phonation, and snoring (Goodenough, 1959). Aserinsky and Kleitman observed a correlation between REM sleep and dreaming twenty-seven out of thirty times. These phases of "activated sleep" (Dement) occur after the first three or four hours of a night's sleep and last an average of about twenty minutes each. From these observations it seems most probable that there is a statistically significant relation between dreaming and REM sleep. This fact appeared so clearly established that Dement attempted to explore the "safety valve" function of dream activity by preventing his subjects from dreaming (by interrupting their sleep at the start of eye movements). Over a period of forty uninterrupted nights, eight young boys spent about 20 percent of the night dreaming. After having their night's dreaming reduced for three to seven nights, five subjects averaged more time in dreaming (27 percent of night spent in dreaming), as if a certain amount of dreaming was necessary. But, as Kleitman points out, nothing allows us to say that dreaming does not occur throughout the whole time we are sleeping; only the dream which can be reported during the several minutes which follow the interrupted REM sleep appears to be closely related with the eye movements or at least with this stage of "light" sleep which has its own characteristics. This brings us to one of the most controversial points involved in the neurophysiology of dreaming and its relation to REM sleep.

For Kleitman, who is in general agreement with Loomis's classical description, four stages or levels of sleep can be distinguished. The first is characterized by a low voltage, irregular alpha pattern, interspersed with slow waves and without spindles. The second is characterized by low voltage spindles and K complexes. The third is characterized by a higher voltage, with delta waves and some spindles. The fourth has waves of 100 μV with an activity of 1–2 cps or slower and is without spindles. For Kleitman and his school, *it is during stage I, but only when sleep is coming out of its deepest levels,* that REM sleep appears to correspond to dreaming. The electrical characteristics of the sleep during which dreaming occurs are thus very similar to those of the waking state. But what distinguishes this stage of sleep is that it is extremely unyielding to external stimuli (as if the reaction threshold to the external world was particularly elevated, while at the same time muscle tone is absent). For these reasons, Jouvet has called these stages of sleep, where the dreamer appears to be hypnotized by his dream though sleeping very lightly, "paradoxical phases."

Jouvet later came to call this stage of sleep "rhombencephalic sleep phases," making the problem one of cerebral localization (on the basis of transections carried out over three years on sixty-five cats).

Paradoxical sleep is characterized behaviorally by a *general atonia,* by the total disappearance of any electromyographic activity of the neck muscles, and by the appearance of eye movements, "which are one of the most constant indices" of this stage (movements which are rapid and explosive, horizontal or vertical, conjugate, rarely dissociated, sometimes nystagmus, occurring in saccadic movements, along with extreme miosis). These movements occur in 2– to 5–second bursts and are repeated five to ten times per minute. They disappear at the end of this stage. The animal's EEG shows a rapid cortical, diencephalic, and mesencephalic activity (20–30 cps) of low voltage, similar to that of the waking state. The hippocampus has a slow (5 cps) and regular activity, whereas at the level of the nucleus reticularis pontis caudalis there appears a rhythmic 8 cps activity of high voltage with spindles. These stages of paradoxical sleep average ten to fifteen minutes in length and are particularly invariable in the same animal. They take up about 30 to 40 percent of its total behavioral sleep. In man, this stage of sleep has a low voltage EEG, whose frequency is close to alpha and sometimes slightly more rapid, interrupted by polyrhythmic theta elements and by triangular Rolandic waves. We have verified the principal characteristics of this description in sleep-dream studies of mental patients. Jouvet calls this type of paradoxical sleep "rhombencephalic sleep."[30]

3. EXPERIMENTAL CEREBRAL TRANSECTIONS OR LESIONS AND THE PROBLEM OF THE LOCALIZATION OF WAKING AND SLEEPING

The idea that the cortex itself regulates waking and sleeping has lost much ground, but periodically regains some of it. This can be explained by the ambiguity of the concepts which are used. (If the cortex is the "seat" of higher activity, it is the "center" of wakefulness. Since the cortex is capable of inhibition, it would also be a center of sleep, etc.) Over and above all these discussions, there is one fact which remains constant and which has been known since Goltz's decerebration experiments: the decerebrate or, more exactly, the decorticate animal continues to pass from waking to sleeping; on the behavioral level it can awaken or fall asleep. Of course its waking is less differentiated from sleep than in the case of the intact animal; but the animal can be observed not to be always asleep. Thus, if an animal which has been deprived of its cortex can either wake or sleep, the mechanism which regulates this behavioral change can, by supposition, only be subcortical. The experimental confirmation of this hypothesis came as a result of a fundamental fact established by Bremer's famous transection, called the *"cerveau isolé"* (1935). On an anesthetized cat, Bremer[31] showed that transection at the level of the union of the mesencephalon and the pons, leaving the telencephalon and its blood supply in place, produces a state of sleep (the electrical activity of the cortex being similar to that of a cat in barbiturate sleep). On the other hand, transections below the medulla oblongata *("encéphale isolé") allow the possibility of wakefulness; this state of more or less attentive wakefulness is interrupted by periods of somnolence or of more or less profound real sleep.*

We thus arrive at a second important fact which relates to this problem. Since the brainstem's connections with the cortex must be intact in order that the animal might come out of the sleep state, the question arises as to whether or not Bremer is right in holding that sensory deafferentation, that is, the interruption of extero- or interoceptive messages produced by this section, is responsible for the lack of wakefulness. As we have seen above, electroneurophysiological experiments (Magoun, Moruzzi, etc.) have shown that the mesencephalic reticular formation has an autochthonous dynamogenic influence on cortical arousal. It has effectively been demonstrated that the convergence of specific messages maintains, partially, only the activity of this reticular formation, which has the ability of autonomous activation. Pretrigeminal transections and gasserectomies (Rossi, Roger, etc.) have shown that if sensory afferents play a role in the phasic tone of the reticular formation, they are not required for it to be able to exercise its activating influence. This shows that the reticular formation of the brainstem can be considered to be an "ascending activating system" and, on the whole, verifies Ranson and Ingram's view that what exists is not a subcortical center of sleep but instead is a subcortical center of waking.

But this has not brought an end to the debates to which we have alluded. In effect, "next to," or more exactly "above" (thalamic intralaminar substance) or "below" (pontine or caudal segment of the reticular formation), numerous pontine (pre- or retrotrigeminal) transections have shown that certain parts of the reticular formation have a power of inhibition and not of facilitation with respect to cortical arousal. The research of Dell, Hugelin, and Bonvallet (1954), Bremer and Terzuolo (1954), Hugelin and Bonvallet (1957), Batini and Zanchetti (1958–1959), and Cordeau and Mancia (1959) has shown that there is a segment which activates not waking (desynchronization) but cortical inhibition (synchronization). Bremer has thus conceded (1960) that there could exist a hypnogenic center (as Hess had claimed) whose action is the reverse of that of Magoun's ascending reticular activating system. The same basic opposition between "center" of sleep and "center" of waking arises at the level of the brainstem, as occurred in Hess and Ranson's experiments of excitation and destruction at the level of the hypothalamus.

It is most interesting to note that the mechanisms which regulate the homeostasis of waking and sleeping necessarily involve a double oppositional power of activation or of inhibition of waking. Waking itself involves processes of cortical differentiation which in their turn imply reciprocal modulations of the processes of facilitation or inhibition of the various functions which they integrate. This homeostatic regulation essentially depends upon mesodiencephalic structures. These structures are, moreover, certainly in relation with the rhinencephalic formations, whose "schizophysiology" with the isocortex is well known (Gloor, etc.) and whose influence incontestably extends over the rhythm of waking and sleeping (Green, Arduini, 1954; Cadilhac, Passouant, etc.) by means of the limbic midbrain circuit (Nauta, 1958).

If "waking" is not a simple and uniform state, and if the field of consciousness which it constitutes involves an "architectonic," the same is true for sleep. This is one of the most interesting facts to come to light in the neurophysiological research which we have been considering. The dynamic stratification of unconsciousness during sleep thus no longer appears only in the heterogeneity of the lived experiences of the sleeping person. It has become objective. We have already pointed out that for Kleitman and his school (Aserinzky, Dement, Wolpert, etc.) there is a period of "light sleep" which comes after "deep sleep" and which is characterized by eye movements, apparently corresponding to the visual imagery of dreaming, since 85 percent of the subjects awakened at that moment declared that they were in the process of dreaming.

This stage[32] was termed by Jouvet "paradoxical," for though the EEG shows fast rhythms, there is a lack of muscle tone and sensory stimuli encounter an extraordinarily high reaction threshold. Jouvet later called this stage of sleep the "stage of rhombencephalic sleep." His research on this subject has been most interesting. Here is a short summary[33] of his work:

1) Two types of sleep can be observed in the *intact animal:* a stage of slow EEG activity ("slow sleep") and a stage of rapid EEG activity (paradoxical sleep).
2) In the *decorticate animal* there are no slow waves or spindles at the level of the subcortical formations; spikes

appear in the rhinencephalon. On the other hand, the stages of paradoxical sleep exist along with rapid activity in the hippocampus. High voltage spindles appear at the level of the nucleus reticularis pontis caudalis.

3) In *lateral lesions of the brainstem,* the two stages of electrical and behavioral sleep are identical to those of the intact animal. In *ventral lesions of the brainstem and the septum,* there is no activation (rhinencephalic or cortical arousal) during the stages of paradoxical sleep, and "slow sleep" is normal. In *lesions of the mesencephalic tegmentum,* there is an absence of cortical activation during paradoxical sleep. It thus seems that the nervous pathways which are responsible for cortical activation during paradoxical sleep are distinct from the ascending reticular activating system, because cortical arousal can be electively suppressed during waking as can cortical activation during paradoxical sleep: these pathways make use of the ventral part of the mesencephalon, the subthalamic region and the septum.

4) In *high sections of the brainstem* (chronic mesencephalic animals, corresponding to the *"cerveau isolé"* preparation), there are slow rhythms in the anterior portion of this section (auditory or nociceptive stimuli do not bring about cortical arousal). In the posterior portion of the section, by way of contrast, there is a periodic rapid activity in the mesencephalon, with a total disappearance of all muscular activity.

5) In *lower sections of the brainstem* (pontine animals), total section at the level of the mesodiencephalon suppresses slow waves definitively, but allows the periodic apparition of stages of paradoxical sleep with absence of muscle tone. (Eye movements disappear, however, after this prepontine section.) It thus appears to be established that the structures responsible for these stages of paradoxical sleep are situated below the mesencephalon.

6) *Sections of the brainstem below the pontine protuberance* (retropontine animal) produce a rapid, low voltage electrocorticogram, as in the mediopontine preparation performed by Batini, Moruzzi (1959). During sleep, EEG readings are similar to the slow stage in intact animals. Below the section, there exists a state of wakefulness with continuous muscular activity. The structures re-

sponsible for the stages of paradoxical sleep are therefore situated above a retropontine section and below a
prepontine section.

Following these experiments, and to confirm them, Jouvet
showed that the destruction of the nucleus reticularis pontis
caudalis[34] brings about the disappearance of EEG and peripheral phenomena in the stage of paradoxical sleep, while the
phases of slow sleep remain normal.

Jouvet concludes: 1) that the stages which were first called
"eye movement" stages (Kleitman), then "paradoxical phases"
(Jouvet) are phases of rhombencephalic sleep (PRS) which disappear after a lesion of the rhombencephalon; and 2) that this
"rapid sleep" is opposed to the essentially cortical "slow sleep,"
since the latter disappears after decortication.

Slow sleep demands that the neocortex be intact, according
to Jouvet. The subcortical slow waves and spindles observed
during physiological sleep, barbiturate anesthesia, hyperpnea
or anoxia depend upon the neocortex, and the frontal cortex
appears to play a predominant role. This slow sleep is accompanied by spikes in the hippocampus which appear to manifest
a paleocorticifugal inhibitory activity. For Jouvet, this slow
sleep transforms cortical synchronizations into an inhibitory
mechanism in the Pavlovian sense (rhythmic stimulations). It
is worth noting that in the decorticate animal sensory or reticular stimulation of the thalamus does not cause the animal to
fall asleep. Only stimulation of the hippocampus can bring this
about, as if the limbic system relayed the decaying cortical
activity.

Jouvet considers rhombencephalic sleep to be a primitive
sleep *(archéo-sommeil)*, a sleep which would be "closed off"
from the organism, and different from neocortical sleep in that
it does not interact with the organism's system of vital relations. In this Jouvet opposes the views of Kleitman, Dement,
etc. Since this type of sleep is a periodic stage of hypnagogic
unfolding, it would be "deeper" than slow sleep. Being especially refractory to auditory or reticular stimuli and characterized by a drop in muscle tone, this sleep can be defined by the
activity of the nucleus reticularis pontis caudalis (having a
rhythm identical to that of the hippocampus; in the cat it has
irregular spindles of 8 cps which are related to eye and whisker
movements). The nucleus reticularis pontis caudalis thus ap-

pears to be related to the limbic system in a manner analogous to the way the tegmentum is related to the cortex.

We are now in a position to examine the whole problem of the "localization" of sleep. Just as we say that "we abandon ourselves to sleep" or that "sleep overtakes us," there are two ways of entering into this disorganization which occurs in the superstructures of the waking brain. One of these is "conditioned" by the cortical system of vital relations; the other by the profound rhinencephalic or rhombencephalic demands of dreaming.

This duality is present not only in the manners of falling asleep, but also in the types of experiences which take place during the destructuration of the field of consciousness. At times, in the early and essentially negative periods of sleep, the sleeping person enters into a restful "nirvana." At other times the sleeping person is transformed into a dreamer, that is, within the destructuration of the field of his consciousness he lives the experience of the imaginary in that form of dreaming which we all know and which we have described above.

Everything takes place as if sleeping and waking were not simple states, but involved an unfolding of events which was regulated by the processes of organization, disorganization, and reorganization of the brain. When the individual stops organizing his field of consciousness in its verticality and the facultativity of the movements which allow him to adapt to reality, he then vacillates in sleep. In sleep he can abandon himself to the annihilation of a world, where a dream, as an instantaneous flux, appears only to disappear; or he can again set himself up as an "analogue" of the world. It thus seems that the brain itself "overturns" its own organization: sometimes by raising itself to the highest possibility of its organization which is open to the world because of the wakeful constitution of its field of existence and the activation of its *cortical* functions; sometimes by closing itself off to reality and abandoning itself to the depths of the imagination by giving in to the archetypal processes of its subjectivity in the *rhombencephalic-limbic* vegetating of its imaginary experiences outside the order of "worldly" time and space. Everything takes place as if the apparatus which regulates this vacillating process is truly localized in the centrencephalic system but depends upon the cortex, as if one of these two types of cerebral organization was higher and cortical, without, however, excluding the basal formations which condition it, and the other was inferior and subcortical, without excluding the cortex, which is subordinated during sleeping and dreaming to the forms of the archaic organizations of an essentially regressive system of vital relations which goes to the point of cutting itself off from the world of reality.

4. PATHOLOGICAL PAROXYSMAL DISORGANIZATIONS OF THE BRAIN (EPILEPSY)

As William G. Lennox notes in his work *Epilepsy and Related Disorders,* "the most extraordinary characteristic of the central nervous system is the relative rarity of epileptic seizures in a nervous system which possesses all the potential conditions necessary for its irruption" (Gastaut). If it is true that any brain will react to certain conditions (electric shocks) by an epileptic seizure, only certain brains will enter a partial or generalized epileptic state under certain pathological conditions.

Whereas the mass of cerebral neurons pulsate partially and in succession, massive "synchronization" forms the essence of the epileptic state. This state is expressed by two fundamental phenomena: convulsions and loss of consciousness.

Clinical work[35] distinguishes the following: 1) partial epilepsy of Jacksonian type (hemifacial convulsions, convulsions of a limb or of a segment of a limb); 2) *grand mal,* or major epileptic attacks which are ictal, or generalized, from the onset, and *petit mal,* which is characterized by a sudden loss of consciousness; 3) more or less complete or generalized forms of epilepsy which stop at a stage of psychical dissolution, or gradually propagated epilepsy. As concerns the pathology of the field of consciousness, these last forms are the most interesting, because of the twilight states, auras, and attacks of psychomotor automatisms which occur in them.

These states involve a bioelectrical discharge which is massive (recruiting) and repeated (afterdischarge phenomena), involving a large number of neurons. There is an electrical "conflagration," which, by way of synaptic or ephaptic pathways, spreads to the proximate, then the remote medial structures. This conflagration may be localized in certain functional centers, or it may fulminate the whole brain, setting off all these superstructures and reducing them to a spray of rhythmic movements and to an anarchical disorganization of the field of consciousness. During crises of *generalized epilepsy*— that cerebral hurricane and the paroxysmal hypersynchrony which characterizes it—in the electrical patterns recorded on the EEG (or on the electrocorticogram, or in certain experimental or exceptional conditions by microelectrodes implanted in the various cerebral structures), there occur discharges of rapid diffuse spikes during the tonic phase, followed by slower and slower polyspikes and polyspikes and waves during the clonic phase and ending in a phase of extinction through exhaustion. In *petit mal* there is a pattern of synchronous, bilateral spikes and waves at 3 cps which begin and end abruptly. Seizures with localized partial discharges are characterized by an uninterrupted succession of very rapid spikes which progressively augment in amplitude and which are localized at first at the level of the focus. In seizures with diffuse partial discharges (Gastaut), there occurs a propagation of the process of hypersynchronization, the progressive invasion of more or less distant structures through the effect of bombardment of the discharges which spread over these neurons, which are more excitable the more closely they are "allied" to the epileptogenic focus.

Naturally these clinically and electrically diverse varieties of epilepsy have raised some important questions concerning the seat of epileptogenic foci (or the mechanisms which initiate the epileptic explosion). For many years epileptic seizures were reduced to a phenomenon of cortical excitation. This is because, after the experiments of Fritsch and Hitzig (1870) and of Ferrier (1876), the excitability of sensorimotor centers (which was brought to light by means of electrical and chemical [strychnine] stimulation) appeared to be the only mechanism of epileptic discharges. The same is true of epileptic seizures due to irritative lesions in the cerebral cortex. These cases are exceptional forms of Jacksonian type partial epilepsy.

However, a major neurophysiological evolution has fundamentally modified the cerebral physiopathology of epilepsy. This development is based on the importance of centrencephalic formations in the pathology of epilepsy. Penfield, in 1938, was the first to advocate this position, basing his view on his own research and that of Jasper, Drooglever-Fortuyn, Hunter and Jasper, Gastaut, etc. Penfield distinguishes four

major types of epilepsy which are related to the centrencephalic system: petit mal, myoclonic epilepsy, ictal grand mal,
and the psychomotor seizures with automatism and mental
confusion of "temporal lobe epilepsy."

According to Penfield's fundamental thesis, these forms of
epilepsy are bilateral at their onset and bring about an immediate loss of consciousness. They must therefore be related to a
medial formation which is responsible for this modification of
consciousness. The hemispheric cerebral cortex does not correspond to this double condition. In the light of the research done
by Dempsey and Morison and by Moruzzi and Magoun, the
mesodiencephalon appears to play this central role. The study
of temporal lobe epilepsy, in Jackson's work as in recent research on the hippocampus and the amygdala, shows a strong
connection between the profound and archaic structures of the
temporal lobe and the centrencephalic system (Penfield, 1957).

Petit mal is dependent upon the "centrencephalic system."
Its spike-and-wave complex forms its electrical characteristic.
It appears to be determined by an alteration in the thalamocortical diffuse projection system described by Dempsey and Morison. In 1944, Jasper and Drooglever-Fortuyn could thus
provoke, in cats, patterns similar to those of petit mal (recruiting, augmenting phenomena, etc.). For Penfield and his school,
the spike-and-wave complex is not an autochthonous cortical
phenomenon, since the cortical cells (single cell recording) are
passive during petit mal and do not undergo postictal exhaustion, and sectioning of the corpus callosum (Hensch, 1945) does
not modify the bilaterality of clinical and electrical phenomena. Though it appears to be indisputable that the intra-
thalamic reticular formation plays some part in petit mal,
numerous objections (school of Gibbs, 1952; Ingvar's work in
Penfield's laboratory, 1955) have nevertheless been raised
against the hypothesis of the thalamic origin of spikes and
waves.[36] In spite of Williams's (1953) objections, it seems that
we must admit the cortical mechanism of these spikes and
waves, even though the cortical origin of this bioelectrical complex may not be recognized. Whatever their EEG patterns
might be, even if they should sometimes be asymmetrical (Ingvar, Terzian, etc.) and should be initiated by cortical foci, it is
nevertheless true that the reticular formation (perhaps even
that of the brainstem) is one of the systems responsible for
these absences.

The role of the centrencephalic system in attacks of *grand mal* which are generalized from the onset has given rise to a debate and to criticisms analogous to those we have just examined. For Jasper, Gastaut, etc., this form of seizure (essential or idiopathic epilepsy) has its origin in the same structures as petit mal. Its electrical discharges are bilateral, synchronous, and symmetrical. Tonic-clonic convulsions are observed in the diencephalic and even in the rhombencephalic animal (Gastaut). Gastaut holds that the spark which ignites the epileptic conflagration occurs on the level of the subcortical formations.

Since 1935, discussions and research on the physiopathology of epilepsy have especially focused around temporal lobe, or rhinencephalic, epilepsy. For a very long time (Bouchet and Cazauvieilh, 1825; Lallemand, 1834; Hughlings Jackson, 1876; Sommer, 1880) the attention of neurophysiologists was directed toward the epileptogenic role of structures deep within the temporal lobe (Ammon's horn, uncus). In the last few years, two types of facts have been the subject of more thorough study: 1) the relation of epilepsy to the foci and stimuli of the rhinencephalon; and 2) the relations of epilepsy to sleep and dreaming.

1) The *temporal* localization of an epileptogenic focus (temporal lobe epilepsy) encounters a whole series of problems. A focus of the temporal pole does not always have the same significance; a deep-seated focus can project its electrical patterns to the surface, while it remains difficult to distinguish a focus on the lateral convexity from a rhinencephalic focus. There is also a tendency to confuse temporal lobe epilepsy with localized or partial epilepsy; there are clinical generalized seizures with a focal EEG, and clinical localized seizures with a generalized EEG (Michelle B. Dell). Be that as it may, clinical study frequently shows foci which are temporal and focal; it is during these electroencephalographic modes that confusional states and twilight states occur, with or without automatism and vegetative symptoms (Penfield and Jasper). Though generalized seizures or seizures which are generalized at the outset do occur, it is "abortive" or incomplete seizures which are the most typical (equivalents, auras, absences). The deep temporal (rhinencephalic) origin of certain foci with midtemporal projection has been brought to light by J. R. Hughes and R. E. Schlagenhauf (1961).

It seems to be well established that stimuli from the amygdala provoke a remarkable facility for afterdischarge (only the hippocampus and the motor cortex have a lower epileptogenic threshold). Electrical stimulation (40–100 cps) induces a biphasic discharge whose amplitude augments regularly. The propagation of these discharges takes place in the ipsilateral insulotemporal cortex of the basal part of the anterior brain, in the basal nuclei, especially those of the hypothalamus, and in the mesencephalic tegmentum. It then occurs in the area of the hippocampus and the reticular formation of the brainstem (Gloor, 1954; Walker, 1954; A. Roger, 1954; Naquet, 1953; Morin, 1955; J. Cadilhac, 1955).

The electrical stimulation (or stimulation by stereotaxic injection of aluminum cream) of the hippocampus (Liberson and Cadilhac, Aridy and Akert, 1953) induces analogously propagated afterdischarges.

These experiments performed upon animals, and even certain observations of human subjects (Chapman, Henry, Gros, Sawa, etc.), have thus demonstrated the role of these amygdalohippocampal structures in temporal lobe and especially in psychomotor epilepsy.

The famous dreamy state, the uncinate seizure (which has been thoroughly studied by Audisio, 1959), with its illusions, its ecmnesia, its paramnesia, its rushes of dreams, its anxiety and nightmare-filled atmosphere (Wilson, Don Macrae, Williams, etc.), is generally related to this pathology of the rhinencephalon or the deep regions of the temporal lobe. Some writers, however, notably Hecaen, consider it to be the effect of more specifically temporal lesions, as in Penfield's electrical stimulation of the lateral temporal convexity.

2) The relations between epilepsy and sleep and dreaming here find their strictly rhinencephalic point of convergence (cf. R. Vizoli and C. Morocritti, 1956). All that we have said above concerning the rhinencephalon and the neurophysiology of sleep and dreaming, and all that we have written concerning epilepsy[37] and, in this work, concerning the destructuration of the field of consciousness, all this agrees very exactly with the conceptions of the Montreal school and of the Marseille school. It is generally accepted that these forms of epilepsy are facilitated by sleep (on this subject, Gibbs prefers to speak of "passivation" rather than of activation), that the forms of "sleep epilepsy" (Delmas-Marsalet) have very intimate relations (Levington, Gibbs and Gibbs, Levin, etc.) with the stages

of sleep (hypnagogic states, awakening), and especially that they are perceived in everyday life as imaginary experiences which are engulfed in the destructuration of the field of consciousness. There is no need for us to insist upon this leitmotif of our research. It is enough to point out that these facts have given it irrefutable experimental and clinical confirmation. Epilepsy makes it exceptionally clear that the state of unconsciousness is no more a simple and homogeneous state than is wakefulness or sleep. Unconsciousness admits of a series of levels of loss of structure, which epilepsy brings to light at the same time that it shows us what role the centrencephalic system plays in the structuring of the field of consciousness, whose organization is eroded by its process.

5. THE DYNAMIC ORGANIZATION OF THE BRAIN: CORTEX, CENTRENCEPHALIC SYSTEM, AND THE FIELD OF CONSCIOUSNESS

It is impossible to consider the brain either as a mosaic of isolated functions (the functionalist fallacy, which arises from "objective" observations on an analytic model of experimental isolation) or as a total functioning of a whole excluding any parts (the holistic fallacy, which arises from the intuition of the sense of its situational activity). In the functionalist perspective, consciousness is reduced to a juxtaposition of functions which are traced upon certain anatomical subsystems: the brain is a cluster of isolated and localizable sensorimotor centers which reciprocally activate or inhibit one another. In the holistic perspective, consciousness is the product of an overall activity of a higher functioning: since the brain is the integrative organ of the system of vital relations, it is, both it and the whole body (Hughlings Jackson), the "concomitant" of consciousness. In both cases, consciousness is both everywhere and nowhere at all.

Of course, both of these notions of the brain's structure reflect something of its reality. In fact, contemporary neurobiology leads us precisely to this double necessity. It is no more possible to consider the brain to be a homogeneous structure than to believe that each of its parts is a localized center and that its anterior segments control the others. If this idea of "center" remains valid for certain specific "sensorimotor" functional structures or for certain symbolic coordinating systems (language, *praxis,* etc.), in the area which concerns us the idea of a center of consciousness is untenable. However, this is not to say that the organization of the brain does not enter into the organization of consciousness and specifically into the organization of the field of present lived experience.

In order better to understand this complementary isomorphism (to use Ruyer's expression) of the brain and of thought in the constitution of the field of consciousness, we ought to replace the notion of spatial centers with that of functional patterning. This will allow us to see more clearly how the multiplicity of hierarchical structures of the field of consciousness corresponds to these organizational patterns of the waking or sleeping brain.

To lay hold of this correspondence, we must give up the idea that "consciousness" is a nothing or is a simple function. And, at the end point of the structural analysis of the field of consciousness, we must replace the notion of wakefulness by the image of a hierarchical organization of *present lived experience.* Thus, at this junction of the phenomenology of the field of consciousness and the functional architectonic of the organization of the brain, perhaps we will be able to gain a clearer insight into the problem of their fundamental connection. This seems to be the only means of escaping from the contradictions[38] which are implied in the spatial conception of superimposed centers and in the "simplistic" conception of a "simple" function of wakefulness. It is the only means of understanding the functional hierarchy of both the brain and the organization of the field of consciousness in a real perspective which is more that of the *temporality* of their structure than the spatiality of their localization.

1. PATTERNING AND THE LEVELS OF CEREBRAL ACTIVITY

Whether in its phylogenetic development, in its ontogenetic maturation, or in its real dynamism, the brain is an organization which has a direction, a structural architectonic moving from the minimum to the maximum of its output. As the organ of the system of vital relations (and in conformity with its function), it can reduce or augment its hold upon reality or its ability to adapt to it. The minimum or maximum degree of the patterning of its activity doubtlessly coincides summarily with the inferior or superior levels of the nervous system, in conformity with classical neurophysiological conceptions (Goltz,

Munk, Sherrington, etc.). But the agreement of these views is only relative. After all that recent neurophysiology has brought to light, we can no longer speak of a higher "cortical" level and a lower subcortical level in too absolute a sense, since the activity of the cortex, like that of the centrencephalic formations, is constantly interwoven into reciprocal "homeostatic" reverberatory or regulatory circuits. The different subsystems of the nervous system can never function alone. When experimentation or pathology identify artificial isolated units, only rarely does the interpretation of this type of fact remain conjectural. It is, then, from a less strictly spatial and more dynamic perspective that we should consider the different levels of this patterning of the brain's activity. By placing ourselves in this point of view, we are able to attempt a summary of our most certain knowledge of the brain's activity as it unfolds in the stages of its organization, from its lowest level to its strongest patterning.

There can be no doubt that what corresponds to wakefulness, to neurophysiological cortical arousal, that is, the highest degree of wakeful activity, demands a brainwave pattern characterized by rapid, low voltage waves, indices of "desynchronization" and of "reactivity," and spatial differentiation of its rhythms. The processes of attention and reflection, the ideoverbal constructions of abstract thinking, utilize the "stochastic arrangement" constituted by the neuronal hemispheric mass, which retains and elaborates information. If it were true that consciousness could be defined only by the highest level of mental activity, then it would have its "seat" in the cortex. Its seat would be in the cortex, but also outside the cortex; for the thoughts, actions, and conjectures worked out at this indefinitely open level are rooted in the sphere of mechanisms and motives which are necessary for their achievement. But this is a case in which consciousness's maximal facultativity would be superimposed on the very conditions of its power of choice.

A less elevated degree of organization is what electroencephalography calls "the resting state," a sort of psychical tone characterized by alpha and probably by even slower waves which enter into the composition of the "waking and mature pattern" of rest which is so characteristic of the organization of the human brain. The state of "being disponible" forms the fundamental arrangement of the waking brain in a well-constituted field of consciousness. The equilibrium of this level of

wakefulness seems to demand for its inception and its maintenance bringing into play the functional centrencephalic activating and modulatory circuits which make up the
infrastructure of the field of consciousness.

The destructuration of the field (its manner of being organized at a lower level) proceeds through the stages described by
Loomis or by Kleitman. Corresponding to this process of synchronization is the lack of differentiation and of freedom in the
configurations of consciousness which is characteristic of the
process of falling asleep. Cerebral activity drifts off center or
depolarizes from the cortical structures toward the subcortical
structures. But the cortex is no more absolutely excluded from
this organizational mode than the centrencephalic system had
been from the higher levels. Though it does not exclude all
cortical components, the activity of the centrencephalic system
is closed up inside the world of images and instincts. The
"schizophysiology" which sets up a dialectical opposition between the cortex's activity of differentiating various processes
of adapting to the external world of perceived reality and the
activity of the centrencephalic system, subjects it only to the
demands of the inner world. We then have sleep and its patterns (spindles, slow waves, etc.).

At the very heart of the brain's organization at a lower level,
a new phasic reorganization takes place: the "paradoxical
sleep" which corresponds to Kleitman's "light sleep" or to Jouvet's rhombencephalic sleep. This sleep has neither spindles
nor slow waves. Its threshold of waking, however, is much
higher, and there is blocking of gamma motor efferents (muscle tone) which is accompanied by eye movements and very
probably by dream activity. It is as if sensorimotor relations
with the world were hermetically sealed off, in this new cerebral organization. It is as if the hypnosis by images, which
characterizes the experience of dreaming, was both the guardian and the prisoner of sleep.

These varieties of cerebral patterning correspond to different levels, to a functional hierarchy. Waking activity has its
place here: at the summit. And the activity of dreaming has its
place at the base.

From the anatomical-physiological point of view, the "centering" of cerebral activity obeys the same structural hierarchy. The cortex is indispensable at the operational level of
reflective consciousness. But the dynamic structuring of the

"centrencephalon"[39] is indispensable to the formation of consciousness as a field of presence. It is a dynamogenic condition of the "waking" brain, a necessary but not sufficient condition of reflexive thought. These two levels cannot be confused, since the newborn child and the decerebrate animal cannot rise to this higher level, though they remain capable of waking and sleeping, that is, of a phasic conscious activity.

On the other hand, in Bremer's transection *("cerveau isolé"),* only sleep appears to be possible because of the cutting of relations between the centrencephalic system and the cortex. This fact stands out above all others. It shows not only that the subcortical functions are necessary for the dynamogenesis of cortical arousal, but also that a lesion—here experimental—seriously upsets the reversibility and functional changes of the patterning of cerebral activity. As we have already emphasized, the neuropsychopathology of epilepsy bears this out.

The levels of generalized cerebral activity which we have just described are, in effect, all *reversible.* All of them; for sleep is reversible, given a sufficient stimulus, and even waking is transformed into sleep imperceptibly, when the monotony or propriety of existence so inclines it. But when some functional accident is introduced into the organization of the brain, and especially when introduced into the centrencephalic formations (which hold a central position in the regulation of these varieties of patterning), not only are the higher levels of activity impaired, but, most importantly, the "facultativity" of dynamic modes of organization becomes impossible.

2. THE ACTUALITY OF LIVED EXPERIENCE: THE FIELD OF
CONSCIOUSNESS AND THE BRAIN'S ORGANIZATION

If conceptions of localization tend to hypnotize those doing research into anatomical-morphological problems and hide from them what they are looking for, this is because these researchers consider the brain almost exclusively as an object in objective space. Man is thus reduced to being only a machine which is more or less complex depending upon how, from the medulla to the cortex, one thinks of the superposition of these nerve centers. When viewed thus, in the form of a pyramid of integrative centers, consciousness will exist either at the summit or nowhere at all. But the brain is before all else an organism which winds and unwinds its own time. In contrast to the heart, which is a metronome of mathematical time, whose movement is not a free temporality, the brain is the organ of its own temporality. Upon this relativity of lived time is suspended the space which it creates for itself as presentation and representation. The "field" structure of lived actuality corresponds to this exigency. In other words, insofar as the brain is the nexus of the relation of the subject to its world, it constructs the world as the object which the subject has in view. This world may be a bare outline for the lower animals or the newborn child. Perhaps only a most rudimentary environment, which in the most extreme case would be reduced to the transparency of an "epiphenomenon," is interposed between the stimuli and the organism's responses (conscious awareness is as superfluous an hypothesis in this case as it would be in the case of a machine). But this is no longer the situation for man, whose humanity resides precisely in the faculty of bestowing his own time upon himself, and, along with this, his own space, in which his thought and the world of objects which make up his existence confront one another and are "juxtaposed."

All that we have to say on the subject of the phenomenology of conscious being brings to light its structural heterogeneity, a heterogeneity directly corresponding to that of the brain. To the extent that conscious being is the manner in which the subject exists for his world, that is, the manner in which the subject constructs his world, it is impossible not to recognize that conscious being implies the possibility of stopping in the face of the actuality of one's experience, to organize it in its structural dimensions by means of the order of the cerebral patterning which is necessary to it at each of its levels.

But besides this possibility of *having a present experience* (or organizing the field of consciousness, of maintaining it at a certain level—which can rise to the level of reflection and its facultative operations), another possibility is just as obvious, that of *being someone,* for the synchronistic structure of conscious being necessitates its diachronistic or transactual structure. From this time on, the relations between the organization of conscious being and the organization of the brain can be interpreted and understood only given a triple condition. First, conscious being presupposes an organizational basis for lived experience (invested in the centrencephalic system). Second, in its facultative or reflective operations, conscious being demands a differentiation or, as Freud put it, a connection of psychical processes, which can occur only in the operational and combinative structures (those of the cerebral cortex). Third, insofar as it is a system which integrates the person, his history, and his values, self-conscious being implies a memory which must be conceived not as a simple storehouse of images, but as an organized collection of information which is stockpiled with a view to the programming of means to be directed towards ends. This means of organization can be atopographical. In any case, it is relative to that aspect of the nervous system which represents the genetic apparatus for the *production* of the psychical being as an individual. This genetic apparatus is analogous to the chromosomal apparatus which controls the *reproduction* of the individual as a member of the species. We shall now attempt to sketch the theory of the relations of the brain and consciousness which is implied in this fundamental model.

A sleeping person suppresses his world and gives himself up to the instantaneous kaleidoscopic effect of his fleeting images. When he is asleep he gives himself up to the pure subjective temporality of an intentionality which sets off, in the night of his consciousness, an explosion of chaotic flashes which are doomed to instantaneousness, to oblivion. Sometimes, however, in certain stages of his sleep, he imagines an "analogue" of reality and, on the theme of his desires, creates a scene: he dreams. Shut up in the ipseity of a closed experience, he abandons himself to the flux of a temporality which is in harmony with his instincts. The coalescence of its manifest contents and its latent contents is so intimate that it leaves only the thickness of a symbol between them. This state of unconsciousness is not a purely negative unconsciousness. It is an archaic and lower form of consciousness which is characterized by an almost pure subjectivity in its lived experience. The first and most naive idea that comes to mind is to make the lower portions of the centrencephalic system or even of the rhombencephalon the seat of this dreaming, unreal, imaginary, symbolic, and instinctual activity. But it is incorrect to believe that the sleep-dream state (however inferior it may be to waking) can be localized in this inferior portion of the central nervous system. This sleep-dream state certainly does admit a multiplicity of structural levels and of organization, notably that of dreaming (corresponding perhaps to paradoxical sleep or to rapid eye movements, according to Kleitman, Dement, Jouvet, etc.). It is thus absolutely illusory, or at least never verified, to hold that this state can be tied to some particular cerebral space or center, whether in the cortex, the diencephalon, the mesencephalon, or the rhinencephalon. The lived experience of dreaming during sleep is the reverse of the real and, as E. C. Crosby pointed out, is the reverse of emotional expression. It unfolds in a closed and imaginary space, "outside the law" and in a sort of gratification or pure emotion. This experience appears to necessitate the activation of a type of cerebration which is centered in the old brain (the rhinencephalon). It does not demand a differentiated cortical functioning, though it does not totally shut out that possibility. The notion of a schizophysiology between the allocortex and the isocortex is to be retained as a possible interpretation of this cerebral decentering towards its rhinencephalic pole. In this type of cerebral organization, outside of "worldly" time and space, how can dreaming arise in stages? To what original structures does it correspond? We are now perhaps only beginning to see what the situation really is. The structure of the brain is not displayed either in its space nor in its temporality at this subliminal level of consciousness, which does not manage to be structured as a field (or only barely does so, in flashes). It is not displayed in this lower and unstructured form of consciousness (or of unconsciousness), which is characterized by a flux, a "concreteness" of "immediate givens" with no "axiological relief" and which remains subject to the movements of an enveloped time rather than being coordinated with an enveloping time (Ruyer). Instead, its structure closes up upon itself and becomes immobilized as a closed system. It is deprived of its functions of actualization, that is, of its triple faculty of *presenting* to itself an enclosed content, of *representing* itself in lived space, and of controlling the *present,* all of which functional levels organize consciousness as a structured field of present actuality or actualization, as a field of wakefulness.

Upon waking, a person opens up to his world. The suddenness of awakening makes it appear that the flicking of some switch in the brain is enough to bring about a change from a patterning of darkness and shadows to that of daylight. This may well appear to be the case for the adult, when changing the patterning of his cerebral activity. But the gradations of this patterning, the perplexity involved when waking is not immediate, the psychopathological conditions of the destructuration of consciousness, or the genetic study of the organization of consciousness (from zooconsciousness and the newborn child's first drafts of experience to the awaking of the adult human brain), prove that this awaking calls for the unfolding of a functional architectonic, which, though not apparent, is nonetheless involved in the elliptical brevity of this mutation.

The passage from sleeping to waking involves, structurally and successively, opening to the world (the bilaterality of experience), the arrangement of lived space (the ordered confrontation of the subjective and the objective), and the integration of affective impressions (the direction of the present). These are the three fundamental levels passed through by consciousness as it raises itself vertically. After what we have already said on this subject, there is no need to come back to a phenomenological consideration of these processes which are constitutive of the field of consciousness.

It will be enough for us to emphasize that the first of these levels is not the only one. Consciousness arises in opposition to the world of objects, in the problematic situation of man before his world, and in the external perception of objects, that is, their objective order as subject to the laws of chronological time and mathematical-geometrical space. But this intentionality is only the first way in which the field of consciousness is organized. It is the level reached when the sleeping awareness of oneiric-confusional, confusional, or Korsakovian states is surpassed, that is, when the subject becomes capable of *orienting himself* in his world. We can consider that *mesencephalic-diencephalic structures* are responsible for this first step in the formation of the field of consciousness as it opens to the world of perception; but we can do so only on the condition that cortical arousal corresponds and responds to their activation. For cortical arousal is the infrastructure of any actualization of lived experience insofar as it is open to the world or is attention to life, a confrontation with an objective spatiotemporal order.

To become conscious is not merely to recognize the world and to find or rediscover one's place in it. It is also to "awaken to the consciousness of" or, more precisely, to have the present experience of the "model" which arises and is organized as the environment of intramundane and intersubjective relationships. This world which has appeared is lived by the subject only in the experience which binds him to his body and in the proprietorship which he himself establishes over his thought by raising the problematic of an inner space. Consciousness thus develops only by passing through the exigency of this fundamental discrimination, within any experience, between what belongs to the subject and what to objective reality. In constituting itself and in constituting its world, thought is the prisoner of the duality which it introduces into being. (This is the spectacular dimension of the field of consciousness.) We have already seen that the ability to bring about this *incorporation of experience* into the lived space of the representation could be attributed to the *thalamodiencephalic centers.* Of course they could not do this by themselves, confined within their space or their morphology. This ability depends upon the vast sensitive-somatic-sensory integration which they make possible; and it depends upon the reverberatory circuits which unite them to the cortex and to the rhinencephalon.

This vertical development of consciousness must still rise to yet another level: that of a control which establishes the *order of a temporality* which is in proportion to the present reality and is no longer merely stirred or set in motion by the promptings of its "untimely" impulses. The *formations of the hypothalamus and the rhinencephalon* appear to play a decisive role in this integration of lived time with the ethical temporal structures of the action in progress, which is both desired and restrained. Their role is tied up with that of memory at that moment when the actualization of behavior calls for both the integration of the past and the integration of variations of mood into the present activity. During sleep and dreaming, the drives and emotions, deprived of their means for expressing themselves, pass into images and, as a result of a "rhinencephalic-cortical" schizophysiology, are no longer integrated into the system of reality. The formation of the field of consciousness is accomplished only when this instinctual motivating force is integrated into the stationary equilibrium of a moderated present.

The structural levels of integration thus appear to correspond to the stages through which the vertical movement of the organization of lived experience must pass in order to be formed into a field of consciousness, without, of course, being transferred onto the layers of the centrencephalic system. These intuitions are still too vague to be set forth as scientific knowledge. But it seems most probable that when the functional circuits and mechanisms of the centrencephalic system are better known, this system will certainly be understood in the sense of this dynamic architectonic, playing the role assigned to it by Penfield, Magoun, Moruzzi, etc.

There is not merely a "nonspecific" dynamogenic stimulus which issues from the formations of the centrencephalic system and is transmitted to the cortex to activate it. It is instead a basal and architectonic organization of lived experience which arises at the level of the centrencephalic system as the infrastructure of the field of consciousness.

Once the field of consciousness has arisen, it becomes a field which deepens and becomes more complex in proportion as facultative operations add a discursive structure to this fundamental field structure. Abstract thought, therefore, is formed with all the combinatory resources of the isocortex. But though abstract thought may be the superior and genuine form of constitutive consciousness, it does not constitute its "ground." This ground must already be constituted in order that the dialectical exercises of abstract thought might take place.

But it is precisely through and in these exercises that the Self takes shape—to the extent that it emerges, as we shall see, by itself giving form to the organization of experience. This self, the "oneself" of self-consciousness, superimposes upon the transitory moments of lived experience the axiomatic constant of its own relational system. This relational system both survives this self and glides over the moments of lived experience. The self, which we shall now study as the transcendence of conscious being, constitutes itself through its own historical memory. Though it may depend upon lived experience and consequently "at a second order" upon the the organization of the brain, it tears itself free of these determinations. Perhaps, as we can say of the *cerebral cortex,* it creates its own world of will and representation. This, then, is the perspective from which we must approach any consideration of the relations between "matter" and "memory," no longer viewed in the sense of the dualistic parallelism of Bergson's early writings, but in the sense of "creative evolution." For the brain as seen by an anthropological neurology (Goldstein, W. Riese, Weizsäcker, etc.) is neither an object nor merely a living organism. It is the generator and director of spiritual life. It is the creative organ of the "humanizing" metamorphosis of which Teilhard de Chardin speaks in *The Phenomenon of Man.*[40]

The isomorphism of the brain and of consciousness cannot

be simply and systematically denied. The structure of consciousness as a field of the present actuality of lived experience is embodied in the organization of the brain. Through its own reflection, the field of consciousness at each moment constructs a complement of the experience which rises in the subject's own history only to redescend into a subsequent actualization. Such, in effect, is the circular and reverberatory structure of the relations of the self to experience and, in the last analysis, of consciousness and the brain. Such is the complementary structure of the relations between the brain and consciousness: they are not transferred one upon the other. They engender their reciprocal structures through the process which animates them.

This functional architectonic of conscious being is precisely what is disorganized in mental illnesses. The phenomenon of sleep-dreaming gives us a model of this disorganization of conscious being. By referring to this model, many philosophers (Kant, Schopenhauer) and many psychiatrists since the time of Moreau de Tours and Hughlings Jackson have considered madness, and especially all forms of delirium, as analogous to, if not identical to, dreaming. We ourself have examined this problem numerous times.[41] The "primordial fact" of all forms of delirium is the disorganization of conscious being, the negative structure of all forms of being delirious or of hallucinating. Though it may appear to be only "secondary" to the workings of the delirium which overshadows it in chronic psychoses, this "primordial fact" flares up with perfect clarity in all acute psychoses. These latter thus approximate the phenomenon of sleep-dreaming (as is borne out by the expressions "twilight state," "dreamy state," etc., which are used to describe them). The psychical disorders involved in epilepsy provide us with an essential model of this. Of all these acute psychoses characterized by the destructuration of the field of consciousness, the oneiric-confusional inferior levels are naturally the most analogous (and even, as Moreau de Tours says, identical) to the phenomenon of sleep-dreaming. We can, therefore, easily understand that if the notion of "consciousness" be restricted so as to make it coincide with the notion of "wakefulness," and if the notion of "disorders of consciousness" be restricted to that of an "unconsciousness" which is analogous to sleep, then only the level of acute psychosis would appear to constitute the pathology of consciousness in the strict sense and arise from lesions of a cerebral apparatus which would regulate waking and sleeping. But if, on the contrary, the structures of the field of consciousness be broadened to its natural and complex dimensions, and if the structures of self-conscious being be added, the necessary outcome is a theory of general relativity for the relations between the phenomenon of sleep-dreaming (that is, of unconsciousness in all senses of the word) and the whole field of mental illness.[42] All of mental pathology is thus necessarily enveloped by cerebral pathology. But this is true in degrees and under structural forms which, while they all completely upset the relations between the conscious and the unconscious, could still not be reduced once and for all to the state of unconsciousness of a sleeping person who dreams.

Such an *organic-dynamic* conception of psychiatry and of delirium allows us to arrange research on this subject in the direction of the studies of the neurophysiology of sleep and of dreaming which we have just examined. Our work with Lairy, Goldsteinas, Barros, Guennoc, etc., allows us, perhaps, to begin to see that the various modes of sleeping and of dreaming are *formally* disturbed not only in acute psychoses but also in chronic delirium, schizophrenia, and probably also in neuroses. It is for this reason that we hold that there is perhaps less risk in accepting this general theory of psychiatry in the sense of a "cerebral mythology" of conscious being and its disorganization, than in accepting the hypothesis of an "anencephalous" pathology of the Unconscious.

PART THREE

The Self or
Self-conscious Being

The Self or
Self-conscious Being

By considering consciousness as the fundamental structure of psychical being, as the organization of experience into a *field* of actuality, we have discovered it to be constitutive of lived experience. Its relations with the "subject" can be explained only in relation to the very structure of the subject of its experience, that is, to the transcendence of the ego. In other words, instead of saying that Consciousness = Self, which suppresses the problem of the organization of being, which organization is precisely that of the junction of the transactual structure of the self with the actualization of experience, we must now ask ourselves who is the self that is the subject of experience, and into what relationships does this self enter with the field of experience? More generally, *who* is the conscious being that is not merged with his field of consciousness? The self grounds itself as the ego, the "self" which constructs itself in the individuality of its own being, precisely to the degree that the subject transcends his own experience, grasps it as that which he lives, passes through its successive moments, leaves its field to glide over it or enters into it to elaborate it, and emerges from the necessity of lived experience to constitute itself into a person who is conscious of his world and free from his destiny.

We shall examine later (pp. 229–231) the difficulties involved in the concept of the ego. But before we discuss what concrete and real conclusions can be drawn from the teachings of psychopathology concerning this self which, when all is said and done, should be accepted by all as unquestionable evidence for the Cogito, we must examine the significance of a being's reality, insofar as that being is a consciousness and a person, making special reference to Sartre's 1936 work on the transcendence of the ego.

The thesis which Sartre then defended is that consciousness and the ego are not equivalent. (We have already remarked that this noncoincidence was the ground for the *articulated* structure of conscious being.) As constituted into a transcendental field, consciousness is, he says, "pre-personal"; it does not imply the presence of an "I"; it does not entail a formal egological structure; it is an impersonal spontaneity. The Ego is constituted, so to say, out of a surplus. No doubt it is a product of consciousness; but consciousness constitutes it only as a false representation of itself, as if it became hypnotized by this ego, which is nevertheless neither formally nor materially *in* consciousness, for it is outside in the world: it is a being in the world like the ego of another.

We shall later (pp. 265–266) see how, in *Being and Nothingness,* Sartre came back to this negativity of the ego which is the function of its transcendence. For the moment we must emphasize that Sartre's 1936 position partakes of one of the erroneous conceptions which either (1) identifies consciousness and the self in a single affirmation or a single negation, either of which would be equally naive (this is not Sartre's position), or (2) which makes consciousness and the self so distinct that the abyss of a radical dualism is reintroduced between them. Sartre's first position concerning the transcendence of the ego seems to us to incur this last criticism. We can make this criticism of his position the more freely since for us, also, consciousness and the self are structures which are different from conscious being. However, consciousness and the self are complementary; both are always present at each level and in each step of conscious being's activity. Nonetheless, the self *becomes* transcendental (which is, we agree, a mode of not *being* transcendental in an absolute manner) only through its own development, or through its becoming, which is, as we shall constantly repeat, its being. Its reality is not derived merely from the experience from which it extricates itself. It arises in the very process of its construction. This is not an abstraction or a verbal formula. It is the living dynamic of human individualization through which each of us is someone who is incorporated *into* his body and *into* his field of experience but is also capable of freeing himself from it by means of the movement which projects him *toward* his existence. For the ego does not come from without; it is directed outwards.

This *mode of conscious being* which makes each one of us assume the originality of his existence thus appears both to be joined to the fundamental structure of the field of consciousness and to go beyond this structure. To the extent that the development of the person has already been implied in our preceding descriptions, both the form and the formation of the subject ought now to be examined in the light of what is permanent and systematic in its personal values. At this point, a new manner of being conscious appears, which is no longer simply the consciousness of what I have lived through. We now discover the consciousness of what I am and ought to be.

Insofar as it is radical, we have grasped the *emergence* of the self from experience as the corporeal and organic center of sensing. The subject is the first person to whom are referred the order of the field of consciousness and the constitution of its experience. For this reason, "zooconsciousness" also implies a sensing subject which is not only affected but, because of its own vital requirements, is already engaged in the experience which it inhabits and which inhabits it.

The *transcendence* of the self, which is correlative to the increasing complexity of being (the human phenomenon *par excellence,* according to Teilhard de Chardin), can already be seen coming into being and taking shape in *reflexion* and in the *specular* and *spectacular* structure of lived experience. The self is at the center of the consciousness which is constituted at the end of its *verticality;* it is this self which then exercises its power of choice through its free movements so as to project itself into the *superstructures of the field of constituting consciousness* as an operating subject, as a creator of thought and of action, as the "orator" of its discourse.

In this way, to the extent that it constitutes its own system of values, the organization of the self runs its roots down to the reality of sensing, into the essence ("Platonic," "Cartesian," or "Husserlian") of being; but it fully reveals itself only in the reflexion of the person who is capable of sending not only his roots but his attention down into the constitution of his most irrevocable experiences.

Thus it is not so much a question of the foundations of its experience and knowledge as of what it is in this "conscious being" which constitutes the *historicity* of its person. For "consciousness" in its generality is such that it naturally implies the organization, by the subject, of lived experience in the event which is presently occurring (field of consciousness or consciousness in the strictest sense), as well as the unfolding of the subject as the historical place of the events and values which, by objectifying him, constitute his existence.

This "eccentricity" or these "superstructures" of conscious being are the object of the most radical denial by the "Structuralists," who attempt to place its proper milieu outside the subject *(des armes Ding ... this poor thing ... cette pauvre chose),* to the point of putting it into the absolute impersonalness of a purely geometric or linguistic archeology. Psychopathology is the only thing which can oppose this "murder of the subject." By revealing the sick (insane) self to us, this science guarantees to the self of men in general the structures which permit everyone to be someone—this someone that the person who is subject to delusion can no longer be.

I From Alteration to "Alienation" of the Self

We have already described the modes of the field of consciousness. In order to remain true to our method of grasping "conscious being" through psychopathology, we must now[1] examine another side of mental illness: "madness."*

Around 1855 the problem of the relations of delusion (assimilated to dreaming) and madness was much discussed.[2] These relations are problematic, for madness, in its most authentic as well as its most tragic aspect, is strangely "lucid." The madman is unconscious of his madness; as we have just seen, this means that *his "unconsciousness" is not the same as that of the dreamer who has dropped off into sleep.* What, then, is this "pathology of consciousness" which no longer turns us toward (or at least does not turn us directly toward) the destructuration of the field of consciousness? What information can we derive from the "modalities of unconsciousness" which characterize the mentally unbalanced person, the neurotic, the paranoic, the schizophrenic, or those disturbed persons whose field of consciousness appears to be little or not at all altered? To what structure of conscious being are we referred by that condition of being "unconscious" which is not the lapsing into unconsciousness which we have just studied?[3]

*The French term *"folie"* refers to the mental illness *par excellence.* We translate it by "madness," which corresponds also to the French *"aliénation mentale"* in the broadest sense of the term. Since the French word *"aliénation"* refers also to the concept of alienation in the post-Hegelian sense, we have used "alienation" throughout this chapter, because of the importance Ey gives to the play upon the two senses of the term, in spite of the fact that English usage now limits the word almost exclusively to the latter sense. Cf. note on p. 221 below. —Trans., in collaboration with the author.

Even before we begin its description, we can now say, as we have emphasized in the preceding pages, that it is precisely because conscious being goes beyond the field of consciousness that it is possible to observe mental illnesses which alter conscious being without altering the basic structure of the field of consciousness. And if the conscious being which transcends the field of experience is the self, we can very well consider that the pathology which we are about to describe is precisely the *psychopathology of the self,* its modes of *alteration* and of *alienation.* Thus, the perspective from which we have set out can clarify what is confused and obscure in most psychopathological analyses as regards the distinction between disorders of personality and disturbances of consciousness, etc.: *alterations or alienations of the self are disorders of conscious being insofar as this is the transcendental mode of the person.*

In a work which appeared in 1953, G. E. Störring quite clearly demonstrated that the conscious being belonging to the person who reflects himself in his own order of thought and action is at least relatively separated in its pathology from that of events which are experienced in the field of destructured consciousness. Since the German word *Besinnung* implies knowledge, reflection, and self-control with relation to the self, Störring has been able to clarify a meaning of the word "consciousness" which in French could be designated only by *"escience,"* if we were about to bear in mind what we do, think, and will with full knowledge *("à bon escient").* In the eyes of Störring this important psychopathological fact grounds this distinction: it is possible to have disorders of the *Besinnung* without disorders of the *Bewusstsein;* on the other hand, all disorders of consciousness alter this manner of being self-conscious, the state of full *Besinnung* being that of a perfect self-mastery. The ontogenesis of this conscious awareness thus becomes merged with that of the "maturation" or "historicity" of the self *("Soi-même")* (cf. below, pp. 286–288). Throughout his work Störring holds this form of self-conscious being to be a sort of "function" which has been juxtaposed with consciousness. It is therefore only with great difficulty that he comes to see it as the transcendence of the self. But in the area of psychopathology, no one's views seem to us to coincide with the clinical data better than those of Störring (with the exception of certain confusions in his general framework).[4]

The psychopathology of the personality, which is so often

confused with the psychopathology of the field of consciousness, thus becomes detached from it and shows us certain
forms of mental illnesses which are characterized basically by
a *disorder of self-consciousness,* which is the same as the pathology of the self. What characterizes these disorders of the
self is a certain unconsciousness of the self, a certain manner
of the self's no longer being able to grasp itself. In the pathology
of the altered or alienated self, we encounter the different *ways
in which the self can be what it is not,* that is, its manners of
mixing and reversing the relationships of the self and the
other. In this way *self-consciousness* appears to open upon
the structure of conscious being, which is essentially defined
by *the dialectic of the foundational relationships of the identity, the unity, and the rationality of the subject formed into
a personality.* We shall see this more fully in the next chapter,
which examines the transcendental structure of conscious being as it is derived from psychopathology. But before summarily setting forth the characters of such a decomposition of the
self, we should begin by assigning its fundamental meaning to
this description; we propose to show how most mentally ill
persons are persons who have lost (or who have never been able
to possess) *proprietorship over their being,* which is the most
radical fashion of being neither "reasonable" nor "responsible." For though it is true that the "neurotics" and the "psychot-
ics" whom we shall discuss are "conscious," in the sense that
they are "awake," they are nonetheless disturbed in their self-
consciousness and for this reason are "unconscious" in the
sense that, though lucid, they are not masters of themselves
and no longer are "themselves."

When we described the psychopathology and neurobiology
of the field of consciousness, we first described sleep and
dreaming as the antithesis of well-structured consciousness.
Here we must ask what is the ultimate infrastructure of consciousness as revealed by the pathology of the self. The opposite
of *being someone,* insofar as this is the self-consciousness
which engenders this someone, is obviously *being nobody.*
Doubtlessly no living person is nobody, but is always a someone
to whom we owe the respect due to the human person; the
pathology of the self is never equivalent to a state of animality
which would allow us to treat the idiot or the deranged person
in anima vili. Keeping this in mind, the pathology of the person is what it is, a lack of organization, or a disorganization, in

the human being who has fallen from his personal status. The concept of pathology must not be tampered with to the point that we become unwilling to accept the degradation of human nature under the pretext that even the most fallen of men nonetheless remains a man. The truth is that he remains a man who is not completely someone.[5] "To be nobody" is that form of "limiting" existence in which the differentiation of the self has disappeared, and which we describe as the "demented self" (to which should be joined the "idiot self," unless we exclude the perspective of the impotence of the personality and speak only of its disorganization).

Before undertaking this study of the pathological self, we ought to "take cognizance" of this anomaly of self-consciousness which consists in the fact that the self no longer recognizes itself. How can we consider that the self has "fallen ill" or was born ill, when *it is not what it is,* especially when the phenomenological analyses, the most profound intuitions of anthropological ontology (whether Pascal or Kierkegaard, Heidegger or Sartre), and the most brilliant "structuralist" exegeses (Lacan, Foucault, etc.) show that it is the nature of man *not to be what he is,* that his *inauthenticity* (according to the existentialists), his *cultural and social status* (according to the social psychologists), and his *internal conflicts* (according to the psychoanalysts) are, as it were, the parameters of the precariousness, the relativity, the multiplicity, and the nullity of being? By denying autonomy to the self, or by qualifying it as being "half-way" abstract, we have, since Hegel and Marx, become accustomed to speaking of the "alienation"[6] of man in general as if to exclude his particular alienation. Psychiatry should become aware of this problem and respond to this exigency by referring to the clinical reality of a morbid condition of the human person. Clinical psychiatry's answer is that the alienation of the sick man is not merely the problematic of human consciousness in its generality or its community; on the contrary, it is the particular forms of the humanity of the neurotic or alienated Man which will reveal themselves to us as such, that is, the *deformations* or *malformations* or *"arrests in development,"* which are at the same time both similar to and different from the construction and the problematic of the human person in general. The reality of these forms of alteration and alienation of the self should guarantee the existence of the self to the extent that it will appear to us with precisely those attributes which its alienation eliminates.

1. THE "CHARACTEROPATHIC" SELF

It is generally accepted that our "character" and its "characteristics" constitute a totality of simple properties which are fortuitously distributed in the genotypical constitution of each person in such a way that character pathology can be only "statistical." Since "traits of character" have been isolated and defined in trait tables (some list two or three thousand "attributes" as factors of the human being, others reduce them to several elementary "properties"), each individual can be considered the object of a "factor analysis" which extricates the individuality of his character mosaic; when this is done, the notion of normal or abnormal is represented only by a Gaussian curve. This can even lead to a tendency to reduce both genius and madness to a mosaic of character traits, aptitudes, or dispositions. To do this suppresses the problem of creativity as well as that of mental illness by reducing them to chance. All "trait theories" of personality proceed from this fundamental error of asserting character to be an assemblage of primitive and simple properties.

Though psychopathic personalities (schizoid, manic-depressive, etc.) may be considered deformations or caricatures of character traits, a personality which is schizoid, for example, has not been formed originally from an "essential property" drawn in a genetic lottery. One's character is not totally given; it is also appropriated, or at least assumed. The constancy or the singularity of one's reactions, of his modes of willing, thinking, and feeling, all of which make it possible to identify him, one's "character," in short, rests upon certain corporeal and structural modalities of his form of being, of his "constitution." But this "constitutes" only one pole of his being, that of his determinism, against which (and not merely in conformity with which) his person arises. What we call a person's character is that circular form of being which returns to one's temperament, but which passes by way of his history in doing so. Character is an historical construction.

The clinical study of anomalies of character must not be approached through constitutional prejudices, but rather from

the point of view of the genetic hypothesis of character formation.[7] Anomalies of character structure are not given qualities;
they are the manners in which a person is bound up with his
character.

The judgment which we pass upon others or which others
pass upon us is a "simplification" which is valid only for the
pathological forms of character. When a person thinks of himself, or is thought of by others, as being a hard, or weak, or
greedy, or violent person, this one "dimension" of his personality does not express his total being. In the normal person, this
"character trait" is susceptible of a certain amount of variation
throughout his history or in his relationships with others and
with events; if it is relatively constant, this has happened only
after this trait has become a habit, a constant and systematic
mode of being, a "second nature" which cannot have been
merely constituted but must be and have been adopted. A character's "dynamism" is this relative but fundamental liberty
which opens upon the becoming, or the history, of the person.
It is a flexibility which is constrained by the psychopathology
of the self, to the extent that this is a pathology of character.

The pathological form of a character (characteropathy) begins only with its fixedness and its inevitability, that is, at the
point that it becomes impossible to dominate or modify it in
accordance with one's own history.

The characters of fixation, of fixedness, of constancy, of being a stereotype, are the symptoms of this pathology of a self
which has been reduced to being only a "himself" adhering to
a form which is more fixed than "primitive," which is relentlessly and mercilessly dedicated to its pre-self, to a segment of
its impossible history.

To *have* tendencies which are sadistic or masochistic, schizoid or syntonic, is the condition of each and every person. To
be sadistic or masochistic, to settle into and remain within the
masochistic or anal-sadistic modality of one's existence or
within the summary modality of introversion or extroversion,
is to condemn oneself to be only what one actually is, to be
unable to be what one is not, that is, to be no longer able to
become.[8]

Perversion provides us with a good example which allows
us better to grasp this malformation of the being which is arrested and enslaved to its archaic and primitive forms. To *be*
perverted is not merely to *have* perverted tastes, to *have* a

subversive or scandalous conduct; it is fundamentally and necessarily to *be* unconscious of the values of one's proper existence apart from this fatal "property" (or, what comes to the same thing, to be unable to constitute one's own history by oneself).

Perversity, cruelty, vice, the search for "forbidden pleasures" or "artificial paradises," the manipulation of nature in order to frustrate it, cynicism and faithlessness are found among all men, particularly among certain social groups and structures; even more particularly they are freely chosen by certain individuals. But pathological perversion must be confused neither with the share of perversity possessed by all men nor with its concentration in certain more sophisticated or corrupt men.[9] The structure of perverse being is not defined by maliciousness, subversion, and contrariness, which are aspired to or rejected by all men. The worst, most shameful, most criminal or underhanded actions do not define a pathologically perverse structure. To be "ill," it is not enough to be the most depraved person, the greatest criminal, or the most monstrous of homosexual thieves. Pathological perversion does not amount simply to a quantitative excess. It consists in being caught up in a *malformation* and not merely a *maleficence.* The "constitutional pervert" does not feel the need to rise to summits of scandal, vice, or crime; on the whole, his "acting-out" only rarely attains such excesses. His perversity is more radical and more strict. It is a "willing" of evil which is actually involuntary. Pathological perversion and malevolence lie in this paradox of a malformation which takes away one's liberty only to involve one in an obstinate predisposition towards evil. Pathological perversion is rooted in an anomaly of the structure of the will's movement and of the will's autonomy. It is both an irresistible impulsion and an imperative, in a sort of short circuit which binds guilt to self-punishment, and in which what I desire is a duty to do wrong, a formula which represents the vicious circle of behavior. The consciousness of this obligation, which is at the same time unconscious of its danger and its futility, makes up the very character of this form of perverse existence which is devoted to recidivism and prison, being a prisoner of itself. This perversion is not the effect of a will which chooses revolt and scandal in an existential project which is open upon the world and others, nor is it a simple property or an instinct; it is a law which is formed and closed up within a rudiment of existence and of person. Both the existence and the person of the pervert are truncated and reduced to the scantiness of a ready-made and incessantly repeated history—a seed of violence which explodes in a scene from a Punch and Judy show or in a murder mystery. When the psychiatrist says that this form of "psychopathic personality," since it is an "anomaly" of being, implies at least an attenuated responsibility, he is referring to that state of unconsciousness of one's project, of one's motives and of one's malformation, which is still called the irresistible urge of a "psychopathic" incoercibility. This latter does not merely elude the grasp of the self. It is its constitutional weakness. It is the force and the form which this weakness has taken. The pathologically perverted self is an egoistic self unable to be other than itself and unable to admit anything or anyone other than itself. It is a self which is isolated in its perversity or its perversion, a self which can relate itself only to a *partial* world and to a *part* of other persons or even to only a *portion of the other* in a relationship which excludes the totality of their being and carries out a massacre of the other and a self-mutilation. No matter how conscious the cynicism with which he flaunts himself, the pathological pervert is unconscious of the motivation which forms him.

Those who present themselves to others in this blind singularity, which is a kind of unconsciousness of the possibilities and impossibilities of their existence, are called unbalanced. Psychiatrists designate them as degenerates, persons with character neuroses or psychopathic personalities.

Mental unbalance is eccentricity in the sense that, rather than ordering one's life in relation to others and harmonizing oneself in a coherent unity in relation to oneself, the characteropathic personality develops in the hypertrophic sector of a character trait (the impulsive fanatic in violence, the anxious person in the state of insecurity or failure, the introvert in the refusal of reality, etc.); it develops without being able to construct a manner-of-being which can relate to all its possibilities. In these cases self-consciousness forms as a superficial image, the image of someone who should once and for all be only what he is. The unbalanced person is precisely that being who is only partially fashioned and who displaces his "center of gravity" towards an "eccentric" segment of his relations with others. He is a being whose originality must be understood not as a self which is "too strong" but as a badly formed personality.

The degenerative aspect of these character anomalies refers to the constellation of factors which unites them to a series of biological, morphological, or functional factors which are characteristic of their lack of maturity, of their affective backwardness, of the primitive quality of those characters which remain riveted to the specific mass of primary reactions.

The concept of a neurotic character (Reich) envisions the armature or the armor of a character which forms against itself. The eccentricity and immaturity of the personality are nothing but the regressive structure of a self which, even when it opposes itself to it, models itself upon a pre-self which is both an unconscious and a static core around which the person can only crystalize. All the mechanisms of "self-defense" can be described as bonds which, far from liberating it, chain the self to these impulsive fantasies which singularize its being in its robot-like infrastructure.

Clinical psychiatry (in which Kraepelin, Dupré and his school, Kurt Schneider, etc., converge) understands the term "psychopathic personality" to define the "constitutional anomalies" which can be less radically separated from mental illnesses to the extent that they are better "characterized," though, according to Schneider, they should not be considered as being clearly pathological. The problem of continuity and discontinuity, of quantitative and qualitative, which these anomalies present in the pathology of the personality, is the same problem as that which arises from the notion of personality. If a personality passes over the states of its constitution, it is evident that the pathology of its constitution should be able, at this level of character pathology, to situate itself between the "normal character," the character which is free in spite of its temperament and plastic in spite of its prejudices, and the "neurotic self," which constitutes a malformation or a regression to an inferior level of the organization of the self.

In other words, the very difficulties of the problem guarantee its cogency, that of the ordering of the composition or the decomposition of the system of the self.

We have taken this much time at this first or "superior" level of alteration of the self which is malformed in its character, since the possibility of speaking of a pathological mode of "character" which is at the summit and not at the base of the structure of the self gives its total meaning to the phenomenology of the characteropathic (or psychopathic) self, that is, of the self which has been altered in its character formation. This phenomenology envisions a self which has been truncated in its ethical constitution, in its structuring as autonomous and free. What this self lacks in order to have full self-mastery is the consciousness of its goals and of the projects of its existence; it lacks the transcendental possibility to propose these projects and ends as the ethico-historical values of its own person. It loses its liberty as much in its absolute prohibition as in its absolute permission, that is, when it is carried to the extreme of a choice which is radically impossible for it. An anomaly which makes the self a captive of its character thereby takes away its self-consciousness experienced as the motion and promotion of its own actions. The autonomy of its will has been lost.

2. THE NEUROTIC SELF

The characteropathic self thus lacks freedom, that transcendence which, by appropriating the self's being to its history, grounds the disposition of the self for itself. We shall now describe a distortion of the self which constitutes a more profound incapacity of self-consciousness. It is here a question of an alteration in the formative cycles of the personality which bears more precisely upon *the identity of the person*. At the highest level of the pathology of the self, the self knows itself as such, that is, as "that one" who is the only one to be within the form of his body, of his thought, and of his action; the personality which is morbidly fixated in its characteropathic structure is that of someone who has his own history and has one single history, even though this history may be frozen. The neurotic is a man with no unity, which condition gives rise, in the numerous attempts to define neurosis, to the notions of decomposition or of split personality, or, again, the notion of conflicting structure.

In order to pass more easily from the characteropathic self to the neurotic self, we shall use the example of the mythomaniac, the "inconsistent" person, the person who is given up to a kaleidoscopic multiplicity of roles or of histories. The study of the prisoner of one's own "unconscious lie" will permit us to penetrate into the structure of the neurotic self which is unconscious of its identity or is in search of its identification.

Mythomania offers a pathological structure of the self. The mythomaniac is not merely the author of a simple lie or even of an infinite number of lies. He not merely tells lies and makes up stories; he *is* himself a perpetual lie, a mystification of which he himself is unconscious. The brilliant description of Dupré and his school and the German analyses of pseudologia phantastica seem to have exhausted what can be said about the noncoercibility of the storytelling of these "unbalanced" boasters and liars who are "more or less" dupes of their own lies. The most penetrating analysis of the mythomaniac personality has been made by M. Nayraut.[10] The problem of man's authenticity, the overlapping of his transcendence and the immanence of his facticity, arises in the case of the mythomaniac. More exactly, this problem arises in his case precisely because it does not arise for him. Because he is posited as radically inauthentic, he is situated in a world in which there is no longer any problematic of the authenticity of the self for itself. Earlier we saw the perverted person as a being who has legalized and dogmatized, in his rank prejudice for evil (and thus for its existence), one of the terms of the possibility of the moral conflict which is required in order to exist. Just as the self-punishing, anxiety-ridden person, who is incapable of giving himself up to the fullness of the self, blames a "sub-ego" (which the psychoanalysts have so curiously called the "superego") for acquiescing to an absolutely and implacably moral consciousness, so now in the case of the mythomaniac we encounter a man who, dedicated to falsehood, cannot "tell a lie" because he has lied too much—like the Cretan who could acknowledge his lie only in lying.

The truth which is at stake in speaking is not in itself like an object which can be shown or hidden. It has a dimension in which its problematic is not that of error but of falsehood: this dimension is the sincerity through which the other is constituted as the object of my judgment or through which I constitute myself as the object of the judgment of another. But this offering always remains problematical and demands as much good faith from the person who receives it as it has excluded bad faith from the person who gives it. This happens in such a way that lying, sincerity, and truth have meaning only in relation to the subject's coherence or lack of coherence with himself. Whether one seeks the truth and speaks it or instead hides it, the consciousness of truth or of falsehood is this coalescence of the self with itself, which is the only thing which allows one to know his truth and which makes it responsible for the lie. The trajectory, which in a monologue unites a meaning to its author and in a dialogue unites the subject to the other, is that of an arrow which makes its way through the meaning of the discourse as the very intentionality of a sincere project. And this project, in and through the contingency of its own freedom, can exist or not; it can permit falsehood or not: this falsehood enters into the historical relationship of self with self, into its own relationships in bad faith with itself (in its own dupery), or into the historical relationship of the self with another (whom it deceives). The personality of the mythomaniac, his manner-of-being-in-the-world, exists in another manner-of-being-in-the-world, in an alteration of the self which consists precisely in being unable to establish bonds of authenticity with others or with oneself because this self lacks historicity. The mythomaniac, as Nayraut states, replaces his history with stories. This is similar to the condition of the compulsive swindler who, as M. Zeegers has shown,[11] does not experience his own self as a future possibility, for he involves himself with this self and with others only in the range of an infinite number of possibilities. The compulsive swindler's "consciousness," that is, his knowledge of himself, of others, and of their relationships, which are interlinked and projected into the space of their reciprocity, seems absolutely remote from those around him, always pushing others further and further away from him into a sort of unreality in which all obstacles vanish.

It is thus that the self-consciousness of the mythomaniac and that of the compulsive swindler, with their topsy-turvy anthropological structures, present themselves. In the case of these men, who can live only in a world of myth or can be aware of themselves only in the mirrors of a casino or of a "fun house" in which only the fantasies of the game are reflected, the fluid authenticity of their selves arises recklessly in their non-self-conscious being. The self then appears without definite outlines or character. The mythomaniac "character" consists in not having a character. It is unable to have or to recognize itself as having a definite set of features. Nor can it be aware of the traits of others except in an evanescent universe which is infinitely changeable and superficial, a universe which is simultaneously subtle, elating, and futile.

To the extent that it is the foundation of the inauthenticity of the neurotic, this mythomanic foundation forms the imaginary framework of the neurotic self. The neurotic self can arise only in the mirror-like and game-filled structure of an imaginary person.

As we have already said, the neurotic self is essentially a self without unity, a self from whom the problematic of unity has been excluded. In the construction of the personality, the dialect between the self and the other, the perpetual adjustment of what I am, of what I desire, or of what I ought to be, of what others believe me to be, of what I am only in the eyes of others, etc., this dialectic is doubtlessly a perpetual conflict between the unconscious motivations and the impulses of the self which constitute its being, between itself and the other, a conflict which unceasingly and relentlessly compromises its unity. But to the extent that the self chooses its character in conformity with what it is and what it ought to be, it extricates itself from this ambiguity by offering itself a being which is its ideal.

By way of contrast, the neurotic self admits to being both itself and another. It is to this duality, to the double register of this duplicity, that the artifice of its existence corresponds. The neurotic person thus presents himself, represents himself, and is represented as an inauthentic being who accepts wearing a mask which corresponds neither to himself in his own self-consciousness nor to the consciousness which others have of him. For this reason the neurotic's existence is dedicated to the absolute theatricality of a novel or of a scene from a tragicomedy. On the subject of hysteria, the most spectacular form of neurosis, Racamier has given a prominent place to the alteration of the hysterical person's affects and his compulsion to act while fooling himself.[12] More recently Green has examined the contemporary existential role of Oedipal stages of identification, whose "original text" is that of the drama of "being like the other" or of "possessing the other"; he has shown how this ambiguous role lends itself to this playacting which can be that of either the comedy or the tragedy of the actor, who at the same time becomes the play's author.[13] Any symptomology of neurotics, with their semblances, eccentricities, excesses, caricatural reactions, blackmailing, and, in sum, their insincerity, can be deduced from this overlapping position of the self face to face with itself. The complexity of neurotic conduct, the Machiavellianism and the strategy of their defenses, exhibit the labyrinth in which the self has become lost. But as a final paradox, the self loses itself therein only incompletely; without acquiescing in it, it devotes itself to the "paradox of the actor," whose many facets and reflections have been so well analyzed by Diderot. These facets send us within the self, into the space of a scene or a representation, of which the subject is both conscious and unconscious, so as to have to be or not to be what he appears.

Clinical studies have always given an important place to the "histories" of neurotics; but it is only since Freud that the significance of their symptoms has irrevocably appeared. These symptoms are, in effect, symbolic: on the conscious level, half fooled by the imaginary, the neurotic person manifests a need "to do as if," "to be as if," to borrow one's own self-image from someone *other* than oneself. This "other," who thus enters into a conflict with the self and its history, is the maker of another history, of a history which cannot enter into the historicity of the self, but which unceasingly obsesses, bewitches, and possesses it. This double, which is a *possession* that interferes with the proprietorship of the self, this double, which splits self-consciousness, is now seen to appear (as it appeared to Freud for the first time in his theory of neurosis) under the figure of another who speaks in the self. To be neurotic is to have a self-consciousness which is the captive of the other and of its false history without being able to be conscious of what one wants to say or cannot say. To be neurotic is to be unable to escape from this other, that is, from one's unconscious, without losing the awareness of this doubling, or even by being so absolutely conscious of it that it alone counts. In the last part of this work we shall examine the image which we can form of this unconscious "personage" that is, in the eyes of certain psychoanalysts, closer to being something than someone.

For the moment it must suffice to make note of that particular structure of the neurotic self which is reduced to nonbeing only in order to defend itself against the anxiety which chains it to its unconscious. From this structure arises the illusion that has appeared in psychoanalytic psychology, which, when dealing with the neurotic self, has succumbed to the temptation to consider the self in general only as an ensemble of defense mechanisms. This illusion must be dispelled. But here, in this phenomenology of the neurotic self, this weakened self (which is not "too strong," as has been said abusively) is truly reduced to this defensive (which is also an aggressive offensive) whose vicissitudes recount the mythology of its unconscious. It is their manner of being or of not-being which prescribes the symptomatic signification, that is, the neurotic existential meaning, to these manifestations of an unacceptable and insatiable desire. These images and complexes electively bear upon certain segments of the self's prehistory and well represent the vicissitudes of the libido's object choice, that is, the mechanisms of identification, especially of sexual identification, whose problematic remains indefinitely, in the case of the neurotic, with only a metaphorical solution.

The neurotic is aware of being inhabited by this other, who he is not, cannot be, or does not wish to be, and by whom he is possessed. But this fragmented state of consciousness can constitute itself only as a personage, be it false or falsified, who (like those "characters in search of an author" who are reduced to being only dramatic fragments) can neither live nor become. We thus see that the neurotic organizes his existence along the lines of the imaginary, as if nothing could occur in his history which did not cause his histories to appear in it, these stories being, as it were, the embryonic "organizers" of his destiny. Such is the preposterous, dramatic, and essentially tragicomic destiny of the neurotic person, who "symbolically" displaces his anxiety in his panic before an object, an action, or a situation (phobia or anxiety neurosis), or who dilutes and neutralizes his anxiety in a veritable strategy of prohibitions and magic rites (obsession and obsessional neurosis), or who utilizes all the powers of his psychosomatic expressivity in order to play for himself or for others the comedy of one who is bodily sick, which act takes the place of his sickness, the malformation of his being (conversion hysteria).

3. THE PSYCHOTIC SELF

In passing from the virtually divided neurotic self to the psychotic* self which involves its world in its division against

*This psychopathological form corresponds to the mental illness *par excellence* which Ey designates by the French word *"aliénation."* Cf. note on p. 207 above.—Trans.

itself, we witness a metamorphosis which is familiar to anyone involved in clinical work. The self becomes an other. This is the simplest way of expressing this most radical form of alienation. As we have already noted, since Hegel, and in all the renewed dialectics of *Entfremdung,* it has been repeated that the self is constituted only through its alienation. (We will take up this theme again when we outline the phenomenology of the self, turning our attention precisely to the necessity which the self feels to go beyond itself through its attraction for the other being.) But what moral philosophers and the existentialist anthropologists have repeated so often finds its most absolute justification in psychopathology and more exactly in madness.

This manner-of-no-longer-being-in-one's-world presents itself in the clinic in two modes: that of systematic delusion in which the self becomes an other, and that of schizophrenic delusion in which it is the other which becomes the self. It is not merely through a purely verbal dialectic that these two formulations of the alienated self correspond to these two fundamental forms of delusion; they refer to two aspects of the structural upheaval of the self which is the very basis of all the classifications and clinical analyses of chronic delusional psychoses.

The alienation which defines the most authentic aspect *(der echte Wahn)* of delusion is not a stage of the individual's history, but its end. Is not the most striking and tragic image of the madman that of the person who takes himself for another, not metaphorically or by approximation, mood, sympathy, refined introspection, or metaphysical cogitation, but rather "in complete simplicity" and "absolutely"? From the point of view of common sense, the absoluteness of this alienation finds its most vivid illustration in Épinal's supreme image of madness: he thinks himself Napoleon—he believes that he *is* Napoleon. At this point we enter that sphere of the constitution of the self, the modes of which can be described only in terms of belief, conviction, and judgment. We penetrate at this level into *Unreason* as the form of the "alienated self." The formula "I-am-someone-that-I-am-not" does not suffice to define this alienation, which insists upon the additional, and equally dogmatic, affirmation "I-am-not-mad": unreasonableness is excluded in the name of the reason which it usurps. "Madness is an illness which is not aware that it exists," "Madness is unconscious of itself" are aphorisms which are intended to express this change of place of the self and the other in the frightening lucidity of its denial. The radical inversion of this entirely reversed logic is expressed in statements such as "I am not mad," "I would have to be mad to believe it," "It isn't me who is mad, it's you," "It is everyone else who is mad." This reversal of the revolution of the being in the orbit of his world characterizes alienation. His movements no longer accord with the logic of the world; instead the world gravitates only around his desires, which have crystallized into absolute beliefs. As is the case for everyone else, these desires are no longer the object of a "problematic." They become absolute objects because the dogmaticism of alienation is the total absence of doubt and of mystery. Everything is clear in this mad self-consciousness which is not conscious of itself, that is, which is unconscious of its condition of being a man in his world with others and in accord with common reason.

Before attaining this "truth" which is so absolute, and of which megalomania is the supreme formulation, the alienated person submits just as dogmatically to another who fills his existence, occupies the center of his being, and dislodges his self *(moi-même)* from it. The theme of *persecution* is the objectification of this image of the other who dislodges the self from its place in the world. All the vicissitudes of the delusional novel which the subject relates to himself as the truest of stories are only explanations, beliefs, and convictions which are involved in a judgment which has been enough falsified to transform into truth what is actually the very contrary of true. Such a systematic psychosis develops and crystallizes in and through this Copernican revolution of the self's value system, through this metamorphosis which renders it conscious of being what it is not, what it must not be, and what it cannot be.

To the extent that the self keeps its coherence, it admits delusion only as a "system." In proclaiming this system, the self disguises its delusion under the appearances and the instruments of reason. The self makes this coherence defensible and plausible to itself and to others (with the exception of the validity of its postulates). The self becomes for itself an other whose existence is demonstrated. This paranoic delusion develops, if not like a theorem, at least like a symphony, in the order of the tragic clarity of a perfect but inverted consciousness of the relationships of the self to its world. In becoming an other through the simple and pure reflection of itself in the image of the other, the self retains its own constitution. The persecutor appears as the inverted image of the self.

As is true in the case of the schizophrenic person and of the world of schizophrenics, the disorganization of the personality can cause the self to regress to a phase or an infrastructure of its constitution where the self disappears insofar as it is a system of personal values and the author of its world, and its world disappears by becoming "autistic," or the contrary of a world. The other then substitutes itself for the self and leads the self into its labyrinth. As we shall see in the last chapter of this work, the unconscious becomes conscious, turns itself out, so as to annihilate the person and his world by drawing them into a personless world. Such is the schizophrenic catastrophy: the autistic metamorphosis of the self and its world. The "autistic" self is not a self which has withdrawn from the world, as many somewhat naively believe, "saving" the self from its alienation by basically denying that the self is alienated and attributing to it only a "simple" and reasonable intention to flee in the face of reality. The autistic self is not the subject in its power organizing its retreat. It is instead a mode of existence whose subjectivity is as totally impossible as is the objectivity of its world. The "manner of being" for-the-self autistically to its world is most fully expressed through the semantic distortion of its verbal system. This system loses its communicative value; it ceases to be a means and becomes an end in itself. In all the neologistic or schizophasic forms of his discourse, in his jumbling of words (especially as regards the pronouns used in conjugating verbs), the schizophrenic mixes up all the elements of a conversation. Language no longer says anything; it can be understood only poetically or as a game of mimicry (metaphors, metonymies, neologisms, etc.). It is in this labyrinth that the self's relations with others evaporate and that the consciousness of oneself which has become confused with the consciousness of others and of the objective world dissolves. In this way, schizophrenic thought becomes like dreaming: both find the most authentic language of psychosis in the language of the unconscious.

The autistic self falls within itself only when it loses the very form of its organic relations with its world. The schizophrenic process called dissociation, disintegration, or narcissistic regression of the personality is both an impotency and a need. The need to constitute once more a world of fantasies is creative of the imaginary pseudoworld, of the schizophrenic *Eigenwelt* which is subject to the magic of the fantastic and departs from the natural order and the logic of reality. The impotence, or the "negative structure" of this regression, is the disorganization into which the subject falls when he inverts his relationships with the other, when he ceases to be able to "contain" him (to have him within himself) because he is unable to "contain" him (to be his master).

We can thus follow the alienation of the self from its purity and lucidity (that of a delusional transcendence of the relationships of the self and its world) to the schizophrenic point at which it coincides with (without, however, entirely fusing with) the destructuration of the field of consciousness and the disordering of lived experience[14] which it implies (Bleuler, Berze, etc.).

In this manner the disorganization of the self touches its limit at the point at which reason collapses, that is, when it is no longer possible to integrate its world into a system of logical values and of reality. What separates the alienated self, even in its schizophrenic form, from the demented self is that the totality of its beliefs, determinations, behavior patterns, and feelings still forms a world in which the self is still able to be involved, though it may not actually be involved, as its own producer. As "weakened" as the schizophrenic may be (except, perhaps, in the terminal forms, in which his pseudodementia coincides with dementia praecox), he seems to continue to be what he still is: a man buzzing with the fantastic, but whose intelligence has not yet been radically and irreversibly altered.

4. THE DEMENTED SELF

The self's incapacity to bring about the logical integration of its behavior, that is, the fundamental disturbance of the intellectual structure of its being, defines dementia. Dementia is a pathological form of the self to the extent that the self has lost its power to judge. It is true that in sleep or in analogous states of the destructuration of consciousness (particularly at the level of oneirophrenia, Korsakoff's syndrome, or stupor) judgment is suspended; but this failure of operational actualization is not dementia. What disappears in these disorders of consciousness is the capacity to organize experience according to the intellectual values of the orientation and modalities of the conceptual formation of discursive thought or of dialectical construction. The clinical description of confusional states, in pointing out the more or less complete annihilation of the operational activity of the mind, forces the self to *disappear* or to *fade,* without causing it, in this pathological experience, to appear to itself any other than as a virtuality which renews itself when the unconscious or subconscious state ceases, when the self reawakens. This is not the case with the demented state, for in this state of disorganization of psychical being there is still an alert self, *but one whose wakefulness is itself essentially altered.* The demented person is often confused, but he is generally less "troubled" than the person in a confusional state, both in his "elementary functions" and even in the clinical and electroencephalographic contrasts between his waking and sleeping states. It is precisely in this that he reveals himself as "demented." To be demented is a state in which the self not only is disturbed in its efficiency (in the performance tests which measure mental deterioration and intellectual enfeeblement), but also is radically vitiated in its judgment. This leveling from the base of the system of values is characterized by a loss of self-criticism, a "foolish" indifference to logical and moral values, a lack of importance attached to one's acts, speech, and ideas. Because of this the demented person is profoundly alienated in his personality to the extent that, in its extreme state, there is for him neither world nor anyone; in any case, there is no problematic of existence. This demented void or wasteland draws upon the capital of intelligence or of reason. Any analysis of dementia necessarily leads us to an analysis of intelligence so long as intelligence not only represents a sum of functions or of discursive or logistic schemata, but implies Spearman's g-factor. This factor, insofar as it enters into the factor analyses of intelligence as saturating or transcending all tests, this factor, which animates intelligence with its insight, is nothing other than the self which is the subject and agent of the intelligibility of its world. No logistic can do without a logic; no reasoning, no intellectual schematism, no cybernetics of information can be conceived in the absence of an axiological system which constitutes the very law which gives a judgment its meaning. All intelligence presupposes a subject who not only possesses it but is it. It is this mode of being reasonable, this structure of assimilation (to use a term dear to Piaget, to whom we owe so much in the area of the genetic knowledge of the epistemology which comes into being at the same time as the subject who creates it), which establishes the ontology of reason as ontology of the rational being, that is, of the subject who knows himself in knowing his world. In other words, the construction of the personality comes about through building up a fund of values which constitute the assets of its intelligent being.[15]

Undoubtedly perceptions, automatic responses, memories, and habits remain in the demented person, but his *membra disjecta* do not become integrated into his self-critical consciousness of himself and of situations. The only persons and situations which exist for the demented person are vague reflections of what has existed. The demented person is no longer "historical." His history has stopped. Being incapable of that invention, creativity, and adaptability to new difficulties, which keep one alert by submitting him to a pressing necessity to be constantly resolving "problems," he remains on this side of those interrogations which are the motivating force of his own history. He has forfeited his capacities and his rights. He is "incompetent" in the legal sense of no longer being a person. That this decline is still reversible, that it is still "human," is certain, and certainly more so than the older clinical psychiatrists had thought. But the existential analysis of the demented person can only record his "nonexistence," that loss of a "for itself" which reduces him to the level of a "quasi animality" and in some cases even to the appearance of vegetable life.

This deterioration of the self to the phases or infrastructures of its "nonexistence" can naturally be recovered in the perspective of those impotencies of the personality which constitute states of backwardness or of feeblemindedness. Progressing from the rudimentary or teratological personality of the idiot, from the backwardness of the feebleminded person, to psychoinfantilism and the state of congenital imbalance of the personality, the spectral analysis of the continuum of this disorganization or malformation brings us back to the self, whose levels of disorganization we have just outlined.

If we cast a last glance upon the architectonic accidents which constitute the pathology of the altered or alienated self, this pathology can easily be reduced to the lowest common denominator, which—to the degree that reason is the formative law of the person who constructs his history and his world in the transcendence of a system of individual values which are integral parts of his person as well as integrated into his thoughts in the world of his cultural coexistence—is none other than the loss of reason. For man can form his originality only by conforming to his rational being, that is, by continuing, while constructing his autonomy, to conform to the rules of humanity, from which, while constituting his history, his person cannot separate itself without falling again into a communal history and participating, from his individual place, in its construction. The person and his work in the world are inseparable within that *praxis* which causes the birth and the discovery of the self to be the very dialectic of theoretical and of practical reason through which a man forms himself.

The study of the progressive accidents and anomalies of this construction will permit us to describe (based on our clinical experience) the labor of formation of the self. That is to say, we shall describe that development which the personality goes through (and which is the very opposite of its arrested development) when it passes beyond the stage of the *subject of knowledge* who, in his logical thought, adjusts his being to the constitution of his world, and then arrives at the stage of the *subject who is the artisan of his world* and binds himself to others without depending upon them, while reserving to himself the faculty of his beliefs and of his feelings, in his *Weltanschauung;* next comes the stage of the *subject who becomes identified with his personage,* who is in accord with the motives of its organization (of its needs, instincts, and impulses) and with the imperatives of the roles which he must assume in his social milieu; finally comes the stage of the *subject who is the master of his character,* who is capable of keeping in equilibrium what he is, what he is going to be, what he wishes to be, and what he must be.

As was the case in the preceding chapters and with regard to the field of consciousness, the advance we have made in the study of psychopathology has been in understanding the order of the composition of the rational being, of the self-conscious self, by referring to the decomposition of the personality. This is not and cannot be either an abstraction or an a priori construction, for the clinical reality of its alienation guarantees its existence against all metaphysical or sociostructuralist sophisms.

II The Autoconstruction of the Self

The self is consciousness reflected upon itself and formed into a "system" of values which are peculiar to its own person. This reflection and this formation confer upon the self the existence of a *person* that is both similar to and different from others. These ground the self, for itself and for others, as the reality of that existent which is nominally designated by the pronoun and in the singular as *someone*. It is this "someone" who is the I (you, he, and she), whose dynamic *personality* structure we shall now describe.

When examining the definitions of the self's personality, of psychical individuality and of character, we shall once again encounter all the problems which we encountered at the beginning of this work when discussing the definition of consciousness. "Personologies" (like "antipersonologies") have great difficulty grasping the proper object of their affirmation (or of their negation), that is, the reality and autonomy of the *Ego*.

The negation of that which the natural attitude calls the self, the I, the person (the *Ego* in Latin, the *Ich* and the *Ichselbst* in German, the *Moi* and the *Moi-même* in French), consists in the affirmation that the self is an abstraction or an hypostatization (the product of a reification) or again a spiritual principle which rebels against any method of scientific observation. The autonomy of the self (its transcendence) appears to be as incompatible with any logical analysis of it (cf. above, p. 204) as with its empirical content, that is, as with the facticity—if not the inevitability—of its characteristics, of its character. The possibility of describing the self in terms of objective reactions, conditioned responses, memories, habits, or learning, and of considering it as the sum of its functions and its experiences, seems to exclude the possibility of considering the self in any fashion other than as a cluster of images or an aggregate of empirical data, its nature then being only a "simple" habit.

Behaviorism (in its "molecular" form à la Watson, and even in its "molar" form à la Tolman), because it reduces the totality of the mind and of the personality to manners of behaving, or reflexology, which reduces it to a collection of conditioned reflexes, constitutes the theoretical model which is the most strongly opposed to a phenomenology of the self.

Depth psychology, especially psychoanalytic theory, arrives at an analogous negation from the opposite direction, by embedding the dynamism and the formation of the self in the unconscious (the Freudian topography conceives of the ego as a fundamentally unconscious system when considered in its relations with the id and the superego). Neopositivistic structuralism, as we have pointed out, denies consciousness, the subject, and the self. It replaces them with "impersonal systems."

These negations occur on the very ground upon which they attack the affirmation of "common sense." They take note of the fact that the self does not appear as seen from outside (behaviorism) or as seen from within (psychoanalysis), but they do not perceive that the self is precisely that through which or through whom behavior or motivations are conscious or unconscious. In other words, the self can be grasped in its being only through a structural analysis of its organization which does not stop merely with affirming its reality, but goes on to explicate it. Only by attempting to discover the architectonic of the self, in studies such as the descriptions and conceptions of Mounier, Rothaker, Lersch, and Nicolaï Hartmann, can we hope to discover the self not merely as a "realized" abstraction or an "essential" reality, but as a concrete and original reality. In this way, the self need not be affirmed; instead, it asserts itself against all the empirical or speculative negations to which its very being gives rise.

These are but some of the difficulties which arise from the idea of a self which, if it is to be affirmed, must appear as free while at the same time it is "grasped" in its nature or in its relations with its world and with its unconscious. None of the philosophies which derive from Leibniz and Kant and which uphold the transcendence of the self insofar as it is a dynamic structure of individualization or an integrative autoconstruction can consider its autonomy to be a pure freedom; for the self is "condemned to be free" by its very incarnation. Having submerged the self in the determinism of the organic or social body, the empiricists (Locke, etc.) find themselves in a difficult position because of their own negation.

We shall now quickly scan several "personality theories" which illustrate these positions or these fundamental difficulties. The goal of this exposition is to show that a true "theory of the person" cannot reduce the self to those factors which determine it. We shall see that the transcendence of the self can be described only in its relationships with its immanence, for the self and its character are only "my freedom's mode of being," to use Ricoeur's expression.[1] They are the *nexus* which binds the will to its involuntary powers and motives. The positions of characterology or of personology will thus show us the necessity of going beyond these positions by means of the dialectic of the autoconstruction of the self as the intelligible subject of its existence. It constructs itself by *forming itself* in a strict process which is both in contradiction to and in conformity with itself. Because it implies the opposition between the *given* (heredity, temperament, biotypology) and the *taken* (the autoconstruction and original organization of the person) or, as the Anglo-Saxons put it, the antinomy *nature-nurture,* the self is a being whose problematic is that of promoting itself in and through the knowledge which it has of itself, in its self-consciousness. This is true to the extent that this self-knowledge is not purely speculative but is instead rooted in the *praxis* of existence, and to the extent that the self forms itself in opposition to itself. It exists in and through this very movement.

1. PERSONALITY THEORIES

We shall begin by stating the most basic positions on this subject.[2]

Certain of these theories are reductionist as regards the complexity of the self, reducing the personality to a sort of elementary homunculus, to a mosaic of characteristics, dispositions, idiosyncrasies, or cenesthetic sensations, or else making it the product of impressions. The general thesis of these personality theories is that everything in the personality is either given or received, that in essence the personality is merely a collection of properties or a reflection of its environment.

Other theories emphasize the evolutionary development and the organization of the self. Some are resolutely *generalist*, in that they focus upon the development of the personality, considering that "the person is his history"—a thesis which is correct and which holds good of the most profound aspect of the self's structure, but only on the condition that its development be opened to its transcendence and not be closed up within itself and be unconscious of its relationships. We shall give special attention to the Freudian theory of the self.

Certain theories of the self are designated as *dynamic* in the sense that they emphasize the overall structure of the process of individualization and of the functioning of the self. Their thesis is that the personality is the totality of the psychical being. The person thus risks losing its originality, or its "physiognomy," in the generality of the psychical organization.

Other theories, which we designate by the term "personalist," attempt to describe the human personality at the highest point of its humanity, in its existential and ethical unfolding. They describe the self as the Being of existence, which description is incontestable; but these theories tend to undermine any organization of this free movement of a being in its world.

A. "Elementarist" Theories: The Reduction of Personality to Basal Determinants

These theories consider the personality to be a mosaic which is "pre-fabricated," either by "nature" or by "nurture." It is "ready-made" and "static." It is included in what could be said to be a specific preformation, and can be reduced to such "characteristics" as temperament, character traits, biological functions, and body types, or, on the other hand, to cultural conditioning. Their concern is primarily to treat the personality as an "individuality" which resides within its physiognomy (as within its fingerprints) or within its constitution, whose elements are derived from the characteristics of the species or of the community.

1. THE REDUCTION OF PERSONALITY TO BIOTYPE AND TO TEMPERAMENT: BIOTYPOLOGIES

In this case there is a definite reification of the person which is reduced to its *morphology* or to its congenital *properties* (biotypology, temperament).

It will suffice for the moment to point out that all these biotypologies have their origin in the work of one psychiatrist, Ernst Kretschmer, to show to what point such a reduction corresponds to a pathological "caricature" of the distinguishing marks of the personality. Of course we are not saying that this methodical research into the correlations of temperament, body type, and character are without value or that "biotypological givens" do not enter into the makeup of the person in such a way as to furnish it with its own proper physiognomy and reactivity. We wish simply to state that this "vital" layer of the personality, to the very degree that it is "basal," does not come up to the dynamic and historical structure of the person, no matter what degree of absolute necessity demands that it be grounded upon this stratum. The biotypologies of Sheldon, of the Italian school (Giovanni, N. Pende, Viola), of the French school (Sigaud, Thorn, Mac Auliffe, Corman, Verdun), the celebrated study of the dimensions of the neurotic personality by Eysenck, and Pavlov's typology of the nervous temperament are all monuments of observation. Our basic criticism and the brevity of this reference do not intend to lessen the capital importance of the facts which these masters of biotypology have discovered or established.

2. THE REDUCTION OF PERSONALITY TO CHARACTER TRAITS: CHARACTEROLOGIES

Character traits[3] are innumerable. They have nonetheless been enumerated. Thus Allport and Odbert list 17,963 English nouns or adjectives which designate these *traits,* these particular manners of being. It must be remarked that in order to be "characteristic" of an individual "character," they must be combined in a "personal equation" which at the end of a factor analysis gives a "horoscope" about which we know neither the origins nor the end point. The analysis of "fate" (Szondi), no matter how interesting its prognostic value might be, and *projection tests* of personality, whether thematic (TAT) or structural (Rorschach), indicate only a fundamental orientation or configuration of one's character. This takes place in such a way that in all of these characterologies the infinity of traits or of character possibilities is reduced to a more or less arbitrary choice from among a minimal number of properties, which are, moreover, almost always the same.

The constitutionalist characterologies of Delmas and Boll, or those of the Groningen school (Heymans and Wiersma), are completely typical of this type of reduction of the personality and its essential properties. We must repeat that such a procedure is perfectly well grounded by the importance of the "characteristics" of the type upon which individualization is constructed; but it risks the danger of attributing the total originality of its fate to the being's preformation, to the chromosomal mosaic of its constitution.

Certain characterological systems, like that of Raymond Cattell, react against this simplicity and strive to achieve a factor analysis of character traits, which does regain the multiplicity of its "factors" but only at the price of losing the "pregnancy" of its "types."

3. THE REDUCTION OF PERSONALITY TO CENESTHESIA

This conception, which was developed in the age of Taine and Ribot, would not appear to be relevant here, having been criticized by so many writers—we take special note of the criticisms made by Pierre Janet. However, this "sensationist theory" of personalization is so often incorporated into theories of depersonalization and is once again a subject of such great interest to so many psychophysiologists that we feel obliged to make mention of it here, particularly in its modern form as the psychophysiology of the bodily schema (of somatognosis), as the foundation of the identity and of the identification of the self. We can simply state on this subject that, as Merleau-Ponty has so forcefully repeated, it is not a question of "disincarnating" the self by refusing to reduce the personality to its "feelings," to its sensations or to those interoceptive or proprioceptive inner perceptions which enter effectively into the constitution of the field of consciousness. It is simply a question of not being taken in by the oversimplifications of this reduction so that we do not confuse the self with its field of sensible experience.

4. THE REDUCTION OF PERSONALITY TO ITS SOCIOGENETIC OR CULTURAL BASIS

In this case the personality is not reduced to its intrinsic properties, but to impressions, to a sort of cultural *imprinting*. This class of theories reduces personality to being only the product of its culture or else the sum of one's habits.

Certain Anglo-Saxon schools of sociology, psychology, and psychoanalysis (M. Mead, Linton, Sullivan, etc.) rather facilely reduce *ego involvement* to its sociogenetic or ecological parameters. They consider the *ego* to be a simple phenomenon of acculturation, a cultural *pattern* which is supplied by its sociogenetic nurture. It is hardly necessary to recall here the "basic personality" of Kardiner and Linton, which was studied in great depth by Dufrène (1953).

The reduction of the person to an associative system, whether "stimulus-response" or conditioning by the environment, because of its empiricist, sensationist, and behaviorist foundation, is closely akin to this "socio-reduction." Learning theory, which admits that the learning of habits forms a second nature, reduces the personality to an accumulation of behavioral elements. Numerous theories inspired by a Watsonian molecular "behaviorism" have been developed which advance this line of thinking (Hull). They are generally interpreted on a psychoanalytic model (introjection, frustration) and call upon a mosaic of affective dispositions which "reinforce" or utilize conditioning (Dollard and Miller, Sears, Mowrer). The most resolutely "Gestaltist" or "molar" conceptions of the Anglo-Saxon writers, of which we shall speak later, often tend to ally themselves to this manner of conceiving the personality as an "aggregate" of experiences, an effect of the environment.

However, this "epigenesis" or this "exogenesis" of the personality, which considers personality to be a product only or fundamentally of the influence of the external environment, scarcely holds up after examination. Kurt Lewin, the celebrated social psychologist, has forcefully shown[4] from a "relativist" point of view (which refers explicitly to Einstein's system) that the person is a system which is organized on a *topological* model whose differentiation supposes a continuously reciprocal interaction of variables from the external world and from consciousness in an internal order ($B=f$(P.E.), where B=behavior, P=personality, and E=environment). In other words, we might say that the Milieu (the environment) is at the center *(au milieu)* of the self's organization. For Lewin, the person is an intrasystematic unity. Despite its dynamic concepts, despite its constant recourse to valences and vectors and even to unconscious mechanisms, his theory nonetheless is restricted by stimulus-response theory, by a classical conditioning viewpoint, even though it is more open or more complicated than that contained in the models of Hull, Dollard and Miller, etc.

B. Dynamic Theories of the Ontogenesis and Structure of the Personality

Unlike the preceding theories, these theories do not attempt to find the original and primitive "core" of individualization; instead they attempt to understand it as a *development* and as a progressive *structuring*.

1. GENETIC THEORIES

It is most difficult for an "egology" not to be genetic. The idea that one's personality is not given all at once and that it is structured only in the process of forming itself is as obvious to those who prefer the concepts of "Gestalt" or of "comprehensive structure" to that of the evolution of the organism as it is to those who claim, along with certain phenomenologists, that they restrict themselves to the pure psychical constitution. It is a constant metamorphosis and process of development; it always involves change, mutation, and becoming.

The genetic conceptions of personality recognize its *historical development* and its *maturation*. They concentrate essentially upon its internal organization, the general sense of which is an increasing degree of complexity and a greater freedom of the functional cycles and structures which progressively construct the personality.

Numerous conceptions of the evolution of personality tend to place at its base either primitive man (Lombroso and the naturalistic theories) or the "genius" of the species, the essence of mankind (Nietzsche, Bolk, Spengler, Klages, etc.); but they are all concerned with tracing the process by which it passes from this stage or from this substratum to the more personal forms of individualization.

There have been innumerable genetic theories. We shall first examine the important theory of Henri Wallon. Following this we shall discuss Piaget's theory of mental development, then the theories of Pierre Janet.

a) Henri Wallon

For Henri Wallon, the stages of development of the personality, understood in the sense of the "total physico-psychical being," presuppose "a changing of their total economy" among themselves. This metamorphosis of the being who not only grows but matures is carried out in *stages* (alternation of metabolic and anabolic reactions) and in *crises*.

The stage of *motor impulsiveness* (the level of conditioning) is characterized by the first exchanges between mother and child. In the *emotional stage,* the infant projects himself into his familiar surroundings and incorporates himself into them. This sketchy kind of relationship (syncretic sociability) leaves, as it were, "undivided" those acts which bind it together. Toward the end of his first year, the infant passes to the *sensorimotor stage,* which is characterized by modes of behavior which are directed toward orientation and investigation and which allow him to conquer space and the objective world. Play activity, characterized by the bipolarity of actions and of situations (differentiated syncretism), allows the "I" *("je")* to separate itself from the objects in the "game" *("jeu").* The *stage of personalization* is characterized by the development of the self. This self makes its appearance in and through language as well as through the exercise of seductions (grace period) which, along with his interests and his affective complexes, assert the existence of a person, the first formation of which occurs during the crisis of the three-year-old. Then his character and personality are developed across the changing situations of complementary actions and reactions which become integrated into his patterns of social behavior.

b) Jean Piaget
The genetic psychology and epistemology of Piaget do not center explicitly upon the notion of the personality. But whether he is studying the birth of intelligence, of language, or of thought, the construction of number or of reality in the child's mind, whether he is showing us how intellectual operations, logic, and logistic come to be organized into systems of understanding and knowledge, all these studies which have as their object man's conquest of his world necessarily send us back to the study of man's formation. If Piaget has specialized in the organization of noetic structures, it is in order to emphasize precisely which aspects of the human personality are essential: the architectonic of his rational being. We shall not attempt here to give a complete exposition of this monument of contemporary genetic psychology, but shall be content simply to refer to his theory of the organization of intellectual schemata and to his theory of the construction of the real, so that we might come to understand in what manner his theory of knowledge forms an ontology of the subject who is encoun-

tered in the knowing of his world, that is, how it is a genetic theory of personality.

The constitution of sensorimotor intelligence: The constitution of the operational schemata of adaptation which assimilate and elaborate primitive experiences (the birth of intelligence) can be understood only through a biological model. The fundamental categories (Höffding) of the process of organization which determine this order (totality, relations, ideal or values), and those categories which are tied to adaptation (assimilation and accommodation), are the formal invariables, the models or schemata which enter into the construction of the intelligent organism. From the very first Piaget includes the development of intelligence into his system of coordinates: *assimilation* and *accommodation,* the ability to *construct* schemata and the ability to *use* them. Piaget's great merit is to have followed this operational construction step by step, through a meticulous analysis of the activities of assimilation and adaptation. The purely reflex exercise which is bound to its organization is a process of primordial assimilation (a tendency towards the repetition of assimilated modes of conduct). In a second stage (*first acquired adaptations and primary circular reactions*), when the child acquires the habit of sucking his thumb, assimilation is replaced by a reaction of accommodation which begins a stage of learning in a new capacity of intersensorial or sensorimotor coordination. From this time—and this point is of capital importance—assimilation and accommodation are to be differentiated. This differentiation allows for the possibilities of self-determination which are necessary to it and which must be enduring and systematic. Intentional sensorimotor adaptations are then characterized by secondary circular reactions which form an indefinite cycle of accommodations. It then becomes the *stage of secondary schemata,* and of their coordination so as to allow for their application to new situations in the light of foresight. After this is developed the *stage of tertiary circular reactions* and the discovery of new means through active experimentation. In this way the instrumental apparatus which makes *invention* possible is achieved. Corresponding to this increased degree of complexity are certain aptitudes for invention through *representation.* Action is thus internalized, and this internalization stimulates the activity of the subject who now has a milieu of symbolic mediation at his disposal as means to attain his ends.

Naturally, when reduced to this theoretical skeleton this operational schematism appears to be preposterous, as it would be if it were not supported and animated by the richness of the facts and observations which justify it. These "operations" could just as naturally appear to be valuable only as a part of a pragmatic, behavioristic, or cybernetic catalogue of self-regulated modes of behavior; but we are now going to gain a fuller understanding of where and how the person comes to be introduced into this mechanism, that is, precisely why it is not a question of mechanism, nor any longer of a man who would be merely mechanical.

The child's construction of reality takes place upon the stages and structures of sensorimotor intelligence. After he has shown how the child has directly *assimilated* the external environment to his own activity so as to form an increasingly great number of schemata which are both more variable and more apt to be coordinated among themselves, Piaget then shows how in a parallel manner, or thanks to this progressive *implication* of assimilatory schemata, the external universe is elaborated. This latter, however, depends both upon implicative *assimilation* and upon explicative *accommodation.* While during the first months of the child's existence assimilation remains centered upon the organic activity of the subject, the universe itself is chaotic, with neither regularity nor fixedness (this phenomenalism might be designated by the term "radical egocentrism"); nor is there self-consciousness. This organization of the real is brought about only to the extent that the self organizes itself by discovering itself. This passage from chaos to cosmos is the product of both the construction of the world and the construction of the self. The genetic analyses of the spatial field and of displacement, and the study of the development of causality and of the structuring of the temporal field, clearly point out this autonomy of the self's activity which is the correlative of the organizing of the world. Whereas accommodation and assimilation were undifferentiated at the moment of the birth of intelligence, they have since developed in and through their reciprocal and creative activities.

Without going into either the details of his work or the essentials of its dialectical movement, it is enough for us to emphasize that though to our knowledge Piaget has never devoted any of his works exclusively to the subject of the self or personality, we nonetheless can discover the formation of the self as a rational person in the autonomy of representative, interiorized, verbalized, and conceptual organization which is capable of inventing materials through accommodation (not only sensible materials but those constructed by instruments which have been furnished and elaborated by assimilation), and in the fundamentally relational construction of the inner and the outer. *The development of personality is,* from this point of view, *the embryology of reason.*

Rather than losing ourselves in genetic analyses of schemata which are organized and differentiated to the point of a *reversibility* which turns the subject of these actions into the agent of his plans of action, we shall instead look into the workings of fully constituted intelligence, into the work of the intelligence: the epistemological procedures through which scientific knowledge develops. Having discussed, with great clarity and depth, the problems concerning knowledge, its formation, its external and internal sources, and the idealist, empiricist, Gestalt, and phenomenological positions, etc., Piaget indicates that the process of the growth of knowledge corresponds to a construction of "norms," which is the correlative of the passing from *effective action* to the most *formalized* operations, and of the passing from the efficacy of the *real* act to the status of the *possible.* In this way the development of reason moves toward an *equilibrium* which is operational at the juncture of temporal reality and nontemporal logic. It is not a linear event but rather the evolving circularity of a system of references, the object both of a psychogenetic analysis of mental structures and of a historical-critical analysis. Only in this second sense can *genetic epistemology* resolve the problem of knowing whether such a system constitutes a sort of random juxtaposition of a body of logical-mathematical propositions (logical syntax) which seems to become objective in intelligence (a thesis implied in the position of the "Vienna Circle"), or whether it is formed by coordinating logical-mathematical connections with mental operations. The nature of mathematical beings can in effect be reduced not to a pure logistics but to their operational function and to their reflection upon the operations of physical thinking. Biological thought, that is, the categories which allow us to understand the adaptation and evolution of living beings, expresses more or less directly their psychical embryology. Psychological thought more immediately applies the structure of the subject to its object; it does this in the very stating of its problems, since psychology refers to the facts of consciousness, and consciousness by nature has a structure of *operative implication*. For if it is causality which determines the laws of the world of objects of knowledge, it is implication—insofar as it is the normative potentiality of actions—which constitutes the modality of the relations and operations which are effected by the subject himself.[5]

We have already seen, when considering the birth of intelligence and the construction of the real, that the processes of assimilation and of accommodation create this inner world of knowledge into which the subject is incorporated when he takes himself for the object of his knowing. Now we can see even more clearly that when the subject reflects as a psychologist upon his own thought, he is present at the simultaneously logical and operational construction of his object, which is a subject. This is because the facts of consciousness can be reduced to pre-implications or to implications, and because psychical operations are actions which become mental through the agency of images and signs, which allow them to be executed symbolically. This occurs in such a way that it becomes possible to explain the construction of logical-mathematical operations and to bridge the gap between psychological knowledge and logical and mathematical knowledge.[6] However, if the structure and formation of intelligence are essentially bound, in the activity of the subject, to his organization, reason is animated by a vectorality which is immanent in its own nature. This problem of the immanence and the transcendence of the self suggests to Piaget that the determinations and movements of the subject in his adaptive and scientific procedures emerge on the one hand from a reason which is formed by the succession of implied structures, and on the other hand from a constitutive reason which is composed of those functional invariables which are its own values.[7] It is as if the progress of its organization towards always more and more open schemata, towards an increasingly greater operative reversibility, as if these progressions which cannot be reduced to the physical or even the biological order,[8] were to bring into existence a consciousness of the possible.[9]

It does not seem to be a distortion of Piaget's theory to say that this organization of the *consciousness of the possible,* insofar as it is the very structure of reason, is precisely *the rational structure of the self*. Of course we cannot conclude from this that the self is rational only on the condition that it be the self of a scholar! It is obvious that the subject's reason implies only its rational structuring and not any particular degree of perfection to which this can lead it. Piaget's examinations of genetic psychology and epistemology show us that it is as radically impossible to discuss reason without referring to the structure of the subject as it is radically impossible to discuss the structure of the self without referring to the formation of its reason.

c) *Pierre Janet*

From the pragmatic and social-psychological perspective which has remained the axis of his thought, Pierre Janet also has developed an essentially genetic theory of personality. He has often repeated that personality is a construction which goes beyond a hierarchy of levels of organization. A person's individuality is that not merely of a living being but of a social being who develops his own unity and identity during the process of formation as a social being. The formation of the personality is this working, this hierarchical series of actions and modes of conduct which superimpose a superstructure of social conduct upon the stratum of unconscious biological and reflex responses or of "lower level" actions. "The social point of view is the particular point of view which dominates the personality." "Our personality is an inner labor to achieve unity and to gain distinction first of all from the material point of view and then and above all from the social point of view." "To sum up," concludes Janet, "it is society which creates one's personality." At this point Janet refers to certain ideas from Anglo-Saxon psychology (Josiah Royce, William James, Baldwin) to show not that the self is entirely dependent upon others but that the self forms and is constructed only in its relations with the other —the leitmotif of social psychology and contemporary existential analyses. All his analyses of the contributions of cenesthesia, of the meaning of attitudes and effort, of bodily sensations, etc., show that the dynamic system of the personality is formed on the basis of that which is "mine" in its appurtenances, which adjuncts actually presuppose this "mine" rather than cause it. Janet states that this *invention* of the person is on an equal footing with the possibility of complicated (or "secondary") actions which add *conscious awareness* to the primary modes of conduct.

The analytic study of the functions and types of conduct

which compose the personality is thus the study of social feelings or beliefs whose hierarchical ordering represents psychological evolution. All those types of conduct (voluntary and reflective action, accuracy, calculating, reasoning) and feelings (love, hate, selfishness) which unfold in time and with the language of "deliberating with oneself" and of "relation with others" enter into one's personality. The personality is therefore a combined mode of conduct which involves and subordinates all the others. It merges with thinking to the extent that thought ensures the secrecy of action, that is, the possibility to prepare, suspend, and direct the act.

This functional edifice of the internal and social modes of conduct which are superimposed on elementary actions, Janet continues, separates, distinguishes, and identifies the *person*. It is first of all a separation of the body, then a social separation with the particular feelings which belong to the hierarchical system of classes, and finally a separation of the individual. Such is the evolution of the personality. The person resembles no other person. He is different and other. The ideal of personality which is realized across the history and psychological evolution of the individual, Janet states, constantly supposes that it be formulated and made explicit by means of a "biographical account." This is to say that the personality is essentially temporal, verbal, and social. It is formed by an aggregate of types of conduct which can be narrated as if to order the narration relative to the narrator.

These marvelously Socratic analyses, which at times prefigure the most modern style of sociocultural structuralism, simultaneously touch upon a functionalist, dynamic, and anthropological conception of the creation of personality, of the autoconstruction which the individual, through his own psychological forces, creates in and through behavior which is related to the social forms to which he is bound.

2. THE PSYCHOANALYTIC THEORY OF THE GENESIS AND THE FUNCTION OF THE EGO

When Freud[10] discovered and defined the Unconscious as the "repressed," he gave an opponent to this "instinctual," "sexual," "infantile" unconscious which is subjected to the pleasure principle or which is, in other words, libidinal. This opponent was the "censor," as a force of opposition and of repression. This censor which is aroused in sleep and which waking increases, was thought of by Freud on the model of an optical apparatus (a telescope or microscope), an intuition which Freud states[11] that he accepted, subject to new scientific findings, up until *An Outline of Psycho-Analysis* (1938). In 1900, at the end of *The Interpretation of Dreams,*[12] Freud asserts that consciousness had lost the omnipotence that had been accorded to it and that it is nothing but the sense organ of the perception of psychical qualities (*ein Sinnesorgan zur Wahrnehmung psychischer Qualitäten*). This perception-consciousness system is a psychical apparatus which functions under the influence both of external perception and of inner processes in their relationships with pleasure and unpleasure. Its function as censor consists in the regulation of this equilibrium. What will later become the ego, designated as a faculty of resistance, of defense, of vigilance, in his first writings is reduced to this apparatus, a sort of eye or ear through which reality enters and encounters the inner world of the instincts. In *Beyond the Pleasure Principle* (1920), he returns to the functioning of the nervous system in general and to consciousness in particular, and emphasizes that it is the cerebral cortex that constitutes the system perception-consciousness.[13] The spatial representation of this cerebral apparatus orients it towards the outside through the organs of sense; it is an apparatus of protection and of selection of excitants which come from the external world. From the dynamic viewpoint, this double barrier against the exterior and the interior ensures a regulation of the energies and of the excitations which crop up on its surface. Later, in *An Outline of Psycho-Analysis*[14] (1938), he will speak of a middle position between the drive and its realization, of a *Denktätigkeit* (noetic activity) which represents the structure of consciousness in its role as constructive (*konstruktier Leistung*) of the functions of the ego. It transforms free and variable energy into bound energy. It is this liaison which could be said—with reference to the structure of the field of consciousness—to constitute the legality of its function.

However, that aspect of the psychical apparatus which represents the ego, in other words, the theory of the ego as theory of its genesis and of its autonomy, comes only in the later conceptions of Freud concerning the psychical apparatus. It is this which we shall now examine.

At first the ego appeared, in Freud's view, as the effect of a primary cathexis (primary narcissism). In his memoir "On

Narcissism" (1914), self-love or autoerotism, in the "oceanic feeling" of one's first experiences, is taken to be the pole which attracts and organizes the ego: this feeling of omnipotence or at least of a privileged value accorded to one's self as a libidinal object *(Ich libido)* will remain for the rest of one's life. At this stage of Freud's naturalistic conception, the ego responds to the demands of the pleasure principle. These demands, moreover, are only indirect, since their satisfaction must pass through an *Ichideal*—which prefigures the structure which will be known as the superego in the works of around 1920.[15]

The work on collective psychology (*Group Psychology and the Analysis of the Ego,* 1921) accentuates the process of identification with the father image in the Oedipal situation as that which endows the ego with its ideal or legal sense. This identification at first constitutes an affective attachment to an external "object" (the parental image), but following a regressive (or fantasized) substitution, it comes to be attached to a representation of this object incorporated within the ego, as if the ego was formed and developed through this *introjection.* "Introjection" thus enters as a spectator or a censor in the ego, which it divides in order to form it (a theme which refers to so many other profound reflections on the antinomic structure of the ego). This part of the ego, the ego-ideal *(Idealich)*, is the true heir of the original narcissism *(Erbe des ursprünglichen Narzissismus)* in which the childish ego delighted. It also has its origin in the father image. This double structure of the ego as libidinal object and as ideal is represented in the libidinal structure of crowds; for the crowd can be reduced essentially to the distinction between the ego and the ego-ideal. It has a double kind of tie *(doppelte Art der Bindung)*: identification and substitution of an external libidinal object for the ego-ideal,[16] as if, coming from outside, it was constantly called back to it.

In *The Ego and the Id* (1923) we find Freud's famous diagram (see figure 5).[17]

This topographical outline barely sketches what will become the famous Freudian trinity of the three agencies. The ego already appears there as that "poor creature" of which Freud explicitly speaks in this text.[18] An individual *(Ein Individuum)* is composed of an unknown and unconscious psychical id *(ein psychische Es)* upon whose surface rests the ego *(diesen setz das Ich oberflächlich auf)*, which itself emanates from the system perception-consciousness and preconscious, as

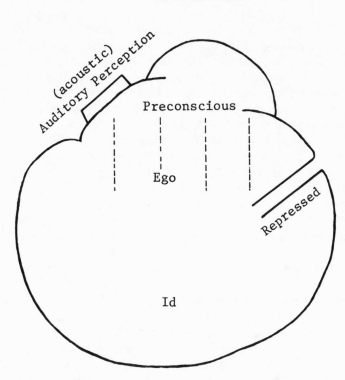

Perception–
Consciousness

Figure 5. 1923 Diagram from *The Ego and the Id*
Consciousness is represented by the system Perception-Consciousness; the Preconscious is in relation with Consciousness
and Perception (acoustic = auditory perception); the Unconscious is represented by the Id; the Ego communicates with the
system Preconscious-Conscious; the Repressed occurs partially
because of pressure from outside (Perception-Consciousness)
and partially through the agency of the Ego.

from a nucleus. Between the id and the ego there does not exist
any sharp separation, especially in the inferior part of the latter where one tends to merge into the other. Here again, in
conformity with the earliest of Freud's intuitions, the ego is
only the representing of the influence of the external world—
to which conception is now added the idea that the substance
of the ego is itself supplied from within by the id (later it will
be said and repeated without end that the ego receives its energy from the instincts). From this viewpoint the ego is above

all a bodily ego *(vor allen ein Körper Ich)* and it is (as in *Beyond the Pleasure Principle*) assimilated to the apparatus of consciousness: it is, says Freud, a surface *(oberflächen Wesen)*, or better still, the projection of a surface *(Projektion einer Oberfläche)*. Thus, even when it has scarcely appeared, the ego is either swallowed up by the id or is considered to be merely a thin film which reflects the external world. Perception plays for the ego the role which instinct *(Trieb)* plays in the id;[19] each of them, from without and from within, stands in opposition to psychical equilibrium (homeostasis).

Freud indicates, however, that the ego undergoes a differentiation into a *superego (Über-Ich* or *Ichideal)*,[20] which does not, however, figure into the 1923 diagram. On the contrary, the text[21] invites us to consider that the development of the ego continues to a certain grade *(eine Stufe,* a certain degree) at which point this differentiation within the ego constitutes the superego *(Über-Ich* or *Ichideal)*, which thus becomes part of the ego *(ein Stück des Ichs)*.[22] Here we are once again retracing the history and prehistory of identification in its relations with the *Oedipus Complex.* Let us point out that the mark of identification with the father and with the mother, in its dual sense as prescribed by the object choice of the daughter or the son, has perhaps nowhere in Freud's works been more strongly exhibited than in this text. The "be thus" and the "do not be thus" constitute the double aspect of this ideal of identification. This ideal can arise only from the repression of the Oedipus complex. The superego is thus the prolongation (which continues during the whole of one's existence) which adds its "morality" to the ego.[23] But there is another origin of the super ego, since it also arises from the sources of the id. Finally, this functional severity of the superego reflects the death instinct, or at least represents the sadistic impulse, the destructive element which violently opposes the pleasure principle. With regard to its function, if the ego is charged with coming to terms with the external world, the superego by differentiating itself opposes itself to the id. In this respect it satisfies all the conditions to which the higher nature of man *(das höhere Wesen im Menschen)* must conform. In this schema of the conflictive nature of the psychical being, the ego is thus grasped between the id and the superego and depends upon both of them. The states of the dependence of the ego *(die Abhändigkeiten das Ich)* show it as a "poor creature" *(als armes Ding)* submitted to a triple enslavement and to a triple danger: the external world, the libido of the id, and the severity of the superego. This ego is itself, like the physician undergoing psychoanalytic treatment *(wie der Arzt in einem analytischer Kur)*, harassed and full of good will. The ego is a locus of anxiety *(ärgentliche Angstätte)*; it exists, we would say, taking up Heidegger's expression, for and through its cares and for death, a theme which concludes *The Ego and the Id.*

In 1926, *Inhibitions, Symptoms and Anxiety* appeared. In this work Freud returns to the inhibition of the ego which "plays dead" in order not to have to enter into conflict either with the id or with the superego. The inhibitions which constitute neurotic symptoms (through the withdrawal of cathexis, or repression, or through defense mechanisms) are restrictions of the ego's functions which can shed some light upon its structure. The connection between the ego and the id is undoubtedly very strong, as is its dependence upon the superego. Thus the problem of the autonomy of the ego is posed. On the one hand the ego is an organization *(Das Ich ist eine Organization)*.[24] It rests upon a free exchange *(auf dem freien Verkehr)* between its parts *(Bestandteilen)*. But on the other hand, it is the organized part of the id *(eine organisierte Anteil des Es)*.

In the *New Introductory Lectures* (1933), the autonomy of the ego, that is, of the conscious being, is once more examined and is clearly rejected. In the third of these lectures, Freud continues the "dissection" of the ego to the extent, he states, that the ego can be taken as an object.[25] For there is in it a possibility of splitting *(sich spalten)*, and for us the possibility of effecting a dissection *(Zerlegung)* of it. Before the formation of the superego, its role is filled by an external power, the severity of the parents; as long as this is exercised from without, we cannot speak[26] either of a "superego" or of a "conscience" *(Gewissen)*. On the contrary, both of these form when one's *imago* is substituted for the fear of parents (Freud emphasizes that the superego can be of an implacable severity even though the severity of the parents has been very weak). The assimilation *(Angleichung)* to an alien *(fremd)* ego, that is to say identification, is characteristic of the first ego *(erste Ich)*. This assimilation has even been assimilated to the oral cannibalistic incorporation of the other person. Object choice, that is, the choice concerning which of the parents the subject desires to *have* and not to *be,* constitutes a second process which is greatly different from the first.[27] The superego is the product of a successful identification with the parental agency. It is not a simple abstraction,[28] or the personification of an abstraction such as conscience *(Gewissen)*. In this text we see that the limits of the ego and the superego are continually fluctuating, since Freud speaks[29] of the superego as a special agency which has its seat in the ego *(eine besondern Instanz in Ich)*. Self-observation, conscience, and the functioning of the ideal are in a special manner vested in the superego. The ego nonetheless has an essential function: that function which appears in its "resistance" in analysis. Having successfully brought about the repression, the ego is unwilling that it should be suppressed.

At this crucial moment in his reflection upon "repression," Freud asks:[30] Are the ego and the superego themselves unconscious, or do they merely produce unconscious effects? Freud chooses the first alternative. He adds that he was at first annoyed by this truly inconvenient *(eigentliche unbequeme)* discovery that certain portions of the ego and of the superego are unconscious[31] in the dynamic sense (that is, they are fundamentally opposed to being conscious); this discovery, he adds, nonetheless facilitated things for him *(wirkt hier wie eine Erleichterung)* by making it clear that there is no reason to call unconscious the psychical region which is alien to the ego *(das ich fremde Seelengebiet)*—a realm which corresponds rather to the personal pronoun "It" *(Es, Id)*, which is particularly appropriate to express the essential characteristic *(Hauptcharakter)* of this province of the mind *(Seelenprovinz)*. To make his point even more clear, he adds that to be unconscious is not the sole characteristic *(sein ausschiessender Charakter)* of this province of the mind. If we understand him correctly, it is thus at the very moment at which he introduces the ego and the superego into the unconscious that Freud hastens to add[32] that "we will no longer use the word 'unconscious' in its systematic sense" *("so wollen wir 'unbewusst' nicht mehr im systematischer Sinn")*. From this point onwards, he says, it will be better to use the word "id." The unconscious which has been replaced by the id is not merely the repressed: this constitutes a rather remarkable turning point in Freud's theory and deserves to be emphasized. From this point onwards, the three systems, the three realms *(Reiche)*, the three regions *(Gebiete)*, the three provinces *(Provinzen)*, through their interpretation and the ensemble of their relationships, which will later be

called "intersystemic" (between themselves) or "intrasystemic" (within each of them), these form a mode of organization, the separate parts of which interpenetrate and merge
with one another. This psychical apparatus is presented as a
dynamic structure which is submerged by the unconscious or,
to speak in Freud's terms, by the id, and of which the systems
ego and superego are themselves "largely" unconscious.

At the end of this lecture explodes this statement which
commands each man to emerge from his unconscious by forming himself into an ego, that is, by himself constructing his
autonomy: *Wo es war, soll ich werden.*[33] This does not state
"The ego ought to dislodge the Id", as the French translation
puts it, but rather "There where was the id, I ought to become
ego." In other words, after having wrapped the psychical apparatus in the gaping depth of the unconscious, Freud returns
to the essential point, the sense of existence, of this autoconstruction of the "myself" which should turn its back upon the
highest form of the Unconscious, that is, upon the id. In this
way, the ego and its ideals (the superego) appear as that which
is rooted in the unconscious, but which I *ought* to transform by
forming myself. This is exactly the sense which, in our view,
constitutes the very essence of the ego. Freud very strongly felt
this necessity, but this formula has remained dead-letter in his
work.

In *An Outline of Psycho-Analysis* (written in 1938, published in 1940), the characteristics which are proper to that
fraction *(Bezirk)* of our psychical life which we call the ego are
once again described, in the first chapter, according to the 1923
diagram: the ego ensures self-preservation and control of voluntary movement; through memory it stores up its experiences.
Freud here repeats that the ego develops out of the id's cortical
layer *(Rinderschicht)*, which has been organized in such a way
that it can enter into contact with the external world. It takes
"conscious perception" as its starting point[34] and submits an
increasingly larger territory and deeper strata of the id to its
influence. But it itself bears the indelible stamp *(untilgbaren
Stempel)*, a sort of official certification (analogous to "Made in
Germany," he says), of the origin which it derives from the id.
It transforms free energy into bound energy. Its constructive
function *(konstruktive Leistung)* consists in interpolating an
intellectual activity *(Denktätigkeit)* between the demand
made by some instinct and the act which will satisfy it. This

intellectual judgment forces the instinct and the physical action to adjust to one another, for it is subject not to the pleasure principle but to considerations regarding its own safety. The ego exercises a sort of control, a reality-testing *(Realitäts-prüfung)*. Insofar as it is a psychical system wedged between the id and the superego, the ego[35] has the function of battling against outer and inner perils: it wages war on two fronts *(kämpft auf zwei Fronten)*. But if the inner enemy is the more dangerous, this is simply because the ego, which "is only a differentiation" of the id, finds more difficulties in getting rid of it.

However, Freud adds[36] that all this is true only of the manner in which the ego is represented up to the age of five years. At this time an external portion of the world has been at least partially abandoned as an object and through the mechanism of identification has been taken into the ego as an integral part of its internal world. This internal agency which thus completes the structure of the ego is the superego in its function as conscience.

Thus at the end of the Freudian itinerary we find that though the ego may be well defined as an agency of the psychical apparatus, this apparatus itself has no autonomy. It remains a prisoner of its own unconscious roots and of two other agencies: the id, which is essentially unconscious, and the superego which is itself the product of an unconscious labor of identification and introjection. *The ego,* for Freud, therefore *remains the prisoner of the unconscious;* since it is in a state of constitutional heteronomy, it has no autonomy. This is the sense of what Freud writes in *An Outline,* when he states that the id and the superego represent the weight of the past (the id that of heredity, the superego that of others), whereas the ego is above all determined by what it itself has lived, that is, by what is accidental and real. The ego has thus never ceased to be the reflection of what is presented to it by the system perception-consciousness, that is, by perception submitted to the reality principle: the ensemble of qualities which experience bestows upon the ego. In Freudian psychology the ego is purely empirical. If Freud has at times spoken of its organization and its dynamic structure, *it has always been in order to reject the ego's autonomy.*[37]

The whole psychoanalytic school has naturally taken up this conception of an ego which has been assimilated to an optical apparatus from the very start, an ego which is burdened with external affairs, with "simple" coming to terms with reality, or which is reduced to being only a "differentiation" of unconscious processes. Paul Ricoeur[38] has emphasized Freud's failure to solve the problem of "sublimation," which (like the problem of repression) cannot be reduced to the economics of the unconscious.

As concerns the development of the ego as ego identification (that is, the intrinsic relationships of the ego and the superego), the very basis of the distinction between the ego and the object during the oral stage, and all the mechanisms involved in this (introjection, incorporation, identification, negation), form the usual subject matter of studies concerning object relationships during this libidinal stage. All these relationships naturally revolve around the person of the *mother*, where the demands of the reality principle awaken in the presence of desire and of anxiety (Melanie Klein, Sullivan, J. Bowlby, R. A. Spitz). Melanie Klein traces the formation of a superego back to this first stage of psychical development, to the moment when the newborn child establishes his *first relationships with an object.* The superego would thus, from its origins, be inseparable from the constitution of objects and of their relation to the ego in the protoexperiences of anxiety and frustration, during the period which Sullivan calls "parataxic." In the mirror stage (Lacan), the first beginnings of language (Sullivan) are thought of as being processes of "personification" in which a first sketch of the psychical apparatus is formed during the pregenital phase, as we have pointed out in relation to other genetic conceptions. Lacan emphasizes the formation of the ego through its own lack of recognition, that is, a knowledge or a recognition which is refracted through the prism of another's image.[39]

During the psychosexual development contemporaneous with the anal-sadistic stage, from one to three years of age, the ambivalence of expulsive and retentive tendencies exercises a strong influence both upon the mastery of those affective states which arouse anxiety and upon the reduction of their tension. Clara Thompson and Erik Erikson have stressed the importance of the cultural environment and of interpersonal relationships at this stage. The relationship with another person and the formation of language open the possibility of negation through speech and through the acts and fantasies which constitute the *first defense mechanisms of the ego* (Anna Freud).

tuitions which they have drawn from the source of the geno-
typic development of the infant, the Ego psychology of these
authors nonetheless ends in defining the *Ego* as a "substructure" of the *Self;* it grants it a certain amount of autonomy on
the condition of reducing it to being only a part of the individual's constitution.

Paul Federn's conception is much more interesting, to the
very degree that this disciple (and even collaborator while in
Vienna) of Freud has felt the need to define the ego through its
organization.[45] Federn starts from a sort of *cogito* applied to an
"Ich-erlebnis" ("Ego feeling"), which, in the succession of the
"states of the ego" (of the moments which are lived in the
actuality of experience), having crossed the successive "cathexes," arrives at the constitution of an ego which is unstable
in its "frontiers." He describes the properties of "His Majesty
the Ego" precisely insofar as they are a cohesion, unity, and
permanence of the ego—a theme which had already been outlined by Freud, and one which we shall develop in the chapter
on the autoconstruction of the self. However, this ego is formed
by the stratification of past states—this is again a theme which
we shall take up later. It thus contains and goes beyond the
internal contradictions of the *libido* and of the *mortido* (death
instinct), which come to a state of equilibrium in its action.
This much too simplified and abstract account of Federn's theory might nonetheless give us some idea of how a psychoanalyst—if not psychoanalysis itself—might be led into a
theory of the ego which, without giving up any of Freud's empirical and intuitive contributions, might add something to his
position: the organization of the ego.

Analytical clinical experience has shown the need for, as
well as many of the difficulties involved in, a theory which
represents the ego as a system of defenses subordinated to the
superego, or a system of cathexes depending on the id. In this
precarious position, the ego reveals itself so that its "responsibility," its "force," and its autonomy might be judged. Daniel
Lagache's report to the Colloque de Royaumont (1960) is the
most important document to consult on this point. Remaining
sensitive to the "personality" character of Freud's second topographical model of the psychical apparatus (of the decade
1915–1926), Lagache underscores the role of intersubjective relations (with others) in the structuring of the personality, that
is, in the construction of the ego-subject in relation to the ego-

object. Freud, when very near the end of his doctrinal evolution (1926), reacted against "the excessive idea which certain psychoanalysts have made of the heteronomy of the ego." For there is, Lagache states,[46] a relative autonomy and even an "autonomism" of the ego with respect to its intrasystemic relations (within itself) and its intersystemic relations (with respect to reality and to other agencies). In opposition to Nacht, Lagache finds himself on this point in agreement with Hartman when he writes: "Many misunderstandings and obscurities can be reduced to the fact that we are not habituated to considering the *Ego* from the intrasystemic point of view. The *Ego* is spoken of as being rational or as realizing certain factors of integration, whereas these are only characteristics of one or another of its functions."

This reflection raises the problem of the inner structure of the ego—without, however, solving it, as we have already seen. In the work of Anna Freud this inner structure appears in its fundamental ambiguity, particularly in relation to the resistances and transferences which send us back to the problematic of the autonomy or the heteronomy of the ego. ("The ego," writes Lagache, "does not control the defensive operations of which it is, however, the agent."[47]) In addition, we should add that even more than its resistances, its abandonment to the "constraints of repetition"[48] (its manner of giving in to the death instincts) comes into play in its dynamics as in its relations with the id and even with the superego. Thus, if it is *constituted* as the agent of defensive, automatic, and unconscious operations, motivated by the id and the superego, the ego is *constitutive* when, through the realization of the possibilities of the subject,[49] it tends to *disengage* the subject from its own defensive operations. But it attains its autonomy (which is at least relative) only by passing through the autonomism of the ego-ideal and by going beyond it.[50] At the end of his report —which we have here reduced to several fragments so as to make these points stand out from their dense context—Lagache concludes[51] that the freedom of consciousness (here assimilated to the autonomy of the ego) "is free in that, connected to a structural plurality, it can in some manner bring one or the other into action. ... Through its relation to unconscious structures, (its) efficacy is bound to the subject's power of 'decentering.' "[52]

The psychoanalytic theory of the ego thus leads definitively to the problem of the autonomy of the ego, a problem which never ceased to haunt Freud (in his theory, and above all in his practice).

By confining the ego to the unconscious, psychoanalytic theory has a tendency to consider the ego as no longer being a person or as being only an evanescent person weaving between the lines of speech, the syncopes of desire, or the conflicts of instincts, either as a reflection or as a residue. In order to restore its proper being to the ego, it must be considered either in its *organization* or in its *autoconstruction.*

As a "genetic psychology," Freud's conception lacks "development," as if being went round and round within the chains of its constitution or the closed circuits of its intersystemic relations. In this perspective of a perpetual turning back, a turning back to the depth of oneself, the famous formula *Wo es war, soll ich werden* remains a formula by which Freud enjoins the necessity of passing beyond his own theory of the ego conceived as "a poor creature" *(ein armes Ding),* of completing it with a phenomenology of conscious being and of its becoming self-conscious, that is, of its "becoming someone." This becoming must go beyond the id in order to arrive at the ego—this is the very sense of the formula. To the extent that the "superego" is unconscious, it forms, like the id, the unconscious part of the ego, which ought, in its turn, to dominate it in order to become itself. In this way we are led to a radical reformation of the structure of the psychical apparatus—a demand to which we shall later attempt to respond.

The Freudian ego, however, remains an "I" with neither cohesiveness nor structure. If it is only an "other" which does not emerge except in illusions, lies, and negation, if it is merely that to which the self of the neurotic (or of the psychotic) is reduced, if on the whole it does not coincide with the self of Man in his normal formation, it inevitably was revealed to us as being something *(id)* which prevents it from being someone *(Ich).* We must also understand how revolutionary the discovery of the unconscious forms which permeate and contain the ego has been. If Freudian theory's own development has caused it to miss discovering the ego because it aimed too low, it has rendered the enormous service of setting forth its meaning, of obliging us to speak of it only as a mode of conscious being in its relationship with an unconscious foundation, prehistory, and prelanguage. The ego is formed in opposition to the id. But it emerges from the depths of itself only on the condition of not detaching itself from it.[53]

3. ANGLO-SAXON DYNAMIC PERSONOLOGY

In the United States a large number of works have been devoted to the dynamic structure of personality.[54] Most of these (G. Murphy, 1947; R. B. Cattell, 1950; O. H. Mowrer, 1950; Murray, 1953; A. H. Maslow, 1954) have been characterized by their *objective method* of statistical observation (tests, questionnaires on attitudes, scales of interests, factor inventories, systematic surveys, controlled observations by teams) and by their common theoretical inspiration: *the person is his biography.* This psychology, which is a Gestalt, organismic, and historical psychology of the person, uses the schemata of genetic psychology and above all those of psychoanalysis, while it constantly applies principles of objective behaviorism which are, moreover, more resolutely "molar" than "molecular."

For Cattell, personality ("that which permits a prediction of what a person will do in a given situation") is envisaged as an ensemble of modes of behavior which can be precisely measured and described and whose coherence depends upon the connection of original and constitutional "traits," and upon their internal psychodynamic structure. The study of behavior and of the reactions of personality traits leads him to take a longitudinal perspective upon the structuring of the personality's tendencies. These manifest themselves through attitudes (hierarchical "dynamic lattices"). The dynamic structures of the person are elaborated on this "ergic" or instinctive (and not energetic) basis. These structures are modeled by the environment under pressure from unsatisfied needs. This organization acts according to the laws of *learning* and of *conditioning,* understood as the effect of a motivated response in a *goal-tension field.* For the action of the external environment takes place only within *dynamic crossroads,* which should not be considered merely as unconscious complexes. Almost the total dynamic analysis of these processes of adjustment and of the defense mechanisms which form the personality is conducted on the model of a Freudian psychodynamics.

Murray's personology (which predates Cattell's analysis by ten years) is situated in a more resolutely historical and thematic perspective. The exploration of the personality[55] was undertaken experimentally by the Harvard school as a team project carried out on fifty-one subjects (all male) over more than two years. These subjects were subjected to a series of systematic explorations (interviews, analysis of real or fictional situations, T.A.T., autobiography, and even "psychodrama"). It was a question, Murray tells us, of blazing a trail between "peripheralist" hypotheses (behaviorism, empiricism, elementarist associationism) and "centralist" hypotheses (dynamism, conceptualism). He defines the concrete personality to be disengaged as a *biographical organization which integrates environmental influences into the system of drives.* This dynamist hypothesis of the activation of "actones" (motor or verbal adaptive conduct) through motivating or impulsive tendencies (drives, needs), is borrowed from William James and W. McDougall. His system of more or less "derivative" (or "secondary") needs constitutes the energetic apparatus of the person and his goals. Murray distinguishes five of these secondary needs (acquisition, conservation, order, retention, and construction) from which are derived one's activities and attitudes (ambitious, achievant, self-forwarding, exhibitionistic, inviolacy, infavoidance, defensive, and counteractive attitudes). Another group of needs is concerned with whether power is exerted, resisted, or yielded to. Still another is formed by the sado-masochistic dichotomy (aggression, abasement). One last group includes person-to-person relationships (giving, exchanging, protecting, etc.). Two additional complementary needs are described: that of cognizance (curiosity, investigation) and that of exposition or giving information. The interrelationships of these needs, their subordination one to another, and their conflicts are naturally described in terms of a homeostatic hedonism, of the relations of objects (positive or negative cathexes). This system of variables carries a "directional vector," a sort of trajectory which regulates its "pre-actions." Finally there appears the most original idea in this generally rather banal qualitative analysis of tendencies: the concept of "themas" (the assemblage or federation of thematic tendencies)[56] which exercise their dominance in all "actual processes" (we would say in the organization of the field of consciousness). It is at this point that a true personology actually begins. Murray's personology consists in finding the process of the historical development of the person in the observer's judgment as well as in the subject's judgment of the observer, as if in the subject's autobiography and in a biography which was objectively reconstituted (with the aid of validated interpretations). This process of development involves continuation and variation, progression and socialization. Thus, to the internal process of the organization of the person there is a corresponding history of the individual and "this is his history."

4. GERMAN STRUCTURALIST THEORIES

Among[57] the "organismic" theories of the hierarchical structure of personality,[58] those of Klages and Lersch merit special attention. They are rigidly bound up with a philosophy of organization which we find also in the theories of Palagyi, 1922; Spranger, 1924; Max Scheler, 1930; Rothacker, 1936; Braun, 1930; H. F. Hoffman, 1935; Nicolaï Hartmann, 1935 (a view which is analogous to that which we find in France from Maine de Biran to Bergson, Janet, Teilhard de Chardin, etc.).

For Klages, the *matter of character* (traits, aptitudes, faculties) is constituted by measurable capabilities. Character itself, which ought to be taken in the sense of "person," cannot be reduced to this "matter." The *nature* or the *quality* of character corresponds to the elaborations of its "matter"; it is a sort of melody which is composed (according to laws whose constancy through the most diverse characterological or personological systems we have had the opportunity to appreciate). The *structure* of character is the organizational law which directs the movements of this architectonic. This structure is built up of layers of the person; it refers to a metaphysics of personal differences which is based on the superposition of two spheres: life and mind. It finds its origins in the Nietzschean image of a combat between the sources of life and of power, between the soul, which is rooted in the body *(Seele)*, and the mind *(Geist)*. "Character" is at the end of this dialectical movement a sort of equilibrium between *pathos* and *logos*.

It is precisely this theme which is taken up by Philipp Lersch in his work *Aufbau der Person.*[59] He, too, attempted to apply a *principle of stratification* to the analysis of the person. As Nicolaï Hartmann has shown, this is not only a psychological principle but the directing principle of any ontology of human being—an idea which is found in so many philosophers since Plato and Aristotle. There are grounds for describing the "tectonic" of personality as a superposition of dynamic structures. Its basis is formed by the *vital ground,* the vital and organic experience of bodily needs (the "profound" or "vital person" of Rothacker and Braun). The endothymic ground is constituted by the *Erlebnisse,* that is, the lived experiences of appetites and tendencies (*libido,* activity) which form into an egoistic system of seeking after individual satisfactions or of transitive systems which are directed towards others. All these affective experiences unfold on the level of emotions which are, moreover, inseparable from their "noetic horizon." Out of this endothymic background the *vital feelings* emerge. Our own analyses have shown that these lower and basal strata of psychical being form the infrastructure of personality at the point where it coincides with the structure of the organization of consciousness into the actuality of lived experience. These basal strata are the vital spheres of the personality. The personality develops only through its connection with the external sector (perception, memory, representation) of its organization, an idea which, as we have seen, Freud has very strongly expressed in his first topography. We ought, however, to say that these borrowings from so many diverse sources, especially from comprehensive and functional psychologies, find their most original outcome in Lersch's analysis of the *higher structure of the personality.*

The fusion, or at least the harmony, of this activity of thought and of will with the endothymic sphere forms the personal *self* (his figure 13 summarizes this *tectonic* of the *Funktionkreis des Erlebens,* which has been, perhaps, too much complicated by its systematic symmetry). Finally Lersch shows (as did Klages) that all the vicissitudes of existence in its relationships with the different levels of experience appear in the conflict or dialogue between this higher layer and the affective foundation. In this way the importance of the unconscious as an internal factor of inauthenticity is introduced. This is because, as Nietzsche so forcefully had shown, the person introduces, as a characteristic of his own structure, the possibility of lying.

As we shall see when we now examine the personalist conceptions which had already been so clearly enunciated by these "personologies," in general *the self is born, is formed, and manifests itself only in a problematic being.*

C. Personalist and Anthropological Conceptions of the Person

The problem of the self and of personality, insofar as it leads to the problematic of the existence of a subject "in his world," that is, insofar as it focuses upon the moral, social, religious, or political person, is fundamentally the problem of the goals and values of the individual, of his own existence, and of his autonomy. We shall here restrict ourselves to pointing out that a certain number of psychologists and philosophers have placed special emphasis upon the specific anthropological structure of the human being as a *personal being,* as *someone* who is self-assertive and resolves the problem of his existence and his freedom by himself. Of course this "personalist" or "anthropological" conception of human personality coincides with what is usually held to be the most intimate aspect of human experience. This does not prevent certain psychophysiologists—those who have been "blinded to the person," as Max Scheler has described them—from denying that this *someone* is anything other than *something.* Against this postulate have developed the "existentialist" and "anthropological" currents which we shall now discuss briefly.

There has always existed in France a psychology of personality animated by notions such as organizing force, autoconstruction and autodetermination, which corresponded to the psychodynamism of Maine de Biran and of Bergson. In Germany, biopsychological romanticism from Goethe to Nietzsche has equally never ceased to uphold the structuralist, Gestalt, and dynamist points of view of an autonomous force of the self. There are a host of authors who, following Dilthey, Brentano, Spranger, etc., have become involved in this psychodynamics of the self. Let us simply recall the work of William Stern.[60] For Stern, psychology is the science of the person considered as having an experience *(Erlebnis)*, as capable of having an experience. From the very outset the viewpoint is taken that the personality is not reducible (as we have emphasized) to "Gestaltizations" of experience; the very contrary is the true situation: "There is no form without someone who forms it" *(keine Gestalt ohne Gestalter)*. All the different aspects of the psychological life whose motivation coincides with its own planning are ordered with relation to the differentiation of the subject. The person commands changes and survives them. This *self* is not the body *and* the mind; it is the mind *having* a body.

This personalist conception has certainly influenced one of the contemporary Americans most interested in the problem of personality: Gordon W. Allport. After having studied in great depth and with considerable documentation all the possible meanings of the concept of personality, he bears down upon this idea and points out that it is the dynamic organization of the personality which determines its original adjustment to its environment; for if the personality cannot be resolved into an objective law, it is nonetheless a law unto itself.[61]

There is no psychology of the "person" and its "character" which has more force than that of Emmanuel Mounier. He does not take as the object of his penetrating analyses a "man without qualities" or a man reduced to his "geology." Instead he analyzes a man whose qualities, far from being "pathic" (that is, considered as simple elements which are passively received and lived), are the product of a creation which is carried out between the abysses of the organic unconscious and the infinite possibilities of personal transcendence. Men are truly these opaque beings who are unable completely to solve their own enigma. The formation of the personality is the history of this problematic and of this deciphering.

In this respect the person is "beyond" its character. It is a never-ending labor which the subject performs upon himself. Of course the emotions and forms which are the internal vicissitudes necessary to the mastering of action are stirred by the constant or variable "provocations" to action which come from society, objects, the natural environment, and the social, cultural, and historical environment, as well as by the biological milieu (the bodily environment) in which the person is rooted. However, the self breaks loose from its own relations with others, as if the inner drama could not escape from the drama of the other except to be bound to the other by its very constitution. By escaping the modeling of imitation and interaction, its constitution is not an immobile architecture; it is rather similar to a musical development, composed in time. Struggle and conflict are the essence of the rivalry between the received self and the willed self. The being of the self lies in this affirmation. It is not an object among other objects—including what are called psychical "functions" or "phenomena." Its identity is not a common denominator of a superposition of states. If it is "lived" before being "known,"[62] the focusing of self-consciousness is operated only across a directed asceticism which implies that self-consciousness asserts itself against its unconscious. It is with justice, says Mounier, that the "excentricity" of the self has been spoken of. It is as much outside itself by its nature as it is essentially within itself. For this reason speech is at least as characteristic of personal being as it is of reflection. The self carries on two adventures at the same time: one in depth towards the sources of time, the other in breadth in the expanse of space.

The self has a sovereignty over space, for its kingdom is first of all its body. Thus grammar rightly places the verb "to have" immediately next to the verb "to be" as a main pillar of human order. What is "mine," the collection of objects which I appropriate to myself, designs a spatial field which could be called "the circle of having." Through it, the self ensures the proprietorship of its properties.[63]

In its centrifugal form *self-affirmation* is presented as *assurance,* which is "the public face" of the self. This corresponds to an inner solidarity which has been acquired through the credit which it has at its command or which it borrows in its relationships with itself and with others. It thus happens that feelings or tendencies such as egoism, ambition, aggressiveness, self-respect, etc., become a part of self-affirmation. This self-affirmation is not only an authoritarian attitude, an attitude of overvaluing the self, but is also the strengthening of a mobile and progressive reality which uncovers itself, is enriched, and grows in inner authority. Personal man is not a monolithic existence, inwardly immobile or punctual and more or less blind to the outside "as both the materialistic psychologies and individualistic idealism would have us believe." He is the inwardly articulated "atom" of forces and movements: a *movement of exteriorization* which regulates its relationships with reality (on this subject Mounier has clearly seen that the autoconstruction of the self is a dialogue which implies the "dramatics of intelligence," for man's involvement excludes his blindness). It is a *movement of interiorization* which is active in the "recovery of the self" and the "deepening of the self."

The *process of transcending* is as essential to personal life as is the reality principle or the principle of interiority. The constancy of the self is not a sort of primary and absolute identity, which would be "as if its death." The self is identical, according to Mounier, in the same way that a person is constant or faithful. For the essence of the self is its system or problematic of values; it is its "valorization." The psychology of the self runs over not only into ethology but also into ethics.

There is an obvious connection between this moral conception of the person and the philosophies of Louis Lavelle and of Gabriel Marcel. In his *Philosophy of the Will,* Paul Ricoeur rejects the attempt to turn the self into an object by reducing it to "tendencies" (a view which is central to the reductionist studies of character which we have discussed above); for it is impossible to ascribe the character which has been put together in this manner directly to the free subject (cf. below, p. 277). To have such and such a character means not only to fit a description of myself, but to affirm "myself" as unique, inimitable, "thrown into my own individuality." ("I yield to myself as a given individual."[64]) My character is my freedom's manner of being, to which I ought myself to consent. This theme of rending, of infinitude, of the struggle of the self against itself, as the affirmation of the self in its own negation, this theme implies a going beyond, a transcendence of the person with respect to its organization which is a sort of index of the involuntary. It is "through a sort of return shock of phenomenology upon biology that the totalitarian pretention of explication through organization can be limited"—limited, we might emphasize, not denied.

This manner of being oneself, of gaining possession and consciousness of oneself, of being for oneself in one's world, is precisely the foundation of any "existential" analysis of the self established in its *Dasein,* according to Heidegger. The transcendental binding of *Dasein* to the world (as we have seen above, p. 53) is preoccupation or concern *(Sorge)* insofar as these cannot be reduced to need or impulses but rather to the relation of the existent's own needs to his own world, which itself is made not of objects but of the tools of his own action. This existential relationship can be found in the ontology of the self, whose being *(Dasein)* is a being-with *(Mitsein).* For the self is a manner of being with others; self-knowledge and knowledge of others are interrelated. In addition, the self is rooted in the community of "one" *(man),* that is, in the manner in which "one" is included in or caught up in or subjugated in a communal interpenetration which is the ground of common and everyday existence—a "one" which renounces its authenticity in order to fall into its world. For this reason the "myself" is possible only as an ideal of authenticity which is *to be for death.* This properly and absolutely ethical doctrine of the ontology of the self, with its Pascalian, Kierkegaardian, and Schopenhauerian overtones, represents the highest summit of the identification of a being with his duty.

Jean-Paul Sartre, especially in *Being and Nothingness,* emphasizes the very relativity of the freedom which characterizes *being-for-itself.* This being-for-itself "is that which it is not and is not that which it is"; it "is to be." On the other hand, being-in-itself is massive, isolated, and has no inside. This being-for-itself is precisely the nothingness which is in being, not as its negation but as its structure as free (it is doubt which grounds the *cogito*). The for-itself as foundation of the self is the up-surging of negation, etc. *"Lacking" is the reason of human being* (human reality is the self as being which is lacking in itself). Through this lack, values are set up (the being of the self is value, whose essence is to be and not to be). There is thus no absolute coincidence of the self with itself. Being is "ex-centric" with respect to itself. It is involvement in its own possibilities. This problematic of being for itself seems to refer more especially to the structure of consciousness than to that of the *Ego,* for in its transcendence,[65] the *Ego* seems to us to be the positive reality of this negativity. The self does not inhabit consciousness. It is the *reason* of the infinite movement through which the reflection reflects to the reflector. It is an ideal, a limit. The *Ego* is the sign of the personality. To form it (make it, *le faire)* and to have it—human reality's principal categories—come to be reduced either immediately or me-diately to the project of being. These few words obviously can-not pretend to give an exposition of or even to make a serious reference to what is important in Sartre's analysis of "reality" considered as being problematic of "man who is condemned to be free." Perhaps, however, it will suffice to have given a brief indication of the degree to which the problem of the self is involved in the organization of being, or rather outside of its organization, to the point that from its historical transcendence it can cause its gaze to fall upon what it is—what it is to be.

Having concluded this exposition of theories of personality, we can now better understand that the self, being someone, is not "ready made," as the "biomechanistic," psychoanalytic, or characterological theories of its formation would have it. The self is always *to be made.*[66] The self, an existence's someone, is constituted by this movement, by this temporality inherent in a process of becoming which is constantly drawn back to its having and its being.

2. THE STRUCTURAL ORGANIZATION AND CONSTRUCTION OF THE SELF (THE PERSON IN THE PROCESS OF ITS FORMATION)

The self is the *problematic form of conscious being,* not because it does not exist, but because its being so makes use of its time that it both asks and answers the problems of its history. The evidence for this remarkable state is dispersed or refracted in the different theories whose fundamentals we have just discussed, the truths of which we must now extract. What, or who, is this someone that I am or that another person is for me? This someone obviously has a "body" and a "description," a "countenance," a "type," a "character" which can identify him. But this is true of any animal which one can actually "recognize." The someone who is "this man" or "the person who I am" has all those individual characteristics and is the object of a physiognomy, a biotypology, or an anthropometry; but he cannot be reduced to this identity or to this physical, anatomical, or functional individuation. The self is a person in the process of forming himself, along with his world. There is "someone" only when the subject forms himself as a "person" or—what amounts to the same thing—when he identifies himself with a personal system of self-determination which, having been brought out of the impersonal milieu, returns to it in order to affirm therein his originality, his identity, his autonomous existence.

To the extent that the self is self-conscious being constituted as a person, the phenomenology of the self must grasp at the same time its *construction,* its *dynamism,* and its *relationships with the field of consciousness.* For the structure of the self is such that by nature it unifies its *temporality,* its *values,* and its *experience:* it is the *duration, the continuity of the person up to its very end.* When we successively set forth these aspects of the *Ego,* we shall not lose sight of the artifice of an analytic exposition which contradicts the very idea of the unity of the self. Even here, if we are able to decompose the self into its elements, it is because, as Maine de Biran very clearly saw, it is susceptible of being decomposed through the prism of its psychopathology. Whatever we might say concerning the *ontogenesis* of the self, or its *structural dynamism,* which is centered around a system of values that are implied in its action and which unfold in its history, and of its connection with its experiences, even if we are forced to describe them in abstract terms, we shall always be brought back to what is concrete in this diachronic or historical structure of conscious being, whose reality has been guaranteed, if not revealed, by pathological models.

A. The Ontogenesis of the Self

At its basis the ontogenesis[67] of the self coincides with the maturation of the nervous functions (especially in the organization of language, of sensorimotor intelligence, and of the structuring of the field of consciousness). However, insofar as it is the construction of the person, its essential development continues throughout its existence.[68]

The development, constitution, and history of the person are one and the same thing. If embryology is not the history of the organism, this is precisely because the adult organism begins only after the metamorphosis of the fetus into the newborn child. The adult organism is substituted for the development of the embryo. But the same is not true for the psychical organism. The psychical organism, through its history, does not succeed its first development. Instead, its earliest development coils and uncoils as does the history which it contains. Its antecedent phases (which are like the future perfect of its development) in effect remain contained within its structure. We shall pay special attention to this point when considering the unconscious infrastructure of conscious being.

The construction of the self which we observe in the progression of its successive forms of organization cannot be conceived as being a series of states each of which would be added to the preceding so as to replace it. This question deserves our special attention. When we shall speak, for example, of a first form of the self's organization as a "subject of its knowledge," we shall not be considering this modality of the self as disappearing below the higher or ulterior form of the self with its status of person and of character; nor shall we be considering it to be absorbed by this higher form. This earliest mode of organization of the self is itself still in the process of absorbing. In other words, the progressive forms of the construction of the person must be conceived as dynamic levels of integration wherein the lower level is not merely "integrated," but itself is always an "integrating" part of the process of formation *("Gestaltkreis")* which progresses towards greater autonomy because of the fact that it is continuously providing a foundation to its legality. To place (as we shall do) the subject, considered as the logical being of its own knowledge, at the beginning of its evolution is not to suppress it at the end of its development, but rather to assign to it the means of its reason along with its end. In the higher or ultimate forms of its organization, the self thus conserves its earliest foundations, the very conditions of its basic and permanent construction. Even when sleeping it carries within itself the prehistoric bases of its being, just as *that* which *I* ought to become or *that* which *I* have become still remains in the depths of myself. Having said this, we can now examine the process of formation of the personal edifice, the "tectonic" (Lersch) of its development.

1. THE FORMATION OF THE SELF AS SUBJECT OF ITS KNOWLEDGE

We have spoken at length of the fundamental *bilateralness* of the field of consciousness. No consciousness can either be lived, described, or imagined without some *experience (Erlebnis)* by which its *subject* is affected. We have heard repeatedly that to be conscious is to be conscious of something. But in the final analysis, it is also to be conscious of being the one affected or attracted by this thing. For this reason, at the extreme limit of consciousness, at the stage of the newborn child, we cannot speak of the infant who is crying or sucking without bringing in, between the stimuli and the responses of his behavior, the subject who suffers or enjoys, who forms his own experience insofar as he lives it. Melanie Klein has attempted to reconstruct the drama and the fantasies of the piecemeal structure of this primitive subjectivity. From the time of this "psychological birth," the self comes to the world only in this hiatus between desire and its object, in this indeterminate zone which is like its cradle, over which both good and evil fairies are bending. The self develops from its power of enfranchisement and isolation relative to both external and internal objects. It develops from its reflexive taking possession of itself as the "object" of its own subjectivity. The self does this in such a way that it fills in the lack of being with which it is born. We shall now trace out the phases of this opening and of the individualization of the self which, as subject of its knowledge, takes possession of itself as an individual object. This supposes the double generation which we are about to set forth: the emergence of the bodily self and the logical construction of the model upon which the self institutes all objectivity as well as the object of its own knowledge.

a) The Emergence of the Subject in Its Object Relationship and in Its Body

Sensibility towards pleasure and pain, muscular tension, spontaneous attention, the movements of a need towards its satisfaction, all the primary vital phenomena which have led us to state that there is a "zooconsciousness" or that the new-born child has experience, those manners of behaving and those sensations which constitute the first outline of the system of vital relations, all these are "irreflexive," "automatic," to the degree to which what is felt is confused with the experienced object itself (the presence or absence of the object of desire). It makes no difference whether we call psychical life at this stage purely subjective or purely objective, for it does not yet include the bilateralness of the subject-object relationship. The first personalization appears only when the subject can detach himself from the object, either by surviving it through memory or by being opposed to it as in perception or in purposeful activity. This detaching of the subject, which we have seen to be inscribed within the structuring of the field of consciousness, can be brought about only because of the resistance which one's needs encounter. No one has discerned better than Freud the birth of the object in the obstacle which it opposes to desire. The subject emerges along with the object from the moment that the object becomes objective, that is, when it presents itself and escapes. And it is the *Aha! experience* of amazement, the *Oh! experience* of disappointment, or the famous "hither and thither" *(dort und da)* of the earliest game of hide-and-seek between desire and reality. This emergence ceases to be transient or ephemeral and is constituted as the "first person" of its relationships with the external world and with others when the possibility arises of a "meaningful" form of those relationships. This form will effectively become the very essence of the person, its *logos*. The epiphany of the self, its manifestation, which is henceforth and forever anchored in its existence as the subject of its discourse, comes with the ability to enunciate the "yes" or "no" of desire, its disappointment or its pleasure; this is the point at which it gains access to the "I" which maintains the permanence of these relationships.

This first appearing of self to self, which sets the myself in opposition to the other and to others, is immediately tied to the affirmation of the "its." In the first instance the "I" is formed only as possessor, possessing first of all its *body* and all the "objects" (the persons who enter into its object relationships) which prolong its desire and perception. In its organs, its temperament, the thrusts of its instincts and of its vital tendencies, in its functions and its movements in the space which is proper to it, in all these the self becomes rooted in its proprietorship; it then strives to master its body without itself ever ceasing to belong to it. On one level what has been so often repeated to us is true, that the self and the "body image" become confused with one another. Though this is certainly not true for the self which has unfolded in its history, it is true for the "I" appearing in its prehistory. This body among other objects is mine. It is in effect the protoexperience of the subject in its own space. It is as a spatial modality or a spatial property that the self perceives itself as an object in its first self-consciousness. This is the reason for the importance of the "mirror stage."[69] It would doubtlessly be naive to pretend that in order for the self to become conscious of itself it would be enough for it to "see itself" or to perceive itself in the reflected image of its body. This is true precisely because the self cannot see itself unless it knows itself. We should instead understand this necessity of the reflection of the self upon itself as the absolute of a fundamental structure: that of the relationship of the self to others. To see oneself appear "as that other" which is the self, the mirror image of which sends back its image to myself, is the objectification of the self, or as is often said, is its "alienation." The self appears as a person opposite oneself, in the eclipsing of the subject, in its "fading" (Lacan's term), and, as it were, in its disappearance. The self is grounded in and through this negation of its absolute ipseity. The too brief but very profound reflections of Edouard Pichon[70] deserve attention here. The grammatical "I" is an agglutinate pronoun which is welded to the verb ("I told you" is an expression which, relative to the strong sense of the verb, expresses a "tenuous" differentiation of persons). The self, on the contrary, is an explicit pronoun ("I told you so myself") which refers to the *substantial person*— let us say to the person who is structured on the model of the objectification of the self, which has already made of this self a "someone" having a personality which cannot be reduced to the simple use of the agglutinate pronoun.

This transcendence of the self in relation to what belongs to it is organized in the formation and then in the course of all existence, in the problematic of what is a part of oneself. More generally it radiates into all the "relationships" and the *praxis* of the "properties" and "ties" which compose my somatic reality and my "having." By prolonging and making more complex the body image, the self image continues to incorporate into itself all the "affective" relationships which are, as the psychoanalysts say, the *libidinal investments* through which it secures the domain of its possessions.

b) The Logical Construction of the Self

On the model of the object which it "assimilates," and "by forming itself," discursive intelligence organizes the subject as an inner object; it causes it to enter into the domain of its *thought.* The self at first emerged in opposition to the object and the other. It is now about to objectify itself first as "content," then as "container" of its own body, in a labor which will detach it from space and project it into the time of its historicity and cause it to fall into its existence.

This brings us back to what we have said about the structuring of consciousness, with which, moreover, the first stages of the ontogenesis of the self almost entirely coincide. But in order that the two coordinates of psychical life between which its conscious being is developed (the field of consciousness and the self) might diverge, the subject must be divided within itself. In that respect the formation of a capital of logical values which are extracted from the operational exercise of thought (Piaget) is the fundamental correlative of the rationality of the self's logical being. This is as much as to say that all that we learn from the comparative psychology of the development of intelligence in infants and in animals (the stages of the genesis of intellectual operations, learning, ethology) enters into the constitution of the self. By detaching itself from experience (without ceasing to adjust to it), the self develops its power of action, foresight, and control as a function of a system of axiological references. In simpler terms we can say that the self constructs itself through its thought, that it thinks itself by thinking and does so on the very model of its thought. By doing this it acquires its essential force, which is that of a power which it exercises upon the external world and upon its corporeal and inner world by subordinating its experiences, its modes of behavior and its representations to the "principles of its understanding." The self subordinates these not to the principles of a formal logic which is external to itself or to principles of an operational logic, but to the rules which are and become the fundamental legality of its thought—as if it had itself been at the source of its information and brought about its formation.

This logical and objective autoconstruction of the self, which forms the primordial stage of the self's ontogenesis, does not cease to develop in the history of the person as the very axis of its rationality. From the time of the "age of reason," the unfolding of this structure of the self enters into the history of the individual in such a way that it represents within it the vicissitudes of the adaptation of conduct to the norms of the cultural community, to the demands of a logical legality to which the lawfulness which is really consented to by the self and which is taken on as its own is always in the process of adjusting itself, but to which it is never able entirely to conform. When it becomes "reasonable," the self assumes the function and the limitations of its own intelligent being. It cannot, of course, be reduced to its "intelligence quotient"; but it is with relation to this that its possibilities of judgment, its "knowledge of good and of evil," are ordered—precisely to the point where its theoretical and its practical reason are conjugated in the formation of a world of values which is substituted for the "motivations" of its animal nature. Since man is neither angel nor beast, throughout the events of his existence he manifests this power of knowing through which he recognizes himself. Because it takes itself as an object and is grasped in the structure of the subject's knowledge, the self is and becomes that "reasonable being" which is first of all, above all—and under pain of death—the human self.

2. THE CONSTITUTION OF ITS "WORLD"

Having emerged of its own power, codified in its reason, the self goes on to develop only as a function of the world into which it is thrown. We know, in addition, that the self's conquest of its world begins at puberty. This "world" and this "reality" are the modalities of its being which have been temporalized in its beliefs and in its ties with others. Because it is giving itself a real world, it is important that the self not only adapt it to the principles of reason but also adjust it to the *movements* which its desires project, which bring it closer to or lead it away from others, etc. This *Weltanschauung* in motion is an image in which, within its representations and its feelings, a state of equilibrium is produced in the reality of its existence, that is, its possibility to clear a path for itself, to make a place—however small it might be—for itself in history. This is essentially a question of the historical *temporalization* of the self. For the self can become itself only as a result of its ability to inscribe outside of itself, outside of its past and of the actuality of its experience, a "history" which will remain forever *its own*, both for itself and for others. The self is linked to its world as an event which is not merely lived but which enters into its history. This tie, which the child making his First Communion, the orphan, or the beaten infant establishes with his world, weaves a network of dramatic, anecdotal, or romantic significations which places in reserve, between his own world and the world of others, that secret and intimate history which is his own private worldliness.

When becoming the artisan of his world, when constructing his reality, the child does not apply only the rules of logical thought and operational precepts. He is building his representation of the world. But it is not a mythical representation, a geodicy, a theodicy, or simply a fairy tale. The world which he constructs around himself is that of his ideas, his needs, and his emotions. He is bound to it by his feelings and his beliefs. *Feelings* and *beliefs* are, as it were, the models of this "affective logic" which, by constantly interfering with ordinary logic, induces beings, situations, nature, one's neighbor, and intimate friends (as well as remote acquaintances and strangers) to belong to the self, to be for the self either the object of its love or its hatred, or an object which enters into its system of ideal values or into its system of reality. The world is constructed for the self only in and through these ties which unite the interest and passion which captivate it to the "objects" of which it is made. In the last analysis, it is only the force of the desires which these objects satisfy or frustrate which allows them to appear, to enter into a context of worldliness with the self. Since it is formed on the basis of these desires, this "worldliness" derives from them the laws of its conceptual, verbal, perceptual, and imaginative organization. The subjective demands, of which feelings and beliefs are precisely the transitory or compromised forms, and the values of objective reality constantly interfere, combine, are set in opposition or are reconciled with one another. These demands and values are irruptive phenomena, intuitions and forces which thrust themselves upon the self. The self adheres to them only at the price of consenting, if not succumbing, to the necessity of the unconscious realm of the other. The model of the world which each person has as his own is a sort of image of the division which occurs in the self between what is desired and what exists.

The "conception of the world" which is raised little by little through the labor of the construction of the self is thus a living tissue of images, ideas, and representations in which the forces of imagination and the forms of reality are more or less successfully brought into a state of equilibrium. The cosmic image to which it leads is proportional to the development of the personality. In the infant who forms it, it is shot through with a dream which no adult—not even the "coldest" or the most "positive minded"—can ever completely exclude from his existence.[71] Insofar as it is a stage in the formation of the personality, one's "conception of the world," one's *Weltanschauung*, fills the gap which the self has developed between its need for figurative "coherence" and its irrationality. For this reason the world view represents a moment of history, that moment which, during the period between infancy and puberty, carves out an abyss between the self which has begun to form its rational demands and its infinite desire to undo them.

3. THE CONCEPTION OF THE PERSONAGE

The "self" whose historicity we are here retracing, this self which first says "I," which takes possession of its body, of its language, of its thought, and thereby gives itself its world, this self is certainly a "person." But to the extent that this person does not naturally recapitulate itself so as to say "I" and abstractly to know its name and its civil status, the consciousness of its own identity is a value which is added to the self at some later time. To be "someone" is to assume a *role*. It is to identify with a personage. This labor of identification has its own history, is its own history. In earliest infancy it first of all passes through the problematic of object choice, the Oedipal situation; it then passes through cultural representations, imposed social status, etc. This elaboration, into which the *imagos* of the parents, imitation of others, attractions of sympathy, injunctions of respect, repulsions of hatred, etc., all intrude, this slow and progressive edification of the "person" who is to be, runs up against its embryology or its prehistory. The "oneself" which is to come to be, that person who accepts himself as a person, as a form of being always the same, in the depths as well as on the surface of the self, with all its character traits and somatic and moral attributes, this person can be formed only through the conjugated consciousness of the being as it is and as it ought to be. The consciousness of the personage which I wish to be cannot in fact be other than that of a *duty. It is necessary* that I be this or that. *I ought* to become this person or that. Now, to assign an *ideal to the self* is incompatible with its prehistoric or unconscious determination. This is why all psychoanalytic theories of the self, because they are unable to detach the *ideal* of the self (that is, its transcendence) from its conformation (that is, its immanence), are condemned to deny it, as we have seen.

Here again it is beyond any doubt that one's choice of whom he wishes to be is never entirely detached from his first "object choices." But the dynamic stratification of the self's ontogenesis, if it is not a myth, implies that being, when it passes from the being of the body (Freud's "id") to that of an historic being, undergoes true metamorphoses in its becoming. The existential problem of personalization cannot be resolved by having recourse to its predetermining factors, whether its preformation or its prehistory: the person is not prefabricated. This can be seen in a special way in the case of twins[72] for whom everything goes to make them identical *up to a certain point* which is precisely where they are not identical.

The whole history of second infancy and of adolescence, the whole psychology of the self at the moment it arrives at that important stage of its formation—puberty—these show us that this is the crisis of the *problem of identification.* It is first of all sexual, with the actualization of all the problems of the Oedipal stage, especially the definitive fixation of object choice, that is, of the opposite sex to the extent that this ought to be what the self should desire "to possess" and not to be. This is necessary in order to resolve the problem of love, which is at stake in this identification. It is social, too. This is the age of vocation, of ambition, and of idealism, when family, professional, and political choice must be made, when the problem of the unity of the self with its social status, with its *role* and its *mission,* is posed. The situation is the same with this process of ideal identification as it was with the preceding constitutions of the self: it will never be wholly completed, for to be "someone" implies that this someone can never completely renounce the possibility of being another, that other who is always there as if to hinder both the possibility and the desire of being the person that one wishes to be. This is why the later unfolding of the person's history, since it never implies the resolution of the problem, perpetually maintains and renews its terms. All the situations through which the existence of the self passes thus take on the sense of a reasking of the question of this "should be" which tends to confer unity and fixity on the self without ever coming to arrest its choice, which is to say, its life.

4. THE AUTONOMY OF CHARACTER

We have often repeated that a person's character is not "ready-made." The characteristic unity of a person which is presented in his personal originality is, on the contrary, the product and the achievement of the successive elaborations of his autoconstruction. From the ontogenetic point of view, this mastery of the self by the constitution of its character—which constitution is not "given" but "taken"—cannot be described as a simple phase of the basic autoconstruction of the self. It proclaims and already is the person's history in the strict sense of the word.

If at seven years of age a child reaches the "age of reason," being formed after the model of a reasonable being, if in second infancy the child constructs his world in the fundamental network of his beliefs and his feelings, if at puberty the role of the personage is fixed as the status of the person, this does not mean (as we emphasized when speaking of these diverse stages of the construction of the self) that the self has acquired its complete intelligence when seven years old. Nor does it mean that the self has formed its world at ten years, or that it has been assigned personal status once and for all at fourteen years of age. Instead, this simply means that the order of the composition and development of the progressive forms of the construction of the self is achieved with its maturation—but as this is done, an indefinite margin of "maturity" is guaranteed from this time on.

This maturity is essentially what is aimed at insofar as it is the *formation of character*. The formation of character is not to be found at the beginning but at the end of the ontogenesis of the self. As the development of personality, it is definitively the temporal unfolding which constitutes the historicity of someone, his "style," his history and his character.

We therefore cannot describe as a simple *stage* in the formation of the self—even if it were to be the last—what is its true *creation* and its completion: the true *personal history of someone,* which we shall later on find to be incorporated into the very structure of the self.

B. The Dynamic Structure of the Self

We have at length looked at the fundamental structure of conscious being insofar as it is constituted as the field of actuality of lived experience. It has become increasingly clear that conscious being is not exhausted by this *synchronistic* structure, that of the simultaneity of the figures which compose its multiplicity. The self emerges from this exigency as the conscious being which, through self-consciousness, adds a *diachronistic* dimension to this series of "states of consciousness," or to this succession of experiences. It is upon this that the self is grounded and presents itself as a systematic organization of the subject in its world.

The self's memory is the transactual structure which assures the self's fundamental characteristics of unity, power, historical continuity. This is not the memory of immediate recall and of habit. Nor is it Bergson's "pure memory." It is instead a memory which is the very form of the existence of the self (Gusdorf, for example, has shown its structural coincidences with the person). We have already said that the self is a being with reason. We are now able to say that it is a being with memory; our point is that the self so commands its time as to be incorporated into it. When we now describe the dynamic structures of the self, setting forth the trajectory or the axis of the values which unify its systematic direction, when we show the power which is implied in the activity it contains, and finally when we discuss the historicity of its existence, we shall only be making explicit the fundamental intuition concerning the diachronistic or mnemic structure of the self—that the self is being which is conscious of its nonactuality. We thus touch upon the antinomic character of the structure of the field of consciousness. We shall consequently touch upon a totally different modality of temporality. Inactuality is to the self what actuality is to the field of consciousness: its fundamental manner of being. For what is essential in the self's being is its virtuality, the potential it contains and the history which it continues. In this sense we can say that the dynamic structure of the self is that of *containing* and *retaining*. Its dynamics ought to appear to us in this perspective.

1. THE AXIOLOGICAL TRAJECTORY AND AXIS OF THE PERSON (THE SYSTEM OF THE SELF'S VALUES)

The dynamic axis of the person is its unity and continuity as these appear, to itself and to others, as a trajectory which has its origin in the constitution of its first experiences and which is directed towards its ulterior experiences and last ends. The finality of the subject, and then of the person as the agent of its existence, constitutes its earliest structural character. The *project of existence,* the very axis of our destiny, is the conducting wire which binds us to our past or to our world. The self appears in its *direction,* as the vector of the temporality of being, the sense of life. This temporality which keeps the self on the alert and projects it outside of itself does not, however, cease returning to its earliest origins and to its own organization. It is as if, without lingering over its successive experiences, the unfolding of time passed through them and oriented them. We shall see later how this protension or this propulsion of the self needs a fulcrum, which it finds in the fixity and the solidity of the field of consciousness, in the transitory immobility which alone can allow it to advance and soar. Let us simply say that the axis of the person is in some way magnetized and polarized, that it is oriented according to a vectorial function which is assumed by the self. Whether awakening or concentrating its attention in reflection, the self can be conscious of itself only when it affirms itself as an agent and not merely as the support of this existential trajectory. The "Kantian" self of obligation, the "Biranian" self of effort, the "Bergsonian" self of duration all coincide in this phenomenology of its axial structure.

The axis of this trajectory is "axiological" in the sense that it does not consist in the interval of two moments of chronological time or of two points of geometrical space. It is neither a line nor a thing: it is *value.* It is the very sense of that movement by which the self fixes its norms and its normativeness.

The self is, in effect, the promulgator of its ends and the creator of its own system of information. It exists by endowing itself with a system of values. These values are not, of course, only its own. For any scale of human values necessarily goes beyond the individual; its law is borrowed from an external or transcendent legality. All this is obvious. But no less obvious is the fact that culture, religion, and values in general must be incorporated into this system, which is capable of forming the information, logic, ethics, syntax, or social rules of this personal *axiology*. The incorporation of this system—whose organizational progress we have outlined above—is the being of the self. In this sense it is true that the superego of Freud is truly in the self, for the self cannot form itself without the ideal which grounds it.

The self, however, is not "formal" or "ideal" as is a sovereign and impersonal Law. It is "at the same time" both the person who gives himself the law and the one who is obliged to obey it. For this reason the trajectory of the personality is not that which the self's direction would follow if it were a projectile. It is rather more an uncertain project, a pursuit of a goal which is itself changeable. The self's direction is in fact probabilistic and problematic. By polarizing its acts, its choices, and its decisions, by having itself accomplish them, the self is constantly bringing its goals back into question. This uncertainty represents the internal variables upon which depends the function of the curve which the self describes in the perpetual movement of its reflection upon itself. In other words, since it cannot be reduced to a uniform movement, this trajectory remains constantly free, animated by a living force.

By thinking its project, the self again calls it in question. This is indeed a fundamental structure of self-conscious being: it is for itself a question which is unceasingly reflected upon itself. Who am I? This problem, which was enunciated tragically by the Sphinx, philosophically by Socrates, and dramatically by Hamlet, is the constant problem of each person, since one can be only in seeking oneself. Its own particular questioning and its own particular response are the operations which propel the self. This is so true that the self's structure as a trajectory or as an arrow can be applied quite exactly to the vectorial form of its movement towards its goal, but only as the segment of an aleatory curve.

2. THE PERSON'S IMPLICIT STRUCTURES (THE SELF AND ITS FACULTY OF CONTAINING)

Though it may not be "implied" in the sense of a logical and formal implication (which states that, whatever the value of its variables might be, such and such a relation implies such and such a term), the structure of the self appears rather as being *implicit*. The ideal line, the trajectory or the vector by which the self presents itself as directed towards the point—more or less sharp or blunt—of its willing, this simplification contained in the word "self," is an ellipse which contains an infinity of virtualities. The dynamic aspect of the self's constancy resides not in its simplicity but in its potentiality.

If a person's self appears as being both so "characteristic" of a certain simplicity of the "character" which "characterizes" that simplicity and so mysterious in the secret of its implications, it is because this structure of implication itself implies the dynamic structure of a being in whom the self's organization represents that power of control and of integration which is the most often recognized and which can be summarized in one word: it *contains* its experiences, its past, its abilities as its own essential possibilities, and especially its capital of logical and moral values. But it also *contains,* repressed in its unconscious, that which in itself is contrary to its fundamental axiological trajectory. These modes of implication and containment must be described by any analysis which attempts an ontology of the self. Without claiming to be able to carry this through to a definitive conclusion and to complete it in all its details, we shall content ourselves with several indispensable remarks. We must now show how it is that in order to be conscious and master of itself, the self must exist as the agent of all potentiality and on this account contain its own possibilities and its own obstacles within itself. This excursion into the implicit structure of the self will moreover give us the opportunity to reflect one last time upon its own reflection and the problems which this engenders in this being whose "for itself" is also an "against itself."

The self implies the body. We must now examine what this reciprocal implication is and what are these relationships of container and contained which, in the formation of the self, affect its relation to *the body.* What is the being of this being in relation to its body, to which it cannot be reduced and with which it nonetheless remains consubstantial until its death? To say that it is a *purely* spiritual being is to contradict the incarnation of the self. On the other hand, to say that the body excludes the person and that the person is only its body contradicts the very structure of the person. The human mind perpetually wavers between the dualism which in an absolute manner separates the body and the person and the monism which purely and simply assimilates one to the other. There is no need for us to add one more oscillation between these two antinomies of reason to the myriad reflections upon this eternal theme. Instead let us state that the problem of the person's being, in its concrete and real form, can be resolved only through the evidence of the constitution of the person by its body, understanding by "constitution" (whatever may be the metaphysics or the faith which leaves in abeyance the very principle of this constitution) the personal being's power of transcendence or emergence from this body. As we have already seen in the case of the problem of consciousness considered as the field of what is presently lived, as well as in the case of the most diverse theories of personality, this power of acceding to reflexive knowledge through the constitution of a reality is a *creation*. This creation is perpetuated in the constitution of the self, that is, in the production of a system of values rooted in its organization but which has as its function to go beyond this organization by superimposing upon it a supplementary motivational and symbolic order. The self can go beyond its body only by deriving through its roots the nourishment of its "information." The being of the self thus appears as a transcendence, but as a transcendence which is always compromised by its submersion in the body, from which it tears itself away only to find itself still bound to it in its representation. The freedom of the self is not absolute. All metaphysical positions can agree upon this point. Sartre tells us that "Man is condemned to be free," just as Ricoeur reminds us that our freedom is only human, that is, limited. The self's "reality" thus proceeds without confusing itself with the reality of the body. Instead it transcends the body by unfolding itself in a system of relations which, as we shall see, cause it to fall from the "body-in-space" into a "body-in-time" which is the historical body. But if it escapes from the body only to be contained by it, the self is the container of the body in the sense that the latter is implied by the former.

In this same sense the self also implies *language,* which is just as much the vehicle of its freedom as it is implied by it. Language is the symbolic reality which constitutes the stuff of the self. It "leaves" the body in both senses of the word: it emerges from it and it leaves it behind. By incorporating a common language into itself, the self, which had at first been possessed by it as by the language of others (Lacan), comes to possess it as it possesses its own body. This relation of the self to its language as being its own (this "second signal system," as Pavlov has called it and which is the first systematic relation of the self with the other) becomes the relational activity of the self-conscious self. To be conscious of what I sense or of what I wish is necessarily to verbalize my ideas, my projects, or my feelings; and it is to have the power to do something about them. This ability to tend to things is certainly not complete and absolute, but it is the condition of the control which I am able to exercise over myself, over others, and over things. This world of meanings, which enters into the composition of the self as another world, ought to be my own. Such is language's mediating function between the self and its world. For this reason the personality can be constructed and can move only as a manner of expressing itself or of speaking to itself and to others. This is, as it were, the milieu and the motivating force of all the intra- and intersubjective relations of its existential movement.

The self also implies *reason* and is implied in it. As we have seen, the self develops only through its dialectic. With Piaget, we have laid hold of the birth of intelligence in the advent of the subject's operational ability. When this ability is being organized and incorporated into the implicit structures of the self, it "catches" itself in its reason. Of course not everything that the self does is "reasonable," and the self does not exist only in the case of the mathematician. But the "capitalization" of intellectual values is a part of the properly juridical and ethical constitution of every person. The self, in fact, finds the source of the effectiveness of its actions upon its world, itself, and others in its obligation to submit itself to a legislative power. The self contains this power within it, but only as a virtuality which implies a constant problematic. The self's reason is not "pure Reason"; it is only that which refracts and contains the laws of the understanding within its own structure.

The self also implies the *construction of the world* which

it contains. The direction of its trajectory is constantly sustained by its representation of the world, which is constantly bound to its own operations. The world and the self reciprocally engender one another. They each refer *one* to the *other,* this "other" being either what is in the world as not being oneself, or even what is in oneself without being oneself. To the degree that it is differentiated and constituted, the self can never separate itself from that which it has been and which rebels against its constitution (the irrational, the fantasized world of imagination, of myth, and of poetry) and which seems to be another world contained within itself and which surrounds and concerns it relentlessly and mercilessly. When discussing the alienation of the self we saw that pathology furnishes us with the "solidified" image of this virtuality of the fantastic. The person's trajectory—recalling here the trajectory of the field of consciousness, with which it can maintain very close relationships, as we shall discover later on—is in control of enough processes and reversibility that the excursions from one sphere to another which are allowed by judgment guarantee to the self enough freedom in its movements to allow it to bind or to unbind itself. This elasticity of judgment, this modality of accommodating itself to reality and of admitting the irrational, the magical permission to tolerate an osmosis of the world of subjective and objective values, a supportable dosage of feelings, and, in a word, a certain ambiguity and, as it were, a penumbra of certainty, all these are manifested through one's *beliefs.* These are judgments of good or of bad faith which make us accept our believing even though we lack certainty. In the same way, our "conception of the world," which is itself as changeable as we ourselves are, can allow itself both to submit to the reasonable structure of our system of values and to find in the verbal structure and the tolerance of judgment enough resources to resist it, if not to escape from it. To the extent that it is "inauthentic," the whole existence of everyday life is a fabric of beliefs which are a compromise or a transition between the rational world of objectivity and the irrational world of subjectivity. The temporal structure of the self, with the freedom of the practices which it implies, allows for this "game" or this ruse of the subject with himself and his world, which—as psychologists have noted and moralists have denounced—enters into the human condition.

The system of the self also contains the *personage* which is n author; he is his own author. By *becoming* itself, the self installed in its character, that is to say, in its history. For a n's history creates his character just as his character creates history in and through the indissolubility of the bonds ich unite the "constituted" person to his constituted world. The history of the person is not, however, reducible to that story in novel form which oneself or another can extract m the existence of the person. It is more than that: it is the hrownness" (in the sense of abandonment, of *Geworfenheit,* use Heidegger's term) of man in his world. Obviously this anner of being "thrown" or "cast out" into the "haecceity" of xistence, into *Dasein,* is the tragic destiny of every human erson. But it is also his proper manner of participating in istory: coexistence with others *(Mitsein).* This manner of taking one's place in history—even if it be in the most modest osition of an obscure existence—and of directing oneself to ne's task is indeed a constitutive modality of the self as it is settled in its "worldly temporality." As we have pointed out above, it is precisely by getting beyond the space of the body in such a way that it lands in the time of history that the self produces its fate. It is very true that the self's transcendence is its possibility of inscribing itself outside of itself (as in its photograph, its memory, its image, or its works) in the consciousness of those others who form History (which is interwoven with the self's own history). The self is completed as it begins in its relationship with the World, of which its own person, its own history, and its own world are a part. From the first moment of its constitution it has *become* what it had not been and what it always has trouble being: self-conscious. It has become conscious of its ends, of its person, and of the history which receives and contains its being.

3. THE SELF AND THE FIELD OF CONSCIOUSNESS: THEIR RELATIONSHIPS OF RECIPROCITY AND OF SUBORDINATION

Conscious being is therefore neither simple nor homogeneous. It cannot be reduced to an "agency" or to a "function." It represents in the first person the integrative realm of relational life, that is, the system of relations which submit life to the exigencies proper to an existent which is structured according to the model which we have described in the first chapters

implied in its identification with that which it ought to be. The role's obligatory aspect is not naturally as exterior to the person as certain psychologists or social psychologists represent it to be. We have already shown how the reduction of the person to the "basic" cultural personality could appear to be both accurate and incomplete. It is obvious that the individual's *social status* and his *encounter* with loved, feared, prestigious, or exemplary personages can induce models of imitation, that is, of identification. But if the "mask" of the personage can be and is borrowed, it does not depend merely upon its form and characteristics being taken on. In addition, it is necessary that the role be assumed. In this way it happens that the problematic of this consenting is posited as well with regard to the form which is imposed by nature as to the figure which is offered by the environment. In this respect the movement which prompts a being to become a personage involves, here again, a freedom of choice which leaves relatively loose the bonds which unite what I am with what I wish to be, without on this account causing the self to cease being structurally committed to pursue the conformity which is necessary to its being, the cohesion whose *identity* is as if the "end" of its own identification. Approximations, combinations, contradictions, and changes are also, to some extent, possible or even prescribed. What I am in the eyes of others or of myself always puts a certain element of risk into the trajectory and the distance which separate me from or draw me toward that being which I as yet am not and the very ideal of which attracts me without determining me. In the last analysis, to the question "Who am I?"—which implies that in my identity I achieve the ideal physiognomy which haunts me—I can never give a simple answer. For through the vicissitudes of its composition, the personage that I compose for myself always remains to be completed. The self runs after its identity. It creates it without achieving it, leaving to its civil status and its name the task of establishing that which it is unable itself to attain completely before its death. In this dialectic of the identification of the self with its own ideal we once again come upon the contradictions of the one and the many and of the self and the other which are the inner progression of self-consciousness. The desire to be the person he loves, or to be the person by whom he could not be loved unless he were symmetrically different from himself, this desire is for the self the very model of the original Oedipal problem. However, we find always persisting in the self those internal and reversed movements of its demand which urge it both to attain the ideal object of its desire and to submit it to an ideal of itself which would necessitate its annihilation. In this way, once again the identification of the self through self-consciousness implies an internal division, a conflict which enters into the existence and the structure of the self.

At the extreme point of the dynamic trajectory of its manner of being in the world and of inserting into it the arrow of its potential for originality, the self culminates in the manifestations of its *character.* This, as we have seen, is the "spearhead" of the Ego, insofar as the self is presented from this point of view as the master or proprietor of itself. Thus the "objectification" of the self in character constitutes the highest degree of its personalization. But if by asserting itself the self gains its highest degree of mastery, this ultimate form of its proprietorship remains a domination and a conquest. Though it could not reduce itself to its given character, the self does not cease to be concerned with it. Here again, by acting at the extreme point of its "personal characteristic," the self contains within its organization the very thing in opposition to which the self establishes itself. We have thus arrived at precisely that level of the architectonic of the self where its character and its history merge.

3. THE HISTORICITY OF THE SELF

Since the being of the self is its becoming, its ontology sends us back to its development or its ontogenesis. Through its character the self culminates in its historicity, if it is true that it has no character but that which it has constructed for itself in the originality of the events of its own existence. In this way the self reveals itself as that personal temporalization which in effect constitutes its history.

To the extent that it is the structure of the self, its history is within the self's reach and at its discretion. This history is essentially intimate; it unfolds in its secrecy. By its very nature the historical self keeps its history to itself as the most inviolable of its properties, that to which it refers back by itself and alone as if to gain consciousness of its most personal aspects. The historicity of the self is not merely its manner of enveloping itself in what is secret and private in its existence. It is also the unfolding of the events which enter into and follow each

other in this existence, the sequence of dramatic plot of the self.

The *historicity* of the person is incor of the self, for all the explanations which its memory and out of its self-consciousne historic order of the events of its existe who is (this *Dasein* of the being who is forr not belong in the category of actuality. He c his actual presence; more precisely, his present moment. This history is not merely mulation of past experiences or of sensation has *had.* It is the very unfolding of the met takes place in the being who proceeds thro incorporates into himself the events of his ex is the temporalization of the succession of eve riences in that it takes upon itself the choice r and its projects, but of its memories. The suc one's biographical vicissitudes, this fundamen the identity of his person, is not a chain or which would be imposed upon him from outsic gration of those values which are retained th labor of edification. The winding and unwindin personal history in the temporal structure of his movements of his cohesion and his homogeniza tory of the person can effectively be recounted b were the object of a narrative or a novel. An auto a diary is an extreme illustration of this film of the creation of the person in and through the e history.

If it has often been possible[73] to study, along wi the person as the subject of the novel or the novel as of one or several persons this is precisely because th development of the person falls into the novel of when it emerges from the infrastructures of the bod the process we have outlined above. We have, in effec at the transition from the simplicity of the "I" to the cc of the self. To its complexity, but also to its plasticit Lowenthal has remarked, just as a person in a nc comedy (and he cites Shakespeare's Caliban) is not nec fixed to the unity of his personage, so the living perso any more given up to the constancy than to the simplici character: he is not like the characters of Pirandello, in

of this work. By examining once again, and in the most sche-matic manner possible, the reciprocity of the relations of the "field of consciousness" and the "self," which are the two modalities of being conscious (being conscious of *something* which is lived as something, and the consciousness of being *someone* who is oneself), we are now better able to understand the relations, the connection, and the order of the organization of conscious being in its generality.

When we described the structuring of consciousness, we saw that it is organized as a *field of actually lived experience* only in relation to the subject who constitutes it. In effect, the ontogenesis of the self has its roots in the constitution of con-sciousness, in its formal invariants and its cerebral montages. It is in this way that the incorporation of language, the institu-tion of an inner world of symbolic, verbal relations and of intel-lectual operations, can be described both as the foundation of consciousness and the source of the self. But the field of con-sciousness and the self then diverge in their direction and their organization.

The structuring of "constituted consciousness" as a "*field of actual experience*" and the organization of the corporality of experience as a *"lived experience"* are the condition of those "facultative" movements whose "verticality" is the guarantee of freedom. This is the reason that consciousness is often de-scribed as a "flux" (William James, Bergson), whereas its con-stitution as a field is a sort of fixed pole, the anchor which makes possible the mobility of its operational pole.

The *self* derives its substance from experience, but tran-scends it. It "flies over" experience and breaks loose from it so as to become constituted as a "rational" being, as the personal being of which we have outlined the possibilities, structures, and the individual history it involves, along with its develop-ment and its dynamic trajectory. We thus clearly see that the *Ego* is the transcendental being of self-consciousness in rela-tion to the field of consciousness in which its experience is lived. Since conscious being can be reduced neither to a pure subject nor to the momentary object of its experience, it ap-pears as being structured by the juncture which binds it to its world, insofar as it *has* the experience of its world and *is* its master. In fact, there can be no conscious being without the absolute proprietorship of one's experience and without the ability to have it at one's command in one's own history. As we have so often repeated, to be conscious is, by turns and at the same time, both to *live an experience* in its actuality and to *direct one's existence* through one's fields of actuality.

To say that Consciousness and the Self are the same thing is one of those ideas which are "generally accepted" and incessantly passed on by most ethicists, philosophers, psychologists, and psychoanalysts. This book has been written precisely against this oversimplification. There is no need for us at this point to drag out all the arguments involved in it in order to reject this thesis.

Nonetheless, it is not enough for us to have made explicit the fundamental relationships between the field of consciousness and the self. We must consider what is the meaning of these relationships and especially whether their relationships are of pure reciprocity or of subordination.

It is obvious that the field of consciousness is subordinated to the personality system in the normal adult when awake. This means that I am someone who integrates into his history the successive moments of the actuality that I live. This "integration" is the "functions" which classical psychology distinguished as attention, memory, reasoning, affectivity, and which are realized more totally as a taking possession of the field of consciousness through the self's intentionality. When the self actively directs its experience to this "summit," to this supreme region of the psychical being, then the self and the field of consciousness coincide. But this relation of coincidence should be interpreted neither as an identity nor even as a relationship of total reciprocity. If conscious being appears as a reflecting structure, subject to its fundamental law of reflection, the juncture of the field of consciousness and the self is not organized in a relationship of pure and simple reciprocity, but rather in a relation of subordination.

These two modes of being refer back each to the other as does the figure and its ground in the coming and going of experience in which at one moment I *feel* myself living an event (from the most trifling to the most dramatic), and at another I *know* myself to be pursuing and directing my history through the events which make it up. The subordination of these two modes of existing is evident.

The field of consciousness is constituted only as an organizational order which, as we saw when we studied the neurobiology of the field of consciousness, is tied to the very order of the organization, that is, to the organism and in the last analysis to the brain. It is impossible to consider this modality of conscious being not to be rooted in the nervous functions, in the bodily apparatus which organizes lived experience's order into a field of actuality. As we have seen, the self is born of this basal structure. It emerges from the "I" of a vague subjectivity and, by flying over it, goes on to the point of forming itself into the legislator of experience. Thus, the relationships of the field of experience and of the self are not simply reversible but are open in a sense which is the sense of the transcendence of the self. The law of this organization is that *the field of consciousness is the necessary but not the sufficient condition of the formation of the self,* such that while it influences the relationships of mutual solidarity, these two modes of conscious being admit a difference between them which, as we have seen, can be conjugated in the mood of to be and to have. Self-conscious being envelops being conscious of actual experience in the same manner that being transcends having.

PART FOUR

The Unconscious

I The Problem
of the Unconscious

The structure of conscious being which we have just described is not and cannot justify a "Psychology of Consciousness" if that means a psychology which excludes the unconscious or—which amounts to the same thing—which reduces it to an insignificant mode of conscious being. On the contrary, all that we have said concerning the structure of the field of lived actuality and of self-consciousness implies that the unconscious exists within the constitution of consciousness and within the autoconstruction of the self. This is so because the "generating line" of the figures of consciousness is a movement which organizes human experience and existence and which causes them to move away from that which is not amenable to entering into the modes of conscious being, to its appropriation into the domains of the field of lived experience or the domain of the self. Nothing, then, is more contrary to the doctrine of the transparency of the self to itself, as postulated by the Cartesian *Cogito,* than the exposition of the "conscious and organized" being which we have just completed. If we have often used the term "problematical" to designate the constitution and the proceedings of this conscious being, this has been precisely because the ontology of conscious being is "ambiguous," "ambivalent," "bilateral," "conflicting," etc. This leitmotif should be interpreted as the exigency of the "thrust" of the unconscious into all the structures of consciousness.[1]

This comes down to saying that neither a monism nor a dualism of psychical being can be reconciled with what exists. For this being is not one and immobile like that of Parmenides, entirely reversible in and through its knowledge. Nor is it

295

formed of two juxtaposed parts, the unconscious body and the conscious mind. On the contrary, we have constantly been led to describe the movement of conscious being, in its complexity and its reflections, as unfolding in a "milieu" in which the continual "back and forth" of consciousness and the unconscious are "mediated." We therefore believe that we are in agreement with all those phenomenologists who ground psychical life in the problematical constitution of being, as well as with the psychoanalysts who ground it in the negation of its desire. In both cases there is necessarily a reference to a dynamic stratigraphy which not only makes possible but even necessitates the interrelationships of the imaginary and the real, of the automatic and the voluntary, of the unreflective and the reflective, of the given and the "taken," in sum, of the unconscious and the conscious.

We shall first of all make a short inventory of "unconscious phenomena," in order to try to lay hold of the total description of the unconscious. Next we shall consider which theoretical positions oppose and which tend to admit the *reality* of this unconscious. We shall then examine in more detail the psychology and the metapsychology of the Unconscious according to Freud, as representing the sole valid conceptualization of the being of the unconscious. Finally we shall attempt to articulate the structure of the unconscious along with that of conscious being in the dynamic organization of human beings. We shall thus have one last opportunity to explain our views on the validity of the connection of the field of consciousness and the self, this time in its application to the unconscious being which corresponds to these two modes of conscious being.

1. UNCONSCIOUS PHENOMENA

All unconscious phenomena are characterized by the fact that they do not appear to consciousness as belonging to it. In other words, *they escape it.* However, these manners of escaping from conscious being, of being unknown or misunderstood, denied or repudiated, are very diverse. They can be classified in relation to the two fundamental forms of conscious being.

1. THE UNCONSCIOUS AND THE FIELD OF CONSCIOUSNESS

Ricoeur's statement that consciousness is not a totality is especially true of the field of consciousness. Consciousness is essentially selective and thematic in and through its actualization. We have already seen that its "topic" or the "Gestaltiza-tion" of its lived experience involves fringe areas, implications, and exclusions.

To the extent that lived experience presents itself and is grasped as the object of an experience (of a "perception" in the broad sense of the word), it implies that what I think or per-ceive or represent to myself draws out of my past, out of my memory, all the antecedent experience which is necessary for the constitution of the actuality of my lived experience. And it extracts nothing but that from my past. This extraction neces-sarily presupposes a "reservoir of memories" whose virtuality constitutes the most universally accepted form of the uncon-scious (mnemic unconscious). Another form which is scarcely distinguishable from this material or this "stockpile" is consti-tuted by the "reservoir of automatic actions" and of "habits," the mechanisms of which come to haunt, to uphold, and to relieve the actuality of experience (this is the *habitual or un-conscious automatism*). All this is obvious.

It is also obvious that the actualization of experience im-plies a whole series of harmonies, of psychical phenomena and operations, which are a sort of "subconscious" or "infracon-sciousness." These phenomena occupy an eccentric position relative to the present field, but they are always ready to occupy its center. This is the "peripheral" unconscious of the *"petites perceptions,"* of the subliminal fringes, of the obscure percep-tions as conceived by Leibniz and Maine de Biran.

Lived experience appears to be even more deeply rooted in the sphere of the unconscious when we observe in a secondary manner in our own case, and still more easily in others, that this lived experience (in its noetic-noematic structure or in its function of positing the categories of the real) obeys an uncon-scious intentionality—as, for example, when I seem to see what I desire, and am unconscious of the hallucinatory or illusory relation which has been introduced, without my knowledge, as a trick or a practical joke which I unconsciously play on myself. This sends us back again to the problematic of the subjective and the objective which is inherent in experience (this has been made explicit, categorized, and analyzed in any number of studies of perception, in Gestalt psychology, etc.). I may also, however, be unconscious of my own desire to be aware of it only in the second degree of its expression, that is, only in its mani-fest content. All these "manifestations" of the unconscious in "daily life"—lapses, slips of the tongue, unsuccessful acts, these hundreds of ways of saying one word in place of another, of doing something other than what was intended, of forgetting or of being mistaken, etc.—these can all be understood in relation to an affective motivation which escapes the law of the constitution of experience.

This *affective unconscious,* which shuffles the cards of perception and, more generally, of the organization of the field of consciousness, becomes apparent in an even more radical manner. First of all, in the phenomenon of the *irruption of affective impressions.* These latter, which are given as a vital thymic tone or as a coercion on the part of drives, emotions, or feelings, surge forth as a "motivation," a "bestowal of sense," whose initiative escapes our conscious awareness. Next—and here we touch upon the depths of the unconscious life which is reflected and masked in lived experience—the very sense of the consciously lived affective impression (anguish, for example) can appear as the inverted reflection of its unconscious intentionality (the pleasure connected with the desire to hurt oneself, for example). To admit this ultimate manifestation of unconscious life is to admit what is essential to the Freudian theory of the Unconscious, as we shall see. If at this point we remain strictly with the facts, we find it to be perfectly clear that through their ambivalence, feelings and emotions are "given" not as simple and direct vectors but as pairs of forces whose poles—which blend together in the obscure labor of their unconscious germination—are inseparable.

More generally, we can state that whatever makes inroads into actually lived experience represents the unconscious, whether it is found in experience as an originating intentionality or as an incongruous automatic element. We thus see that even if the presence of lived experience in the field of consciousness always reveals itself as an *irruption,* whether it seizes us from without in the perception of objects or arises from within (as an intuition or automatic response) in our thought or action, the origin of the motivation and the meaning of our lived experience always escape us, only partially but necessarily. And this "partially" is the very facticity of unconscious intentionality, which is constantly interwoven with the conscious direction of what I cause to appear to myself. This compromise, halfway between what I present to myself and what presents itself, appears as the limit of our power of initiative over our actually lived experience..

All actualization of lived experience thus involves some aspect of unintelligibility, something which resists the noematic legislative power of experience. The task of consciousness is precisely always to will to take possession of that which can never be entirely grasped or justified.

The lively force of the drives and impulses enters into the composition and the equilibrium of lived experience, though its opaqueness does not appear to be a "half" of the field of consciousness but rather one of its coordinates. An "order" of lived experience cannot be spoken of unless its organization suppresses disorder by going beyond it and, all in all, by implying it.

A more in-depth study of its structure shows language, which is consubstantial with consciousness, to be the operation which forms the unconscious by hiding it in the discontinuity of its discourse. Being the environment or, more exactly, the vehicle of the dialectic between being and having which is constitutive of lived experience, how would it be possible for it not to ground the unconscious, through the exclusions of what it does not say? What is said is indeed what sets its sights upon the "thing" of the lived experience. But this sighting remains a sighting in that it retains a certain distance, a certain withholding of sense. De Waelhens emphasizes this when he states that through its displacements and its metaphors, language is a dialectic of absence and presence. Let us say that it is always a "play" on words, following the model of the famous phantasmagoria of "little Hans." At the two extremes of this game are idle chatter (as a "common" manner of speaking so as to say nothing) and poetry (the poet's manner of speaking is not that of other men). Between these two extremes, between sterile talking and poetic creation, language fills experience with its ambiguities and gives to consciousness an infinite ability to say without saying, to "play" symbolically with things. Later on we shall examine the problem of verbal structure as involved in and structuring the unconscious.

All that we ordinarily refer to as being a manifestation of the unconscious in the formation of experience thus refers to its essential structures, for consciousness is not established merely on an unconscious pedestal. It cohabits with its unconscious. It never ceases to happen along with it.

For this reason any psychology[2] of psychical "functions" (memory, attention, perception, discursive thought, affective impressions, etc.) is forced to admit that in their surging forth, their articulation, their signification, or their operational combinations, all these "phenomena" admit an unconscious current (engrams, *Vorgestalten,* impulses, formative activity, schemata) which is charged with meanings and "virtual fantasms" which make up the system which projects its unconscious even into the heart of its field of consciousness.

An infrastructure or an intrastructure of unconsciousness shows through not merely "under" but "in" the organization of experience. In fact, no individual or social human psychical structure[3] can be constituted without referring to that which is within and in the depth of itself and which it manifests only in its actuality and its facticity.

2. THE UNCONSCIOUS AND PERSONALITY

When we raise the question of the relationship of this latent system, this chain of unconscious phenomena, with the *personality,* we discover the unconscious in its historical or prehistorical dimension. It appears as one of the terms of the dialectic between the self and the other, as the other which is contained within the self.

The manifestations of the other are there, in this *Dasein* which is radically unconscious for itself. They are perceptible only to others because the nature of Self-consciousness is precisely the "transcendence" of the self in relation to the other. As we have so often insisted in this exposition of the configurations of consciousness, this transcendence is only a relation to a system of ideal values existing in the depth of this "axiological being" which is the self (and which tends to become what it wishes or does not wish, but ought to be). The "Hegelian" alienation of the self is there as if to remind us that it is precisely the self which, in its "promotion" of objectivity, contains this contradiction within itself. But the self contains it in such a manner that the self is conscious of this contradiction only through the contradiction's effects, that is, through the trials of the self's history. On the contrary, the self is not easily (and in some cases is never) conscious of the bad faith of its rationalizations, of the motives of its sublimations, of its inabilities which it transforms into principles, of the desires which it projects into its duties. These are all blindnesses which "are a part" of the self, but only as "objects" which are radically excluded from it through its own denial.

This paradoxical unconsciousness of the self as a dimension of the *Ego* is not a simple (and even less a conjectural) Freudian interpretation. It is—with all due deference to certain French or foreign phenomenologists for whom phenomenological idealism would reject the unconscious—at the very basis of any existential analysis of "being-for-itself-in-its-world," since, being a lack, this being implies a nothingness in its being and a reality which can be only the being of the unconscious. The unity of the self-conscious person is an existential value which grounds all interhuman relations. To the extent that it defines the character and the identity of each of us, it is rooted in its own consciousness of being someone. But as we have pointed out with respect to the ontology and the ontogenesis of the self, if this self-affirmation is taken in a system of values which demands absoluteness from this unity, it does not remain any less problematic in the reflection of its "for itself," and especially in the reflection of others upon the self. This is because the "myself," the self in the absoluteness of its affirmation, is constantly in conflict with the Other from which it is born and which it never ceases to reflect in its own speech, in the dialogue of its constitution. The Unconscious is precisely *that which* at the same time compromises, demands, and grounds the unity of the self.

When forming both its personage and its world, the self never ceases, in the denial of that other which inhabits it, to affirm its own proprietorship. At the same time that the Unconscious "manifests" itself, or becomes transparent in the difficulties of this task, it is absolutely denied by the self. This is because no matter how exacting this other whose image interferes with the self might be, it is the self which "is right." Through its autoconstruction—even if it is upon the knowledge of the other that it has built, along with its self-knowledge, the model of its proprietorship—this proprietorship must be one which is willed by the self. It is through its development and in its history that the self takes the place of the other. A person's history is a sort of text of the conscious discourse of the self, just as his prehistory is the text of his unconscious discourse. This unconscious inscription *(Niederschrift)* can only with great difficulty be discovered[4] in this structure of consciousness, covered over as it is by this "History" in which it *ought* not to be and in which only the self *ought* to be found. However, even if it be pledged to silence as far as expressed language is concerned, it speaks in the prehistoric depth of the self as an echo which never uses up its "archaic" or first communications.

The paradoxical and furtive appearing of the "unconscious" or of the "other" at the level of this higher form of self-conscious being shows clearly enough that the dialectic of the "self-consciousness" which grounds the self and the dialectic of the "consciousness of something" which grounds the field of lived actuality are in some way opposed to one another. Through its flexibility the latter admits the unconscious only on the condition that it be categorized as unreal or insignificant. On the other hand, through its manner of proceeding, the former excludes the unconscious from its proprietorship.

Once again we repeat that in this way *the unconscious appears under the form of images which are deprived of reality in the destructuration of consciousness and under the form of the language of the other in the decomposition of the self, in its alienation.*

3. PSYCHOPATHOLOGICAL MANIFESTATIONS OF THE UNCONSCIOUS

In relation to the field of consciousness, the Unconscious is revealed as being a counterreality (an imaginary entity). In the constitution of the person it is revealed as a counterself (an alienation). It is in this latter form that it is the most unconscious, that it manifests itself with the most difficulty—much more so than in its function as a counterreality. In any case, and no one should be surprised at this, manifestations of the unconscious are by definition, or more exactly because of the very fact of the structure of the psychical apparatus, rare and problematical in the experience of man's existence. When we seek out the unconscious we must necessarily seek its manifestations there where they appear. Since the very nature of conscious being allows the unconscious to appear only furtively or only to the "objective" gaze of another (or more exactly in his "interpretations"), it becomes obvious that we must go to *psychopathology* (a realm which can correctly be defined only through the inversion of the structures of consciousness and the unconscious) in order to find it. If it were not for psychopathology (or for dreaming, which is its counterpart in all existence which has been interrupted by sleep), the unconscious would never have appeared, not even to Freud, who is truly its discoverer.

In his "Note on the Unconscious" (1912), Freud asserts that psychopathology is a privileged realm for the unconscious: *"So-*

lange das System Bewusstein Affektiwität beherrscht, heissen wir der psychischen Zustand des Individuum normal.[5] In effect, the "royal road" which leads to the unconscious passes through *dreaming, madness, neuroses, and delirium.*

The modalities of unconscious being which form the "clinical tableaux" which we have previously examined are set forth in an often blinding clarity by the "clinical material" of cases of mediumistic trances, hypnotic states and sleepwalking, delusions of multiple personality, hallucinations, oneirism, epileptic auras and twilight states, schizophrenic dissociations, hysteria neuroses, obsessions, and phobias.

Psychopathology has in fact shown us: 1) that whenever (as in dreams) the field of consciousness loses its structure, the unconscious appears to the subject as a lived "reality," in and through its unconsciousness; 2) that whenever the self loses its structure, the unconscious appears to the subject as an Other, in and through its alienation. This is because "unconsciousness" as the collapsing of the organization of present experience is rigorously antithetic to the "unconsciousness" of the alienation of the self. One causes the unconscious to appear only by having it enter into the field of its destructured consciousness. The other causes the unconscious to appear only by excluding it from its property. One reveals the unconscious as a symbolic world of things whose reality varies along with the categories of lived experience when the field of consciousness becomes disorganized. The other reveals the unconscious as the language in which are articulated the relations between the self and the other, which relations are inverted when the self becomes alienated. However, even though the source of interminable discussions concerning the Unconscious in its relations with the Unconscious and with a consciousness which is sometimes denied, sometimes made into a thing, and sometimes unified to the point of absurdity or multiplied to infinity, these two manners through which the Unconscious appears as the opposite side of the two modes of conscious being do not necessitate a division of unconscious being. On the contrary, we shall see that unconscious being is and must be the root, the common trunk of psychical life.

For the moment it will suffice to have shown that the manifestations of the Unconscious are both hidden in the structure of conscious being and obvious in its disorganization; that the Unconscious and conscious being refer back one to the other.

2. THE THEORETICAL NEGATION AND
AFFIRMATION OF THE UNCONSCIOUS

We have already, from scarcely differing points of view, looked at this problem in relation to the negation or the affirmation of consciousness in general, then of the self in particular. The problem now arises in the form of a double interrogation: is not the concept of the unconscious psyche a contradiction in terms, and if not—that is, if an unconscious does exist in psychical life—what is its being?[6]

In order to gain a good understanding of the theoretical positions on the subject of the negation and the affirmation of the Unconscious, it is necessary to grasp thoroughly what fundamental positions they postulate. The negation of the Unconscious is the affirmation of the homogeneity of psychical life (either everything or nothing is conscious). The affirmation of the Unconscious is the affirmation of the reality of the psychical *organization* insofar as this is a composite structure, an *unitas multiplex.*

The *negation* of the unconscious is implied by "any psychology of consciousness" which accepts the Cartesian idealist postulate[7] of a complete transparency of the object in its being known. Traditional, academic psychology has been grounded upon this theme of the perfect intelligibility, the absolute equivalence of the object and its cognition. Its fundamental thesis asserts that consciousness and psyche are synonymous and thus that a phenomenon is *either* unconscious and physical *or* conscious and psychical. This attitude which negates the unconscious is the most widely accepted. It is that which Freud most directly attacks. It can be found in innumerable classical psychological and psychiatric writings. One of the most famous examples of this negation of the unconscious is that which Bumke and his disciples caused to triumph in the domain of German psychiatry, in which the influence of this school is still alive. The "anti-ontological argument" (the proof of the inexistence of the unconscious god) is formulated thus: an unconscious psychical phenomenon can exist only by ceasing to be, for a psychical being must be the object of its own knowledge. This argument is based upon the "observation" that anything designated as unconscious is unable to pass or to be passed through consciousness—neglecting simply that psychical phenomena are not things in space but rather apparitions in time. (An "unconscious" memory either has been lived in consciousness or else could be so lived.) For this reason an idealism which will not admit any obscurity into being, or a realism which will admit no light, must be condemned to a "plane psychology" (that of the mind, or in the inverse interpretation, that of behavior).

It is in this sense that Ricoeur has been able to say that Politzer's famous critique, in his *Critique des fondements de la psychologie,* remained the prisoner of an "idealism of the senses" which would even out all the structures of being in their meanings. For "concrete psychology" the facticity of the senses and of lived experience entails "no under side," "no genesis." ("What is 'on scene' in consciousness, as at the theatre, involves an identity of the meaning of the action, the text, and the theme.") However, for Politzer, Freud's "metapsychological" hypothesis incurs two other criticisms: that of *abstractionism* and that of *realism.* The abstract character of the Freudian unconscious lies in its "enunciation"—outside of the first person, which causes it to fall into impersonal factors—of a machinery of abstract psychological entities. The "reification" of the Unconscious appears in the analysis of the dream when its latent meaning is "hypostatized" as if it were a text which would be the Freudian object.[8] All in all, Politzer has been equally critical both of the notion of consciousness and of that of the Unconscious. This is especially true when he writes that his concrete psychology "has no need of the notion of the unconscious, precisely because it does not consider that the subject's ignorance concerning his own being is a particularly remarkable fact."[9] In effect, it is all interconnected: if all that constitutes the possibility for the subject to understand or not to understand himself should be suppressed from psychical being as being an epiphenomenon (conscious) or as being a thing (unconscious), and if "concrete psychology" be reduced to a linear series or to a flat strip of lived experience, there nonetheless remains a subject in the first person who can be conjugated neither with others nor with himself nor with things. This criticism, which itself is subject to criticism, has come from a most vigorous mind. It has had extraordinarily far-reaching repercussions throughout French philosophical, psychiatric, and even psychoanalytical circles. It has had the beneficial effect of making us aware of the dangers of turning the unconscious into a thing; but it has gone beyond its mark by taking up a prejudicial position against the unconscious, in the manner of a "sophisticated intellectualism."

There is another prejudicial negation of the unconscious which has often been touted: that of Husserlian or Heideggerian phenomenology. Even the most important of the phenomenologists themselves, with Jaspers, Heidegger, and Sartre, etc., have often repeated that phenomenology excludes the very possibility of a psychical being which would be refractory to the constitution of consciousness or which would not enter into *Dasein*. Nonetheless, Merleau-Ponty,[10] de Waelhens, and Lanteri[11] have recently shown that even if the immediate certainty of consciousness is "unassailable," its constitution is neither immediate nor given in the intuition of its complete unintelligibility. De Waelhens, along with Fink (in his famous *Krisis*), remarks that the essential dimensions of experience (those which we have discussed in the chapter devoted to the phenomenology of the field of consciousness), its potentialities, and its horizons are all related to what is implicit, referential, allusive, virtual, and anticipatory. Though it appears to be susceptible to multiple or ambiguous modalities, consciousness is not and cannot not be refractory to being grasped in its totality. Lanteri states that even in the perspective of a "phenomenological psychology," if conscious being "cannot recapture the whole of its transcendence," we must then say that it implies —as if being a remainder, an exclusion, or an inclusion—an unconscious which is "that whole part of nonthetic consciousness which man cannot recapture by his reflection." Thus "the essence of human transcendence necessarily implies the unconscious." And if, in the last analysis, Husserl and Freud are not as far apart from one another as is so often emphasized, or hoped for,[12] neither is Heidegger's position necessarily a negation or a denial of the unconscious; for as Lanteri again states, without assimilating the inauthenticity of existence to its unconsciousness, it can nonetheless be said that this inauthenticity grounds the possibility of the unconscious. In order to exist it must take itself for other than it is and must flee from itself into an exteriority in which it is unaware that it is to be found. In his "Meditation" on *The Unconscious and the Conscious* (to which we shall return later), Paul Ricoeur does not appear to be very far from this rapprochement of existential analysis and psychoanalysis when he validates the dialectic of the conscious and the unconscious through the reversibility of two "hermeneutics."

We must therefore assert that both existentialist philosophy, which places the accent on the relativity, incompleteness, and conflicting structure of *the existent,* and depth psychology, which is necessarily dynamic and genetic[13] in its theoretical conception, have broken with the very foundations of the negation of the unconscious considered as nonbeing, by affirming it as a manner of being without appearing, or of appearing to be what it is not.

If Freud is the brilliant theoretician and practitioner of the *affirmation* of this unconscious structure of being, it nevertheless preexisted in certain vague but pressing intuitions which have and still do set their sights upon a certain number of aspects of "unconscious life."

First of all, it is in the form of a *reservoir* that the unconscious asserts itself as a "recipient of memory," a "warehouse of the past," or a "storehouse of remembrances"; for it must truly be the locus of recordings, of engrams, of traces (Hering). It is impossible to speak about *memory* without saying something about the *Unconscious,* insofar as this is an automatic conservation and a potentiality of memories. For this reason one must posit with or against Bergson a thesis concerning the relations of matter and memory. However, the models of associationist psychology, especially its theory of the reversibility of the image and of perception, do not allow the appearance of the dynamism of the unconscious, which, along with the dynamism of consciousness, is suppressed by it. Considered in its mnemic aspect, this dynamism demands that memory should be considered as the very temporal organization of the psychical order. It demands that memory be a faculty of its choice with respect to the acts which permit it to remember this or that—as well as to forget this or that—and, in sum, to annihilate in order to reproduce according to the inclination of its needs.

This operational aspect of memory sends us back almost simultaneously to the intellectual operations (the "unconscious cerebration") which can be effected outside of consciousness under the form of logistic automatisms or of unconscious discursive thought. Since Hervey de Saint-Denis (and even before), there has been no end to the descriptions and demonstrations which have been given of the force of the unconscious both in this faculty of thought which underlies waking thought and in the thinking of dreams.

No matter how discursive or logical it may be, this "unconscious labor" appears more generally as a matrix *germination* of schemata or of intuitions. Through this the Unconscious asserts itself and is affirmed as an *intuitive power* which is the source of thought, Bergson's "profound self." We know that Eduard von Hartmann has unfolded his philosophy of the Unconscious, considered as the genius of intuitive knowledge, out of this force of the Unconscious. This function of knowledge which has been recognized in this mysterious and profound activity can be found throughout an uninterrupted chain of the history of thought, particularly in the Asiatic roots of detachment and contemplation, where the attention is closed to the world and opened to what is within oneself. We especially think of Schopenhauer, who saw in human existence the artifice of a will which supports the world of its representation.[14] This assimilation of the unconscious to a biological force, to a "psychoid" which through its vital urge animates the whole "psyche" without unfolding itself in the sphere of consciousness, as if better to preserve and conserve the creative power of all of humanity through its symbols, its archetypes, its fantasies, and its myths (panpsychical visions), this reminds us also of the "German romantics" (C. G. Carus, Herder) and, closer to us, of the neurobiological conceptions of Monakow or of Bleuler. It would thus be possible to speak of a "genealogy" of its spirit—a term which establishes an obscure correspondence (Szondi) between the "genetics" of the species and the imperishable germ of its "genius." ... This short discussion shows us in what sense the affirmation of the unconscious is in danger of being lost by attributing to its intuitive or irrational nature, to its power of symbolizing, the totality of the destiny of a man and of humanity. In this hyperbolic affirmation the unconscious turns its back upon the individualization of the person.

We have just traced the history [15] of the passage from the use of the adjective (which attributes the characteristic "unconscious" to such and such a psychical phenomenon) to the use of the noun—the Unconscious, raised into an autonomous and, in some manner, omnipotent being. This might be considered a passage from the negative concept of the unconscious to its positive conception. At this point we arrive at the advent of the Freudian Unconscious.

Freud's discovery, we repeat, sprang from his psychopathological material. In his clinical treatment of neuroses this discovery clashed headlong against this "something" or this "someone else" that, though imprisoned in consciousness, escapes from it in hypnosis, dreaming, and neurosis. For this reason, these states appeared to him to be the means of access to this closed-off world. Later we shall examine the Freudian theory of the Unconscious. We must now content ourselves with stating that it is inscribed in the historical movement of the affirmation of a true reality of the Unconscious.

A simple comparison of Freud and Pierre Janet shows the diverging sense of their positions with respect to the unconscious. From his experience of hypnosis and his remarkable studies of psychological automatism, Janet has derived the idea that these maladies no longer have the strength to oppose themselves to the mnemic or verbal ideomotor systems of their unconscious. The unconscious thus appeared to him as a force derived from the weakness or the dissociation of consciousness. For Janet the unconsciousness of hysterical manifestations and of somnambulism is a psychological automatism freed from the constraints which constitute the hierarchical organization of the psychical being whose unconscious is only a mechanical infrastructure. This conception of the relationship of the unconscious to the conscious, which, as we shall see later, remains valid for us, led him, however, to underestimate the meaning of the sphere of the unconscious and to overestimate the formal organization of conscious being. It is in just the opposite direction that Freud exploited his discovery and deepened the sense, the dynamics, and the structure of the unconscious by turning his back (after long periods of hesitation) upon the structure of the field of consciousness and, above all, upon the self. Apart from the individual genius of each one of his great clinical therapists, it can be said that the route followed by Freud has been infinitely more fruitful, for two reasons. First, he brought to light an unconscious which was so unconscious and so unknown only because it is its nature to be badly known or to be denied. Second, Janet's theory, in spite of his brilliant expositions and his profound analyses, has not been capable of giving a true explanation of the structure of conscious being.

The historical confrontation of this success and of this half-failure obliges us in our turn to become conscious of the sense and the limits of an apportionment of being between its Conscious (which some deny, against the very evidence of its being) and its Unconscious (which some deny, once more in the face of the evidence of its manifestations). However, no "apportionment," no division of the totality of psychical being could be accommodated to the affirmation that only one or the other of them exists. Each of them does exist; but they exist only in relation to one another.

It is impossible to read Ricoeur's meditation on this fundamental theme without being fascinated by it, just as it would have been impossible to understand how it should come to be formed. The question of consciousness, he states, is as obscure as is the question of the unconscious. If immediate consciousness has any certainty, it is not a self-evident knowledge; all reflection sends us back to the consequence of an intentional evasion of the self, which also is not a true knowledge of the unconscious. This true knowledge is indicated and furnished to us by Freudian realism. For its unconscious is commensurable, which implies that the being of the unconscious, its manner of being only as "diagnostic" or "deciphered," passes through the consciousness of others. Consciousness is the opposition of this unconscious. There is a relationship of opposition which appears between them and which subsists definitively, not merely as a distinction between things, but as an object of two hermeneutics which move in opposite directions: the one "reads" the unconscious by moving backwards towards its origin; the other "reads" the conscious by moving forwards towards its goal. Since both of these readings are possible (an example of this is given in the double reading of *Oedipus Rex*), they lead us not to a separation of being into two parts or to an eclectic mixing of two entities, but rather to a single unity.

This problem of the dialectical articulation of these two modes of being is the true problem which is posed when *the existence of the unconscious* (which for us is intimately united to *conscious being*) is thus validated. We shall now see that by wishing too much at the beginning to separate the unconscious from the conscious, Freud was later placed in the situation where he could not accord being to the unconscious without refusing it (or very nearly refusing it) to consciousness.

3. THE FREUDIAN THEORY OF THE UNCONSCIOUS

If, as Freud himself has said, the ideas of Theodore Lipps, or Freud's visits to La Salpêtrière, or his visit to Bernheim helped bring to birth the psychoanalytic theory of neuroses, of dreaming, and of the psychical apparatus, which theory is wholly built upon the notion of the unconscious, it is nonetheless true that we have here a veritable creation *ex nihilo.* The idea that the unconscious constitutes the "greatest part" of the psychical realm is a discovery which is due to his genius alone. The whole problem obviously consists in evaluating not the quantity but the meaning of this "greatest part."

The earliest form of the theory was suggested to Freud by comparisons between the cases of Anna O. (treated by Breuer) and Elizabeth v. R.: the hysterical symptoms spring from the force of repressed memories.[16] From this comes the fundamental schema of a force of *repression* (a "Russian censor," he wrote to Fliess in 1897) which is exercised over whatever is *forbidden.* Repression and the repressed, such is the binomial which forms the psychical apparatus in the earliest form of the Freudian doctrine, in which the unconscious is clearly defined as the "repressed."

However, this primitive schema, which opened up to human knowledge a forbidden realm simply by recognizing it as forbidden, was to become more complicated because of the fact that the sense of this prohibition had to be made more precise: *what* was forbidden, by *whom,* and according to what *law.* Thus, to describe the Freudian unconscious consists in following, along with Freud himself, the progress of his discovery, from his earliest works and his theory of repression of 1913–1915, up to his theory of the three agencies (Id, Ego, Superego). We would not dream of giving a complete account of this fascinating and methodical research into the Freudian truth at this point; but it is indispensable for us to present a rough outline of it, asking the reader to excuse any gaps and obscurity, or perhaps inexactness, in a domain which is more intuitive than logical and in which even the best psychoanalysts sometimes become lost.

The two fundamental, or primitive, theses of Freudian theory are these: 1) The Unconscious in the strict sense is the repressed (the repudiated); 2) The Unconscious *(Unbewusst, Ubw)* is radically separated from consciousness *(Bewusst, Bw)* and from the "preconscious" *(Vorbewusst, Vbw),* which is as if its anteroom.

By studying first of all the theory of repression, we are going to follow the development of Freud's thinking up to the point where the Unconscious is no longer merely the repressed and where the "repressed" is, in short, repressed by itself, that is, without having to appeal to its primitive exigency, that of a repressing force.

We shall then see how his topographic theory of the psychical apparatus comes in the end to admit a less radical separation between the Unconscious and the Conscious.

Finally we shall examine how these theoretical modulations leave the problem of the nature of the unconscious in suspense, for want of having suppressed the problem of conscious being from its very wording.

1. THE THEORY OF REPRESSION

The "absolute" Unconscious,[17] radically separated from consciousness, is constituted by all those psychical phenomena which *ought* not to accede to consciousness, which are separated from it by a law of prohibition.

a) The Repressed

Considered at first as a scene *(Urszene)* the memory of which was not permitted, the repressed almost immediately became identified with the pleasure which is more or less directly attached to it: the repressed was the *libido* (sexual hunger), which is the most intensely and universally desired but also the least totally demanding of all the satisfactions which are bound to the pleasure principle. We should add that it is also the most precociously desired of satisfactions, for the repressed is constituted by the *infantile memories* of sexual desires which appear outside of their unconsciousness precisely from the moment that it is permitted to manifest them (in therapeutic analysis). This is the theory of the *Three Essays on the Theory of Sexuality.*

This "repressed material," which receives and retains the unconscious, is not formed by the instincts, which, insofar as they are biological forces, do not enter into the domain of the psychical unconscious. It is rather formed by the drives, or still more exactly by the ideational representative of these drives *(Vorstellungsrepräsentanz)*. Thus it is increasingly accepted that the repressed is neither a really lived past (memory) nor the instincts themselves, but is that milieu in which figurative and substitutive formations swell (*wuchern,* says Freud).

Consequently, the "repressed" neither always nor necessarily represents the frustrations, pleasures, or anxieties of the "reality" of an infantile life (which precisely is not real). It represents the fantasies which represent the dialectic of desire. The repressed is not the instinct as such. It is a desire's disposition taken in a tissue of images which accompany it, or in a context of words which carry it along, of substitute-formations *(Ersatzbildungen)* which disguise it. It is in this sense that we should understand all the vicissitudes of the relations of the subject with objects (the libidinal investments), all the psychical derivatives *(Abkömmlingen)* and the representations which are related to it and which constitute the formations of the unconscious, the complexes or the key fantasy situations which are presented in the succession of the oral, anal, and genital stages and which naturally emerge in images of nourishment, of fear, and of the first libidinal "relations" of the infant with himself and with others, with the parts of his body, or with the image of his parents. The first of these complexes, or in any case the most crucial, the one which provides us with the model of our knowledge of the unconscious, is the *Oedipus Complex.* In it the libidinal investment *(Besetzung)* is revealed. Once this is detached from the infant's own body, it is affixed to one or the other of the parents (of the same or of the opposite sex). From this arises the possibility of affective constellations, of a "combining" of the relations of the desire to its object in which the dramatic vicissitudes of identification (crime and the punishment of castration) are knit together in the conjugations of *to be* and *to have* (centered around the paternal problem, that is to say, around the phallus). In the last analysis, what is repressed—and which has never been conscious (in opposition to the earliest theory which demanded the witnessing of a lived event through a recovered memory)— what is repressed and can appear only after the gratification ceases (as in the dream or in the course of the incomplete discourse of the psychoanalysis patient who hears and understands the psychoanalyst), is an amalgam of fantasies which were "prefigured" in the structure of being and which are like the already "developed" buds of the instincts, but to which access is forbidden to consciousness.[18]

The analysis of repression in the writings of 1913–1915 defines the repressed as that which is opposed to instinctual pleasure, as that which enters into conflict with the "conscious-preconscious" *(Bewusst-Vorbewusst)* system. This latter system demands that in order for this pleasure not to be an unpleasure, it be "repressed" and come into consciousness only through substitute-formations.[19] When examining the theory of repression, we shall see that the "repressed," like repression itself, is heterogeneous, for it can be prohibited or averted by various mechanisms which are rather different from those of the earliest theory. In any case, it involves representations which are more or less directly tied to instinctual impulses *(Triebregungen)*. It also involves unconscious feelings, to the degree to which the impression to which they give rise and which enters into consciousness does not correspond to the repressed representations.[20] This is so true that the repressed is not a scandalous or prohibited lived experience; it is rather a substitute for a tendency. It is not a "tabooed memory" but a deep part of the self, or something whose "topographic" abode is the unconscious system of depth psychology *(Tiefen-psychologie)*.[21] Insofar as it is the active structure of the repressed, this *endogenous* nature of the repressed is the proper object of the dynamic theory of the Unconscious. The repressed is not immobile. It involves stages and derivatives which are more or less invested with energy. In the Freudian theory of this period, the quantitative factors *(Quantitative Faktors)* of the quota of affect *(Affektbetrag)* seem to be as important as the selective cathexis *(Besetzung)* for constituting this force which constantly maintains the possibility of the return of the repressed *(Wiederkehr des Verdrängten)*. Thus, little by little and to the extent that the Unconscious ceased being uniquely the repressed, the repressed itself ceased being the product of a conscious repression and became a sort of *automatic and unconscious repression*.

Later, in 1923, the repressed[22] will be principally constituted by the id. In Freudian theory this id is generally considered to be the source of instinctual energy (the reservoir of the *libido*) and to be subordinate to the pleasure principle alone. It is necessarily amoral and illogical. Being the storehouse of ancestral experiences, it is composed of drives which are derived from the instincts. Thus the Unconscious which is represented by the id is the "repressed *per se*" (that is to say, from the "nonrepressed," since it is anterior to the law of prohibition and of censorship). This naturalistic conception of the id, its "positivity" being in some way biological (cf. below, pp. 355–365), has naturally given rise to an enormous number of discussions which have not yet been exhausted.[23] But we cannot avoid examining the way in which the psychoanalytic theory of the repressed developed in Freud's own mind. The concept of the "repressed" has changed so much that this concept could now be said to suppress the function of repression, for something can be repressed at the very outset without having been put to the test of consciousness. This repression is then closer to a sort of flight *(Flucht)* than to a condemnation *(Verurteilung)*.

b) The Mechanisms of Repression

We shall gain a better understanding of this degradation of the function of repression by examining the theory of the repressive agencies. In succession these are: the censor, consciousness, then the ego and the superego. Far from "repressing" and constituting the Unconscious, these agencies are definitively a part of this Unconscious. They consequently lose the capacity of constituting it to the extent that it is "repressed."

In the theory's earliest form, the censor is the living force which actively represses what is forbidden. This earliest form of the "agency of repression," which determines the aptitude to be conscious (*bewusstseinfähig,* says Breuer), was first conceived as the moral and collective interdiction which is directed against sexual pleasures—especially incest. The theory moved almost immediately towards an ethical and social interpretation of "taboos." This idea of a sort of censorship, or rather of a "censor," of a permanent watcher *(ein ständige Wächter),* was taken up again, especially in his 1913 work on repression,[24] where he shows that "someone" can prohibit the access to such and such a part of the psychical apparatus. Naturally the superego will later play the role of this vigilant censor, but it will then itself be unconscious.

The consideration of one of the most characteristic situations of the return of the repressed through the weakness of the suppressing—that is, in the case of the dreamer[25]—has certainly not been missing from the theory of the relations of the conscious and the Unconscious which was formulated around 1915 in "The Unconscious" and in "Repression." *Consciousness,* Freud states, is the surface of the psychical apparatus.[26] It shows itself as a sort of thin film or porthole through which the psyche enters into contact with the external environment.[27] It represents the locus in which the psychical phenomena which become conscious unfold. It is both a perceptual and an effector system of reality. Consciousness and perception-consciousness are always synonymous in Freud's works. This consciousness has no activity by itself. It is only the reflection of reality with which the pleasure principle must "come to an understanding." The Unconscious is thus repressed by what is external, by means of consciousness, which is its "representative." Hereafter this repression will depend also on unconscious conditions which will gravely compromise its initial sense, that of a condemnation by the conscious censor.

From this period onward, the Freudian analysis of repression increasingly emphasizes the somewhat unconscious processes of repression.[28] Repression no longer works only through the conscious agency. Instead it works as if from underneath, through the attraction which the unconscious sphere itself exercises.

Let us now follow the development of the theory of repression through the two works from which we have just quoted. Repression is destined to put off unpleasure *(Vermeidung von Unlust).* It cannot, therefore, repress the instincts themselves. It acts upon the instinctual representatives. *Primal repression (Urverdrängung)* constitutes a first stage of this repressive process. This primary repression *refuses* to allow the instinctual representative to have access to consciousness. It *fixates* its content by binding it to the instinct. This process is not, we repeat, the effect of conscious repression, but is instead that of an unconscious force (its countercathexis and its registering as *inscriptions,* which are "absolute" in the same way that a reflex is said to be absolute). Perhaps this process can be assimilated to the mechanisms of reversal into the opposite *(Verkehrung ins Gegenteil)* or of turning round upon the subject's own self *(Wendung gegen der eigene Person),* which are described here (1915) as the stages of the inevitable development of instincts, but the "vital" sense of which is later modified by Freud in *Beyond the Pleasure Principle* (1920). The very least that one can say is that in any case we have a repression which excludes the conscious agency of consciousness. This is not true of *repression proper (eigentliche Verdrängung),* which is also called "afterpressure" *(Nachdrängen)* or "secondary repression." This latter bears essentially upon the psychical derivatives of the repressed representation or the chains of ideas *(Gedankenzüge)* which are associated with it. This repression is brought about by a withdrawal of cathexis *(Entziehung von Besetzung).* That is to say, the unconscious representations (perhaps we should say, paradoxically, "repressed," rather than "unconscious," since it seems that they are already the object of the primal repression) are not invested. They are, then, unconscious because they are not invested with energy which belongs to the conscious system. We can here see a sort of lack of energy in its cathexis, a primal repression *(ein Urverdrängung)* substituted for the selective and positively active action of the repressing agency. All in all, for the theory of repression is substituted a theory of a *retention.* This radically changes the sense of the unconscious. When the dynamic standpoint is substituted for the topographical, the suppression of this agency is confirmed, by making it depend upon investments. The theory then falls into a tautology and into contradictions which scarcely permit it to be followed and even less to be analyzed.[29] We can understand that the "repression" which was at first envisaged in its topography *(in ihre Lokalität),* that is, as being active on the threshold of the Unconscious and of the preconscious-conscious *(an der Grenze der System Ubw und Vbw-Bw),*[30] is then presented in its dynamism. For the double inscription of the topography in two places is substituted the passage from one inscription to another; that is, the displacing of preconscious cathexis, the maintaining of unconscious cathexis, and finally the replacing of a preconscious cathexis by an unconscious cathexis. In other words, the repression takes place only through graduated combinations of libidinal charges, without the intervention of a repressing agency. The same transition, which is substituted for the fundamental opposition of conscious-unconscious, can be noted in the case of both substitutive representations and derivatives of instinctual excitations. It produces the same difficulties in both cases. Freud himself feels a certain dissatisfaction *(gewisse Unzufriedenheit)* as a result of considering these derivatives *(Abkömmlingen)* of the Unconscious in their relations with the conscious system:[31] on the one hand they are highly organized and bring all the advantages of conscious organization, from which they are not distinguished; on the other hand they are unconscious and incapable of becoming conscious. What had been the very basis for the definitions of the Unconscious through repression and of repression through consciousness,[32] this all becomes blurred and confused in this penumbra— which is perhaps the justification for this other statement of Freud's: "From the theoretical point of view, it is not easy to deduce *(abteilen)* the possibility of repression."[33]

The theory of repression becomes lost in the reciprocal interactions of the three agencies found in the last Freudian topography, without being able to explain the repressed either by the repressing action of the ego or by that of the superego, both of which actions are themselves unconscious.

We have already seen (p. 251) that the ego is a system which is overwhelmed, submerged, as it were, by the Unconscious. Especially in his later formulations, Freud considers the ego itself to be unconscious. It is only a part of the id, developed, it is true, "under the influence of consciousness, that is of reality"; but it represents only a "superficial differentiation" of it.[34] It is similar, Freud says, "to the rider who controls the horse, but who is also obliged to be led by it." (A. J. Westerman Holstijn has remarked that the substantial union of the ego to its Unconscious ought rather to be compared to a centaur.) This repressive system thus finds itself in the position of being repressed by the forces of the id. The specificity of repression by the ego is, on the other hand, better guaranteed by the assimilation which Freud established between resistance and repression. This comes down to turning its "defense mechanisms" into the natural accompaniment of repression by the ego. As we have seen, the theory of repression by the ego had to lead to the development of an "ego-psychology," as Freud seems to have foreseen.[35] When examining the contradictions in Freud's theory of the ego, we found that the ego, which at this point is considered as a part of the Unconscious, had for a long while been invested with a function corresponding at first to the reality principle and then to the libido (narcissism). In *Beyond the Pleasure Principle*,[36] the ego was transformed into a "bearer" of the instincts of death and destruction. This metamorphosis of the ego-censor into a censored and unconscious ego, and into an ego which is a slave to its own unconscious tendencies, again places it in question as being the agent of repression. At the twilight of this Pyrrhic victory, the Unconscious wins the whole of psychical being. "It is not only that which is most profound in us which can be unconscious, but also that which is the most elevated."[37] And as if to repress the ego even more into the unconscious, Freud adds that it is "above all a corporeal ego" *(vor allein ein Körper Ich).*

Because the agency of the superego is also essentially unconscious, it does not help us to understand any better its repressive function. Under the name of *"Ideal-ich"* or *"Über-ich,"* the "superego" is, Freud tells us, not so much an autonomous agency as a stage *(eine Stuffe, eine Differenzierung)*[38] of the ego which is itself bound to the id. This superego is nothing other than an identification (itself unconscious) with the father. This identification is so unconscious that we can say that it is an immediate identification, anterior to any object cathexis *(frühzeitiger als jede Objektbesetzung).* However, this superego is not a simple residue of the id's first object choices. It also has the signification of a formation which is destined to react dynamically against these choices. It is therefore fundamentally ambivalent in its assimilation and its introjection of the father image. It is the heir of the Oedipus complex, while at the same time it represents its solution. Relative to repression, this superego behaves towards the ego exactly as does the id. If, as would be indicated by its name and its functions, it could represent an agency which is repressive and constitutive of the Unconscious, it is itself buried in the Unconscious, in the repressed, about which one never knows either why or by "whom" the access to consciousness has been forbidden to it.

We thus seem to be well-grounded in saying that what is most lacking in the Freudian theory of the Unconscious is a theory of repression. Though it ought to have grounded the Unconscious in the strictest sense—the Unconscious which is radically different from the conscious and the preconscious—the power of repression ended by losing its ability to constitute the Unconscious. Whether it constitutes the genus or the species of the system of defenses or of countercathexes, the system of repression is abundantly described in its means. These means can, at the very extreme, be described in terms borrowed from the formalizations of Carnap and Nagel, as Peter Madison has proposed (1961). But the sense and the force of repression continue to hang in suspense. They can come to it only from consciousness, to which, Madison tells us, they are "inextricably bound" so as to become even essentially bound. For in its symbolic representations, every repression is the correlative of a significant (and not simply signifying) "context," of conscious being's structures, projects, and legalities.

This is as much as to say that by following Freud's thought through its meanderings and its patient labor of conceptual elaboration, the basic schema, the foundational intuition of the Unconscious defined as the repressed, whose access to consciousness is prohibited by consciousness itself, this schema has undergone several profound modifications and even, in a certain sense, a revision which places it once again in question.[39] Repression has ceased being the effect of a conscious censor; because of this the unconscious has ceased to be defined by the repressed.[40] We shall now see that once it comes to be confused with the id, and to the degree that its ulcerous development has absorbed the whole of psychical being, the thesis of the radical separation of the conscious and the Unconscious finds itself profoundly modified.

2. THE UNCONSCIOUS AND THE PSYCHICAL APPARATUS

The absolute separation between consciousness and the Unconscious has undergone a reduction which is proportional to the degree that the Unconscious has become omnipotent and has been extended throughout all of conscious being.

This can already be sensed in the first diagram of the Freudian topography (cf. above, p. 246). It becomes increasingly obvious as Freud complicates his topographical conception of psychical systems to the point of merging them all.

In this general aspect of the theory, we shall find all those contradictions which we have already encountered in our analysis of repression. It is easy to understand that once the conscious system is excluded as a sort of epiphenomenon or thin film which reflects reality, everything else—which is almost the whole of psychical life—is unconscious.[41] The idea of repression is then reduced to a reciprocal antagonism between the parts which make up the almost completely unconscious psyche. At the same time, the topography of the psychical apparatus is compromised, if not destroyed, in its functional significance.

In discussing the theories of the ego (pp. 243–257) and of repression (pp. 316–318), we have already set forth the Freudian theory of the psychical apparatus in its successive "topogra-

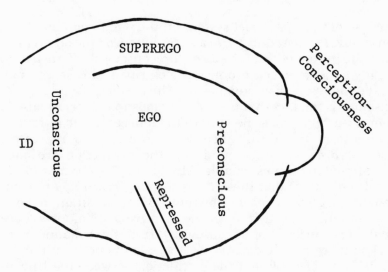

Figure 6. Diagram of 1933 *New Introductory Lectures on Psycho-Analysis*
   In this diagram the superego and the ego are coupled together and both plunge into the Unconscious. Repression is represented as a sort of lateral pressure, as if the separation of the Unconscious and the Conscious was no longer effectively its responsibility.

phies." We have seen how Freud, in the *New Introductory Lectures* (1933), moved from a position which considered the unconscious to be distinct from the person, to a triad of agencies which compose psychical life (cf. figure 6). (In Freud's early theory, the censor opposed a waking consciousness, open to the reality it reflected, to a closed Unconscious, both of which were separated from one another by a barrier, which only the symbol could cross in such a way as to manifest its latent content in consciousness.) We also saw[42] that these systems "are not even as rigorously delimited as different countries artificially are in political geography." The id represents the "reservoir" of the instincts, that is, of internal forces, while the ego and the superego represent the pressure of reality and of the ideal. The *ego* has an executive function: it controls the motor and perceptual apparatus. (It represents there what we call the structure of the field of consciousness.) The *superego* is a sort of second ego which represents the incorporation of the parental image as ideal or as law. In this respect there is a most characteristic evolution of Freud's thought concerning the separation of the

Unconscious *(Unbewusst)* system on the one hand and of the Conscious *(Bewusst* and *Vorbewusst)* system on the other. First of all, the introduction of the term "preconscious" *(Vorbewusst)* already appears to compromise the clarity of this separation. What doubtlessly distinguishes the Unconscious from the preconscious is the fact that the Unconscious in the strict sense is "repressed." But just as he later found it necessary to introduce another term (the "third" unconscious, which is not repressed, *nicht verdrängt*), the grounds for the distinction are once again found to be questionable. Already in *The Ego and the Id* Freud indicated[43] that these three terms *(Terminis)* are commodious *(bequem)* concepts, but only on the condition that one does not forget that if from the descriptive point of view there are the two varieties of unconscious, "from the dynamic point of view there is only one." Now it seemed to be from the dynamic point of view that the distinction between the Unconscious and the preconscious had been most strongly delineated. We must therefore resign ourselves, Freud adds, to giving a double sense to the Unconscious (if we correctly understand this to be the repressed and the preconscious, or the nonrepressed unconscious). From the economic as well as from the dynamic standpoint, it is the id which definitively represents the Unconscious in its generality. From it comes the energy of the whole psychical system. From the topographical standpoint, that is, from the standpoint of the functional relations between the various parts of the psychical apparatus, this apparatus is conceived in the manner of those famous schemata in which Freud tried to mark out, by their "bizarreness" and by the confusion of their outlines, both the "organic" interpretation and the nondifferentiation of these three persons in one single person. But this "trinity" of the psychical being seemingly remains constantly open—as does the unconscious "demand" which it expresses—to another person: that of consciousness, that "true" person which the psychoanalytic school has so much trouble admitting in its autonomy and *which alone, however, can give any meaning to repression*. In other words, by causing the whole of the structure of conscious being to sink into the Unconscious, the psychical apparatus is dissolved.[44]

   In our opinion this is the most important contradiction in the Freudian theory of the Unconscious. For Freud himself this constitutes an inversion of his fundamental and first intuition concerning the Unconscious. In the logical coherence of his system, the Unconscious is and ought to be "autonomous," that is, radically able to elude consciousness, if it is to avoid being merged with the preconscious and losing its absolute sense of repudiation and denial. Because of a sort of empirical exigency which this concept has, its "autonomy" doubtlessly cannot be so radical; without this, any awareness and any psychoanalysis would be impossible. But this is one of the exigencies of his doctrine, radically to separate the Unconscious and the conscious, which was constantly affirmed by Freud (until 1915) and reaffirmed by all his disciples as a dogma. In order to become convinced that Freud has reconsidered on this point, it is enough to refer to what we have just seen concerning the infiltrations and merging of the three agencies or concerning the questionableness of repression. This is notably the case in "The Unconscious,"[45] where the separation between the two systems conscious-preconscious and unconscious is completed by the theory of "derivatives" and that of the double censor. Or again in *The Ego and the Id*, where he asks us not to forget that there are not two varieties of unconscious but one only, and where he consequently brings together rather than separates the preconscious and the Unconscious.[46] To the extent that practical facility was gained in rendering conscious the unconscious, their separation appeared less certain and less necessary to the theoretician.

Another contradiction which is just as evident and which has been long recognized, and which we consider to be a corollary of the preceding, is that the Unconscious ends in no longer being the repressed. It is no longer the unique product of repression, and comes to admit a variety of meanings (*Vieldeutigkeit,* Freud says in "The Unconscious").[47]

At the end of Chapter One of *The Ego and the Id*, he states:

> We have found in the ego itself something which is as unconscious as the repressed tendencies.... Because of this fact, we come up against innumerable difficulties and obscurities in our work when we attempt to keep to our usual definitions; for example, when we try to reduce neurosis to a conflict between the conscious and the Unconscious. We must admit a third Unconscious, one which is not repressed.[48]

Freud himself suggests the direction which ought to be taken in doing this: "We should," he adds, making reference to

Beyond the Pleasure Principle (in a note which is not present in the French translation), "substitute for the pairing of conscious and unconscious, the opposition between 'the coherent ego' *(Zusammenhängenden Ich)* and the fragments which are repressed by it *(von ihm abgespalten Verdrängten)*."

There is, finally, another contradiction—or another mutation—which has been introduced into the theoretical system of the Unconscious. This contradiction belongs not to its topography but to its dynamics and economics. The Unconscious had first been conceived as an exigency of the *Lustprinzip* (pleasure principle). Against this exigency, the censor of consciousness exercised its control, in the name of the reality principle. This was perfectly clear but, alas, much too simple! On the one hand, during the evolution of the theory, the structure of the self and that of consciousness have undergone ever increasing libidinal investments, up to the point where, in *Beyond the Pleasure Principle* (1920), the necessity of the antagonism between the "life instincts" and the "death instincts" appeared. Freud then reduced all the constructive and destructive forces of psychical being to the play of the impulses of Eros and Thanatos, as if the original distinction of conscious and Unconscious lost its importance in a perspective in which the only thing which should any longer have any importance would be the equilibrium between the tendency to go to the extremity *(bout)* of life and the tendency to renounce it. Freudian theory thus substituted the opposition "life instinct–death instinct" for the opposition "conscious–unconscious." This happened because the two forces which are confronting each other are the ego instincts *(Ichtriebe)* which struggle against the *libido*.

Since the unconscious obviously cannot be defined through repression (which nevertheless remains its prototype), since it can no longer be distinguished as one of the systems (which are all more or less unconscious of psychical life), and since it can no longer represent the life instincts *(libido)* which oppose the death instincts, or vice versa, in a word, since it cannot set itself up in opposition to what is truly its foundation, that is, conscious being, the Unconscious ends up being a being without quality and, in any case, without causality. The Freudian Unconscious is conceivable only in the first model of the theory of the psychical apparatus, that is, when it was defined as the effect of repression, which implied that there was a structure to conscious being. When this disappeared and the whole apparatus became fundamentally unconscious, the Unconscious dissolved into a plethora.

3. THE NATURE OF THE UNCONSCIOUS

These problems, set forth by Freud in his very patient clinical and therapeutic research, with all the hesitations and contradictions which they involve, all amount to presenting the *symbolic structure* of the unconscious at the very heart of the theory of the unconscious. Whatever might be the contradictions that Freud's genius was unable to overcome, in this realm which is "naturally in opposition to logic," the basic nature of unconscious being has been shown to be its *function of occultation and of negation (Verneinung)*. For to say that something escapes consciousness is to make it present itself to consciousness in such a manner that it is both present and absent—as a text to be decoded. The reality and the problematic of the Unconscious is constituted by the obligation, the fatedness, of this hieroglyphic. As we have already seen (pp. 296–300), all appearing involves a background against which it stands out and in which it hides. It is only when the fragmentary text, the cryptogram, is deciphered that the Unconscious appears to whomever has known how to break through its opacity. This is why dreaming (and free association), to the extent that it is the language of the Unconscious, is the major means of access to it. It seems unnecessary for us to give examples of this symbolism, of these metaphors, of these metonymies, of these displacements, of these condensations, and of these dramatizations which "give an impression" or "speak" so as both to reveal and to hide the Unconscious. In its "apparitions" the Unconscious manifests itself as a world which is other than that of its enunciated desire. It is a more or less dramatic caricature of itself. All the characteristics which the psychoanalytic school recognizes as specifying the Unconscious are, as it were, attributes of this being, which either is or is not "subterranean."[49] It is the symbolism of unconscious phenomena and their relation to the imaginary and to language (to the extent that the Unconscious is condemned, or condemns itself, to speaking a particular idiom) which are the eidetics or the grammar of its closed relations. The characteristics of the Unconscious, which we have described by referring basically to what Freud himself has said,[50] are determined by the symbolic shadow which spreads over the Unconscious.

The Unconscious is composed of *isolated derivatives* which "represent" the instincts and which are "exempt from any essential contradictions." This is to say that they can associate themselves with one another without being combined. They do not come into agreement with each other; they form a system with gaps, a text without syntax.

Unconscious processes take place *outside time*. They do not change according to it, but change according to the whim of the cathexes (displacement, condensation).

The processes of the unconscious system, since they are subject to the pleasure principle (a point which was questioned in 1920 in *Beyond the Pleasure Principle*), also have little consideration *(Rücksicht)* for reality.

Within the Unconscious there is no negation; nor is there doubt, variety, or degree of certitude *(keine Grade von Sicherheit)*. These are all formal characteristics which are the attributes of a consciousness which is constituted as we have seen it. That part of the Unconscious which manifests is presented in the positivity of a presence or an affirmation which is the mark of its unconditional isolation. The *imago* is there as a thing.

It is also said that the Unconscious *excludes pronominal declension*, or more exactly, that it merges together pronouns and persons and objects. More generally it can be said that, according to its whim, it can bind any words together in metaphor or displace them in metonymy, at least in the isolated sphere in which fantasized meanings unfold or are linked together.

All these processes connote it as a *primary process (Primärvorgang)* which is a kind of symbolic current of a system of images or of words which lives its own life. In this way the unconscious life unfolds as a *doubling* of conscious life. This is the origin of the problem of the double inscription of the Unconscious which records the inscription *(Niederschrift)*, the lines that lie below the "reach" of memory, and which draws toward its own constellations all that it succeeds in attracting to itself from the preconscious-conscious system.

Having completed this brief enumeration of the characteristics of the unconscious, in which Freud's marvelous clinical and theoretical contributions are summarized, we find ourselves, in terms of this symbolism, ready to approach the ultimate problems concerning the Unconscious. These all come down to this essential question: Is the Unconscious made of *images*, or of *words*? Let us first of all set aside the question of knowing whether or not symbolism, as the constitutive law of unconscious being, presupposes that the eidetic structure refers to the verbal structure. Let us rather say that both interpretations, both hermeneutics of the sense of the Unconscious, focus upon two divergent "theses."[51]

The first is, in fact, that one which is found in Freud's original thought: the Unconscious is autonomous. It can be said to be below any formulation, to the degree that a formulation is constructed only in consciousness and is already present in the preconscious. The dynamic Unconscious is therefore composed only of *images* (charged with their specific libidinal investment), which are, in a way, inner perceptions, or of fantasms, which are, in a way, crystallized events of its prehistory. This theory of the Unconscious includes what is essential to any psychoanalytic study of libidinal development or of the anachronism of object relations. What is essential to the Unconscious is the mechanism of repression and forgetfulness—which can be said to be absolute. What is essential to conscious awareness, on the contrary, is memory, aided by the arrangement of a transference relationship which both interprets and is itself interpreted.

The second is more sensible to the transitions and mediations which language introduces between consciousness and the system of impulses. From this time on, the Unconscious can no longer be absolutely separated from the conscious (a thesis which Freud finally accepted, as we have already seen). It resides in the zone of its symbolization, in precisely that area where the preconscious is the locus of verbal formulations. The Unconscious doubtlessly is destined to resist entering into consciousness. But the incompatibility of the unconscious and the conscious systems, the distance which separates them, stems from the thickness of the figures of speech in which the situations or the principal imagos of primitive existence are knit together. The Unconscious is structured *as* is a language. Consequently, "one can converse with it." But only on the condition that one *understands* it. This essential thesis involves the fecundity of its perspectives and of its issuing into linguistics and, even more generally, into the role of speech in human institutions and existence.[52]

The first of these positions is subject to the reproach of "realism"; the second to that of "nominalism." Moreover, these reproaches can be reversed or added to one another, as in Politzer's critique.

It is obvious that these two points of view are not irreconcilable. They should be reconciled; but each of these theoretical conceptions should encounter the other, pursuing whatever historical aspects might be found in the structure of the unconscious, as well as whatever is structural in its history.

It would seem, then, that we ought to seize the Unconscious as it appears to us as the *rejection* (the objection, the negation and the condemnation) of a past which does not move beyond itself, and the *incarceration* within its fantasies of a fatal resolution not to speak except to say nothing. This has resulted, whether this had been intended or not, in situating the sphere of the Unconscious in this "profundity" of being where reign— in their symbols and their internal and reciprocal contradictions—the pleasure principle and the instincts of death, anxiety, aggressiveness, desire, love, and hate, that is, of all that is opaque, of all that which, being forbidden by the very sense of existence, cannot and should not be said. The death instinct does not lend its force to the ego and its defenses. On the contrary, it places it in the service of the Unconscious. It does this not because the Unconscious is the "id" which moves towards pleasure or is the superego which enjoys forbidding, but because the id and the superego are those contradictory forces in which seethes the being's discord, which provokes and necessitates its formation into an ego in opposition to this background of itself. By its very existence, the Freudian Unconscious is in fact a counterexistence which gives existence its value, not by governing it, but by instituting it through the danger which its mortal forces cause conscious being to withstand.

From this perspective, *a psychology of the unconscious which would reduce all psychical activity to the unconscious is no more sound than is a psychology of consciousness which would reduce the whole of psychical being to conscious being.*

Freudian analysis is an *analysis*. We must neither forget nor be surprised by the fact that his theory of the Unconscious leads to a pulverization of the psychical organization into shreds and pieces or into systems of dynamic cathexes which are incompatible with the very idea of this organization. As we have attempted to show by pointing out its vicissitudes within the Freudian theory, the notion of the unconscious demands this organization as the sole foundation of the theory of repression and of the equilibrium of the conscious and the Unconscious within the psychical apparatus. Psychoanalytic theory could give birth and substance to the Unconscious only on the express condition of making it depend upon, be born of, and live upon the constitution of conscious being. We must remind psychoanalysis of what the intoxication of discovery has caused it to forget of its first fundamental intuitions: there is no Unconscious without the structure of consciousness.

The theory of an omnipotent Unconscious, whose censor would be merely the reflection of an occasional external constraint, was only adumbrated in the first conception of the repressed Unconscious (which presupposed precisely that this conscious being have a certain force of repression of its own). It was then transformed into a sort of *theory of generalized Unconscious*, which can be summarized as follows: the Unconscious is the absolute of being. It is this which directs the reactive or defensive dispositions of the ego. But what is the nature of this force by which it becomes master of the ego, as if of its slave (the ego itself being essentially unconscious), if this force does not conflict with a force which is other than itself? If the Unconscious is both "other" and "something," the ego can only be other than what is unconscious and must be someone. We thus find that the thesis of the radical separation of the conscious and the Unconscious and the thesis of the absolute identity of the ego and the Unconscious are equally unacceptable, for the very good reason that both the theory of repression and that of "unpression" are equally impossible.

Let us rather say that the Unconscious can be grasped in its being only as a mode of conscious being: as a relation of *container* to *contained*. Of course this is only on the condition that we understand by this relation not a *position of reciprocity* in space as described by solid geometry, but a *dynamic relation of implication within the very structure of conscious being*. Through this relation the Unconscious shows itself to us: 1) as the *reverse side* of conscious being, of which it is a "consubstantial" part; 2) as *that against which* conscious being is organized and constructed.

As we have remarked above, this problem of the Unconscious is *naturally* to be found within the organization of psychical being. Insofar as it is the form of a system of vital relations, this organization implies a constant confrontation of "conscious being" with its "Unconscious." The *Unconscious* must be given an absolutely *positive* sign: that of desire. *Conscious being* must be given an absolutely *negative* sign: that of the law which controls all the relational movements of the being in its world. This is to say that the relations "conscious-unconscious" are *organic* relations of an order of subordination or of integration. It is this order which grounds the ascending movement of *conscious becoming*.

PART FIVE

Conscious Becoming

I The Organization of Psychical Being and the Problem of Human Values

The Unconscious is a part of, in fact it is, the body of conscious being. The latter can be constituted only in a first movement against the former; and the former can be organized only in a second movement against the latter. Following this dynamic relationship we ought now to consider the general structure of what Freud called the "psychical apparatus," which would be better designated as the *psychical organism* which is superimposed upon the vital organism, which it prolongs and surpasses. This organism itself involves a hierarchy. It is structured in a certain way: *conscious becoming* is a higher form of integration of being. For us the relationships of the conscious and the Unconscious are thus inscribed in the organizational scheme of psychical being, not in a proportion from zero (the conscious) to infinity (the Unconscious), as too many psychoanalysts are prone to represent it, but rather following a dialectic which assigns to the conscious the sense of an integrating system and to the Unconscious that of an integrated system.

We shall first show the manner in which the Unconscious is subordinated to the conscious, of which it is a property. We shall then attempt to present the general structure of psychical being, that is, of that conscious being which possesses, which *has*, an Unconscious, in an attempt to understand the dialectic of the diverse regions of being which compose it. Finally, at the conclusion of this study of conscious being, the real nature of which has been revealed through its psychopathology, its disorganization, we shall ask what effect our structural analysis of psychical being can have upon the debates whose stakes are human values and freedom.

1. THE UNCONSCIOUS AS A PROPERTY OF CONSCIOUS BEING

To say that the relation of the conscious to the Unconscious[1] is that of container to contained is to say that the container is the form which it imposes upon the contained. It is in this sense that the Unconscious can be said to be a property of conscious being (conscious being *has* an Unconscious). We must first examine whether or not the subject *controls* his Unconscious when he becomes conscious. What we call the appearings of the Unconscious are only attacks against the property of conscious being: either something slips away from its property, or it gives it away itself. Since it is by itself constituting itself (by becoming conscious) that conscious being places the Unconscious outside its domain, if the conscious does not control the Unconscious, it places it in the depths of itself. This shall become clearer when we examine the two categories of conscious being which will appear as a manner of expelling the Unconscious, that is, of "assuming ownership."

In the field of actuality belonging to a consciousness which has submitted to the *law of reality*, consciousness can appear only on the condition that what appears be subordinated to the law of objectivity. Whatever enters as a "content" into its field is effectively constrained to submit itself to its formal setting: I can allow an angel to enter this field only if at the same time I cause it in some manner to leave it. Undoubtedly the proprietorship which conscious being exercises over its own experience by the very disponibility of what is in its jurisdiction to include or to exclude, this proprietorship admits a certain flexibility which is regulated by its structure as a field of actuality, that is, as the field allowed by the condition of its reality and freedom. The Unconscious nevertheless remains that "more or less unconscious" obscurity or profundity which can cross the allowable limits of the field by escaping the control of its organized striving, without, however, gaining any rights to reality. The Unconscious can appear in the activity of conscious being only by eluding its vigilance (its censorship), by a trick or by some incongruity (once again let us refer to the psychopathology of the forgettings, the slips of the tongue, and the failures of purpose which occur in everyday life). The Unconscious is the reverse side of the field of consciousness. It is both that which is excluded from it so as not to belong to it, so as not to be able to be "contained" within it, and that which is "contained" (kept at a distance) outside its area of proprietorship. We thus come to recognize the relativity of both the conscious and the Unconscious, as well as the dependence of the Unconscious upon the conscious. To the extent that it is "repressed" (or arises as a result of repression), the Unconscious is the negation of conscious being, the nonbeing of the intended object. It is a necessary but necessarily exceeded dimension of what arises as an actual experience with its own index of reality. Further on, however, we shall see that this negative aspect, included in the word Un-conscious, does not correspond to a void or a nothingness. On the contrary, it corresponds to the dynamic positivity of instinctual impulses to the extent that it is denied, repelled, or repressed by "consciousness" and is constituted by it.

With respect to the other mode of conscious being, which consists not in being conscious of something which enters into its experience but in *being conscious of being someone*, the self instead *excludes* the Unconscious by a *Verneinung* (negation or denial) of whatever is not in conformity with the law of its identity and of its autonomy. In this case the Unconscious is not merely excluded from the contingent space of a property, of a field; it is condemned to be foreign, to be the other who could never appear in or be a part of the domain of the self. Thus, when the self's autonomy asserts itself, when, for example, the self decides to be a husband, socialist, or actor (or resolves to be neither a thief, a priest, nor a father), whatever is opposed to its wish, to its vocation, or to its proposal is rejected as something which should not be. Such a categorical imperative abolishes the other as an ideal, but leaves it subsisting in his examination of conscience as that someone that he is himself guilty of wishing to be, by whom the self has allowed itself to be tempted, even possessed. The Unconscious thus never appears, and is absolutely unable to appear in that self-consciousness which excludes the other to the point of always and unceasingly calling it to account only to deny it. It is the negation of the sense of existence, the existential antipode of an objectivity which can appear only to others but never to itself. It can well be understood that Freud should especially and freely refer to this mode of the Unconscious in the systematics of the ego. Of course when Freud spoke of the absolute-Unconscious, he was referring to this reverse side of the absolute-

Conscious. For "to be self-conscious" is for the subject always to make use of his property in such a way that he distributes it between the ideal values of good and evil which he intends to take upon himself by choosing what he intends to be.

Be that as it may, these two manners for conscious being to have an Unconscious—an Unconscious which, because it does not want it, it has command over—are made much more obvious by psychopathology, which, much more successfully than the *Daseinanalysen* of the existence of all men, shows us how "to become unconscious" consists in being dispossessed of the Unconscious. But, here again, this happens according to two modes of disappropriation.

Our case study of Jean-Pierre is worth noting here.[2] This 60-year-old epileptic, in a "twilight state" of his destructured consciousness, murders his mother in an apocalyptic and Dostoyevskian atmosphere of crime, punishment, and incest. Unfortunately, the death of his mother is real. But there is no crime, either for him, who did not will it, or for society, which held that his responsibility had been destroyed. He acted in a total lack of consciousness, the structures of the field of consciousness having collapsed. He no longer knew where he was or what he was doing. He had become the pawn of his unconscious incestuous impulses to the point of actualizing *in an imaginary world* an act which dropped down, like the forbidden fruit of his desire. He had lost hold of the underlying property which makes it possible to possess the things of the world: reality.

We have observed another case which should be mentioned here: that of a 23-year-old young man who attempted to rape and shoot his mother. In this case he was not in an unconscious state. He was in fact quite lucid, "in full possession of his faculties," as the classical formula puts it. He was, however, unconscious of his incestuous desire (a desire which was nevertheless expressed in his tattoo *"A ma mère"* ["Mom"], which avowed it in spite of his ignorance of the direction of his desire to the inevitability of his Oedipal relationship): when he pursued young women, as if to take his mother both into his confidence and into his bed, he did not acknowledge the passion which devoured him. His unconscious showed itself there—in the hermeneutics of the observer—only through the projection of a paranoid system of aggressiveness towards his mother. In this crime, once again there was no crime. Not because the mother was not killed (she did, in fact, escape death), but since in spite of, or rather because of, the lack of awareness of his illness, this illness appears as a delirium, a derangement *(aliénation)* which suppressed the crime by making the criminal lose his self-consciousness, not knowing that he was what he desired to be: his own father. He had alienated the proprietorship of his own person.

The dialectics of the Unconscious, of unconscious becoming, differ in these two cases. In the first case, the Unconscious appears in *epileptic unconsciousness* as projected fantasies, to the point that the symbol is inverted until it becomes the murderer of the "thing." In the second case, on the contrary, it is transparent in the "alienation" which allowed the subject to be someone other than himself—in his *lack of self-consciousness*.

But, it will be said, these two modes of the Unconscious with relation to conscious being are precisely what Freud had seen so clearly when he set up the system Conscious-Preconscious-Perception-Reality *(Bw-Whn-Vbw)* in opposition to the system of the *Unconscious in the strict sense (Ubw)*. This is true, but only on the condition that we see just as clearly that Freud's division of the Unconscious corresponds to two modes of conscious being rather than to two modes of unconscious being. As we have emphasized above with reference to Freud himself, it is not quite correct to oppose the system Conscious-Preconscious-Reality to the Unconscious in the strict sense, as being two impenetrable and radically heterogeneous spheres. Instead of this, the Unconscious is the same whether in its preconscious or its radically unconscious form. All that differs are the modes of conscious being which repress it, at one time in the name of the reality principle, at another in the name of moral censorship. This is so true that it is the same Unconscious that manifests itself in both modes of the Unconscious (in simple terms: dreaming and "alienation").

At first Freud started from a division of the Unconscious (preconscious and absolute Unconscious) which was untenable, even in his own eyes, because it forced upon him an inextricable complication of this Unconscious which was monstrously formed out of whatever was taken away from conscious being (the ideal of the ego, then the ego itself). In order to restore order (yes, order; and to aggravate this determination with respect to the extollers of the "cultural," we even say a natural order) to the psychical apparatus, it is necessary, and sufficient, to note: 1) that conscious being includes both the ego and the ideal of the ego (the ego in the strict sense); 2) that the Unconscious is composed of the id and its counterimpulses (the death instincts and the sub-ego strictly speaking, abusively called the superego). Such is the model of psychical organization (the topography), whose dynamics we must now describe.[3] When we say that the Unconscious is the property of conscious being we of course do not mean to reduce it to being only a thing. Instead, we consider it to be a region of psychical being which draws its limits from the conscious being which contains it and, by that very means, consecrates it as such. To say that conscious being *has* an Unconscious is not simply to assert that it contains the Unconscious by repressing it, that is, by instituting it, but that it contains the Unconscious as an other self: in the last analysis it is to say that it has an Unconscious as it has a body, but a body which it itself has created.

2. THE DYNAMIC STRUCTURE OF PSYCHICAL BEING AND THE DIALECTIC OF POSITIVE AND NEGATIVE

Far from leading us to separate radically the two systems conscious-Unconscious as Freud has done (a position which he himself appeared to have abandoned on several occasions, as we have noted, pp. 322–323), all that we have just said about the Unconscious as a property of conscious being persuades us instead to associate the Unconscious and the preconscious as two different modes of repression corresponding to the two modes of conscious being. We now consider the Unconscious not as the negative effect of repression but in the positivity of its being. The Unconscious appears as the sphere of the it (the id) which is opposed to the order of conscious being. We must now explicate its dynamic schema, the only one which clearly emerges from Freud's system. To the extent that it is the impulsive being as controlled by the pleasure principle, in the absoluteness of its being, the Unconscious is a being of desire. If it becomes the repressed Unconscious, it is because conscious being exercises its right of proprietorship and keeps it out (this is the negative function of conscious being), as we have so often repeated. But it is also because at its very origins it has a tendency not to enter into the order of consciousness. Freud constantly embroidered upon this theme. We, too, shall take it up in our turn. But when we do we shall emphasize the dialectic of the negative and the positive which envelops the forms of the Unconscious and of the conscious, so as to set forth the organization of psychical being. The structures of the psychical apparatus, its topography or its dynamics, can be ordered only in relation to the subordination in which conscious being holds the Unconscious, not under its pontifical domination, but at that distance which, by separating it from itself, leaves it to the unbound energy of its constitution, to its *positivity*, which can be said to be absolute since it is constant if not total.

1. THE POSITIVE STRUCTURE OF THE UNCONSCIOUS AND THE
NEGATIVITY OF THOSE STRUCTURES OF CONSCIOUS BEING
WHICH ARE IMPLIED IN THE NOTION OF INTEGRATION

The opposition which certain psychologists, physicians, or philosophers feel towards "consciousness" can be equaled only by that which certain others—and sometimes the same persons—feel towards the notion of the Unconscious. One cannot take away man's consciousness without destroying oneself; nor can one deny the Unconscious without denying man's consciousness.

As we have seen throughout this work, it is a question of two dimensions of psychical being which maintain between themselves certain dynamic and strictly vital relationships which are the very organization of man's psychical life. What characterizes man is not that "he *is* conscious," but rather that he *has* an Unconscious. This signifies both that his conscious being is not the totality of his psychical being and that his Unconscious is not merely a negative being, a shadow which would disappear in the light of consciousness.

These relationships between the conscious and the Unconscious are not merely relationships of simple reciprocity or of equipotential probability. The conscious does not act upon the Unconscious as the Unconscious acts upon the conscious. The phenomena which unfold in the Unconscious and the conscious do not form two entirely reversible series in a symmetrical functional structure. On the contrary, the equation for representing this formal structuring of psychical being can only be a differential or integral equation which introduces a function of dissymmetry. Since asymmetry is characteristic of all living systems or molecules, we should not be surprised to encounter here a relational, dynamic, or topographical model, which we have already adopted by using the term "structure" in the sense of "organizational plan" of an "organism." It is, in fact, this asymmetry and this irreversibility with respect to the structural relationships of the system Unconscious-conscious which give the psychical organism its sense. The organization of this organism is such that both subtotalities of this totality are subordinated to one another. As regards the sense of this subordination, it very naturally constitutes the "problem of values" which is implied in the problem of the relationship of the conscious and the Unconscious. The Freudian doctrine, which we have examined above, of the omnipotence of the Unconscious reduces the conscious to being only "a poor creature" and a "quasi nothingness" which could exist only as a precarious, artificial, and cunning line of defenses against the Unconscious, from which the conscious could draw only the being of a shadow or a reflection. Such a submersion of psychical being in the Unconscious has provoked and will always provoke the most savage and the most justified "resistance"[4] to the degradation of man which it implies. Here is the pet topic for argumentation between the noble souls and the great minds in the turmoil of modern times.

The whole debate over this interpretation has been carried to its highest level of moral and philosophical drama in the meditative and polemic reflections of Paul Ricoeur. At the end[5] of his long and detailed reading of Freud, he shows that the teleology of the subject cannot tolerate its archeology. He shows especially strongly that it is not possible to move from the oneiric to the sublime in a theory of sublimation of existence which would bind existence to its embryology. As we have already remarked, the psychical organism is constructed according to a model which, while reproducing the model of the living organism, differs from it in that the embryo whose development it constitutes subsists in its structure, as though the temporality of psychical being demanded that its past should be contained within the unfolding of its becoming.[6] By going beyond Freud to Hegel's dialectic, Ricoeur takes up this theme with great vigor, emphasizing the fact that the exigencies of life and of desire are certainly unsurpassable and ceaselessly assert their demands; but they are *"integrated"* into the formation of man according to the Kantian model, gaining freedom only by conforming to the Law, to the autonomy of Reason.

Biology, especially neurobiology, has demonstrated that the nervous organization has precisely this sense: that of a memory of the past which is constantly taken up again in the exigencies of action. Let us reflect a moment upon the meaning of this *"integration,"* which is the key notion in the whole problem; for, to say that a being is organized is only to say that it is integrated. The notion of *integration* implies a sense of construction or of surpassing of the lower which is kept in a state of subordination. This notion, fundamental in neurophysiology, of the *highest level* of superior nervous activity represents the idea of an *order* which imposes its organizational law upon the inferior agencies which it controls. The *"positivity"* of any integration (its value or its efficacity) is always and necessarily reduced to a function of choice, of differentiation, or of control. It is reduced to the obligation of submitting to some order. For this reason the function of integration can be said to be essentially *inhibiting*, as neurophysiology since Hughlings Jackson and Sherrington calls it; or, as we shall show, it is a *function of negativity.* Do not both the ontological structure of psychical being and Freudian theory clarify precisely this? Freud's own description of the dynamism of the Unconscious prevents him from assimilating it to the conscious, as is perfectly obvious. It does, however, necessarily subordinate it to the structure of conscious being because of his conception of the Unconscious as repressed, which implies the negative action *par excellence* of conscious being: the order and the prohibition which forbid its transgressing the law of its constitution.

To say that the Unconscious is that region of being in which there is neither negation nor law of contradiction is to say that this "locus" of the psychical apparatus which is subordinate to the pleasure principle, to the sphere of the instincts, their representatives, and the conflicts between these instincts and the objects which represent them, is the reign of an absolute desire (or of its equivalents), of a sort of radical positivity, that of the exigencies which *push* being to assert itself according to the only law which it recognizes at this level: the law of pleasure. The whole dynamic structure of unconscious being can thus be envisaged only from an economic-dynamic point of view which takes it to be the seat of opposing forces. The forces which provide the dynamism of psychical being are first and foremost those which it draws from the needs of the body. Even when, in man's case, these needs and instincts are always and necessarily caught up in an equally vital dialectic of desire and anxiety (of Eros and Thanatos), and even when desire and counter-desire mingle to form the configurations, the "complexes,"[7] the fantasies, the "imagos" of love, of hatred, and of fear, they always exert their influence as impulsive vectors in the direction of an insatiable desire. If desire can always be described as a lack, as a gaping, it is the *positivity* of this gaping which constitutes the fundamental reality of unconscious being.

From this point on, a nonsymmetrical but dominating structure of being—that of the negativity of this positivity— necessarily opposes itself to the positivity of this being, which being has, however, been designated as a negation (the unconscious). For this reason, even in Freud's eyes, conscious being appears as the locus of negation, of *Verneinung*, insofar as its function is precisely to subordinate the Unconscious's forces of fantasy to the forms of the conscious which can be constituted only as orders, as imperative and selective rules. Nothing in the Freudian theory of the Unconscious can be understood —especially repression and the symbolism which emerges from the repressed—that does not postulate this function of negativity which incessantly opposes its law (what Freud called the censor in his earliest writings) to the impulsive forces of the Unconscious. The structures of conscious being represent this power of "legislation," of "control," of "order," of "direction"—all of which are concepts whose form is derived from the notion of integration (the "negentropic" negation of disorder), a form which is traditional in neurobiology.

All the advances which have come about in the field of neurophysiology can be ascribed to the theoretical model inaugurated by the structuralist and architectonic evolutionism of Hughlings Jackson, which model has replaced the mechanistic schema of reflexes and their associations. The *processes of differentiation and of inhibition* are interpreted after the model of the integration of the nervous system. Even in the case of conditioning or of learning (which have too often been interpreted in terms of reflexes or of simple associations), these processes cannot be understood without a *"Gestaltung"* which *subordinates* the functional parts to a restrictive totality of meaning. The concepts which belong to information theory (codes, feedback, programming, negative entropy) constitute the mathematically constructed formulation of this higher nervous activity, which, "finalized from the very outset" by instinct, can direct the adaptations of the organism to reality only by means of a semantics and a logic which are inscribed in the functional structures of the brain. *The nervous system is logically organized*. It represents that algorithmic logic (or logistic) which allows its cybernetic models to be reproduced in electronic computers—and not vice versa. We need only refer to the stochastic constructions of artificial brains in order to find the cybernetic diagrams of the nervous system. Even if it is not possible to forget that they are not merely images of the thinking brain but its products, these models show us that, to a certain point, our brain functions like a computer. The apparatus which classifies, distributes, chooses, and processes information functions much in the manner that a logical operation unfolds. On this subject we can refer, for example, to the diagrams representing the cascade of neuronal synapses, following Boole's model of algebraic functions,[8] or to W. R. Ashby's use of Bourbaki's *Éléments de mathématiques* in his *Design for a Brain*. These studies should be enough to convince us, if not of the truth, at least of the possibility of a geometric-mathematical treatment of the connections, of the intersynaptic network of the nervous system. The very organization of the nervous system implies the *obligation* to apply a certain rule, to conform to a certain order.[9] Of course this assimilation to the schematism of mathematical-logical structures could never cause us to forget that the human brain is more than this order-giving computer. But it is important to remember that whenever neurophysiology and neuropathology (from the time of Jackson, Sherrington, and Head to that of Goldstein, Lepique, Eccles, etc.) are based on the evolution and hierarchy of the functions of the nervous system and on the fundamental idea of its integration, they more or less implicitly refer to the logical structuring of the nervous system or, in Köhler's words, to the isomorphic relation of the brain and thought. This is what Freud had foreseen in his "Project for a Scientific Psychology" (1895), with this difference: that then (as again much later), he was much more inclined to consider the "bound" activity of the brain in its relations with the system perception-consciousness along the lines of a dynamic, homeostatic, and thermodynamic model than along the lines of a logical and probabilistic model of information theory.

It is enough for us here to take note of this fact, which becomes evident whatever interpretations of it might be given:

the structures of consciousness are in effect inseparable from those organizational functions which above all impose an order. This order is an order, that is, a prescription of rules, which must be obeyed.

It is in this sense that we can now turn toward another manner of apprehending acts of consciousness. We shall turn to *phenomenology*, in order to restore concreteness to our increasingly abstract reflections. Though the answer is given by Heidegger or by Sartre, we must return once again to Hegel. What Paul Ricoeur has written on this subject is especially illuminating and fruitful. When he is investigating the tendency toward destruction, toward the death wish (which Freud assimilates to negation), he discovers[10] that this functional modality, this negativity, is the function *par excellence* of consciousness.

As Ricoeur writes:

> But just what type of negation is this? Very definitely it is not located in the unconscious; the unconscious, let us remember, contains neither negation, nor time, nor the function of reality. Therefore negation belongs to the system *Cs.*, along with temporal organization, control of action, motor inhibition involved in every thought process, and the reality principle itself. Thus we meet with an unexpected result: there exists a negativity that does not belong to the instincts *but defines consciousness*, conjointly with time, motor control, and the reality principle. (Our italics.)

Ricoeur then insists upon the second degree of this negation, which concerns "reality-testing," adding:

> ... we know that the conditions of becoming conscious and those of reality-testing are the same.... The negative judgment ... is truly a judgment of real existence only when it goes beyond the viewpoint of the pleasure-ego, for whom to say "yes" means that it wants to introject into itself what is good, i.e. to "devour" it, and to say "no" means that it wants to eject from itself what is bad, i.e. to "spit it out." The judgment of reality is a sign that the "initial pleasure-ego" *(anfängliches Lust-Ich)* has been replaced by the "definitive reality-ego" *(endgültiges Real-Ich).*[11]

It is in this way that we should understand how conscious being assumes a basic function of negation. Its activity of "defense," of "control" or of "prohibition" (or, as neurophysiology most often calls it, of "inhibition"), and all the other various aspects of the order by which it restrains the totality of the system of vital relations, are only the functioning of conscious being insofar as it submits itself to the reality principle by opposing the Unconscious, where the pleasure principle is master. It is in this sense that we stated that the absolute positivity of the unconscious (of the pleasure-ego) is opposed, as a power and a duty of order or of repression, to the negativity of the acts of conscious being, which is the form which conscious becoming imposes upon psychical life in order to constitute itself as such.

We find the same viewpoint put forth by Sartre in his exposition of "being for itself."[12] In the whole first part of *Being and Nothingness* it is a question only of the constitution of being for itself in response to its interrogation and to its negation:

"The being through which nothingness comes into the world ought to be its own nothingness. The human being is a being of 'negativity' through which one is a being of freedom and is an uprooting of himself," as Sartre reminds us. Hegel saw this very clearly when he defined mind as mediation, as the Negative. This disengaging of consciousness which "conditions all negation, all negative transcendences, all the interrogatory behavior of being for itself, causes consciousness to surge forth as a 'no.'" The for-itself *is* in virtue of a "being-which-is-not-what-it-is" and "which-is-what-it-is-not." It is a crack in being. It is a "being of value," a normative and dispersed existent, a being of possibilities. It slips into time as a totality which is for itself its own achievement pursuing itself. But "the for-itself, through its self-negation, arrives at the in-itself which it is not." All these formulas, so often repeated, tend only to make of being-for-itself, of conscious being; an essentially problematic being.

This is what we mean when we say that the being of consciousness forces into its problematic the being of the unconscious which asserts itself (in its positive impulse as well as in its negative counterimpulse), without burdening itself with any problematic.

Thus, whether we refer to the neurophysiological model which is applied to the highest structure of the level of integration (to which the system of vital relations, with all its subsystems, its infrastructures and lower systems, is subordinated), or to the phenomenological model of ontological structures of conscious being, conscious being appears both as a system of coordination and constraint and as an aleatory and problematical system. In this way, whether it controls through the order which it imposes or is indeterminate because of the freedom of its indefinitely facultative movements, it is indeed a being which imposes its negation and which carries it within itself as the form of its law. *It is a being of contradiction or of negation which asserts itself only by negating its own negation.* In this sense it is the very contrary, the antonym, of unconscious being.

Having thus justified the generality of our theory concerning the organization of the psychical organism by using the model of a complementarity of positive (Unconscious) and negative (conscious) structures, we shall now attempt to describe each of these from this perspective.

2. CONSCIOUS BEING'S FUNCTION OF NEGATIVITY (INTEGRATION
OF THE SYSTEM OF REALITY)

Having abandoned ourselves for an instant to these neurobiological, logical, or metaphysical speculations, let us now examine how all that we have said concerning conscious being and becoming can acquire its complete meaning in relation to the integrative function, or the function of negativity, of conscious activity.

The synchronistic and diachronistic modes of conscious being which we have described must now be examined insofar as they are legislative structures of reality, insofar as they are coercive, or normative. Their dynamics is that of a *labor* which, by obeying certain rules governing their efficacity, imposes these laws upon the whole of psychical being, so that it opens up to its world by becoming conscious. It is in this way that "reality-testing" is a test: it is an experience which has been subjected to a law; it is a putting to the test of a system of values. Because all legislation is a power which opposes order to disorder, and because all values imply some ideal whose end subordinates the means, the structures of conscious being are those of a negation, a repression, which opens onto the construction of reality only to the extent that these structures are a "denial" (or a double negation) of *that* which I ought not to be, so that I might become that which I ought to be. We must therefore transpose this function of negativity or of constraint into structural terms.

a) The Field of Consciousness

As has been discovered in the process of developing its structure, the field of consciousness appears first of all as essentially *circumscribed*, such that it might obey the demands of its constitution. Its constitution can be realized, that is, can organize all actually lived experience, only through certain determinations which are, as everyone knows, negations (*omnis determinatio est negatio*, one of Spinoza's formulas which was taken up again by Hegel).

The first time that conscious being appears, the field of experience is constituted (the first waking of consciousness in the newborn child or the moment of waking from sleep). The confrontation of desire and its object, the first face-to-face contact of the desiring subjectivity and the objectivity which escapes it, rises up as a harsh reality which resists its satisfaction. By thus opening itself to the world of possibilities, the first form of reality, the field of consciousness stakes out a line of demarcation between the amoral subject and the laws of objectivity. He becomes involved in what he must know, and for this reason his centrifugal movement carries him to his "ex-centricity" by opposing him to the environment in which his appetitive tendencies swarm and boil.

The second act in the actualization of experience is the distribution of the lived space of representations. It is here a question of the preeminent thetic function of consciousness insofar as it is constituted in experience by the order which it establishes when it submits to the judgment of reality (to the first reality-testing, as Freud says). At this level of the constitution of lived actuality into a field, what is lived is set only in a heterogeneous space (lived space is precisely *not* the homogeneous space of the world of objects), which is composed not merely of *partes extra partes*, but of subjective and objective. Everything, therefore, can be lived within this space, but only on the condition that it is given its proper place in the hierarchy of realities. The problematic of the orders of thought and of extension is here the exigency of the appearing of a fundamental connection which organizes the lived field by attributing to the subject's thought what comes to it, and to objects those results which thought receives from them. This is the very heart of the *structure of perception*, to the extent that it requires both thought and the language which forms it—as well as the provocation of the external world which is communicated to it. This perception can thus constitute itself sometimes as external perception, sometimes as perception of the imaginary, and most often as a composite which itself must submit to the control of the perceptive act. This perceptive stratum of lived experience is therefore characterized by the repression of the unreal and the imaginary, or at the very least by the recognition of what they are when they appear in the field of consciousness. The unconscious can enter this field only if it triumphs over the intentionality of the thetic function or over the organization of the field by deluding the surveillance of consciousness in hallucination or delirium. When these penetrate consciousness through imagination or speech, these latter are taken into the normally organized field as they are, either as illusions or as scoriae, that is, as capable of separating and choosing, of exercising their lucid and vigilant discriminatory function.

The third level of the constitution of the field of consciousness as the field of its own experience is attained through the organization of its temporality, that is, of the order of urgency which, in conformity with the demands of the present, regulates the necessity for conscious phenomena to occupy only that moment of time which turns its back on the past and does not encroach upon the future. This temporal structure is evidently a formal law of the constitution of experience into actually lived experience. It imposes upon lived experience the speed and succession of its movements as well as its agreement with the principle of equilibrium, an agreement which is necessary to maintain that pause suitable for present action. This ethico-temporal regulation of experience is nothing other than the controlling of the tumultuous demands of the Unconscious, which does not obey the laws of time and so tends to force the reversibility of these symmetrical and interchangeable configurations upon the moment at which the diaphragm of the field of consciousness insists upon the ordering of the presentation, of the presence, and of the present against the disorder and the chaotic telescoping of the instincts. The structure of the field of consciousness which is "well tempered" in its attention, in its expectation, and in its mastery of the time which it contains

and maintains in the equilibrium of a stable system is an imprescriptible law of the field of consciousness. It is therefore
the very negation of the disorderly atemporality of the untimely movements which, coming from the Unconscious, lure
lived experience into the vertigo and fatality of the past or into
the omnipotence of an indefinitely open future.

The legislation of the field of actually lived experience is
thus its very structure insofar as it is constantly and without
intermission the guardian of its constitution.[13] It is this structure of systematic negation and opposition which bestows upon
the being of consciousness the severity of its vigilant censor
and its inexorable function of the vigilant application of a law
which is constantly cruel towards the pleasure principle, a law
which is somewhat villainous in its repression of an unconscious unreality in the name of the reality principle.

b) Reflexive Consciousness and the Facultative Movements
of Conscious Being

Upon the pedestal of its constitution, conscious being has
depicted the forms of those facultative exercises which range
from the unconstraint of free association, of a roving imagination, to the operational acts of its reflexive constitution, all of
which are modes of its manner of filling up the moments of its
existence.

When thought hesitates, it allows itself to be overrun by the
free play of its instincts. In this state, in subjection to the thetic
function which maintains it within the brackets of reality,
whatever is presented to the field of consciousness coincides
almost completely with the play of the Unconscious upon the
ground of the automatism of meanings. When it ceases to be
controlled, imaginative thought demonstrates both the force of
the Unconscious, which force has been allowed to manifest,
and the organizational force of conscious thought, which force
has thus been suspended.

By asserting its rights, conscious thought exercises its power
only in and through its turning to certain rules of constraint,
which alone allow discursive thought to produce something in
the category of the possible. A *production* of this sort can be
accomplished only at the price of this constraining discipline
of normative thought which constitutes the logical body, the
methodology of thought. It is at this level that the dynamic
structures of conscious being which organize its experience

carry this "production" to its highest degree as a test of reality, that is, submission to the directing principles of the understanding. The law of causality, the principles of contradiction and of the excluded middle, all the laws of knowledge are then applied to the strategies of thought. For thought can progress only when the subject learns how to adjust himself to the prescriptions of the art of thinking in order to gain mastery over his own operations as well as over those irrational complications which seem to be the fermenting of the affective sphere of the unconscious instincts. For even when, by breaking away from the laws of two-valued Aristotelian logic, he invents a many-valued logic, such as the "negationless" logics of Bromer, of G. F. C. Griss, and of Heyting, these logics must still submit to new laws of incompatibility. The very freedom of logical constructions of thought necessarily implies those constraints of abstract thought which it imposes upon itself in order to bring about the fundamental negation of its attachment to that which, in the unconscious, constitutes the essence of the irrational.[14] By tying the steps of discursive thought to the very operations that fuse it to the subject and that then unfold as a function of their axiomatics, and by admitting the interdependence of the real and the possible in the *states of equilibrium* that bring about the junction between the temporal real manipulated in logical operations and the temporal logic which governs them, Piaget's genetic epistemology makes it very clear that the construction of the real by the subject realizes and requires the subject's own transformation. This transformation or ascent from the empirical to the logical level can be brought about only by the "absolute" flight (to use Ruyer's expression) of the subject who directs this formation, which cannot be reduced to information. Since it involves an infinite number of possible combinations, information becomes effective only under the influence of an encompassing consciousness (as Ruyer points out[16]). The debate concerning the origin of information and its relation to entropy, to Carnot's second principle, and to thermodynamics began precisely because the cybernetic models of information theory postulate the conversion of information into negative entropy.[17] These references and reflections may appear to be rather far removed from the problem of consciousness's reflection upon itself (as can be seen by consulting the enormous literature, especially the writings of Boltzman and of Norbert Wiener, which is devoted to these subjects and

which continually brings up the problem of the relations between consciousness, knowledge, logic, information, computers, and living organisms). They are, however, indispensable if
we are fully to understand that the *secondary process of conscious thought* is active in its own sphere, a sphere which can
be said to be totally opposed to the domain of unbound energy
which is represented in the structure of psychical being by *the
primary process of the Unconscious.*[18]

c) The System of the Self and of Self-consciousness
   The model which the subject uses in order to know himself
and to recognize his place in the world constitutes the diachronistic dimension of conscious being: the self. Through our preceding analyses we have established its ontogenesis and its
dynamic structure. We shall now take up this exposition once
again, in order to situate it in the dialectic of the organization
of psychical being.
   The ontogenesis of the self—its development—is its history.
It is of the very essence of being-for-itself to be thrown into
existence so as to manifest itself and to fulfill its destiny in it.
Nothing in the organization of a being is more external to it
than this relation to others, which relation becomes a part of
the structuring of the self through the events which arise because of their encounter. But on the other hand, nothing is
more internal to it than this organization, for the identity of the
self is the knowledge which it has of itself when pretending to
be, all in all, an object, an in-itself. Since it is not the other but
is like the other, since it is alone but has relationships with
others, since it is objectivity without ceasing to be the very
subject of this objectification, and since the self's being is always in the process of taking shape and will not be completed
until death, this being is indeed the most problematic being
which each one of us has to be. Corresponding to the problematic of these ambiguities centering around the subject is the
rationality of the construction of his world. I am able to bring
about the objective status of the someone who I am only
through the epistemological utilization of my method of knowing in general, by turning to the logic of noncontradiction. The
subject constructs his person as a correlative to the development of his reason. To the extent that the reflexive models of
thought in general are subject to the rules of the understanding
and of its discursive progress, all that we have said concerning

352 / Conscious Becoming

the utilization of these models can and must apply to the construction and elaboration of the judgments which the subject passes on himself as he becomes intelligible to himself. This is so true that the converse generally becomes obvious on this account, namely, that the subject's action upon his own reflection demands of him that he carry it out only by projecting his own rational structure into the apprehension of the real, in the course of all the low or high voltage exercises of his intellectual operations. The principle of the identity of the self throughout the occasional changes and the mutations of his becoming, the rigorous separation of the self from all others, the distribution of the attributes which qualify the substantive nature of his own person, the conjugation of "to be" and of "to have," the syntactical forms of all the relationships to which his speech and his action give rise, all these enter into his objective status. His self-knowledge and his system of reality are grounded in his judgments of perceptual reality concerning the form of his body, his physiognomy, his properties, and the differences which separate him from others. The self-image is thus constituted by a sort of objectifying abstraction which causes the self to become someone who is both like others and different from them. But this rational mechanics of the construction of the self always leaves a halo of doubt, incompleteness, and confusion around this privileged object, the self. This is so because the self can never grasp itself without leaving some remainder, without some perplexity. As is the case with objects, its being carries within itself its shadow, its Unconscious, even if (and especially if) its lack of knowledge and misconceptions are themselves unconscious. Self-consciousness is brought into being only through the affirmation of the Unconscious, of the other who I am without knowing it. For when I cause myself to enter into the reality system of the world which I construct or of the person that I believe myself to be, I must place that which I ought not be between the brackets of a radical annihilation, whether this "I-ought-not-be" is the formulation of an obligation or only a consciousness of doubt and bad faith. Obviously nothing more is needed for the problematic of this reality to be sometimes considered as a problematical reality, or for this selective annihilation of what I ought not be to pass for a nothingness of being. We have already pointed out the myth of "this poor creature" which is the self and is precisely that being-for-itself the essence of which lies in its structure of negativity.

This negativity is the reality of this being, which is the surest reality of our existence. It is our own essence. We can then put it more simply (!) by saying, with Sartre, that self-conscious being, or being-for-itself, is a being filled with the negativity of the consciousness of its being. "To be someone" is "obviously" this. It is asserted in this negation, as the child's self is asserted first when he says "No." For the ontological law of reality is the belief that one is someone, which belief is posited by opposing oneself to any other person, whether that other be beyond or outside of himself.

The negativity of the self-conscious being considered as a self is a negation which is applied to whatever does not enter into its consciousness. If this raises the question of what is real in this being which is encompassed by the shadow of illusion, this negativity is even more evident if we consider the dynamic structure of the self, which we have described as the axiological trajectory and implicit structure of the person. For this ideal form of the self must be approached with even greater care. If the being of the self consists in its *belief that it is someone*, what value can this being have, since it is subject to self-delusion? When we turn to the ideal which it would like to realize by identifying with that which it is not but would like to be, do we not find that it is doomed to be only this mirage? Do not such a mirage and such an illusion have to be considered as such, as a pure unreality or a projection of the Unconscious, the seat of the imaginary? We here touch upon the problem of the superego and of sublimation, which notions attempt to bring a negative response to the affirmation of the self. This affirmation is condemned equally by the superego and by the id, by these agencies of the Kingdom of Shadows which intend not only to hold it prisoner but to condemn it to death. We thus find ourselves in the midst of the dialectic of the positive and the negative, of the Conscious and the Unconscious. We are brought back to the point at which we began, to the dialectic of the negative and the positive in the overall structure of psychical being. The reality of the self raises the question of what reality in general could be. It does this because the self's reality is frozen within the negativity of the Unconscious by self-consciousness, which "really" depends upon the single positivity of desire, or is only an illusion. For if the negation of the other is merely a pure nothingness, and if the negation of desire and, still more generally, of the structure of conscious being opposing the Unconscious are nothing, then no reality is possible for this "system of reality" other than that of an illusion or a projection of desire. When we touch upon this furthest limit of the dynamic structure of conscious being as it is constituted as a "person," we find that this person draws its reality, its manner of being someone (and not no one), from the exercise of this power which the subject has of becoming other than it was not *(Wo es war soll ich werden).* This comes down to recognizing, at the end of this dialectic of the positive and the negative, the creative function of reality, which is affirmed through the negation of the forces of the pure subjectivity of desire. What causes that self-conscious being which is constituted as a person to remain constantly problematic (or grounded less upon an apodictic judgment both of value and of reality) is that the dialectical movement of the negation of the Unconscious, which is contained within the configurations of conscious being, opens upon that reality which gives rise to this movement without ever suppressing its vital connection with the sphere of instincts. We shall return to this problem, which is basic to the dialectic of conscious becoming and to the questions of sublimation and of values, when we examine the generation of conscious being and its connection with the Unconscious, whose different modes of repressing constitute the organization of the synchronistic and diachronistic structures of consciousness.

The negative function of the integration of conscious being in its different structures consists essentially in forming an order which conforms to the constitutive law of reality. This "reality-testing" culminates in the acts of actualization of lived experience which form the field of consciousness by putting a constant and more or less solid bar between what can and what cannot be admitted into reality. To this synchronistic function of conscious being is joined its diachronistic function. This latter is the function of the integration of the identity of the person into his world, in an historical system of values, which integration consists essentially in containing, or annihilating, anyone other than the self which this integration posits and maintains. This "anyone other," whether the unconscious other or another person, necessarily conflicts with the system of the self in the problematic which constitutes it. It is evident that through the dialectical movement involved by it, this negative or negating function of conscious being (considered as the organizational principle of the system of the organization of reality) *transforms this negation of the Unconscious into the affirmation of the reality both of the objective world and of the self.* This affirmation, which corresponds to the negation of the Unconscious, is really a negation of that negation, in that all the operations which expel the imaginary from the field of consciousness, and even more especially those which oppose the self to the other, consist in *taking back the imaginary and the other so as to integrate them,* after having first opposed them. This is the somewhat Hegelian sense of the dialectical movement of the mind and of consciousness, to which we shall return later. All the structuring activities of consciousness, the order which it organizes through the labor of thought, the categorical forming of all the modes of reality, including its own, these all *realize* a construction which is nothing other than that model of the self and of its world, which it dominates by creating it, by engendering it as that being which enters into the world through its acts, which moves from lived time into the objective time of history. This phenomenology, this progressive dialectic of the constitution of *conscious being,* makes it appear with all the attributes and categories which oppose it point for point to the Unconscious. This unconscious region of being is in some ways more geographical, geological, and archeological. It is discovered only through induction, intuition, or recurrence, through the negation or denial of conscious being, as that "thing" which it finds to be repressed as not fit to enter into its own constitution.

3. THE RADICAL POSITIVITY OF THE UNCONSCIOUS

The being of the Unconscious, for which there is no negative, is a "conative" being. This term is not frequently used, but it is perfectly definite and very exactly connotes the essentially dynamogenic nature of that sphere of being which is usually designated by attributes such as "instinctual," "impulsive," etc. The general concept of affectivity or of affective motivation catches its meaning to the extent that it expresses desire and, this side of desire, the needs or instinctual demands of the body. However, as Freud had seen, it does not include the specific tendencies of these "instincts" merely as a "reservoir of instinct." It is also the "laboratory of the instincts." Instincts, needs, and desires enter into it only as being prefigured (ideational representative, *Vorstellungsrepräsentanz* or instinctual representative, *Repräsentanz des Triebes*). We here encounter one of the first modes of the "embryological" organization of the Unconscious (we have already shown that it never ceases to retain its original constitution, even in the most highly evolved adult): its "plication," duplication, multiplication, reduplication. No word expresses this structure better than does "complex," which remains the clearest idea which can be had to express the increasingly complicated knots in the Unconscious (in spite of the fact that contemporary culture has popularized this term ad nauseam). It is enough to recall that the Unconscious is a dynamic concept which points to an association of the forces representing the instincts. The terms "drives" and "complexes" point to this embryonic organization of the "forms" which constitute internal and unconscious stimulation of psychical being and of its motivating and propelling forces. What are these forms, and how do they arise so as to remain on this side of conscious awareness? Any theory of the Unconscious must come to grips with these questions, as we have noted (cf. above, pp. 311 ff.) when examining both the aporias and contradictions involved in Freud's theory of the Unconscious, as well as the fundamental meaning of this theory, which was such a brilliant discovery by the founder of psychoanalysis. We shall now briefly summarize this theory, following the order of its development. We shall attempt to preserve what is essential to this theory, both as it has been represented (especially in recent publications and discussions), and insofar as we can here reproduce it closest to its "organic" conception, or rather to the organic-dynamic model which will serve as a point of reference in our structural synopsis of psychical being and in the dialectic of the negative and the positive which organizes it.

a) The Heterogeneity of the Instincts of the Id

It is remarkable that Freud very naturally and simply used an extension of the concept of instinct to defend himself against the charge of "pansexualism" which was so quickly brought against him. It is obvious that at this primordial level, the subordination of the Unconscious to the pleasure principle, that is, to the principle of an economic homeostasis in which satisfaction and tension are in a state of equilibrium, includes all the instincts as well. The instincts cannot be reduced to sexual hunger. The whole history of psychoanalysis shows this. There are other hungers and ends which figure into the movement of desire. For this reason there was first of all an extension of the erogenous zones and functions, which allows more or less all pleasures to enter into the pleasure which the subject derives from the genital organs and orgasms. Then, most naturally, arose the need to gather together the selfish drives of the ego into this sphere of "instincts" (or of their representatives). Finally the aggressive instincts and the death instincts came into evidence. We must therefore examine this heterogeneity of "instinctual life."

The libido both represents and is the servant of the instinct of the preservation of the species. Our species is perpetuated because of the pleasure derived from a drive which is enveloped in the radical unconsciousness of the reproductive function of the organism. But at the individual level another need very naturally makes itself felt: that of self-preservation. This instinct to live finds its satisfaction in the pleasure of breathing, of eating, and in the general use of the body, as well as in the other satisfactions of the subject's system of vital relations, such as his language, his thought, and his actions. From this arises a system of autoerotic, narcissistic impulses which invests upon the physical and psychical ego the principle of a pleasure which is destined to preserve the individual, to cause him to persevere in his being. Scarcely had the unconscious roots of individualization, of this unrestrained desire to live and to survive, been discovered when, "beyond the pleasure principle," another "instinct" made its appearance: the death instinct. This is not the place for a detailed study of Freud's most profound meditation, which best shows the depth of his profoundly biological spirit—the same spirit which animates the works of Bichat. We must be satisfied with noting that this fundamental tendency is engraved in the being's unconscious as a refusal of life—much like an entropy of a system of vital energy. But instinct, even in this almost physical state, is present in man only in its impulsive forms. It takes form in the Unconscious, not as a pure negation of life but as a force which opposes the forces of the life instincts and of the libido through the very form it takes on. Anguish, the tendency to destruction, to inertia, to repetition, to retroactivity, to aggression directed against oneself (against the instinct of self-preservation) or against others (through displacement or inversion of libidinal fixations or aggression), these are all present with their constant demands. What is the origin of these instincts which cannot be reduced to one another and which, moreover, in the theory of their interconnections or their disassociation sustain certain interrelationships of "conflict," of "substitution," of "collusion," or of "transformation" across a system of dynamic charges in which cathexes and countercathexes counterbalance one another and exist in equilibrium? The idea of a fundamental heterogeneity of the instinctual apparatus results from the psychoanalytic theory itself and from the numerous studies made by Freud and his disciples concerning the instincts and their fate. That the instinctual apparatus is completely subjected to the pleasure principle does not mean merely that the search after pleasure is the *primum movens* or the unique impelling force of these instincts. For the instincts of death and aggression, which are necessarily generators of anxiety and repulsion, are more or less intermingled with the desire for pleasure and satisfaction. We thus find not a single but a bifid root in the rootedness of unconsious being. All the tendencies, all the instinctual systems which carry on a sort of "civil war" (Freud, in *New Lectures*) between the "id" and a "counter-id," are subjected to the *pleasure-pain principle,* which constitutes the fundamental conflict to which we are referred by all the studies on narcissism, sadism, and primary masochism, which can be considered to be the primordial and contradictory movements of human being. Human being can never be determined without coupling one's desire with these fused instincts *(Triebmischung).* Nor can it develop unless these two fundamental tendencies join together to manifest in their positivity the direction of desire, even if it be the desire for death or for suffering.

As Ricoeur has so forcefully shown, any hermeneutics comes up against the dynamics of the instincts as this level, where, because the defusion of the instincts has not been accomplished, the id is reduced to being only a play of forces, the object of a dynamics and not of a hermeneutics. Since it is a radically primary process, this dynamics can be reduced neither to the unity of an absolute libidinal force, as we have just seen, nor to a "topographical" distribution, that is, to a structuring by "agencies." For these agencies are to be found at the

origin not of the instinctual system and of the id but of whatever should be repressed in it, since it appears only with secondary repression, which is brought about only by whatever
will enlarge the id, not merely by attraction and retention
proper (primary repression). The thesis of the heterogeneity of
the instincts at least partially nullifies the conflict between the
agencies, and shows this conflict to be largely superfluous. The
agencies represent only the heterogeneity of the id (instincts of
pleasure and of life; instincts of death, anxiety, and aggression), not the diverse effects of repression, which are ensured
by the ego, or, more generally, by conscious being. The trilogy
id, ego, superego, which is intended to account for this
heterogeneity, cannot be completely submerged in the Unconscious, since the trilogy could then no longer explain the Unconscious without being a tautology. This heterogeneity must
therefore be described as one which opposes the Unconscious
and the conscious. By restoring to the conscious what belongs
to it (the ego and the ego-ideal, which is called the "superego"),
we leave the Unconscious with only the id which constitutes it,
with its play of contradictory forces (cf. above, p. 356).

The Unconscious represents the primordial framework
which organizes psychical being's development. This development presupposes that the formation of its vegetative, animal,
fetal, neonatal, and infantile forms—which are as if the ar-
borescence of the life of both the species and the individual—
arises in accordance with a sort of formative instinct (a plan
of specific organization, of production, and of reproduction)
which is opposed to these forces of the antibiological, antibio-
psychological disorder of the death instincts. These latter instincts do indeed form part of a being's finality, but only as
representing its end. The works of such diverse thinkers as
Freud, Bichat, Driesh, Bergson, and Heidegger make this appear to have a certain self-evidence. Its self-evidence can be
found in the very organization of human beings, and at the
primordial instinctual level, even in every animal "psychoid."
For a being which is reduced to this "mechanics" (or to this
"dynamics") of instinctual life is, in fact, the unconscious being. At the very most we can and must concede that it possesses
that degree of consciousness (cf. above, p. 8) which belongs to
the feeling of lived experience as pleasure and pain. This instinctual sphere is thus essentially dynamic and seems to be

governed by a thermodynamic principle of the homeostasis of cathexes in which conflicts of force come to a state of equilibrium.

However, this primary structure of the instinctual substratum is obviously not the Unconscious which was discovered by Freud. It is the unconscious only of the "unconscious being," in the sense, let us recall, that an animal *is* an unconscious being but does not *have* an Unconscious—that Unconscious which Freud has grasped for what it *is* by nature (the id) and for what it *should have been* (the repressed). It is because Freud added the "repressed" to the "common" Unconscious (which is commonly recognized) that he truly discovered the Unconscious (which is commonly misunderstood). It is obvious to Freud, and to us, that at least one of man's instincts is stamped "forbidden": the Libido. Once conceived on the model of this taboo, the Unconscious stops being a mere attribute and becomes a substantive. For the Unconscious is then no longer a mere negativity but is that positivity in which the force of instinct is multiplied by that of repression. It could even be said that the Unconscious slips from the third person towards the first person, for (as we shall examine in the third section of this chapter) the Unconscious belongs to the subject "when situated" in the area of the relations of the id and the ego. *In other words, it can be formed as the Unconscious only through the very organization of the conscious being which represses it.* For Freud, the primary Unconscious (which he strangely called "primary repression," *Urverdrängung*) is constituted by the forces of the id "as such." But the Unconscious *par excellence* is constituted only as a result of two successive processes: first, the constitution of conscious being; second, the repression of the id by this conscious being.

We must now penetrate into the "true" Freudian Unconscious, the effect of true repression (or as he calls it, secondary repression). In order to describe the Unconscious in its heterogeneity and its generality, it was first necessary to take a reverse look at the progress of Freud's thought and look for it "there where it is to be found," beneath the "secondary unconscious formations." We must now examine these latter for what they in fact are: the true "unconscious agencies." We must thus leave behind the dynamic sphere in order to gain access to the unique topography, which is valid and simplified in the sense that we have stated: the relations of the id (and of that "counter-id," the superego) and conscious being.[19]

b) The Complex Formations and Unconscious Agencies
Formed through Repression

Unbound energy within the sphere of the Unconscious, that is, the charging and discharging of instinctual desires, is a sort of abstraction in man. It is an abstraction of a radical disorderliness, which is, strictly speaking, impossible given the level of organization which is presupposed by life, however unconscious it may be, and by psychical life, however rudimentary. As Freud pointed out, the Unconscious thus involves some sort of embryonic organization. At this point, the "anthropological" problem raised by the Unconscious emerges, for "unconscious formations" receive their forms precisely from the constitution of conscious being, whose repression they reflect. The "drives" are thus never instincts; they are already grasped in an imaginary halo (*Vorstellungsrepräsentant,* ideational representative) which is added to the quota of affect. Freud holds this complement to be inherent in instinct itself (it is the extreme point of the theory of primary repression). We must, however, admit that this imaginary, this fantasy which accentuates the instincts, is necessarily and structurally a gleam of the reflection of instinct on the hard mirror of consciousness. This is so because Freud (in his 1915 work, "Repression") derives the meaning (and the existence) of the psychical representative of a drive from the fact "that it constantly refuses to take charge of things in the conscious realm." Setting aside these subtleties and these doubts concerning theoretical interpretation, we can say simply that the theory and practical study of the drives cause the instincts of the id to appear as grasped in these "representations" *(Vorstellungen)* or in the memory traces of things, which are the reflections of lived events and which vegetate in the id as shadows. The instincts which "sleep" at the depth of human nature are not "needs" but forms of desire, which cannot be reduced to simple representations of the past. They are present only in a symbolic configuration whose images (Oedipus, castration, Father, Mother, Narcissus, etc.) are truly archeological (Freud), but also, to be specific of man, are archetypal (Jung). The intervention of the system of reality (of the organization of conscious being) does not simply give a past to this instinctual imaginary. It stamps the forms of its law upon it. In this sense the Unconscious, in the strict sense of the word, is a product of consciousness, a property of conscious being.

We here find ourselves at the heart of Freud's first "truth":

the Unconscious is the repressed. Human existence, the experience one lives in the historical succession of events, the integration of one's system of vital relations into and through the system of his conscious being, is possible only if it conforms to those laws which exclude from the conscious being's thought and action all that should not enter into it and all that one's psychical being cannot keep or tolerate. And it is "that" ("Ça," the id) which, within one's being—as one's body—*has* conscious being, not in the sense of having it at its disposal but of having or depositing it in itself, on the condition of *making* of it the Unconscious. This is the fundamental model of the dynamics of the Unconscious, through which this dynamics is essentially a topography. We are here only repeating what we have already said concerning the relations of the Unconscious and the conscious, which are situated in the category of "containing." Once the Unconscious appears as the repressed (and consequently as a correlate of the constitution of conscious being), it becomes obvious that what we perceive of the Unconscious through all its manifestations cannot be perceived, through symbolic sketches and profiles, in any way other than as a "latent content." The "complexes" or "Imagos" all bear the stamp of the conscious ("Made in Germany," Freud had well said, regarding these formations which are unconscious but for him are stamped by the Unconscious). *The Unconscious is not only masked, but marked by the Conscious.* This is indeed the meaning which we intend the "structure" of the field of consciousness to have. The nature of this field is shaped by a culture which is received only through the structures which belong to conscious being, especially through the mediation of language. For the moment, it is enough to say that the field of the Unconscious appears to be constituted by the interlacing of the derivatives (offshoots, *rejetons*) of the instinct and what is thrown out (sproutings, *rejets*) by consciousness.

Such is the very *positivity* of the Unconscious, of that region of being that adds the dynamics of lack, desire, and avidity to the inertia of what automatically falls into forgetfulness or habit, that adds all the fusions of these forms of desire with anxiety and fear, and also all the complex configurations that represent, on the level of virtual thought and action, the instincts reflecting the forms of social life (and, of course, family life) and that obey, even while they resist them, the rules of the possible (the constraints imposed by the reality principle and by duty, that is, by morality). This complex configuration which forms the strictly "Freudian" Unconscious can only symbolically appear, having been and being *repressed* by conscious being, which is constituted according to the order of its own reason, that is, its logic and its morality. What characterizes this positive pole of psychical being is the *absoluteness* of its aspiration; even when transformed by being refracted in the system of reality by the relativity which subordinates it to consciousness and to repression, it is still as an absolute that this positive pole of psychical being returns and is maintained in the Unconscious. It is this (the id) that desires to be satisfied, whether existing as formed by its primary tendencies or as expressed in the representations which are produced in it by the repercussion of reality,[20] which "fantasizes" it by repressing it. In this respect it is the field of *absolute meaning.* This fundamental process is expressed in "key meanings," which make up the stammerings or muffled (in their symbols) cries of desire and fear. Considered in the totality of desires and counterdesires which are operative within its being, the Unconscious is a being which is a "will to representation." It consequently increasingly demands satisfaction at any price.

If this positivity of the Unconscious, of this "irruptive" being, cannot be resolved into being only a mosaic of specific "reflex" tendencies, it gains the even greater force of a spring made taut by the spirals in which conscious being winds and entangles it. Its positivity is increased because of the "complexity" of the unconscious formations which the principles of reality and morality impose upon the instincts. This, then, is the nature of the dynamism which expresses within the psyche the forces of the Unconscious which are constituted as images, fantasies, and complexes. These latter are like buds of instinct which can grow only in the shadow of conscious being.

c) The Model of the Psychical Organism

In concluding this structural analysis of the psychical organism, and to clarify our own position, we must sketch a model of its organization. This leads us to propose a modification and simplification of Freud's famous diagrams, reducing his topographical trinology to its fundamental dynamics. The Freudian trigon of id, superego, and ego can be reduced to two poles (which we call positive or Unconscious and negative or conscious, in the sense which we have broadly described), between which the structures of the psychical organism are organized.

On this subject, two things are clear: Freud complicated the "agencies" of his Unconscious by placing almost all of conscious being into it; and because of his generalization of the Unconscious, he himself effaced not only the limits but the functions of the opposition conscious-Unconscious.

In the later parts of this work, when discussing conscious being, we have spoken as much of the Unconscious as of "Consciousness." It is important that we be aware of the organic subordination of the Unconscious to the conscious, and transfer one agency, the ego, into conscious being, along with the greatest "portion" of the superego, considered as being the ego-ideal. For even if they have their roots in the Unconscious, they blossom forth "to become what they have to be" in the forms of conscious being. This is the reason we must simplify the topography and clarify how these two regions (Unconscious and conscious) of the psychical organism are strictly complementary in their dynamics. The conscious does not merely submit to the positive action of the Unconscious. By repressing it, it forms the configurations and the complexes of the Unconscious in the strict sense, that is, of the Unconscious which we have shown to be a property of conscious being. We must again examine the three agencies which the Freudian topography distinguishes within the Unconscious and which necessarily express the action of consciousness within the Unconscious. The agency of the ego cannot be reduced to what it is not and does not have to be. For as it takes form, it constitutes the Unconscious, not as it is (Freud's primary repressed) but as it should be (the repressed in the strict sense). The two other agencies in his topography, the id and the superego, join to form the Unconscious (libido-destrudo, instincts and "introjected" prohibitions of Oedipal or pregenital fantasies). At this constitutive level of the Unconscious, it would be better to speak of the "id" and the "counter-id" than to link the id with a so-called "superego," which is in fact a "sub-ego." For the superego in the strict sense, as the "ego-ideal," forms a part of conscious being and not merely of its unconscious determinations, since it represents a sublimation which surpasses them or, more accurately, represses them.

We thus propose the accompanying diagram (figure 7) to represent the topography and the dynamics of conscious-Unconscious relations.

From this sketch we see: 1) that the structure of conscious being frames the Unconscious and exercises its power of repression upon the id by imposing upon it the forms of the complexes which are the symbolic representatives of the instincts; and 2) that the id constitutes the mass of the Unconscious, but that the id is composed of the contradictory forces of the libido and the destrudo—the id is organically interwoven with a counter-id (which is the equivalent of the unconscious superego).

While both retaining and reinforcing what is essential to the Freudian model, our representation of the psychical organism can, perhaps, claim to give to the psychical organism more order than it had had, and even claim to give it a true organization.

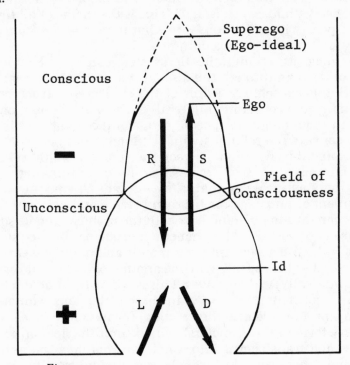

Figure 7.
R: Repression   S: Sublimation   L: Libido
D: Destrudo (Death Instincts)

4. BECOMING CONSCIOUS: LANGUAGE AS THE MILIEU OF PSYCHICAL BEING

If the characteristic of psychical life is the constitution of a milieu between instinct and the world, the characteristic *par excellence* of human phenomena is the constitution of a verbal milieu in which the subject's will is bound up with the representation of his world. Because it has been repeated so often, this leitmotif of all modern philosophy and psychology (including ethology and psychophysiology) has become so commonplace that we are almost afraid to take it up again. That man speaks and is a speaking being is a self-evident truth which has never escaped the notice of a self-conscious being. However, the appearance of the unconscious (that new human characteristic which consists in his *having* an unconscious by ceasing "*to be*" unconscious) can be established only through the possibility, introduced into the organization of his being by his own speech, of an environment in which his relations with himself are linked with his Unconscious. This is the theme of all those contemporary investigations into what in man arises from his nature and what from his culture.

Language as a communication system can never be understood other than through the discontinuous traits of its structure. But as speech, the words of the subject, its structure is essentially and constantly bilateral (emission-reception, natural sign-code, language-speech, sign-signified) and so necessarily conveys the relations which it establishes between the subject and the other and between the subject and himself, in the thousands of ways of expressing himself, of thinking, or of acting only by speaking, that is, by utilizing this institutional monument of language for his own private and personal use.

We can thus understand how both the problem and its solution are to be found in the phonetic morphology of the "statements" which emerge from the mouth and enter the ears of men, whether they speak with one another or alone and "as if" (metaphorically) to themselves. This is where the problem lies, for the information contained in these statements cannot be contingent. But it is also the solution, for its sense appears in the very form of the "functors" which limit the field of possibilities and transform it into a field of apprehension and of meaning, whose context, through its structural totality, designates the intuition of meanings. No matter in which sense the problem of signification and communication is taken, it always comes down to understanding speech as an algebraic construction of meaningless signs so as to compose a meaningful text, to *produce,* as Humboldt expressed it, its own subject matter. Every linguistic, sociological, structuralist, psychological, psychoanalytic, or epistemological school continually takes as the object of its controversies and discussions language at "one or another" or at "one and the other" of these constitutive moments. This is indeed the very problem of language, which cannot be solved unless it is reintegrated, as a product of speech and as an event (Ricoeur), into a hierarchy of moments or of structures which compose it in the subject and through the subject, insofar as it constitutes the specific milieu in which the Unconscious and the conscious are linked, in which psychical being is constructed.

Studies in general linguistics,[21] in perfect conformity with their object, well understand how to deal with signs or significants (that is, precisely that in the sign which is the most detached of meaning and in some way is free to enter into an infinity of combinations) in their sequence, or their paradigmatic connection (as is said, in general conformity to information theory and to a Markovian model), or their syntagmatic connection (which demands, following Cofer, Osgood, Bousfield, etc., a reference to semantic differentiation, which, in the last analysis, implies the anchoring of the system of signs in the intentional sphere of the subject). At a certain level, verbal functioning (insofar as it is a mathematical function of causality and of substitutability) thus appears to unfold according to its own processes and laws. Sometimes this takes place according to sequences prescribed by dictionaries, grammars, or syntax (that is, by the "taxonomical" representatives of the representations of the subject's cultural world); or it may be according to "automatic" connections, whose expressions derive their secondary sense only through their relative position within the spoken series. In such verbal structures[22] language comes face to face with the laws of a general system of language. Language is systematically separated both from the intentionality of speech (that is, from the ontological structure of the speaker and of the person to whom the words are directed) and from its truth or its "decidability" (that is, from its logical structure). Transfers within the linguistic system make up the fundamental structures of the formal apparatus of language. But it is also true that this formal apparatus has its own dynamics according to which one's mother tongue is conjugated,[23] along with what each individual within the group, because of the originality of his particular position, adds to or subtracts from the development of its signs. The individual's originality tempers these formal dynamic laws. Or rather, the subject's reality limits its purely nominalist (or, as we say today, structuralist) interpretation. This is the sense in which Ricoeur considers the semantic level of the subject's speech to integrate the "semeiological" system. For this reason he reminds us that speaking implies not only an ideal use of the sign but also its reference to the system of reality (Frege). We would add that it therefore implies a reference to the subject's own organization in his conscious and unconscious relations to his world.

We are now in a position to examine the connections between conscious language and the Unconscious. Freud has shown that language belongs essentially to the conscious-preconscious system. His view (and ours) is that the gift and use of speech *(la parole)* are a natural index of the structure of conscious being. But—and this "but" is crucial—language involves levels of organization that, when moving from being more or less "automatic" (as the classical authors, Hughlings Jackson in particular, stated), represent nothing other than the very juncture of conscious being and the Unconscious. We must at least briefly examine the fundamental issue of "becoming conscious" in and through the functions of language. This will provide a fitting conclusion to our investigation of psychical being, that is, of those reverberatory structures which allow the conscious subject to carry on that existential conversation with the unconscious subject, by means of which the unconscious subject comes into being.[24]

Language, the symbolic milieu of all the subject's relations, remains in its milieu as if it were suspended (Benveniste) between an intentional and instinctual infralinguistic system, which it *expresses,* and a logical-ethical supralinguistic system, whose law it promulgates. This duality allows for the possibility of both the opposition between and the convergence of the negativity of consciousness and the positivity of the Unconscious. These latter are interwoven "in inverse proportion" in such a way that they describe the processes through which psychical being *becomes* conscious or unconscious.

a) "Becoming Unconscious"

If, in accordance with this work's dialectics, when attempting to understand becoming conscious we look to what it is not, in order to find the traits of what it is, then we should first investigate the meaning of "becoming unconscious." To be unconscious is a certain manner which conscious being has of relinquishing itself, that is to say, of seeing itself as other.[25] Unconscious always presupposes a "certain degree" of consciousness. Any theory of the Unconscious which separates its latent nature from its manifestations holds this to be true. For unconscious phenomena can never appear apart from a certain consciousness, whose language gives an indication of its activity. The Unconscious is thus understood to appear always and necessarily as *the language of the other.* It is a language in which something else is said through the words which it speaks. The more we are concerned with the forms of deep unconsciousness (sleep and acute psychotic states) or systematic unconsciousness ("alienation," which culminates, as we have seen, in the schizophrenic personality, but which can also be discerned in different types of neurotic personality), the more obvious it becomes that becoming unconscious is the condition of allowing what is unconscious to manifest itself in and through language. This is overwhelmingly obvious in dreaming during sleep (or in any delirium or analogous hallucinatory state) when, by becoming "unconscious," the subject causes his unconscious to appear in the symbolism of the dream, which can be lived only as it is narrated. Even at this level of unconsciousness, conscious being is speaking, though it may be muted or only an echo. The subject must "speak" the metaphoric constitution of his dream.

There is another form of being unconscious, in which a delirious person claims to be what he is not, or has himself announced—in his hallucination—as what he is not. In this case the unconscious does not bear upon the absence of something's appearance in consciousness (which thing we can here call a perception, idea, belief, or feeling). It bears instead upon the assertion of an unconscious error expressed in the propositions of a countertruth. The unconscious subject thus errs in giving the unconscious, which opposes consciousness, access to his consciousness, which is the legislator of reality. Any mode of becoming unconscious thus has a tendency to move not towards a zero of consciousness but towards a "manifestation" of the Unconscious, which at the level of symbolic language wins a sort of freedom of the city—that of dreams or of madness.

Becoming unconscious, therefore, obliges us to go even more deeply into what we call the Unconscious and its "manifestation." "Becoming unconscious" points to a mode of being—where the Unconscious is an attribute; but it implies that this mode of being causes the appearance of what belongs to it by nature. The substantive-Unconscious is just this "this" (the id). We shall return shortly to this question of the production of the Unconscious by becoming conscious. In the meantime we shall simply state that becoming unconscious is a certain manner of returning to the Unconscious (of "regressing"). But since becoming unconscious does not lead to a nothingness, it must itself be grasped in those conditions of its appearing which are very naturally called the "manifestations" of the Unconscious. As we have seen, these manifestations are essentially symbolic. They necessarily pass through a displacement of signs which employ polysemia and all the substitutive functions which are to be the resources or the poetic treasures of language. For this reason the Unconscious can be said to be structured *as a language.* For it is necessarily understood as being the inverse of speech, as if it were its negative. Of course the latent being of the Unconscious remains problematic. And problematic in two senses. What can it be *without* being manifested, and how could it not be *underneath* its manifestation?[26] The very demands of this problematic determine its solution. For the Unconscious is a force derived from the milieu of being and not merely from a Milieu reflected to infinity; as we have seen, the Unconscious has positive being (which even the Freudian point of view would have trouble denying). This nonintuitive, fanciful, instinctual force constitutes the *primary signified* or secondarily repressed form of being, that which not only depends upon but gives its meaning to all the subject's figures of speech. This holds true for the Subject to the extent that he becomes unconscious when he abandons himself to the mechanisms of a language which coincides with the movements of his Unconscious.

b) "Becoming Conscious"

If *"to become unconscious"* is to allow one's Unconscious to speak (by allowing it to manifest itself symbolically), *"to become conscious" is to silence it.* For to be conscious is to be unconscious of one's unconscious, just as to be Unconscious is —in a certain manner—to be or to become conscious of one's Unconscious. This designates the relations of reverberation (but not total reciprocity) between conscious being and "its" Unconscious.[27]

For conscious being, to open to its world is to submit to the law of reality, as we have seen. That is to say, definitively and always to subordinate its thought and action, in the general form of speech that sustains and implies them, to the laws that represent the rules of grammar, syntax, and logic, which are the rules of the real or ideal cultural society to which all men must adhere in order to exist. When we emphasized that the field of consciousness and the trajectory of the person are *necessarily structured not only as, but through, language,* we recognized that it is this "Order" and the "orders" implied by it that form the very structuring of conscious being in its two fundamental modes. Yes, as von Humboldt and Cassirer (and, just as profoundly, Buffon) have so emphatically stated, language *is* man. This is to say that the structure *par excellence* of conscious being is language. For, in the Cogito, I most certainly am when thinking, that is, when speaking. And to speak is to conjugate in the present all the modes of the relations which are constitutive of present experience, just as the past, future, conditional, and subjunctive moods structure the arrow of time and of values as a system of the self's coordinates. It cannot escape the fact that the imperative mood lacks the first person precisely because it derives the force of its command from the single direction which it intends. The imperative is only implied and virtual in all the modes in which the self is joined to its world. In whatever manner the self that commands might *appear,* it does so only to obey the injunction of its lack of being, to reply to its wish and fulfill its desire (which is a sort of "gear shift" that forms the singularity of its being). It does this on the condition that it be itself, which entails that it pass through the forms prescribed for the self who speaks in order, by taking control, to gain control of himself and exist as a self. This model has been used repeatedly by all the forms of "Daseinanalysis" and of logical-anthropological or linguistic analyses which are the most frequently used by "psychology." Conscious being is constituted only through language. And when it speaks, its speech contains what it does not say within what it does say.

This is the sense in which we have conducted our analyses of the implicative structure of its being.

"To become conscious" is not merely to make use of an essentially verbal model of one's world; it is also to negate or deny, through the radical unconsciousness of what is not at one's disposal, what cannot or should not enter into the statement of the discourse which has been undertaken. It is to constitute the Unconscious as such, that is, as the repressed of which the subject has no consciousness because he has himself excluded it from his field and from his own system of values and has relegated it to the status of memories which have slipped his mind or of desires which cannot be acknowledged. Through the constitutive act of conscious being, this action of repressing what should not appear in speech (and therefore in thought and in action) causes the Unconscious to become the Substantive-Unconscious, which henceforth *has* conscious being, but has it only for others, that is, for someone other than oneself, for whom one does not exist. What characterizes man is not merely to be conscious (that is, not *being* unconscious) but to have become conscious by *having* an Unconscious which he bears as the shadow of his body. He has this Unconscious, and not vice versa. For the Unconscious does not have him (in the sense of the slang expressions "You have me there" and "I was had"). Such is the connection of the Unconscious and the conscious in and through the mediation of language. Without this symbolic milieu of signs, the reign of prescribed law could not have been established in the individual. Nor could there arise that "human" manner of being conscious which consists in constantly being concerned with what is not said in one's own speech. What language expresses, reveals, or signifies is articulated only when that which forms its relation with the Unconscious is left in the shadows or in silence. We can now see what is necessarily unconscious in conscious being. But we also see at the same time that conscious being controls what is unconscious. It controls it in such a way that the function of its language is to create the event of lived experience, to create that someone that it is, by running opposite to the Unconscious which its own progressive movement has constituted. This "countercurrent" is so strong that it carries away everything in its speech (in its automatic responses and in the free associations which unbind what language binds when it not merely serves but is the form of conscious being) that is beyond its

control and its meaning. In this way the reality of conscious being takes shape in opposition to the Unconscious which it represses. This function of repression is the sole gauge of its problematic "solidity." Repression constitutes not only the Unconscious as repressed, but also conscious being as repressing. However problematical this reality of the subject might be, it still binds, for example, didactic analysis to a hermeneutical exercise which is much more difficult and conjectural than are mental illnesses or sleep. We are well aware that the Unconscious appears in the well-constituted conscious being of the normal waking adult only in certain conditions of everyday life (slips of the tongue, witticisms, failures of purpose), in which he speaks only through the other or by reflecting upon the other.

c) The Incorporation of the Unconscious into Conscious Being

To become conscious or to become unconscious of its Unconscious is always a property of conscious being. This incorporation is the very essence of the activity and organization of conscious being. Whether conscious being in its negativity reattaches itself to the positivity of the Unconscious (sublimation), or whether it detaches itself from its Unconscious by recognizing it (catharsis), the movement of this dialectic demands its own metamorphosis, that of a coupling of the conscious and the Unconscious in the first person.

The Unconscious is constituted only through the action of conscious being, which borrows the form which it imposes upon the sphere of the instincts (repression) from its essentially verbal social milieu. Whether these forms are imagos (figurative representations of the instincts) or words (significative representations of the law), they are always modeled by conscious being, which, by repressing the instinct, bestows its symbolic meaning upon it.

When we examined Freud's views on instinctual representatives and the theory of repression, we saw that the Unconscious comes into being only through the action of conscious being, which extracts the sense of the social environment and of the law which governs its reality and its manner of existing, both through the effect of images (figurative representatives of events) and through words (significative representatives of the law). In emphasizing this, we returned to an inverted form of Freud's formula, that "Made in Germany," which we consider to be *the trademark of conscious being* stamped upon the formations of the Unconscious. These formations are thus seen to be structured as a language; they depend upon language both in their manifestation and in their latency. For through its key signs or its symbols, language so informs the id that it is formed into functional systems (topography) or complexual systems (fantasms). On the other hand, this unconscious "apparatus" never ceases to haunt conscious being, as if to take revenge upon it or, at the very least, to contradict whatever it says (or whatever it wishes and ought to say and do).

Any conception of man (or as Freud put it, of his "psychical apparatus") which hypothesizes the omnipotence of the Unconscious affirms that this is his "true" master. By reading between the lines of his conscious speech that other text which is articulated in a context of signs (of fantasies, complexes, agencies, instincts, etc.—words which express the cohesive force of the systematic organization of the Unconscious),[28] we come to perceive and know that something is moving and speaking in this someone. Of course, this can never force the agent of this hermeneutics not to take account of the self-evidence of the movement and sense of human existence, which self-evidence arises in opposition to the Unconscious to the extent that human existence can progress only by repressing its Unconscious. Even when it discovers the sense of this sense in its unconscious agencies (narcissism, introjection of the superego, Oedipal complex, castration complex, guilt complex, homosexual tendencies, etc.), human existence transforms this sense. This is the most extreme aporia of the problem of sublimation. It is a case of a transformation or a transposition within Freudian theory itself. Freudian theory speaks of displacement, of defusion, of desexualization, of countercathexis —all of which notions point to the economic-dynamic phenomena of a mutation. This *metamorphosis* may well be the law of conscious being, just as metaphor is that of the Unconscious. And this metamorphosis is precisely the organization of conscious being whose constitution both necessarily reflects its *archeology* and requires the institution of its own *teleology.* In these simple bits and pieces we can recognize the thesis which was articulated with such great force by Paul Ricoeur.[29]

Sublimation is that process by which conscious being passes from the positivity of the Unconscious to the positivity of transcendental consciousness or the Ego. This is accom-

plished thanks to the symbolic apparatus which is at its disposal and which is, as it were, the milieu of this mediation. For as we have seen, the functional negativity of conscious being opens onto its action upon the human world as onto the reality of the cosmos. There could consequently never be direct and immediate expansion of the unconscious realm over the motives and the actions of conscious being. But since conscious being is never absolutely separate from the Unconscious, the problem of "sublimation" arises. This is the problem that the moral and rational dialectic inherent in the dynamic organization of conscious being is called upon to resolve. It resolves this problem in that no matter how narcissistic or autoerotic ambition, for example, might be, this dialectic transposes—to the point of inverting it—the motive force of pleasure into the motivation of struggle and the image of the conqueror. Or again, it is "resolved" if the "oral instinct," which drives the newborn child to devour the object of his desire, becomes in the adult the ordering of his life as built upon the ideal of knowledge (to devour books). Or it is "resolved" in the case of an adult woman who projects into her career as a doctor her infantile virile protestation. For these two "states" are not linked merely by the same analogy. They are differentiated by the *change* which is implied by the movement from one state to the other. It is indeed a question of a solution, when across the metaphor which binds them together the disparity widens to infinity through the metamorphosis which distinguishes them, passing from the fatal inanity of primary object relationships to the level of a speech in which the subject articulates his relations with actuality and orchestrates his world of possibilities. This is because only an artificial process can reduce the discursive whole which constitutes the syntax or the semantic field of the existent to an elliptical figure (whether paradigmatic or syntactic) of its closed system of meanings. "Sublimation" can thus be said to be not adherence to the Unconscious but detachment from it. It consists in a double negation of the unconscious so as to repeat in new terms what the Unconscious had mumbled.

The system of the Ego, of conscious being, is often described as a dependency relation, which, though different from "sublimation," is naturally akin to it. The self is thus said to come into being only out of its *resistances* to the Unconscious. Conscious being, then, would "in the last analysis" depend upon the Unconscious, since it exists only in and through its opposition to the unconscious agencies. The "resistances" which the psychoanalyst encounters on the conscious level tell him, very accurately, that something in conscious being is standing in the way of recovery: this something is precisely the force of the Unconscious. On this subject Freud introduced the notion of the death instinct, which is the first and major theme of *Beyond the Pleasure Principle.* "Becoming conscious" here appears as a process which does not give in to the attraction of the unconscious (that is, which is no longer reduced to unconscious resistances). We must therefore say that the conscious self is not the seat of these resistances. It is rather at stake in them. And just as earlier, when discussing sublimation, we emphasized the metamorphosis (and not merely the metaphor) which constitutes the very act of the subject who, reincorporating into his own depths whatever could determine him, transforms this id into the myself that he now intends to become, we can here make the same observations on the subject of catharsis.[30] The act of becoming conscious through which the subject recognizes his Unconscious does not take the unconscious motive force into account. It takes it merely as a starting point from which to go further, to go beyond it. If to be conscious means to be unconscious of one's unconscious, to become conscious of this Unconscious can only add to the property of conscious being what had been alienated in the unconscious thing.

The ascending dialectic (becoming conscious), in its process of liberation, sets its sights on this "back and forth" Conscious-Unconscious-Conscious, as does the descending dialectic (becoming unconscious) in its case. This double dialectic can be carried out only in and through conscious being's modes of being organized, that is, through the articulation of its speech. If words are not things, and if things are not words, this is because the passage from one to the other, the place *(lieu)* which separates and unites them, is a milieu which constitutes the subject to the extent that in order to exist he must think and speak, that is, he must be conscious. To be conscious, to become conscious both of the things which form his world and, by symbolizing them, of their representations, is for the subject to have at his disposal that which cannot be at his disposal (it is the very act of becoming conscious of his Unconscious) by requiring it to become other than that other, to enter into the self's own language, into its dialogue with its real and ideal world. The activity which was a sort of self-analysis in the case of sublimation is, in the case of catharsis, or more generally in any liberation of being through the expression of its Unconscious, an activity which the psychoanalyst helps the subject to do. It is nothing more than the dramatic dialogue which the language of transference (spontaneous, labored, or provoked) assumes: that of "becoming conscious." But in this case it presents a particular difficulty: what is the form of the relationship of conscious being to its Unconscious which has been altered and fixated in its mental disorders?

The dynamic relations of conscious being with its Unconscious are inherent in the organization of psychical being in such a way that they cannot be separated from the structure of language, which is, in effect, the suture which stitches conscious being to its Unconscious. If, in the organization of psychical being, everything works together to take on the meaning of existence against the entropy of the Unconscious, and if to exist is to become conscious by constituting in oneself the domain or the reign of one's own Unconscious, this can mean only that the meaning of existence is a metamorphosis which man normally constitutes or conducts through the organization of his own being; it is his manner of thinking and, in the last analysis, his manner of speaking. When he is not, or is no longer, capable of this metamorphosis, when he falls into the psychopathological forms of existence, it is the speech of others which helps him to become conscious, to make use of the power of passing (of transference) from the id to the ego which he has to be, to become.

The "inferior" position of the Unconscious cannot be represented spatially as a lower region or sphere upon which some pontifical agency would be superimposed. The problematical relationship of conscious being to its unconscious, which we have unceasingly described in all the formations and organizational constitutions of consciousness, sends us back necessarily to the reality of their relationship, to the reality of meaning. No act, no thought, no idea in any category or at any ontological level of human being can radically separate the conscious and the unconscious or bring about the exclusion of one by the other. Even at the deepest levels of the unconscious, consciousness does not disappear. Even in the highest forms of mind, the unconscious is not excluded. The struggle in man which at each moment and in each of the projects of his existence engages the higher and the lower agencies of the subject, this struggle, which is psychical life itself, implies the ontological constancy of a conflict of being which grounds all his choices and all his experiences. Psychical being thus is not divided in two parts. Instead it represents a basically bipolar organization which is denoted by the terms of the sequences "Consciousness-Self-Transcendence-Reason" and "Unconsciousness-Automatism-Instinct."

The distinction between the *"field of consciousness"* and the *"self"* as cardinal dimensions of conscious being does not point to two partial or distinct functions. It corresponds rather to another connection which is as alive as that between consciousness and conscious being—the *connection in time* between the experience which psychical being appropriates to itself when claiming its part of the space which is incorporated into the actuality of its world (field of consciousness), and what psychical being intends itself to be in its history (the trajectory of its personality). Nothing can be said about the phenomenology of the structures of lived experience or about the construction of the self which does not weave together these two complementary forms of psychical life. But another mode of organization for conscious being is its relation to its unconscious. We have seen that language represents the locus of this mediation. For it is through language that psychical being passes from its original state of unconsciousness to the constitution through language of what it does not express or can express only symbolically. It is by speaking that the subject lays down, as it were, two worlds: *his* own and that of *others.* These two worlds would constantly interfere with one another if the sense of the conscious being's speech did not impose its direction upon them.

Thus, the dynamic articulation of psychical being cannot and must not be viewed as establishing simple relationships of interaction or of reciprocity. The development of its hierarchical form, the very structuring of conscious being, constitutes certain relations of subordination or of implication which give psychical being its finality (or, as is sometimes said, with superficial prudence, its "capacity for adaptation"). The direction of its organization and its organization itself specify psychical being's direction. The passage from infancy to adulthood, and that from sleeping to waking, are fundamental indicators of this progress in which the evolution of the phylum and the

development of the person converge. Psychical being is constituted and forms itself in the direction of an opening to a world
of freedom.

Thus does the Unconscious appear in *its place* (representing the positive exigency of the body's symbolized needs) and
in *its function* (opposition to the transcendence of the Ego). As
for conscious being, it discovers its negative function (direc-
torial, regulatory, or legislative) either to organize the field of
its actually lived experience or to ensure the autonomy of
its being, the self; all in all, for every person it plays the role
that the psychoanalyst fills, as Freud has remarked,[31] in and
through the application of the rule of conscious becoming. It is
in this sense that we must say, using Ruyer's words, that conscious being *frames* the Unconscious.

*However, consciousness can be described only in relation
to the Unconscious which it "contains."* The objections which
certain psychologists or anthropologists raise against what
might appear to them to be an abusive or old-fashioned infla-
tion of conscious being are empty, being exactly symmetrical
to those equally abusive objections of the "psychologists of consciousness" who "deny" *("nient")* the unconscious as if, Freud
observes, to "disavow" *("renier")* their own.

The debate between these two philosophies rests upon the
problem of *values,* upon the problems involved in the ethical
structures of the organization of psychical being. Thus, in concluding this work, and to clarify definitively its significance, we
must examine two *fundamental* and *complementary* aspects
of the subordination of the unconscious to conscious being. The
first is that of conscious being's freedom, the freedom of mankind generally in the face of the forces which one's Unconscious sets up to oppose him. The second is that of the loss of
freedom which occurs in breakdowns of conscious being's organization, that is, in mental illness. These two problems are
intimately related to one another. The solution of the second
calls for the solution of the first.

3. THE CONTAINMENT OF THE UNCONSCIOUS BY CONSCIOUS BEING AND THE PROBLEM OF MORALITY

The force of consciousness cannot be conceived as existing
in a state so pure and so powerful that it would completely
separate man from his animality by "mastering" the forces of

his Unconscious (of his irrational or instinctual aspect). Nor can we radically oppose the angel to the beast, or instinct to reason in man, since he is that "antinomic composite" which implies the coupling of that pair of forces which, in the dialectic of his being, represents the battle between his body and his mental and moral faculties. This does not mean that evil and the unconscious are merged in the way that good and reason coincide with one another. This is a good, but simplistic, idea. For on the level of consciousness, freedom consists in being able to choose evil as well as good, as we noted when discussing human violence.[32] Human being is "manufactured" in such a manner that it is constituted in itself only in opposition to the forces which push one blindly, this side of any conscious obligation (as well in the direction of the life instincts as in that of the death instincts; as well towards pleasure as towards the anxiety which is connected with pleasure). The "savagery" of human nature is thus universal and in some way in rebellion against particular systems of good and evil. Man submits to good and evil only when his consciousness gives him access to them through his own history in the History and Geography of his world: "primitive man" is, in this respect and as an individual, as open to morality as is "civilized man." They are both equally "conscious" and organized men, men who are concerned with their Unconscious, but are so in order to surpass it. Nor is there any question of reducing morality to "masochistic" exigencies or to the introjection of parental severity, both of which are equally unconscious. To do this would be, as Paul Ricoeur put it, to reduce the sublime to the oneiric. To say that the superego is unconscious and that the ego is crushed between this phantasmagoria and the symbolic fantasies of the id, without ever coming to reconcile them, this would obviously be to cause *homo ethicus* to fall to the level of *homo mythologicus* and to condemn him to an infantile existence. But as has been said, *"die Welt ist keine Kinderstube"* ("the world is not a nursery").

Such an annihilation of "conscience" by a new force, which has accrued to the ancient Epicurean conception of the nature of man by reflecting on the Unconscious, could not help but give rise to lively discussions and violent polemics. The amorality of Freudian psychology has not ceased to be denounced. Freud was moved to refute this criticism and made the attempt to do so.[33] Some psychoanalysts, such as Charles Odier,[34] have become advocates of a theoretical view of the relation of the Unconscious and the Conscious which grants to consciousness the relative autonomy which certain personalist tendencies of contemporary psychoanalysis (e.g., Daniel Lagache) concede to it. Hesnard discusses the reasons for and against the assimilation of morality to a *morbid universe of error,* to a *morality without sin.*

We feel that the revision we have attempted of the relations between conscious being and the Unconscious—without explicitly insisting upon it in this work (which does not intend to be an apology)—defends man's "nature" against the excesses of a "naturalistic" interpretation of his intersubjective ties or of his duties. The dialectics of being and having, of being and becoming, of depth and surface, to which we have so often referred (though not always explicitly), introduce into the ontology of human "nature" just that problematic which removes it from the laws of nature, even from those of zoology. In defining conscious being as the capacity of being for oneself, for one's goals, and in subordinating the unconscious to the *drama of existence,* our analyses have led us to recognize enough conscious freedom in man's own structure to allow him to enjoy it *and* to suffer it. And we have discovered too little unconscious determinism to hold that man is necessitated to enjoy it *or* to suffer it—this all too absolute alternative not being in conformity with specifically human moral problems. In fact ethics is an existential problematic which does not humanly put up with the law of all or none. From this arises man's anguish in the face of his freedom (Pascal, Kierkegaard, etc.).

Of all the works written during the last fifty years examining the problem of the unconscious determinism of human behavior in its moral incidence, Paul Ricoeur's is the most profound. But how could it be otherwise when, after an exhaustive reading of Freud, Ricoeur investigates the problem of the archeology and the teleology of the subject? In addition, his reflections take on the form of Hegel's phenomenology of mind. Ricoeur definitely does not betray the spirit of the much debated Hegel of the *Phenomenology.* We shall now examine the development of Ricoeur's dialectic.

The rule of the representation of desire does not allow man to be restricted within his infantile model. If the adult has been a child, and if he still remains one, he cannot be reduced to being only the manifestation of his "vegetative" or "animal" life. Representation, Ricoeur states, does not obey merely a law of intentionality which makes of it the expression of something. Instead, it obeys a different law which makes of it the manifestation of life, of some effort or desire. It might be even more accurate to speak of a law of intentionality which makes of this the expression of someone rather than of something. At the basis of the representation of the instincts at the level of consciousness and of language, we can discern the composite which Boerhaave had in mind when he said that man was one in his vitality but double in his humanity. The whole problem of relations, of man's annihilation, or of his transcendence of the Ego, traces back to this composite nature, which is the existential motive of the phenomenology of the mind.[35] The author of *Freud and Philosophy* then reminds us of the sense of the Hegelian dialectic as it constitutes a teleological model of consciousness, a theory of *Bewusstsein* or of *Bewusstwerden,* and links this psychological consciousness to moral consciousness, or conscience *(Gewissen).* The truth of this dialectic resides in the subsequent rather than the antecedent movement. What is in question in such a phenomenology is the production of the self *(selbst)* through self-consciousness. The position of the self is inseparable from its production through a progressive synthesis.[36] This is indeed what Jean Hyppolite emphasized from his point of view when he wrote: "In this act of becoming conscious, self-consciousness is the source of a truth which is for itself at the same time it is in itself. This truth arises in a history through the mediation of diverse self-consciousnesses whose interaction and unity constitute mind *(l'esprit).*"[36] If it can be said that self-consciousness is desire, self-consciousness can attain its own truth only in and through the negation of this desire. This is the point Hegel makes when he states: "Self-consciousness is fulfilled only in another self-consciousness." In the preceding pages we ourselves have sufficiently insisted upon the structuring of *"conscious becoming"* to be able to recognize, at the limits of philosophical reflection (or more precisely of the dialectical process), the act through which mind gives rise to itself by passing through the other. We are thus fully in agreement on this point.

Ricoeur claims to have found in Freud's work the implicit teleology of this imprescriptible dialectical model which separates self-consciousness from its determinations, as the master tears himself away from his condition as a slave.[38] He does this first in the living dialectic of the fate of the instincts; then in the topographical schema. For neither of these can be understood or even formulated without bringing them into the progression of negativity which, being the opposite of a purely economic progression, is the basis for an order of subordination. The problem of identification cannot be resolved by reducing it to an identity in itself and without choice. In a pure economics of dynamic systems, Freudian theory could only sink into a solipsism which denies the theory and the practice of the dialogue.[39] The statements of the principles of the constitution and the action of the Unconscious are incomprehensible if they are not reintegrated into the dynamics, or the dialectic, of conscious being.

In this way, the problem of sublimation—one of the major aporias of the general relation of ethics and instinct and of the specific relation of the Unconscious and the conscious self in the Freudian view—can be solved only by the thesis of a negation of the determinism of the Unconscious in its sublime forms (or, if you will, "sublimated" in the system of good and evil) of conscious being. When discussing the unusual but essential Freudian texts *(Three Essays . . ., The Ego and the Id)*, Ricoeur shows "the inability of Freud to solve this problem of sublimation."[40] All the processes or mechanisms which are set in play by the constitution of the higher agency, which can be called idealization, identification, sublimation, remain incomprehensible in the framework of an economics. Should we attempt to turn our attention to the topological agency of the superego (drawn sometimes from within, sometimes from outside), this agency can appear only as a phantom without substance, because it is not grasped within the constitution of the ego's reality. This reality is its own power and cannot be reduced to childhood images of authority or strictness. (While extrapolating Ricoeur's thought here, we are perhaps even more so formulating our own.)

This critique of the Freudian theory of "unconscious morality," that is, of the "anti-morality" or "a-morality *par excellence*," could not avoid irritating those who "are working" in the Unconscious (as we shall now insist, so as to end in this field of psychopathology) and are led to overlook the process of construction of conscious being.[41] Only one thing else is capable of provoking an equally widespread irritation: the "amorality" of the theory of the omnipotence of the Unconscious, a theory which is basically contradictory to the conception of repression.

Though in its myths, religions, civilizations, and history humanity is not merely governed by its unconscious archetypes, and though all men are not condemned to remain infants, it still happens that some persons are determined in their thoughts, actions, and language by their Unconscious in a different manner than are others and to a degree which is more than their conscious being can "contain." These are the persons whom we call, rightly or wrongly, "mentally ill."

4. THE FIELD OF PSYCHIATRY AND THE ALIENATION OF CONSCIOUS BEING

We have had the boldness to write this book because we felt that we had a rather adequate knowledge of psychiatry. Psychiatry is, we insist, the *pathology of freedom.* If there were no human freedom there could be no madness. For madness consists in the abrogation of this freedom. If it is possible for a man to go mad (or to dream), this is only because the organization of his being both implies and dominates this madness.[42]

The concept of organization as it is applied to the psychical organism implies the "human" order of "human nature." More exactly, it implies the appropriate Law to which conscious being submits its nature, which is represented and symbolized in its Unconscious. Man truly is that desiring and reasoning being who must balance his existence if he is to actualize it. It is therefore not a question of falling into a psychophysiological naturalism which sees mankind on this side of itself or in man's purely moral or cultural transcendence. But—and there is a but—one part of mankind—and not all of mankind[43]—by becoming an object of psychiatry, falls into its nature, or rather falls again into its body, its needs, and the symbolic fantasies which represent the vital dialectic of pleasure and pain, of life and death. Psychiatry must concern itself with these men—and only with them—if psychiatry itself is not mad. Psychiatry, therefore, can be only this *Natural History of Madness* which the "organic-dynamic" perspective establishes as the methodology of psychiatric medical science. In order to be neither a deception nor an illusion, psychiatry *must* consider mental illnesses for what they are: disorganizations of conscious being. For in man they attain precisely those categories of his being which remove him from the reality principle and more generally from the principle of practical and theoretical reason which gives him access to the rule of his freedom.

What we have said in this work concerning the very nature of the manners in which the field of consciousness can lose its structure and in which self-conscious being can lose its organization summarizes the character of man. For in his diverse "manners-of-no-longer-being," man is objectified in the in-itself of his Unconscious, which was so accurately seen by Freud to be an "It" ("Id"). An "It" which is not a natural object, but is rather the organism constituted as an object which represents the animated body of its anxieties and its desires.

From this point on, the function of psychiatry in the social sciences is to guarantee human values, insofar as it becomes aware that they are lacking in some people. It guarantees them by causing them to appear. It does this by contrasting them with the rule of servitude to the embryonic forms of psychical being, by contrasting them with the different forms of determinism which attach these persons to their past childhood, to which the normal, waking adult cannot be reduced. On the other hand, itself gaining a benefit which is parallel to that which it renders to humanity, psychiatry draws the principle of its classification of mental illnesses out of the structure of the suspended or abolished conscious being. We have often shown this to be the case, in our writings,[44] in our attempt to outline a theory of the general relativity of conscious being's loss of organization, throughout all the different modes of being or becoming unconscious. The phenomenon of disintegration of psychical being and the inversion of the relations of conscious being with its Unconscious are discovered not only in dreaming during sleep or analogous states of the destructuration of the field of consciousness. This evidence asserts itself in all the forms of psychoses and neuroses. This general law, which governs the whole field of psychiatry, sets it up on the model of the general concept of a disorganization of conscious being, and not merely on the single dynamism of unconscious forces. By pointing out the *negativity* of conscious being's active function, we have shown a possible annihilation of order to which —whether to deny it or to refuse it—conscious being yields the positivity of the Unconscious. When, in agreement with Hughlings Jackson, we asserted that the essence of mental illness is the "negative disorder" which conditions it, we only stated this obvious truth: *when no longer exerting his capability of negating the Unconscious, when he becomes himself unconscious, the subject surrenders to the positivity of his unconscious.* This is the basic model of any possible psychiatric science. It cannot be emphasized strongly enough that when speaking of the negative function of conscious being, we have validated the possible configurations of the Unconscious (positive disorders) which this function allows to appear by negating itself (negative disorder, in Jackson's sense of the term). The disorganization of conscious being implies that whatever it contains will manifest itself, since the function of conscious being is a function of negativity, of neg-entropy and of choice.

There remains the question of whether or not this object of psychiatry is real. As paradoxical as it may seem, a certain manner and method of thought appear under the scrutiny of that antianthropological structuralism which denies this reality and considers it as a myth. Within psychiatric and psychoanalytical circles everyone is aware that many psychoanalysts, carried along by the impetus of the theory of the omnipotence of the Unconscious, have, at the end of their "analytical" decomposition, come to dissolve the notion of mental illness more confidently than they have succeeded in curing mental illnesses. For example, in *The Myth of Mental Illness,*[45] Thomas Szasz prides himself in intrepidly defending a theory which so many others assert with embarrassment and even regret. Such is the illusion of those who consider mental illness to be only an illusion and believe, as J.-G. Panti imperturbably put it in the title of his work: *The Madman is Normal.*[46]

Mental illness, however, appears with the exigencies of a hard reality. And how else could it appear to man, who is ceaselessly subjected to the exigencies of his fantasies, his "dreams," his Unconscious, and for whom the construction of conscious being appears as the precarious miracle of his humanity? If, as we have shown in our historical studies of the birth of psychiatry (especially in our *Études,* numbers 2, 3, and 4), this appearing is itself conditioned by cultural and historical factors, it could not be said to depend upon a mere "rationalist" myth of a humanity which is so intoxicated with its reason, in the "Age of Reason," that it wanted only to sequester in the "Ship of Fools" those flamboyant bearers of the irrational, who, like the poets, were madmen! Here we recognize, barely exaggerated in its formulation, Michel Foucault's thesis, *Folie et Déraison.*[47] In this work, which is so well documented and so profoundly thought out, Foucault presents all the good reasons for keeping the balance evenly weighted between Irrationality and Reason—and perhaps even for giving more weight to the former than to the latter. On the one hand, a too mechanical and inhuman conception of psychiatry incurs the reproach of performing a magical reification, which is justified in certain respects by socio-juridical necessities or prejudices. On the other hand, a psychiatry which is based upon a concrete study of the pathological variations of the organization of conscious being (and is not based merely upon the faculty of imagination or fancy which, fortunately, men bear within themselves as the genius of humanity) takes as the object of its theory and of its praxis the vicissitudes of a consciousness which is not simply unfortunate but is affected by the misfortune of its disorganization. Such a psychiatry also can have very good reasons for considering itself not to be an illusion and for considering mental illness to have a reality to the extent that it is an illness of reality.

In other words, in spite of what certain "great minds" making light of "noble souls" might say, psychiatry founds man's freedom, his Reason, upon the specificity of its object. It is because of the fact that most men are reasonable that some, and only some, of them are mad. Psychiatry necessarily sends us to the normative modes of conscious being. It sends us there through the disorganization of the field of consciousness and of the self, upon which is grounded the "negativity" of mental disorders. It does not refer us simply to those modes of experience and of existence which form the "positivity" of what still remains in these possible pathological modalities.

This is especially obvious if we consider the goal and the methods of psychotherapy. Unless we say that the neurotic is a person who has fallen under the yoke of his Unconscious, from which he must be freed—and not the contrary—how else could we envisage the constitution of the reign of the symbolic which characterizes neurotic existence and, as a consequence, the goal sought after and sometimes attained by the psychoanalyst, or more generally by the psychotherapist? And how can we not add very simply and as a direct consequence that though he does not, of course,[48] cease to be a man, the neurotic is not a normal man, he is not a man like other men? To go even more deeply into the problem of pathology, how would it be possible not to say that it is conscious being's malformation or disorganization, that is, its *weakness,* which clearly displays the *force* of its Unconscious? After all, such truisms and first truths are all that need be said to those whose thought sometimes evaporates into too volatile subtleties.

We have thus provided a firm foundation for the continuity of our attempt to reestablish the real function of conscious being. Some may see in our view an excess of *rationalism,* others a naive *naturalism,* still others a *spiritualist* position. But how would it be possible to lay hold of human consciousness without holding firmly to the intersection of these perspectives? For human consciousness is precisely man's *reason* embodied in his *brain* in order to be opened to the *freedom* of his existence. We hold to this intersecting not in order to juxtapose these perspectives in a prudent and odious eclecticism, but in order to describe them as they are integrated in the organization of psychical being.

If the psychiatrist has something worth saying about *consciousness*—and he does—this can be done only by taking it for what it is: *Reason.* For the *Madness* which the psychiatrist intends to cure is the contrary of human consciousness.

Notes

Preface to the English Translation

1. This is the task of clinical expurgation that I undertook in the third volume of my *Études* (1954) in order to break down the artificial barrier that has classically separated disorders of consciousness (confuso-oneiric states) from what are called "dysthymic" disorders (manic-depressive or affective disorders.) Nothing seems to me to be more false than this arbitrary distinction, for it is impossible to separate so radically an attack of depression or of mania from twilight states. In this respect, the clinical study of the whole field of the psychopathology of epilepsy is of capital importance. Cf. on this subject the works by J. C. Eccles (1973), Gordon C. Globus, et al., eds. (1976), and J. W. Brown (1977), on the relations between the brain and consciousness.

2. Henri Ey, *Des idées de Hughlings Jackson à un modèle organodynamique en Psychiatrie* (Toulouse: Privat, 1975.)

3. Cf. the work which I have recently published in collaboration with my students: Henry Ey, G. C. Lairy, M. Barros, and L. Goldsteinas, *Psychophysiologie du sommeil et Psychiatrie* (Paris: Masson, 1975.)

4. Report to the *IVᵉ Congrès mondial de Psychiatrie,* Madrid, 1966. Abstract in *Excerpta Medica,* 1967, pp. 139–157. This report has been published in full in *Evolution Psychiatrique,* 1970, No. 1, pp. 1–37.

5. This notion of "psychical body" (corps psychique) (which I prefer to Freud's term *"psychische"*) has been presented and developed in the two principle works that I have written during the last years: the *Traité des Hallucinations,* 2 vols. (Paris: Masson, 1973), cf. especially vol. 2, pp. 1074–1176; and *Des idées de Hughlings Jackson à un modèle organo-dynamique en Psychiatrie* (Toulouse: Privat, 1975), cf. especially pp. 226–237.

Preface to the First Edition

1. Henri Ey, *Études psychiatriques* (3 vols.), Paris, Ed. Desclée de Brouwer:

Volume I: *Historique, méthodologie, psychopathologie générale,* 1st ed., 1948; 2nd ed. revised and enlarged, 1952. Étude no. 1: Folie et valeurs humaines; no. 2: Le rythme mécano-dynamiste de l'histoire de la médecine; no. 3: Le développement mécaniciste de la psychiatrie; no. 4: La psychiatrie dans le cadre des sciences médicales; no. 5: Une théorie mécaniciste: G. de Clérambault; no. 6: Une conception psychogénétiste: Freud; no. 7: Principes d'une conception organo-dynamiste; no. 8: Le rêve "fait primordial" de la psychopathologie.

Volume II: *Aspects séméiologiques,* 1st ed., 1950; 2nd ed., 1957. Étude no. 9: Les troubles de la mémoire; no. 10: La catatonie; no. 11: Impulsions; no. 12: Exhibitionnisme; no. 13: Perversité et perversions; no. 14: Le suicide pathologique; no. 15: Anxiété morbide; no. 16: Délire des négations; no. 17: Hypocondrie; no. 18: Jalousie morbide; no. 19: Mégalomanie.

Volume III: *Structure des psychoses aiguës et déstructuration de la conscience,* 1st ed., 1954; 2nd ed., 1960. Étude no. 20: La classification des maladies mentales et le problème des psychoses aiguës; no. 21: Manie; no. 22: Mélancolie; no. 23: Bouffées délirantes; no. 24: Confusion et délire confuso-onirique; no. 25: Les psychoses périodiques maniaco-dépressives; no. 26: Épilepsie; no. 27: Structure et déstructuration de la conscience.

Preface to the Second Edition

1. We are, of course, referring to the work of Paul Ricoeur, to Michel Tort's critique of Ricoeur, to Maurice Merleau-Ponty's posthumous writings (*Signs*), to Jacques Lacan's *Écrits,* to J.-B. Pontalis's *Après Freud,* to Michel Foucault's *The Order of Things,* to the symposium held at Bonneval on the Unconscious, etc. The vigor of the controversies which have arisen out of these discussions bears witness to the elating excitement of these authors but even more so to the acuteness of a problem which is (with all due deference to those named above) none other than the problem of *human nature.* The works which have been written about the Unconscious borrow their meaning from the theses which they assert or imply concerning man insofar as he is or is not a conscious being, that is, a being who by nature *is* not unconscious but who, because of his organization, *has* an unconscious. We insist upon this relation of having because it implies an arrangement of parts within the whole, and implies an organization.

2. For our part we thus (agreeing with Lacan) place between the brackets of anecdote or of children's tales what Oedipus is not. It thus becomes a "pre-Oedipal" fundamental relation.

3. Especially in *Métapsychologie,* French trans., p. 182.

4. The reprobation by certain persons of the values attributed to conscious being can be equalled only by the reprobation of those who hold the Unconscious in contempt. This is so because from the "moral" or "political" point of view, from the viewpoint of each individual's *Weltanschauung,* men can be divided (among themselves or within themselves) into the "partisans" of reason and order and those of the irrational and instinct: into the "Apollonians" and the "Dionysians." If one were to make up his mind from the outset and refuse to consider that man is a being who must be subject to the rules of his reason, in the eyes of the theoreticians of the absolute Unconscious he could doubtlessly pass for being unconsciously governed by the narcissism of the omnipotence of the self and the conscious (a criticism which is constantly renewed). In the same way one could systematically suspect that those who attempt to liberate themselves from reason and posit the omnipotence of the id are unconsciously governed by their unconscious desire not to be a person or to resist becoming attached to a fetish-ego. The truth of the matter is that insofar as it is the object of scientific knowledge, the organization of psychical being cannot depend upon the motives of each person's conception of the world, and that insofar as its phenomenological description is a grasping of the reality of psychical being which is organized in its person, this description necessarily implies these two modes of psychical being: that of being a subject having an Unconscious. Neither the transcendental idealism of an absolute sovereign self nor the sensationist empiricism of a cluster of images can claim to be set up as the epistemological canon of the organization of the psychical organism.

5. On the notion of structure, cf. Deschamps's article in *Sens et usage du terme structure dans les sciences humaines et sociales* (Paris: Mouton, 1962); *La Pensée,* October 1967; and the special issues devoted to this problem by *Esprit,* November 1963, May 1967, and by *Les Temps modernes,* November 1962. Cf. below pp. 35, 54–56, and especially pp. 91–95.

6. Lacan's view that the Unconscious is "structured like a language" is what has most strongly irritated his adversaries. Ricoeur—among others—has emphasized Lacan's inconsistency with the texts of Freud. To this Michel Tort replied pertinently, but without removing the inconsistency, that an image is itself inseparable from the language which it conveys even in dreams. These internal arguments do not concern us directly, for in the final analysis, the Unconscious can appear only through and in language, only through its refraction in the enunciation of speech, that is, when it flows onto the surface of consciousness. To say this is to maintain (which is our own position) that insofar as *language* is the *form of conscious being,* language is the mediation and juncture between the conscious and unconscious

systems. By referring to Freud's most profound conceptions, Lacan has magnificently illustrated this thesis. But this also asserts (which is again our position) that the verbal form in which unconscious phenomena appear leaves unsolved the problem of unconscious language and thought, which Ricoeur (like Politzer, though he employs a totally different dialectic) calls into question. To state that the unconscious is structured in the manner of a language can be done, he writes, only if we emphasize the word "like" as much as the word "language." He reminds us that for Benveniste the Freudian mechanisms are both intra- and supra-linguistic.

7. It is interesting to note that those who most insistently assert that all is meaning are the most easily taken in by the mirages of the combinations of meanings of signs which are conjugated among themselves, without a "reference," to use Frege's term, that is, without meaning.

8. Michel Foucault, *Les mots et les choses* (Paris: Gallimard, 1966), pp. 390–391.

9. On this subject, cf. what we have written concerning the primordial fact of sleep and dreaming in psychopathology, in our *Rapport au Congrès de Madrid* (1966).

10. In general we write the word "Unconscious" with a capital "U" when it is employed in the sense of the Freudian substantive. [We shall continue Ey's practice of capitalizing "Unconscious" where he does when referring to the substantive Unconscious, and of writing "conscious" with lowercase type. Also, in the French text Ey sometimes uses Freud's "*abbréviations Cs (Conscient) et Ics (Inconscient)*"—as Ey explains in a note (now eliminated) at the beginning of Part Five. When reviewing this translation, Ey suggested that this is perhaps unnecessarily cumbersome and that it would be better to eliminate these abbreviations in order to make the text more readable. We have conformed to this suggestion.—Trans.]

PART ONE. CONSCIOUS BEING

Chapter One. The Problem of the Definition of Consciousness

1. In his *Dictionnaire,* Lalande cites Hamilton's statement, "Consciousness cannot be defined," an opinion which has been repeated by so many other writers on the subject. The behaviorists are the most intransigent. In his interesting work on the problem of consciousness in modern psychology, Hans Thomae (*Nervenarzt,* 1962) draws attention to the fact that the word "consciousness" appears in the indices of the *Annual Review of Psychology* only once since 1953, and that it does not appear at all in Gerald Blum's *Model of the Mind* (1961.)

2. Paul Chauchard, *Les mécanismes cérébraux de la prise de con-*

science (Paris: Masson, 1956), p. 106: Consciousness (*la prise de conscience*) is a simple but limited process.

3. P. Lersch attributes this formula to H. Driesch.

4. Cf. Roman Ingarden, in *Husserl et la pensée moderne,* 1959, pp. 190–214.

5. Cf. the first studies of Raymond Ruyer (1932), those of Latil (1953), the recent work of Ruyer (*Revue philosophique,* 1962), the article by E. Delaveney (ibid.), and a most interesting work by Buytendijk and Christian (*Nervenarzt,* 1963, pp. 97–105); also, cf. below pp. 91–95.

6. Maurice Merleau-Ponty, *Signs,* trans. Richard C. McCleary (Evanston: Northwestern University Press, 1964), p. 184.

7. On the subject of "psychical structure" and of "Structuralism," cf. the Preface of this Second Edition, and below, p. 55.

8. Angelo Hesnard (*Evolution psychiatrique,* 1959, p. 353) finds consciousness to be more structuring than structured. Daniel Lagache (*Evolution psychiatrique,* 1960, p. 491) finds it to be "less bound" than bound. Both authors therefore find the idea of a structure of consciousness repugnant. But consciousness is and should be both structured and structuring, both bound in its constitution but not bound in its activity.

9. Biologists, psychologists, ethologists, etc. have dealt with this fundamental problem at length.

The thesis of the continuity of zooconsciousness and human consciousness is based upon the intelligence of animal modes of behavior and upon the indeterminateness of bioneurophysiological processes, or inversely, upon the determinism or synergetic probabilism of modes of behavior and the information which governs them. We must draw attention to two important works which maintain this thesis in both its forms: Henri Piéron's *De l'actinie à l'homme,* 2 vol. (Paris: Presses Universitaires de France, 1958 and 1959); and U. Ebbecke's *Physiologie des Bewusstsein in entwicklungsgeschichtlicher Betrachtung* (Stuttgart: Thieme, 1959). For Piéron, to the extent that it is a symbolic activity and a conditioned mode of behavior, consciousness is to be found in animals in a rudimentary form which is correlative to the development of their nervous system. He illustrates this thesis with numerous examples ranging from the phenomenon of the adaptive and rhythmical anticipation found in actinia to the intelligence of the primates of Yale, passing by way of the orientation of ants, the memory of molluscs, the processes of recognition and orientation among bees, the autotomy of crabs, etc., which modes of behavior all show that animal organization is not radically different from the human psychical organism, though they do not impel us to leap over the abyss which separates them. (On this subject, cf. Part IV, Chapter I.) For Ebbecke, the *phylum* of human consciousness is found in the

394 / *Notes for pages* 12 *to* 19

functional representation, at the level of the simplest living things, of a dynamic structuring, of an autonomous organizational foundation (he takes his examples from unicellular organisms among coelenterates and insects). Ebbecke describes the neurophysiology of neurons and their systematic continuum (*Assoziate, Konzentrate, Aktivate*) on the model of the organization of consciousness, which would comprise only their growth in complexity.

Most "spiritualistic" authors maintain the thesis of absolute Cartesian discontinuity, holding that the human mode of existing is in some way supra- and even extra-animal. But most frequently only the relativity of this thesis is put forward, as, for example, in the work of Paul Chauchard (*Les mécanismes cérébraux de la prise de conscience,* pp. 118–131), for whom the advent of language constitutes a mutation in the course of the "complexification" of living beings.

I have examined this important problem in the study which I devoted to the animal psychoid (*Psychiatrie animale,* 1964, pp. 12–40). I there established that plasticity of behavior was the index of what is called intelligence in animals, on the model of conscious being. Referring to C. G. Carus (1866), J. B. S. Haldane has said, in the Singer-Polignac Symposium, that "all living beings accumulate negative entropy (order)." If, in the eyes of a scholar who would, I believe, easily pass for the opposite of a spiritualist, the nervous system is presented and represented as an order which is interposed between the organism and its environment to the extent that it is the environment of this relation, it would seem that everyone could come to agree concerning the organization of the animal psychoid to the degree that it resembles, without being identical to, consciousness.

10. Edmund Husserl, *Ideas,* trans. R. Boyce Gibson (New York: Macmillan, 1943), §43.

11. Information theory (Attneave, Make, Klemmer, and Freik, etc.) comes up against this ambiguity when it attempts to apply itself to perceptions which cannot be reduced to simple probabilities.

12. Husserl, *Ideas,* §§36–44.

13. Cf. Merleau-Ponty, *The Phenomenology of Perception* and, more especially, *Signs,* particularly the section on the body and perception.

14. Cf. William James's article in *Archives Suisses de la Psychologie,* 1906.

15. Merleau-Ponty, *Signs,* p. 19.

16. Or at least insofar as it implies being in communication, for this latter can affect other "empathetic" forms than language (affective or motor exchanges), as can be observed among deaf-mutes, whose consciousness can well be structured, though it is almost always enigmatic.

17. Henri Ey, "Force et faiblesse des concepts génétiques et éner-

gétiques de la psychopathologie de Pierre Janet," in *Bulletin de psychologie,* 1960, 14, pp. 50–55.

18. The working of thoughts during dreams, about which so much has been written since Hervey de Saint-Denis, prepares or prolongs thought rather than replacing it. It automatically brings into play schemata which are, however, always *implied* as germination and orientation of thought which is asleep.

19. Husserl, *Ideas,* §97.

20. Like Sartre, we shall discuss the question of transcendence of the ego. For us it consists in the possibility of distinguishing itself from the actuality of lived experience. (See below, p. 204.)

21. We shall discuss later (pp. 204–205) Sartre's thesis on the transcendence of the ego, a thesis in which he opposes to "impersonal" and "spontaneous" consciousness (in our terms, the field of consciousness) the ego, which transcends it while in some way remaining foreign to it. For us, the transcendence of the ego is its autoconstruction, that is, its manner of being first bound to, then separated from its experience, and of being able to reflect itself in it.

22. Which is a priori only in the presentation of the thesis, for what we are placing here at the beginning of our work is actually its conclusion.

23. As an internal structure of consciousness, temporality is distinguished as experience, or rather as the mastery of its movements, of the notion of time and of the perception of time (*chronognosie*). Paul Fraisse, in his *Psychologie du temps* (Paris: Presses Universitaires de France, 1957), shows which interlacings of sensations, ideas, and judgments form the totality of psychological time. But he (pp. 150–196) is careful to extricate the temporal structure of experience, its actualization and its project as a "temporal horizon" which coincides with the field of actuality which we envision here. However, this coincidence is not total, since for us, as for consciousness, the actuality of lived experience is not a synonym for its present, but only for its presentation.

Chapter Two. Philosophy and the Problem of Consciousness

1. Cf. Aron Gurwitsch, *The Field of Consciousness* (Pittsburg: Duquesne University Press, 1964), pp. 60–70.

2. To the extent that Hegelian phenomenology is a phenomenology of mind (*Geist*) rather than of consciousness, it leads precisely to self-consciousness or the transactual structure of conscious becoming. (Cf. Ricoeur, *Freud and Philosophy,* pp. 447–450.)

3. Henri Bergson in the Introduction to the French translation of William James's *Pragmatism.*

4. Originally published in *Mind,* this article became the central chapter in his *Principles of Psychology.*

5. William James, *Talks to Teachers on Psychology and to Students on Some of Life's Ideals* (New York: Henry Holt and Company, 1899), Chapter Two.

6. William James, "La notion de la conscience," in *Essays in Radical Empiricism* (New York: Longmans, Green and Co., 1947 [1912]), p. 222.

7. Ibid., pp. 232–233.

8. Aron Gurwitsch, *The Field of Consciousness*, pp. 307–375.

9. William James, *Principles of Psychology* (New York: Holt, 1890), Vol. 1, p. 278.

10. *Signs*, p. 185.

11. Henri Bergson, *Matter and Memory*, trans. Nancy Paul and W. Scott Palmer (New York: Macmillan, 1913).

12. Henri Bergson, *Creative Evolution*, trans. Arthur Mitchell (New York: Holt, 1911), p. 145.

13. *Matter and Memory*, p. 225; *Creative Evolution*, pp. 262–263; *Mind-Energy*, pp. 58–60.

14. *Creative Evolution*, pp. 236–243.

15. Ibid., p. 261.

16. *Mind-Energy*, pp. 7–8.

17. Ibid., p. 172.

18. Henri Bergson, *Time and Free Will: An Essay on the Immediate Data of Consciousness*, trans. F. L. Pogson (New York: Macmillan, 1910), pp. 129–137.

19. *Mind-Energy*, p. 39.

20. *Time and Free Will*, pp. 80–111.

21. Emmanual Linas in *Revue philosophique*, 1959.

22. *Ideas*, §75.

23. For example, by R. Boehm in his article in the *Revue philosophique*, 1959; or by Roman Ingarden in *Husserl et la pensée contemporaine*, 1959.

24. The attitude adopted after 1907 (cf. the text published in the *Revue philosophique*, 1959, by H. Dussort, p. 438), but which he seems to have abandoned later.

25. *Signs*, pp. 161–166. To go to the "things which are simply things" (*blosse Sachen*) is in effect to seek by an ascending movement not to break out of the *Weltthesis* (from the natural attitude), but rather, in Merleau-Ponty's words, to encounter what originally forms them in the clear-obscure of the opinions (*doxa*) of this attitude. The phenomenological attitude thus definitively (*Ideen II* and *Ideen III*) turns toward the pretheoretical constitution, the "pregivens," of consciousness. In this sense Merleau-Ponty concludes (p. 165) that phenomenology is in the last analysis neither a materialism nor a philosophy of mind.

26. The following works are indispensable to this excursion into

such an arduous domain: Paul Ricoeur's translation of *Ideen I* (1913) and the Preface to his translation; the 1930 work of E. Levinas; the articles of Durvort, Vuillerman, R. Boehm, and Murall in the *Revue philosophique,* 1959; the chapter which Merleau-Ponty devoted to Husserl (*Signs,* 1960, Chapter VI); and the volume *Husserl et la pensée contemporaine* (1959). We shall center our exposition around *Ideen I,* which is the first and most fundamental work in which Husserl attempted to grasp the structures of "pure consciousness." We nevertheless emphasize the importance of *Ideen II, Ideen III,* and of the *Husserliana* (t. IV) for what concerns the "descent" of phenomenology into nature, into the sphere of the *Urpräsentarbar* and the "prereflexive," the sphere to which Merleau-Ponty has given such passionate attention.

27. *Ideas,* §27.

28. *Ideas,* §§31–32.

29. *Signs,* pp. 173–174.

30. *Ideas,* §38.

31. *Ideas,* §§40–46.

32. Paul Ricoeur, Introduction to his translation of Edmund Husserl's *Idées directrices pour une phénoménologie* (Paris: Gallimard, 1950), p. xxii.

33. *Ideas,* §84.

34. *Ideas,* §85.

35. *Ideas,* §97.

36. Paul Ricoeur, "Introduction à *Ideen I* de E. Husserl" (Paris: Gallimard, 1950), p. xxiv.

37. These "noetic" phases are, states Husserl (§ 88), the redirection of the pure self's gaze towards the object focused upon by the self in virtue of its bestowal of meaning. They are, in addition, the grasping and uninterrupted awareness of the object when the gaze is turned toward other objects. These phases are, again, the functions of explaining, of relating, of total apprehension, the various stances of belief, conjecture, evaluation.

38. *Ideas,* §§95–126.

39. *Ideas,* §§38, 69.

40. ". . . That the constitution should in the last analysis be a passive constitution indicates that the constituting transcendental subjectivity, the absolute constituting 'transcendental life,' is not the Cartesian *Ego cogito* which is master of itself; on the contrary, the constitution in its ultimate form is an event beyond the mastery of this transcendental life but which happens to it. . . ." Ludwig Landgrebe, "Husserl et notre époque," in *Husserl et la pensée moderne.*

41. We ought to have here reserved an important place for another stratified ontology of the levels of reality: that of Nicolai Hartmann (*Grundlage eine Metaphysik der Erkentniss,* French translation by

R. Vaucourt [Paris: Aubier, 1948]. Cf. the three studies by Jean Wahl, Centre de Documentation Universitaire, and the Thesis of R. P. Breton.)

42. *Ideas,* §60.

43. *Ideas,* §17, and *Ideen II.*

44. *Ideas,* §§54, 105.

45. On this subject, cf. Hesnard, Lanteri (*Congrès de Neur. et Psych. de Tours,* 1959), and Buytendijk's article in *Husserl et la pensée moderne* (1959), pp. 78–114.

46. Cf. especially *Ideas,* §76.

47. *Ideas,* §76.

48. Edmund Husserl, *Cartesian Meditations,* trans. Dorian Cairns (The Hague: Nijhoff, 1960), especially IV, §38.

49. Naturally Gabriel Marcel's work *Être et avoir* also directs our attention to the problem of the proprietorship of conscious being and of its dominion over itself. Cf. also G. Brand, *Welt, Ich und Zeit nach unveröffentlichen Manuskripten Husserls,* and Robert Klein, "Appropriation et aliénation," *Filosofia,* 1961, pp. 53–64.

50. *Signs,* p. 178.

51. Ibid., pp. 166–171.

52. Alphonse Waelhens, *La philosophie de Martin Heidegger* (Louvain, 3rd ed., 1948).

53. Das Sein des Seienden kann am wenigstens je so etwas sein "dahinter" noch etwas steht was nicht erscheint.

54. Cf. "Les modèles de formalisation du comportement." Colloque 1965, Abstract published by the Centre National de la Recherche Scientifique; and especially B. Matalou, "La vérification des hypothèses en psychologie formalisée et non formalisée."

55. Cf. the work of Claude Lévi-Strauss (1955–1956); the writings of Jacques Lacan (1967); *Les mots et les choses* by Michel Foucault (1966); *Pour Marx* by Louis Althusser; *Le système de la mode* by Roland Barthes, etc. Several discussions on this "structuralism" took place in the literary and philosophical milieu of Paris (*Esprit,* November 1963; *Temps modernes,* November 1966; *Esprit,* May 1967). Cf. the 1968 book of J. Prayet.

PART TWO. THE FIELD OF CONSCIOUSNESS OR THE ACTUALITY OF LIVED EXPERIENCE

Chapter One. The Destructuration of the Field of Consciousness (Sketch of a Phenomenological Psychopathology of the Field of Consciousness)

1. *Études psychiatriques,* III. *Structures des psychoses aiguës et déstructuration de la conscience* (Paris: Desclée de Brouwer, 1954). Since the publication of this work there has been a great increase of

interest in the psychopathology of consciousness. Cf. on this subject the *Comptes rendus du Symposium de Saint-Moritz,* published by H. Staub (Thieme, 1961), and the works of Binswanger, J. Zutt, von Auersperg, Buytendijk, etc.

2. Cf. our *Étude,* no. 8, and our *Rapport au Congrès mondial de Madrid* (1966).

3. The German noun "*das Erlebniss*" more strongly implies the immediacy of experience than this past which is in the process of passing. But this can be translated into French only by the past participle. In any case, the *Erlebniss,* the "*vécu,*" the "lived" aspect of immediate experience sends us back to its "passive" formation, of which the "past" is an imprescriptible form.

4. When examining the neurobiology of the field of consciousness, we shall take note of the problems presented by the relation of dreaming to the depth of sleep.

5. In *L'imaginaire,* the most rigorous, if not the most vigorous of his works.

6. "The dream is the guardian of sleep," Freud has said; but we shall see that it is also its prisoner.

7. It is with reference to this double sense, to this reverberation of the process of dissolution of the subject who is undergoing dissolution and of the subject who brings it about by desiring it, that Henri Michaux says "at times being drawn along by the hemp, at times drawing it along with me" (*Connaissance par les gouffres* [Paris: Gallimard, 1961], p. 145). We shall return to this ambiguity when examining the state of the nervous system during sleep, more especially when examining the experiments of Jouvet (Cf. below, pp. 180–182).

8. Cf. our *Étude,* no. 24.

9. We are well aware of the fact that it has often been stated that phenomenology generally excludes from consciousness anything which exists as a representation or image. It is correct in doing so on two counts: firstly, because lived experience is lived as such, and does not allow any mediation; secondly, because the image and the representation are only reflections or epiphenomena which would render the structure of consciousness "evanescent." But phenomenology would be mistaken if it were here to prevent us from grasping the imaginary as being the lived experience of consciousness which becomes caught up in the nets of its representation, of its power of living the imaginary while taking the risk of accepting it as a reality. If representation were not a structure of consciousness, consciousness could never become the plaything of its own illusion.

10. Cf. the long structural analysis (given in our *Étude,* no. 26) of the case of "Jean-Pierre." Everything that we have just described in abstract terms is to be found there in the terrible concreteness of this epileptic twilight state. P. Schmidt's thesis (Paris, 1950) is a document without equal for the description of these twilight states.

11. Cf., for example, the marvelous autobiographical descriptions published by Mayer-Gross (cf. our *Étude,* no. 23).

12. Cf. our *Étude,* no. 23, p. 290.

13. On this point we can take Merleau-Ponty's analyses (*Phenomenology of Perception,* pp. 334–345) as support and as guide:

> Hallucination causes the real to disintegrate before our eyes.... A hallucination is not a judgment or a rash belief, for the same reasons which prevent it from being a sensory content.... The hallucinatory phenomenon is no part of the world.... The hallucinatory thing ... is an implicit and inarticulate significance.... Nor is hallucination, like perception, my concrete hold on time in a living present. It glides over time as it does over the surface of the world.... Hallucination ... has no place in the "geographical world" ... but in the individual "landscape" (as Straus says) through which the world impinges upon us, and by means of which we are in vital communication with it.

My own attempts during the last thirty years to understand hallucination as the correlate of the overwhelming of psychical being have been sufficient to keep me from subscribing to this conception of hallucination as forming the opposite of perception. We here are especially concerned with hallucination considered as lived experience, as primary delirious experience (Jaspers), or as the primordial state of delirium (Moreau de Tours). Though it is not radically different (or at least is not without ties to these experiences), hallucinatory alienation in chronic psychoses can nevertheless be distinguished from this structure of hallucinating consciousness. I have dealt with these problems in my *Traité des Hallucinations,* 2 vol. (Paris: Masson, 1973).

14. We emphasize this obvious point in order to maintain the basic plan and order which ground the significance of our description.

15. From our point of view, the lower levels of destructuration necessarily involve this *fundamental disorder.* We have made only slight allusions to this, because these levels can be defined precisely by that element which turns the verbal experience occurring in twilight state or dreaming into a relative structural contingency, by being added to the destructuration which we are here examining (according to the method of our hierarchical description).

16. Cf. our *Étude,* no. 23 (pp. 282–300), of which I am here giving only a brief summary.

17. Maurice Merleau-Ponty, *Phenomenology of Perception,* p. 339.

18. Cf. the book by Hécaen and Ajuriaguerra, and our discussions with these authors in *Les rapports de la neurologie et de la psychiatrie.* The problem of anosognosia was the principle topic throughout these discussions. If we make special note of this problem here, it is so that we might "situate" it within an "unconscious" sphere of being

which is constituted by the automatic implications which normally escape consciousness and are manifested only as heterogeneous figures in its destructuration. But we must insist that even though one part of the body can become unconscious without distorting our consciousness of it, this can mean only that the lesions or functions which are connected with this cortical pathology do not directly and comprehensively affect the structure of consciousness (Cf. Chapter Three). In other words, disorders of the body image are not experiences of depersonalization.

19. Henri Michaux, *Misérable miracle* (1956); *Paix dans les brisements* (1959); *Connaissance par les gouffres* (1961); *Les grandes épreuves de l'esprit* (1966). Cf. my *Traité des Hallucinations,* especially the chapter on hallucinogens.

20. This profound relationship of depersonalization and of the structure of lived space with the unconscious mechanisms of the symbolism of *imagos* has been elucidated and developed ad infinitum by psychoanalysts (Paul Schilder, Nunberg, Oberndorf). The work of M. Bouvet (*Revue française de Psychanalyse,* 1960) constitutes a rather deceptive model of this type of analysis, which is most often diffuse and confused.

21. Cf. *Études psychiatriques,* t. III, pp. 140–171.

22. Cf. *Études psychiatriques,* nos. 21, 22, and 23.

23. Indicative, imperative, subjunctive, and conditional as well as future, in the sense that since the future is itself in the present it suppresses this present's necessity not to be a future perfect.

24. H. Tellenbach's *Mélancolie* (Heidelberg: Springer, 1961) contains a psychopathology of melancholia and of *Schwermut* which validates what we presented in 1954 (Cf. *Études,* no. 22). We draw the reader's attention also to Binswanger's penetrating analysis which completes his study on manic-depressive psychosis (*Melancholie und Manie,* Ed. G. Nerke, 1960) and to the psychoanalysis of Dürer's *Melencholia* by Ebtinger (1966).

25. Cf. *Étude,* No. 26; my article "Disorders of Consciousness" in the *Handbook of Clinical Neurology* (edited by P. J. Vinken and G. W. Bruyn, 10 vols., Amsterdam and New York: North Holland Publishing Company), vol. II, pp. 112–136; and what I shall say later, pp. 182–187, concerning the neurophysiology of epilepsy.

26. The importance of the psychophysiopathology of Moreau de Tours, which is nowadays referred to sometimes to point out how astonishing it is, sometimes to rediscover it, has been explicitly emphasized in our article in the *Annales Médico-psychologiques,* 1934, later in the memoir which Mignot and I devoted to the conceptions of Moreau de Tours (*Annales Médico-psychologiques,* Oct. 1947), and finally in my *Étude,* no. 8 (1st Edition, 1948), which I dedicated to this great precursor.

27. J. Zutt, in *Nervenarzt,* 1962, p. 483.

Chapter Two. The Field of Consciousness (Outline of a
Phenomenology of Lived Experience)

1. Cf. *Talks to Teachers,* Chapter Two, and the pages which Aron
Gurwitsch has devoted to William James's theory of knowledge in *The
Field of Consciousness,* pp. 21–30 and 309–318.
2. Husserl, *Ideas,* §91.
3. Ibid., §78.
4. Ibid., §165.
5. Cf. *Erfahrung und Urteil,* p. 20. Also cf. H. Kuhn's "The phenomenological concept of horizon," in the book *Philosophical Essays
in Memory of Husserl* (1940), and also what Aron Gurwitsch has said
on this subject in *The Field of Consciousness,* pp. 192–221.
6. The same concern, however, will be found in the works of
Merleau-Ponty, especially in the comparison, or confrontation, of his
two principal works, *The Structure of Behavior* and *The Phenomenology of Perception.* The writings which A. Hesnard devoted to these
problems at times seem to approximate this rapprochement.
7. Edwin G. Böring, *The Physical Dimensions of Consciousness*
(New York: The Century Co., 1933).
8. Paul Guillaume, *La psychologie de la forme* (Paris: Flammarion, 1937,) "L'organisation du champ total," pp. 115–119.
9. Aron Gurwitsch, *The Field of Consciousness,* p. 18.
10. Ibid., p. 53.
11. Maurice Merleau-Ponty, *Phenomenology of Perception,* p. 63.
12. Ibid., pp. 329–331.
13. Ibid., p. 242.
14. Ibid., pp. 411–412.
15. Ibid., pp. 414–415.
16. Ibid., pp. 429–433.
17. If the notion of "perceptual field" appears to be more easily
acceptable, it is because this notion is presented as the spectacle of the
world of objects with its spatiotemporal dimensions. But if the field of
consciousness is not radically different from that of perception, and if
perception itself is an "intracampine" field (that of the corporality of
things and of itself, of *sensing*), what can be said about the part can
be said of the whole, for the field of experience includes all that is lived
(perceived or imagined, external or internal, corporeal or psychical,
subjective or objective).
18. On this subject it can be remarked that what has been so often
said of consciousness— that it is a "state," a "form of subjectivity," a
"flux of lived experience," a "simple concrete content," etc.—can be
more accurately applied to consciousness which has lost its structure
than to consciousness which is organized as we describe it here. For,
let us repeat it once more, it is through its psychopathological negation

that the structure of the field of consciousness validates its reality, or, if you will, its affirmation.

19. Henri Bergson, *Creative Evolution,* pp. 252–308; *The Creative Mind,* pp. 12–16.

20. Bildlich stellen wir uns das Bewusstsein als die Bühne auf der die eizelen seelische Phenomenen kommen und gehen (Karl Jaspers, *Psychopathologie generale,* 7 ed., 1959, p. 115).

21. The same reflections apply to the *temporal field* of hearing, which has been described so well by Wundt (t. III, p. 80–98). Delacroix refuses to compare the "field" of consciousness to this field; lacking an adequate phenomenological description, the "field of consciousness" remains purely metaphoric for him.

22. It is when this time falls into space that the delirious and hallucinatory experiences of a consciousness which has lost its structure arise, as we have seen.

23. "Beneath the crossed but distinct orders of succession and simultaneity, beneath the train of synchronizations added onto line by line, we find a nameless network— constellations of spatial hours, of point-events. Should we even say 'thing,' should we say 'imaginary' or 'idea,' when each thing exists beyond itself, when each fact can be a dimension, when ideas have their regions?" (Maurice Merleau-Ponty, *Signs,* p. 15).

24. Cf. J. Zutt, 1955; B. Lorscheld, 1962.

25. Weizsäcker (to whom we make special reference in these descriptions of lived space and time) states that biological time is not a three-dimensional time, but is instead a process of formation *(Gestaltkreis).* Cf. J. Zutt, *Auf dem Wege zu einer Anthropologische Psychiatrie* (Heidelberg: Springer, 1963), pp. 364–380 and 406–425.

26. Maurice Navratil, *Les tendances constitutives de la pensée vivante* (Paris: Presses Universitaires de France, 1954), I, pp. 140–257.

27. As we shall see in the next chapter, this occurs at the point at which the EEG arousal response appears to be the threshold of these free rhythms.

28. A constant "putting at a distance" (*immerfort heraustreten,* states Guardini, as cited by Zutt) which is a fundamental characteristic of consciousness.

Chapter Three. The Neurobiology of the Field of Consciousness

1. The idea of a center of consciousness is formally denied by Stanley Cobb (1952), for example. The ideas of Gilbert Ryle in *The Concept of Mind* (London: Hutchinson, 1949) are often taken up by Anglo-Saxon neurologists. "A stick of wood," he has written, "tends to break. Consciousness is the force which opposes, in the brain, this tendency." Whether it is defined by the activity of an omnipotent cell or by the

general property of the nervous system, consciousness loses any structure of reality.

2. D. O. Hebb (*Brain,* 1959), however, refuting Walshe's criticism,
believes, as we do, that his psychophysiological position does not condemn him to the position adopted by Jackson.

3. The title of Paul Chauchard's book is significant: *La Morale du
cerveau* (Paris: Flammarion, 1962).

4. For a more complete study of this problem, cf. my *Études,* Volume III, *La conscience et l'organisation du cerveau.*

5. Ibid., pp. 720–731.

6. Cf. Barbara Tizard, "The Psychological Effects of Frontal Lesion." In *Acta Psychiatrica et Neurologica Scandinavica,* 1958, 33,
pp. 232–250.

7. Cf., for example, Hartwig Kuhlenbeck, *Brain and Consciousness. Confinia Neurologica,* 1957, 17, Suppl. iv, pp. 237–255.

8. The abstracts of the Colloque de Moscou (1958), which dealt
with the EEG and with higher activities of the nervous system, are
very relevant to this topic. P. K. Anokhin's paper on the role of the
reticular formation in conditioning is of particular interest.

9. Cf. Jouvet, "Approches neurologiques des processus d'appren-
tissage," in *Biologie médicale,* 1960, 49, pp. 282–360; J. F. Le Ny, *Le
Conditionnement* (Paris: Presses Universitaires de France, 1961); the
Symposium *Brain Mechanisms and Learning* (Oxford: Blackwell,
1961).

10. Cf. B. Cardo, *Année psychologique,* 1966; H. Laborit, *Biologie et
structure* (Paris: Gallimard, 1968) pp. 13–21; and the 1968 Symposium
directed by Eccles.

11. The work of A. Brodal (1937), J. Olszewski (1954), and the
monograph by J. M. Cuba, *Les formations non segmentaires du tronc
cérébral de l'homme* (Paris: A. Delmas, Mémoire du laboratoire de la
Faculté de Médecine de Paris, 1962), should be consulted regarding the
anatomical and hodological (connectionist) question of this "reticular
formation." Concerning neurophysiological and bioelectrical questions, the following works are especially useful: The Proceedings of
the Symposium de Sainte-Marguerite (1954); P. Dell's article in *Journal de physiologie et de pathologie générale* (1952); the article by Rossi
and Zanchetti (*Archives italiennes de biologie,* 1957); the Proceedings
of the Ford Foundation Symposium (1957); Magoun, *The Waking
Brain* (Springfield, Ill: Thomas, 1958); André Hugelin, *Étude anato-
mo-physiologique de la structure et des connexions de la formation
réticulaire du tronc cérébral* (Paris: Thèse, Faculté de Médecine, 1954.
No. 532); Hugelin's article in *L'Encéphale* (1956); Frédéric Bremer
(*Archives suisses de neuro. et psych.,* 1960, 86, pp. 34–48); Magoun's
paper at the Galesburg Symposium (1960); the *Ciba Foundation Symposium, The Nature of Sleep,* (Boston: Little Brown, 1961).

12. Cf. Dell and Lairy's contribution to the Florence Symposium on *Motivation,* 1959.

13. W. R. Hess, *Psychologie in biologischer Sicht,* 2nd ed. (Stuttgart: Thieme, 1962.)

14. Bremer, *Archives suisses N.P.,* 1960, p. 45.

15. The following works should be consulted for the nuclear structures and pathways of the thalamus: the classical works by Dejerine and Roussy (1905); A. Earl Walker, *The Primate Thalamus* (Chicago: University of Chicago Press, 1938); the *Atlas d'anatomie stéréotaxique* by Jean Talairach and Marcel David (Paris: Masson, 1957); and the works of P. Tournoux, M. Corredor, and T. Kvasina. There have been numerous works on the neurophysiology of the system of diffuse projection since the experiments of Dempsey and Morison (1942) and those of the Montreal school (Jasper, 1942; Hunter and Jasper, 1949; Jasper and Fortuyn, 1947; Ajnone Marsan, 1948; etc.).

16. Cf. Roussy and Mosinger, and the articles on this subject in *Biologie médicale,* 1962.

17. On the anatomy and physiology of the hypothalamus, cf. Fulton's *Treatise;* W. R. Hess, *Hypothalamus und Thalamus* (Stuttgart: Thieme, 1956) and *Psychologie in biologischer Sicht* (Stuttgart: Thieme, 1962); and the articles which appeared in *Biologie médicale* in 1962, especially André Soulairac's "La topographie des noyaux hypothalamiques."

18. J. Delay, *Les dérèglements de l'humeur* (Paris: Presses Universitaires de France, 1946).

19. Papez adds "and from the reticular formation via the subthalamus." (P. 1607)—Trans.

20. Cf. Angelergues and Hécaen, "La douleur hemispherique." In *Journal de Psychologie,* 1958, nos. 1 and 2.

21. In addition to older studies such as Potzl (1924) and Pap (1934), we must point out that since the first edition of this work, numerous very important reports were presented at the Twenty-ninth National Meeting of the Italian Psychiatric Society which have shed light on a number of facts concerning thalamic psychical disorders and psychical functions. Especially worth noting are the reports of D. de Caro, G. Cozzo, D. de Martis, P. Sarteschi (*Il Lavoro Neuropsi,* 1967). Cf. also W. Klages's important work in *Archives psychologiques,* 1965, 206, pp. 562ff.

22. Jouvet, *Biologie médicale,* 1960, p. 319.

23. Cf. Theophile Alajouanine, editor, *Les grandes activités du rhinencéphale* (Paris: Masson, 1961). Cf. also the Colloque de Montpellier, 1961, on the *Physiologie de l'hippocampe.*

24. This hippocampothalamic circuit would be lesioned in Korsakoff's syndrome (Lhermitte, 1967).

25. Detlev Ploog's exposition of all these experiments is exhaustive: *Die Psychiatrie der Gegenwart,* I, 1964, pp. 290–443.

26. Cf., for example, Mortimer Ostow's article in *The Psychoanalytic Quarterly,* 1955, 24, pp. 369–423; and Gut Heilbruner, "The Neurobiological Aspect of Three Psychoanalytic Concepts," in *Comprehensive Psychiatry,* October 1961, pp. 260–267.

27. The problem of *sham reactions* (especially sham rage) typically is bound to this structuring of experience. Of course, there is no problem for those who speak only of behavior: all rage is only an appearance of rage, and any appearance of rage is rage, since no reference to feeling is involved. But for those who are attempting to reintroduce lived experience into neurophysiology, they must choose either to separate the emotion from its expression (Masserman) or to return to the view of William James and hold that the lived emotion and its expression cannot be separated. The expression "lived experience" is certainly precisely correlated with the whole structuring of consciousness at all its levels. For it is the organization of sensible experience which actualizes sensing and permits it either to be integrated into the lived aspect of an immediate experience or to be detached from it so as to be expressed and to become "problematic." We can now see where a correct interpretation of these emotional or behavioral fragments, which neurophysiology observes and interprets in "objective" (i.e., "artificial") terms, should lead us: to the realization of lived experience as the object of these investigations, which consequently could not deny them without denying themselves.

28. For Eccles (1953), the cortex is indispensable to attention, which requires at least a tenth of its mass for it to function as a "mind detector."

29. G. C. Lairy, *Revue neurologique,* 1956.

30. Numerous studies have already appeared concerning this subject (Catherine Lairy, S. Ridjanovic, R. Faure, L. Goldsteinas, A. Guennoc, M. Barros, etc. Cf. below p. 198.)

31. Bremer, *Comptes rendus de la Société de Biologie,* 1935, 118, pp. 1235–1244, and 1936, 122, pp. 460–467.

32. This stage is designated in French by the initials PMO; and in English, first by PEM, then by REM; and by Jouvet by PP or PRS. [We shall accord with established usage and refer to this stage of (active) sleep as "paradoxical sleep," since rapid eye movements do not occur after prepontine sections. What Jouvet calls "slow sleep" is often referred to as "quiet sleep" or "NREM sleep."—Trans.]

33. *Archives italiennes de biologie,* 1962, 100, pp. 125–206.

34. This nucleus, which can be identified in the cat, does not exist in man, at least in an anatomically identical form.

35. Cf. our *Étude* no. 26.

36. This is not the place to discuss the experimental and electrobi-

ological facts and discussions of thalamocortical interaction, the arousal response, slow dysrhythmia, or recruiting and augmenting phenomena. As far as the nonspecific influence of the reticular formations of the mesencephalon or diencephalon upon cortical synaptic potentials is concerned, these latter are considered to be the "stuff" of cortical rhythms (cf. Mary Brazier, *Journal of Nervous and Mental Disease,* 1958, 126, pp. 303–321).

37. Cf. our *Étude* no. 26, 1954.

38. Through the interference of these two perspectives, these contradictions have the effect of placing "on high" what is superior, as if the "superior" or the higher did not depend upon the inferior or the lower. They also have the effect of perpetually confusing facultative and constituted consciousness, intelligence and lived experience, and, in the last analysis, of reducing lived time to mathematical space.

39. Penfield's ideas have been widely discussed by the English neurologists. In spite of the violent criticisms of Walshe (1957), and after Lord Brain's restatement (1958), it is difficult not to admit the existence of this subcortical activating and regulatory apparatus.

40. Pierre Teilhard de Chardin, *The Phenomenon of Man* (New York: Harper and Row, 1959), p. 170.

41. Cf. *Étude* no. 8, the chapter "Troubles de la conscience" which we have written for the *Handbook of Neurology,* and our report to the 1966 Congress of Madrid.

42. A thesis which is examined in my "Rapport au Congrès de Madrid" (1966) and in my *Traité des Hallucinations* (1973).

PART THREE. THE SELF OR SELF-CONSCIOUS BEING

Chapter One. From Alteration to "Alienation" of the Self

1. This chapter is only an approximation of the *Études* which we propose to devote to "mental illnesses," which are chronicals to the extent that these illnesses distort or derange the permanent system of the person.

2. Cf. our *Étude* no. 8.

3. This problem was the object of my report to the Congress of Madrid (1966) on a theory of the generalized relativity of the phenomenon of sleep-dreaming to the totality of mental diseases, to the extent that they are all the effect of a disorganization of conscious being of which the disorganization of the field of consciousness is only a particular case.

4. This is especially true when Störing (1953) describes the disorders of the *Besinnung* by referring to disorders of the field of consciousness (pp. 50–85.)

5. To say that he is not someone like others is to affirm a fact to

which what is called moral psychiatry should accommodate itself in order both to guarantee morality and to ground psychiatry.

6. In German the play on words which allows this confusion between this "alienation" *(Entfremdung, Entausserung)* and mental alienation is not possible.

7. Cf. J.-P. Lauzel, "A propos des constitutions," *Entretiens psychiatriques,* 12, 1966, pp. 241–279.

8. One of the most well-known psychologists concerned with factor analysis of personality, Raymond B. Cattell, is referring to this distinction of *being* and *having* when he says: "Character traits are adjectives through which we describe the normal personality; types are nouns which describe the abnormal personality." (Raymond B. Cattell, *Personality.* New York: McGraw-Hill, 1950, p. 7.)

9. Cf. our *Étude* no. 13, in Vol. II of *Études psychiatriques.*

10. M. Nayraut, "A propos de la mythomanie," *Évolution psychiatrique,* 1960, IV, pp. 533–559. This work won the Prix de l'*Évolution psychiatrique* for 1960.

11. M. Zeegers, "L'escroc dans ses relations avec la réalité," *Évolution psychiatrique,* 1959, III, pp. 437–467. This exhaustive analysis is of an incredible richness, due in part to the relationship which this psychiatrist from The Hague has with the Dutch phenomenologists (Van der Horst, Janse de Jonge).

12. P. C. Racamier, "Hystérie et théâtre," *Évolution psychiatrique,* 1952, II, pp. 257–291.

13. A. Green, "Le rôle. Contribution à l'etude des mécanismes d'identification," *Évolution psychiatrique,* 1961, V, pp. 1–32.

14. This point is of capital importance. It has formed, and shall continue to form, the leitmotif of all our studies on schizophrenia. Cf. especially the chapter "Schizophrénie," in *Encyclopédie médico-chirurgicale: Psychiatrie,* III, 1955, and our reports to the "Journées de Bonneval" (*Évolution psychiatrique,* II, III, 1958), and to the Congrès mondial de Psychiatrie (Zurich, 1957).

15. Following Eugene Minkowski, we have often opposed the mental "assets" *(fonds)* which have wasted away in dementia, and the mental ground *(fond)* which is disorganized in mental confusion.

Chapter Two. The Autoconstruction of the Self

1. Paul Ricoeur, *Freedom and Nature: The Voluntary and the Involuntary,* trans. Erazim V. Kohák (Evanston: Northwestern University Press, 1966), p. 369.

2. We have condensed as much as possible this exposition, the details of which formed the subject of an unpublished conference in our "Cercle d'Études." We plan to return to this topic in one of the forthcoming volumes of our *Études,* which will be devoted to the psychopathology of the personality. In addition there is in the excel-

lent book by Filloux a clear, though incomplete, documentation of the fundamental concepts and types of personality theory. Cf. the works of Gordon W. Allport (1937 and 1950), Raymond B. Cattell (1956), H. A. Murray (1938), Emmanuel Mounier (1947), and, for a (very cavalier) view of American personality theory, Harry Bour's article "Personality Theory" in the *American Handbook of Psychiatry,* edited by Silvano Arietti, 1959, vol. I, pp. 88–113.

3. Cf. the critical study by P. de Gaudemar, "Le développement de la caractérologie," *Journal de Psychologie,* 1957, 54, pp. 326–352.

4. Kurt Lewin, *A Dynamic Theory of Personality,* 1935; and "Field Theory in Social Science," in *Selected Theoretical Papers,* 1951.

5. Jean Piaget, *Introduction à l'épistémologie génétique* (Paris: Presses Universitaires de France, 1950), Vol. 3, pp. 133–187.

6. Ibid., p. 296.

7. Ibid., pp. 306–313.

8. Ibid., pp. 324–326.

9. Ibid., p. 327.

10. We use the abbreviations *GW (Gesammelte Werke)* to designate the collected works of Freud in the German edition (London: Imago, 1940–); *SE (Standard Edition)* to designate the *Complete Psychological Works,* ed. James Strachey (London: Hogarth Press, 1953–1966).—Trans.

11. In a sentence omitted from the French translation (cf. *GW,* 17, p. 67).

12. *GW,* 2-3, pp. 620–623; *SE,* 5, pp. 615–618.

13. *GW,* 13, pp. 23–34; *SE,* 18, pp. 23–33.

14. *GW,* 17, pp. 129–130; *SE,* 23, pp. 198–200.

15. *GW,* 10, pp. 167–170; *SE,* 14, pp. 99–102.

16. *GW,* 13, p. 145; *SE,* 18, p. 130.

17. This diagram was omitted, for some unknown reason, from Jankélévitch's French translation, *Essais de Psychanalyse* (Paris: Payot, 1951). Jacques Lacan (*Psychanalyse,* 6, 1961, p. 132), while recognizing "its technical merits," considers this celebrated figure "of an egg 'on the house' " as fit, he says, "for stuffing into one's head."

18. *GW,* 13, p. 286; *SE,* 19, p. 56.

19. *GW,* 13, p. 253; *SE,* 19, p. 25.

20. In his work "On Narcissism," Freud spoke both of the *Ideal Ich* and of the *Ichideal.* In *Group Psychology and the Analysis of the Ego,* Freud speaks only of the *Idealich.* He now uses the term *Ichideal* as a synonym for the *Über-Ich.* These two expressions, one placing its emphasis on the immanence, the other on the transcendence of the Ideal *in* the ego or above it, have naturally given rise to innumerable exegeses and interpretations (cf. Numberg, Fromm, Lagache, etc.).

21. Chapter 3 (*GW,* 13; *SE,* 19).

22. *GW,* 13, p. 256; *SE,* 19, p. 28.

23. *GW,* 13, p. 264; *SE,* 19, p. 36.
24. *GW,* 14, p. 125; *SE,* 20, p. 98.
25. *GW,* 15, p. 64; *SE,* 22, p. 58.
26. *GW,* 15, p. 68; *SE,* 22, p. 62.
27. *GW,* 15, p. 69; *SE,* 22, p. 63.
28. *GW,* 15, p. 71; *SE,* 22, p. 64.
29. *GW,* 15, p. 75; *SE,* 22, p. 69.
30. *GW,* 15, p. 76; *SE,* 22, p. 69.
31. *GW,* 15, p. 78; *SE,* 22, p. 71.
32. *GW,* 15, p. 78; *SE,* 22, p. 72.
33. *GW,* 15, p. 86; *SE,* 22, p. 80.
34. *GW,* 17, p. 129; *SE,* 23, p. 195.
35. *GW,* 17, p. 130; *SE,* 23, p. 199.
36. *GW,* 17, p. 136; *SE,* 23, p. 205.

37. The address given by S. Leclaire to the Congress of Rome (Abstract given in *La Psychanalyse,* I, 1956, pp. 233–242) is well worth examining. It ends with a moving question which has remained unanswered, for in Lacan's system as in Freud's the ego is imaginary, is in short a fetish.

38. Since its first edition, Ricoeur's treatise *Freud and Philosophy,* a *"Summa"* of labor, intelligence, and courage, has brilliantly demonstrated that the archeology of the subject cannot validate its teleology.

39. In his article "Le stade du miroir comme formateur de la fonction du Je" (*Revue française de Psychanalyse,* 1949, 13, pp. 449–455), Jacques Lacan describes identification as the joyful assuming of one's own specular image, which forms the exemplary situation, the symbolic matrix of a line of fiction to which the image of the self is originally dedicated. The ego establishes itself in the function of a radical misconception or denial *(Verneinung).* From this point on he does not hesitate to contradict[a] Freud, claiming that the self is not centered in the system Perception-Consciousness in such a way as to draw out of it any structure of reality, as if it was only the object of an illusion, of madness. It is unnecessary for us to emphasize that we place ourself at the very opposite of this position.

[a]For example, cf. what Freud has written in his last works for the very purpose of confirming the importance of the system "Ego-Consciousness–Perception–reality principle": "We have repeatedly had to insist on the fact that the ego owes its origin as well as the most important of its acquired characteristics to its relation to the real external world." *GW,* 17, p. 132; *SE,* 23, p. 201 (*Standard Edition* translation).

40. On this subject cf. David Rapaport, "The theory of Ego autonomy," *Bulletin of the Menninger Clinic,* 1958, 22, pp. 13–35; the article of Edoardo Weiss (disciple of Federn), "A comparative study of psychoanalytical Ego concepts," *International Journal of Psychoanaly-*

sis, 1957, 38, pp. 209–222; Vol. 6 of *La Psychanalyse* (1961), which is devoted to "structural perspectives"; and the work which was edited in homage to Heinz Hartman (1966).

41. Glower, *Psychoanalysis,* 1949.

42. Franz Alexander, *Psychoanalysis of Total Personality* (New York: Coolidge Foundation, 1949).

43. *The Psychoanalytic Study of the Child,* vol. V, 1950. Cf. also Lowenstein's article in *Revue française de Psychanalyse,* 1966.

44. *Revue française de Psychanalyse,* 1951, pp. 569–576.

45. Cf. *Ego Psychology and the Psychoses,* Imago Publ., 1953; this work has been analyzed by P. C. Racamier (*Évolution psychiatrique,* 1954, pp. 321–332); also cf. the article by E. Weiss (1957), which has been cited above.

46. Daniel Lagache, in *Comptes rendus du Colloque de Royaumont,* p. 23.

47. Ibid., p. 31.

48. Cf. *Beyond the Pleasure Principle.*

49. Lagache, pp. 34–35.

50. Ibid., p. 46.

51. Ibid., p. 53.

52. In his noteworthy criticism of Lagache's report, Lacan (*La Psychanalyse,* 6, 1961, p. 111) returned with great ingenuity to the system of images of optical reflection and refraction, to this fundamental idea: the ego, the place of the subject, is in the chain of meanings; in short, it is constituted in its status as imaginary. This intuition, which rejoins the dialectic of being and nothingness, will be taken up again in our account; however, we shall place our emphasis on the reality of the autonomous movement which frees "selfhood" from the illusory and the imaginary when *it develops.* In any case, Lacan reproaches Lagache for conceding too much autonomy to the ego and refuses to consider, with him, that to be someone is as illusory as a reflection in a mirror.

53. Because of their fuller recognition of its autonomy and autoconstruction, Jung and Adler have granted a more important place to the ego and to conscious being. Alfred Adler's "individual psychology" (*The Neurotic Constitution,* 1912; *Des Sinn des Lebens,* 1933) is no longer grounded upon the defenses which the *libido* encounters, but upon the obstacles against which the "Nietzschean" will to power collides. The analytic psychology of Carl-Gustav Jung (*Psychology of the Unconscious,* 1912; *Modern Man in Search of a Soul,* 1931, etc.) reveals a process of individuation in the formation of the person which is exercised both against and with the unconscious images (notably collective *archetypes*). The person *(persona)* always involves a shadow, a sort of otherness which is repressed by the resistances it encounters: this is notably the *animus* (masculine element) in women

or the *anima* (feminine element) in men. From this arises the dialectic of the ideo-affective conglomerations which intervene, of the *complexes* which enter into conflict with the human forms of individual consciousness.

54. Cf. in particular *Theories of Personality* by Calvin S. Hall and Gardner Lindzey (New York: Wiley, 1957).

55. H. A. Murray and others, *Explorations in Personality* (New York, London: Oxford University Press, 1938). More recently Murray has published, with the anthropologist Kluckhohn, an important study which appeared in H. A. Murray and C. Kluckhohn, editors, *Personality in Nature, Society and Culture,* 2nd ed., rev. and enl. (New York: Knopf, 1953).

56. Murray defines a "thema" as "the dynamical structure of . . . a single creature-environment interaction" (*Explorations in Personality,* p. 42). He later states, when discussing this concept, that "In our experience, the unconscious *(alter ego)* of a person may be *formulated best as an assemblage or federation of thematic tendencies*" (Ibid., p. 123). —Trans.

57. This "classical" structuralism is diametrically opposed to French "structuralism."

58. Most of the theories which we have just examined, especially those of Piaget, Janet, Murray, etc., are very naturally related to this architectonic perspective.

59. Philipp Lersch, *Aufbau der Person* (Munich: Johann Ambrosium Barth, 1938; 7th ed., 1958).

60. William Stern, *Allgemeine Psychologie auf personalitischer Grundlage* (The Hague: Nijhoff, 1935).

61. Gordon W. Allport, *Personality: A Psychological Interpretation* London: Constable and Co., Ltd., 1937), p. 558.

62. A capital distinction which, without radically separating them, sets in opposition the structures of experience and those of the organization of the self as being which takes possession of its own being through its own sight.

63. As we have seen, this appropriation of experience is what incorporates the self, insofar as it is the personal subject of lived experience, into the actuality of the field of consciousness.

64. Paul Ricoeur, *Freedom and Nature: The Voluntary and the Involuntary,* trans. Erazim V. Kohak. (Evanston: Northwestern University Press, 1966), p. 368.

65. When discussing the self and the range of ipseity, Sartre takes up the ideas he had expressed concerning the transcendence of the *Ego* in *Recherches philosophiques* (cf. above, p. 204).

66. The fixedness of the biography of President Wilson, fixated upon his father (Sigmund Freud and William C. Bullitt, *Thomas Woodrow Wilson, Twenty-eighth President of the United States.* Bos-

proceedings of the Symposium of Cuernavaco, Mexico, 1960, *Zen Buddhism and Psychoanalysis,* by Erich Fromm, D. I. Suzuki, and Richard de Martini (New York: Hayer, 1960) and the article of A. Ben-Avi in Arieti's *Handbook* (1959).

15. Cf. the works of Dwelshauwers (1916), of Donald Brinkman, *Probleme des Unbewussten* (Zurich-Leipzig: Rascher, 1943), and of A. C. MacIntyre, *The Unconscious* (London: Routledge and Kegan Paul, 1958).

16. The passage from the definition of the Unconscious in a descriptive sense to that of a dynamic theory is expressly indicated (cf. "A Note on the Unconscious," 1912, *GW,* 8, 430–443) as determined by the exact comprehension of posthypnotic suggestion which brings to light the selective-repressive and efficient nature of the unconscious, that is, its active function of defense (*Abwehr*), of resistance (*Widerstand*), and of rejection (*Abweisung*).

17. Cf. especially the works which have been translated into French under the title *Métapsychologie* and which are related to the following texts: "The Unconscious" (1915) and "Repression" (which also appeared in 1915).

18. "Repression," *GW,* 10, pp. 247–249; *SE,* 14, pp. 146–147.

19. Cf. "Instincts and their Vicissitudes" (1915), *GW,* 10, pp. 210–230; *SE,* 14, pp. 117–140.

20. Cf. "The Unconscious" (1915), *GW,* 10, pp. 275–279; *SE,* 14, pp. 177–179.

21. Ibid., *GW,* 10, p. 272; *SE,* 14, p. 173.

22. In Freud's works between 1915 and 1925, this "repressed" will be a part of the Unconscious, but will not entirely constitute it, since "there exists an unconscious which is not repressed" (*"ein nicht verdrängte Unbewusste,"* in *The Ego and the Id, GW,* 13, p. 244). In 1915, he had already written: *"Das Verdrängte ist ein Teil des Unbewussten"* (The repressed is a part of the unconscious) ("The Unconscious," *GW,* 10, p. 264).

23. Cf., for example, Daniel Lagache, in *Psychanalyse,* 6, 1961, pp. 18–22.

24. *GW,* 10, p. 213; *SE,* 14, p. 120.

25. Moreover, the first sketch of the relations of the Unconscious and the conscious appears in *The Interpretation of Dreams* (1900).

26. *GW,* 2–3, pp. 620–622; *SE,* pp. 615–617.

27. When discussing the psychoanalytic theory of the self (p. 243), we have shown how in *Beyond the Pleasure Principle* (*GW,* 10, pp. 25–28) consciousness, the cerebral cortex, and the organs of sense are presented as a system of protection and of the selection of external "excitations" which are wanting in the face of internal "incitations."

28. Man tut übrigens unrecht, wenn man nur die Abstossung hervorhebt, die vom Bewussten her auf das zu Verdrängende wirkt ("Re-

pression," *GW,* 10, p. 250). (One would be mistaken however, to emphasize only repression, which, starting from consciousness, acts upon that which is to be repressed.)

29. Cf. *GW,* 10, pp. 279–295; *SE,* 14, pp. 180–195.

30. *GW,* 10, p. 279; *SE,* 14, p. 180.

31. *GW,* 10, p. 289; *SE,* 14, pp. 191–192.

32. The relations between the conscious, the preconscious, and the unconscious and the theory of double censorship all proceed from the same confusion of plans and of agencies.

33. *GW,* 10, p. 248; *SE,* 14, p. 146.

34. *GW,* 13, p. 252; *SE,* 19, p. 24.

35. "Research in pathology has too exclusively directed our attention towards the 'repressed' and we would still like to know more on this subject," he wrote in 1923 (*GW,* 13, p. 246). He adds immediately afterwards, "since we know that the ego can itself be unconscious in the strict sense of the word," as if, in opposition to his earliest intuition, only the unconscious could decidedly account for the repressed.

36. *GW,* 13, pp. 55–58; *SE,* 18, pp. 51–54.

37. *The Ego and the Id, GW,* 13, p. 255; *SE,* 19, p. 27.

38. *GW,* 13, p. 256; *SE,* 19, p. 28.

39. *GW,* 15, pp. 76–79; *SE,* pp. 69–73.

40. Cf. *The Ego and the Id, GW,* 13, pp. 239–245; *SE,* 19, pp. 13–18.

41. Even more than "pansexualism," the thesis of a "panunconscious" could be the object of a crucial objection to Freud's theory. As becomes clear at the end of Chapter II of *The Ego and the Id,* this thesis is neither episodic nor contingent.

42. *GW,* 15, pp. 84–85; *SE,* 22, pp. 77–79.

43. *GW,* 13, pp. 240–245; *SE,* 19, pp. 14–18.

44. One of the most incisive minds in French psychoanalysis, Edouard Pichon, was ever sensible to this contradiction in Freud's work: the attempt to make of the unconscious a force which was independent of consciousness.

45. *GW,* 10, p. 289; *SE,* 14, pp. 191–192.

46. *GW,* 13, p. 242; *SE,* 19, p. 15.

47. *GW,* 10, pp. 271–272; *SE,* 14, p. 173.

48. *GW,* 13, pp. 239–245; *SE,* 19, pp. 13–18.

49. This is why Freud's deviation towards a total hegemony of the unconscious is opposed to his own fundamental theory of the unconscious. It is also why a psychoanalyst cannot spread out psychical life on its surface, or be reluctant to admit the notion of strata and of levels of being, without repudiating himself.

50. Notably in "Repression" (1915, *GW,* 10, pp. 248–261) and "The Unconscious" (1915, *GW,* 10, pp. 285–288).

51. It seems to us that when these two theses encountered each

other at the "Journées de Bonneval" (1960), they gave rise only to
sterile polemics. But one finds that this was the heart of the matter, if
one attentively reads the reports of Diatkine and Lebovici, of Green
and of Stein on the one hand and those of Leclaire and Laplanche on
the other. It must be noted that it was much more profoundly dealt
with in the reports of Leclaire and Laplanche and in that of Stein than
in the discussions between the psychoanalysts.

52. In his critical work (cf. "La chose freudienne," in *Évolution
psychiatrique,* 1956), Lacan intentionally excludes its "genetic" or
"prehistoric" dimension from the structure of the unconscious. Lacan
sees it as a fundamental structuring of the psychical being which is
the reverse of his speech (cf. especially "Fonction et champ de la
parole et du langage," in *La Psychanalyse,* 1, 1956, pp. 82–166; and
"L'instance de la lettre dans l'inconscient ou la raison," ibid., 3, 1957,
pp. 47–81). Referring to the synchronistic and diachronistic structuring of language which we owe to Ferdinand de Saussure, he finds in
chains of "meanings" an articulated structure which is discontinous
and void of any meaning. It is like the "language of another," the
speaking ("*Ça parle*") while saying nothing other than responding to
the other person—not to his voice but to his wish and to his desires—
through the echoes of an impossible discourse. The unconscious is
thus not only structured as is language, but it is implied by language.
This enunciated or virtual word is as if inscribed in the movements
of the body, the archives of memories or of traditions. It is this word
which forms the Unconscious. These "things" effectively form a fluctuating "rebus" which exists as a symbolic interposition which marks
with its presence the anticipated response of the subject to the demand
of the desire of the other. Such is the second characteristic of the
Unconscious: it is essentially symbolic insofar as it slips into the inter-
stices of speech through the blanks in history, so as to represent the
language of desire in its "first" form (*La Psychanalyse,* 1), a language
which is always (according to Jones) related to the body itself, to kin-
ship, to birth, to life and to death. However, the thing which the symbol replaces or repudiates is done away with by the very nature of the
symbol which is introduced into intersubjective relationships by the
constitution of the being in relation to the other. ("The symbol appears
first as the murder of the thing; and this death constitutes in the
subject the eternalization of its desire." *La Psychanalyse,* 1, p. 163.)
For Lacan, conscious being is formed by the chain of meanings into
which the phallus insinuates itself—this symbol *par excellence*—the
fantasized pivot of the Oedipus complex (the relation to the father, to
his name, or to his law, that is, to his function, which is to be significant of desire). This desire becomes occult through the metonymic
function of meanings. It is satisfied through its metaphoric function,
except in the case of a radical repudiation (*Verwerfung,* which Lacan

translates by "*forclusion*") which excludes this imago from its insertion into its unconscious language for it to be other.

The richness of the teaching which Lacan lavishes in his seminars is constituted by such vertiginous acrobatic feats as his substantial exegeses of Freud's texts, his brilliant excursions into clinical studies, myths, institutions, and even into the most trivial experiences of prestidigitation, all of which unceasingly play at hide-and-seek with reality in everyone's case. And between one another they play out the transparent relations of the game of love and chance.

Many problems remain open, or obscure, notably that of the diachronics of unconscious speech, that is, of its rootedness in needs which, being fantasized, are no less weighty in the balance of the algorithm meaning-meant. The wavering of the symbolic order, of the unconscious, at most can be only the object of a mathematical axiomatization, if it is not a mere "that." But if it is only a language which can be understood merely as a tinkling, like an optical illusion which introduces successive or simultaneous "alienating constitutions" into the interplay of mirrors, if it still is only a "this" (only the "id," to be precise), what then can be its relations with the ego and with consciousness? Fascinated and fascinating because of the magic of this rhetoric of the unconscious, Jacques Lacan holds the autonomy of the ego to be "the last fetish introduced into the holy of holies" ("La chose freudienne," *Évolution psychiatrique*, 1956, p. 240). He seems to ground the *Self* only as the locus of speech, as a virtual or complementary specular image, a reflection which can find its place only "in an elision of meanings." He thus rejects the personalist interpretation of Lagache. But we still are left with the problem of the organization of the psychical being "around," "over," "within," or "at the periphery of" (as one prefers) this unconscious. In this respect, Lacan appears perhaps to feel this necessity more strongly, especially in his construction of a model representing the relations between the subject and the sign (cf. the graphs published in the abstract of his lessons of 1958–1959, in the *Bulletin de psychologie*, XII, 1958, p. 254, and XIII, 1959–1960, p. 264). For the person, or the psychical apparatus, must somewhere examine the connections between the chain of signs, in which the meaning is hidden, and the chain of things meant, which necessitate the meaning. The confirmation of their coincidence must be accomplished within the reality of their organization. We must discover either the juncture of the conscious and the Unconscious, or that of the id which was and the ego which it ought to become. Any theory of the Unconscious which shirks or omits this problem reduces the Unconscious to be either all or nothing, or to be a thing which is nothing at all, for want of being connected to an organization of conscious being, which absolutely cannot be reduced to the Unconscious if it is to *exist.*

PART FIVE. CONSCIOUS BECOMING

The Organization of Psychical Being and the Problem of Human Values

1. This analysis presents the relations of the conscious and the Unconscious under the category of having, under a necessarily juridical form: the property rights of conscious being. But again it must be remarked that, even more than the rights of property, this "order" grounds the right of man to decide for himself, the "rights of man" to freedom and to free speech being inseparable from an ontology of psychical being which assures self-determination.

2. *Études psychiatriques,* Vol. III, no. 26.

3. Cf. the general diagram of the psychical organism which we propose below, p. 365.

4. This "resistance" is obviously exactly symmetrical to, and of the same order as, that of those thinkers, however wise or analytical they might be, who "resist" the evidence of the reality of conscious being.

5. Some of his opponents reproach him for having incorporated this already in his "principles" and his "prejudices."

6. The German term *"Aufhebung,"* which corresponds to the dialectical movement of sublimation, i.e., to the mutation of the Unconscious into the conscious, implies not only that the prohibition of something which is unconscious be *lifted,* but also that this something should *remain.*

7. This term which has become so popularized is the term which best corresponds to the notion of this demanding and embryonic dynamic structure of the Unconscious.

8. Cf. MacCulloch and Pitts, 1943; Kuhlenbeck, 1957.

9. The order of the organism which is organized as a living being is a reproduction of the order of the species which is buried in the organic unconscious. But the order which is implied by the organization of the living being's nervous system participates both in the specific organization and the personal organization and has the function of binding them, through its function of integration. Therefore, even if organ transplants are possible, it would be impossible to transplant a brain, for reasons involved with the substitution of one personal memory for another in a different body. With complete safety we can predict that such a transplant will never be made (unless, of course, two brains are reduced to a single brain which would continue to live and to think on its own, but in a different body), just as the circle will never be squared.

10. We must indeed speak of a "discovery" here to indicate the merits of having become aware of this "unexpected result." It is, however, a result which becomes obvious once a person is no longer subju-

gated by the incorporation of all of psychical life into the unconscious, including the repressing instances which, according to Freud's own theory, cannot enter into it. Once the unconscious has been discovered, it is necessary, in effect, to rediscover the conscious which recovers the unconscious.

11. Paul Ricoeur, *Freud and Philosophy: An Essay on Interpretation,* trans. Denis Savage (New Haven: Yale University Press, 1970), pp. 315–316.

12. Jean-Paul Sartre, *Being and Nothingness,* trans. Hazel Barnes (New York: Philosophical Library, 1956), pp. 73–218.

13. We have remarked several times during the course of our analyses of the structure of consciousness that consciousness can be formulated only in and through juridical concepts which point to its judgment and its jurisdiction. This is certainly the reason why in Latin and Anglo-Saxon countries a single world, *"conscience,"* designates *Bewusstsein* and *Gewissen.*

14. It could be said that works such as Bachelard's *La philosophie du Non* (1940) or St. Lupasco's *Du devenir logique et de l'affectivité* (1935) and *Logique et contradiction* (1947), which are unable to move beyond the radical illogicality of any affective logic and which therefore tend toward a valorization of the irrational, are subject to a sort of romantic effusion.

15. Cf. especially pp. 25–51 of his "Introduction."

16. Raymond Ruyer, *La cybernétique et l'origine de l'information* (Paris: Flammarion, 1954).

17. Cf., for example, these two works which are very different from each other: *Problèmes et pseudo-problème du dèterminisme* by J. Moreau (Paris: Masson, 1964) and *Le second principe de la Science du temps* by Costa de Beauregard (Paris: Seuil, 1963).

18. Costa de Beauregard, having encountered Bergson after he had emphasized that the biological and psychological arrow of time (an "anti-Carnot" arrow) transmits its direction to information to the extent that transition, negative entropy, and information imply an essential connection between the two senses of the word "information" (the current sense and the Aristotelian sense), suggests that "there is no good reason for subjecting the Unconscious" (he uses the word "subconscious") "to the same law as consciousness, if it is neither methodical nor logical" (p. 124).

19. In his discovery, Freud went from topography (the radical opposition of Consciousness to the Unconscious) to dynamics (the Libido and the instincts). On the other hand, in his much more debatable theoretical exposition, he moved from a dynamic to a topographical theory.

20. The repercussion of the structures of conscious being, whose form forces it to conform to the demands of the environment, lan-

guage, custom, and Laws, imprints upon the sphere of desire these dramatic, one might even say stereotyped, forms that gravitate around the fundamental Oedipal situation occurring in one's system of vital relations, which system is governed by Law.

21. The major works are well known to all: Ferdinand de Saussure, Troubetzkoy, Roman Jakobson, M. Malle, Ernst Cassirer, Rudolf Carnap, Andre Martinet, L. Tesmire, Noam Chomsky, Émile Benveniste, Louis Hjemslev, Gottlob Frege, Ludwig Wittgenstein, Jacques Lacan, C. K. Ogden and I. A. Richards, Charles E. Osgood and T. A. Sebese, etc. Analyses and references can be found in the excellent reports of Fr. Bresson on "La Signification," *Comptes rendus du Symposium sur les Problèmes de Psycho-linguistique* (Paris: Presses Universitaires de France, 1963), and of G. Lantéri-Laura on "Les rapports de la linguistique à la psychiatrie contemporaine," in *Comptes rendus du Congrès de Psychiatrie et Neurologie* (Paris: Masson, 1967), and in works such as those of Algirdas J. Greismas (1966), Émile Benveniste (1966), and Paul Ricoeur (*Esprit,* May 1967), etc.

22. Or more exactly, in that perspective which causes language to appear as a flood of signs which are borrowed from others and which, so to speak, make love among themselves (to use André Breton's expression) without signifying anything other than themselves, without even a subject and, all in all, without words.

If "histories without words" are signs which are oversaturated with what is signified, in a rebus the sequences of signs are oversaturated with meaninglessness; they are not merely "words without history" or signs which speak only for speaking's sake. For they originate in a *subject* who, when involved in conversation with another person, shows him his own personal being at the same time that he hides it from him.

23. The legal system of the structures of society are derived precisely from this.

24. For it is not the subject, insofar as it is the conscious self, which disappears in the analysis of language, but the unconscious subject that can appear to the conscious self only in the discourse which constitutes this unconscious subject.

25. Our *Traité des Hallucinations* clarifies this thesis.

26. The different psychoanalytic schools have very energetically discussed this problematic, especially with reference to the *Écrits* of Jacques Lacan, who attempts precisely to eliminate from the Unconscious and from psychoanalysis the myth of an "underneath," which would be lost in biology, by substituting an "alongside," which is itself lost in sociology. However strong Lacan's positions might be (reinforced with all the resources of his culture and his reflections), however fundamental might be the interconnection of language and conscious being at the point at which the unconscious *phenomenon*

crops out, for reasons which Ricoeur and, from a different point of view, Politzer have both made clear, it is difficult to attribute the faculty of speaking, which is inherent in the function of conscious being, to the Unconscious—in either its latent or its virtual state. This would be possible only on the condition that all psychical activity be reduced to the level of linguistic models of signs. Perhaps Lacan will understand me better than anyone if I point out that, having devoted the first part of my psychiatric work to attacking Clérambault's mechanistic theory of mental automatism, I now find myself obliged to take sides against the structuralist models, of which he has been the genial architect. These two extreme positions join to reduce man to a geometry or an algebra, which he cannot believe himself to be without becoming delirious.

27. We are now in a better position than above (pp. 320–323) to understand that though the absolute separation of the systems Conscious-Preconscious and the system Unconscious may be convenient and even indispensable for a theory which demands a radical duality within the psychical apparatus, such a separation is incompatible with the dynamics of intersystemic and intersubjective relations, that is, in the last analysis, with the very theory of the constitution of the Unconscious—and with the practice of analysis. The barrier separating them can never be anything more than a penetrable dotted line.

28. On the subject of the analysis of the dream of the Unicorn, Leclaire and Laplanche interpret the myth of the birth of the unconscious—I believe that we could say the Unconscious constituting itself as myth—by considering "that it is a result of the instinctual image becoming ensnared in the net of signs." These "snares" of signs, these more or less fragmentary structures of language appear as the "organizers" of the unconscious.

29. We shall speak later of Paul Ricoeur's conception of the "question of sublimation" (*Freud and Philosophy,* pp. 483–493). In his reflections, which are the most directly in harmony with our own reflection upon the meaning of sublimation as this is conveyed through language, as if caught at the moment of its emergence, Ricoeur denounces the empirical "realism" to which psychoanalysis sometimes seems to be condemned. To be constantly speaking of the "reality" of unconscious phenomena as though they were "more real" than conscious phenomena is to ignore the hierarchy of the real which is implied in any symbolic system. Since it exists functionally as a double meaning, the symbol already contains within itself both its meaning and its interpretation. Interpretation is not merely the recollection of the meaning but is a progressing in the sense of this meaning which occurs through reflection. Interpretation is not limited to the work of hermeneutics. It is also to be found in the structures of symbolic thought. In this it proclaims its openness to the world, its access to reality. Ricoeur prescribes its sense to the symbolic function

in such a way that this sense must be that of passing from the necessity of the *reproductive* function of images in dreaming to its discursive development in reflection, where the symbol becomes the ideal (or motive) of *production* by being refracted in the creation of language (*Freud and Philosophy,* pp. 9–36). This at least seems to be the meaning of Ricoeur's interpretation of the symbol, which at the end of his book led him to find even in Freudian theory this ascending dialectic which is conscious becoming.

30. We use this word in its general sense of a curative "act of becoming conscious" (*"prise de conscience" curatrice*).

31. *GW,* 12, pp. 3–12; *SE,* 17, pp. 137–144.

32. In the *Semaine des Intellectuels catholiques,* 1967.

33. Cf. what Freud wrote on the subject of the superego, in *The Ego and the Id,* Chapter Three.

34. Charles Odier, *Les deux sources inconscientes de la vie morale* (Neuchâtel: La Baconnière, 1947). Other works to consult on this topic are: Charles Baudouin, "De l'instinct à l'esprit," *Études carmélitaines,* 1950; O. Pfister, in *XIIIᵉ Congrès international de Psychanalyse* (Lucerne, 1934); Nuttin, *Psychanalyse et conception spiritualiste* (Louvain, 1950); R. Money-Kyrle, "Psychoanalysis and ethics," *Inter. J. Psychoanal.,* 1952, 33; the supplement to *La Vie spirituelle,* 1952, "Foi, Religion et Psychiatrie" (French translation) (Ed. du Cerf, 1957); Igor A. Caruso, *Psychanalyse und Synthese des Existenz* (Vienna: Herder, 1952); Erich Fromm, *Sigmund Freud and His Mission* (New York: Hayer, 1958); Masserman, *Psychoanalysis and Human Value* (New York: Grüne and Stratton, 1960) (cf. especially C. Redlich's article); Richard Lapierre, *The Freudian Ethic* (New York: Duell, 1961). Many recent works have been devoted to this problem. Two which are especially noteworthy are Ishak Ramsy's "The Place of Values," *International Journal of Psychoanalysis,* 46, 1965, pp. 97–106; and, in the same journal, Racker's article (1966, pp. 63–80).

35. Ricoeur, *Freud and Philosophy,* pp. 457–458.

36. Ibid., pp. 462–465.

37. Jean Hyppolite, *Genèse et structure de la Phenomenologie de l'Esprit de Hegel* (Paris: Aubier, 1946), I, p. 144. English translation: *Genesis and Structure of Hegel's Phenomenology of Spirit,* trans. Samuel Cherniak and John Heckman (Evanston: Northwestern University Press, 1974), p. 149.

38. Ricoeur, *Freud and Philosophy,* pp. 430–483.

39. We have attempted to express this same view in our discussion of the articulation of conscious becoming in and through the mediation of language.

40. Ricoeur, *Freud and Philosophy,* p. 488.

41. In his penetrating critical analysis, Michel Tort (*Temps modernes,* nos. 237 and 238, 1966) is not mistaken concerning the most profound significance of Paul Ricoeur's Freudian interpretation *Freud and Philosophy.* Most especially he has discerned that, as we

have noted above, the cogency or lack of cogency of the antithesis which Ricoeur sets up against Freud lies in the very analysis of the overdetermination of symbols. While recognizing that "from Freud's point of view" the concept of sublimation binds conscious being to its Unconscious, to us it seems more accurate "from Ricoeur's point of view" to say that the manifestation of the Unconscious never occurs unless conscious being declares itself two times—as if to reduce the Unconscious to silence. The first time occurs when the Law declares the prohibition by ceasing to be merely an anonymous or collective law and becomes the law of the very organization of conscious being which is in the process of constituting itself as such. The second occurs when, appearing in speech, the Unconscious hides there until the time it can be accepted and said by the self, which becomes more or less conscious of it. Such is, from our point of view, the manner in which the Unconscious is radically subordinated to the conscious as the very foundation of all human action, that is to say, of all morality.

42. On this subject, the discussion which has been carried on between Jacques Lacan and myself since 1947 has remained an open issue (as he states in his "preliminary question" to any treatment of psychosis, in *La Psychanalyse,* 4, 1958, p. 42). For us, man's being not only could not be understood if it were not for madness; it would not even be man's being if it did not carry madness within it as the limit of his liberty. Madness and existence are opposites, as are death and life.

43. The "madness of men," that of evil, of the evil genius of mankind in its historical and individual vicissitudes, is not exactly the madness of those who are called mad. We have developed this point in our lecture in *Rencontres internationales de Genève* (September 1964).

44. Cf. the *IVᵉ Congrès mondial de Psychiatrie,* held in Madrid in September 1966.

45. Thomas Ssasz, *The Myth of Mental Illness* (New York: Huber, 1962).

46. J.-G. Panti, *Le fou est normal* (Paris: Delachaux-Niestlé, 1956).

47. Michel Foucault, *Folie et Déraison, Histoire naturelle de la folie à l'âge classique* (Paris: Plon, 1961); English translation: *Madness and Civilization: A History of Insanity in the Age of Reason,* trans. Richard Howard (New York: Pantheon, 1965).

48. For, "of course," if mental illnesses are "moral illnesses"in the eyes of a psychiatry which is called "moral" and which naively destroys both psychiatry and morality, this either means nothing or else agrees with what we have been saying, that these illnesses are degradations of the ethical problematics of men whose conscious being is disorganized or is poorly organized—men who obviously do not cease to be men, and who remain always worthy of this name but are impaired in their humanity.

Bibliography

Allport, Gordon W. *Personality*. New York: Holt, 1937.

———. *The Nature of Personality*. Cambridge: Addison-Wesley Press, 1950.

Alquié, Ferdinand. *L'expérience*. Paris: Presses Universitaires de France, 1957.

Auersperg, Prince A. von. "Die coincidential Korinzpondenz als Ausgangsprunkt der psycho-physiologischen. Interpretation des bewusst Erleben und des Bewusstseins." In *Nervenarzt* 25 (1954), pp. 1–11.

Bergson, Henri. *Oeuvres*. Édition du centenaire. Paris: Presses Universitaires de France, 1959.

———. *Creative Evolution*. Translated by Arthur Mitchell. New York: Holt, 1911.

———. *The Creative Mind*. Translated by Mabelle L. Andison. New York: Philosophical Library, 1946.

———. *Matter and Memory*. Translated by Nancy Margaret Paul and W. Scott Palmer. New York: Macmillan, 1912.

———. *Mind-energy*. Translated by H. Wildon Carr. New York: Holt, 1920.

———. *Time and Free Will: An Essay on the Immediate Data of Consciousness*. Translated by F. L. Pogson. New York: Macmillan, 1959.

Binswanger, Ludwig. *Grundformen und Erkenntnis menschlichen Daseins*. Zurich: Niehans, 1953.

Blum, Gerald S. *Psychoanalytic Theories of Personality*. New York: McGraw-Hill, 1953.

Brach, J. *Conscience et connaissance*. Paris: Rivière, 1957.

Brinkmann, D. *Probleme des Unbewussten*. Zurich-Leipzig: Rascher, 1943.

Brunschvig, Léon. *Le progrès de la conscience dans la philosophie occidentale*. Paris: Alcan, 1927.

———. *De la connaissance de soi*. Paris: Alcan, 1931.

Chauchard, Paul. *Les mécanismes cérébraux de la prise de conscience*. Paris: Masson, 1956.

Delacroix, Henri. *Les grandes formes de la vie mentale.* Paris: Alcan, 1934.

Delhomme, Jeanne. *Vie et conscience de la vie. Essai sur Bergson.* Paris: Presses Universitaires de France, 1954.

Dwelshauvers, Georges. *L'inconscient.* Paris: Flammarion, 1916.

Fessard, A. E. "Nervous Integration and Conscious Experience." *Symposium: Brain and Consciousness.* London: Blackwell, 1954.

Filloux, Jean Claude. *La personnalité.* Paris: Presses Universitaires de France, 1957.

"Filosofia della alienazione e analisi essistenziale." Articles by R. Klein, P. F. Cascano, I. Mancini, D. Cargnello, et al. *Archivio di Filosofia.* Padua, 1961.

Foucault, Michel. *The Order of Things (Les mots et les choses).* New York: Pantheon, 1970.

Fraisse, Paul. *The Psychology of Time.* Translated by Jennifer Leith. New York: Harper and Row, 1963.

Freud, Anna. *The Ego and the Mechanisms of Defense.* Rev. ed. New York: International Universities Press, 1966.

Freud, Sigmund. *The Standard Edition of the Complete Psychological Works of Sigmund Freud.* Translated from the German under the general editorship of James Strachey. London: Hogarth Press, 1953–1966.

Grappe, J. *La génèse réciproque. Introduction à la psychologie de Maurice Pradines.* Paris: Presses Universitaires de France, 1949.

Guillaume, Paul. *Psychologie de la forme.* 2nd ed. Paris: Flammarion, 1948.

Guiraud, P. *Psychiatrie générale.* Paris: Le François, 1950.

Gurwitsch, Aron. *The Field of Consciousness.* Pittsburgh: Duquesne University Press, 1964.

Gusdorf, Georges. *La découverte de soi.* Paris: Presses Universitaires de France, 1948.

———. *Mémoire et personne.* Paris: Presses Universitaires de France, 1951.

Hartmann, Nicolai. *Grundzüge einer Metaphysik der Erkenntnis.* Berlin: de Gruyter, 1941.

———. *Zur Grundlegung des Ontologie.* Berlin: de Gruyter, 1935. Cf. R. P. S. Breton. *Le problème de l'être spirituel dans la philosophie de N. Hartmann.* Paris: Vrin, 1960.

Heidegger, Martin. *Being and Time.* Translated by John Macquarrie and Edward Robinson. New York: Harper and Row, 1962.

———. *The Essence of Reasons.* Translated by Terrence Malick. Evanston: Northwestern University Press, 1969.

———. *Was Ist Metaphysik?* Frankfurt am Main: Klostermann, 1949.

Hesnard, Angelo Louis Marie. *La relativité de la conscience de soi.* Paris: Alcan, 1924.

————. *Psychanalyse du lien interhumain.* Paris: Presses Universitaires de France, 1957.

Husserl, Edmund. *Ideas: General Introduction to Pure Phenomenology.* Translated by W. R. Boyce Gibson. New York: Macmillan, 1931. French translation by Paul Ricoeur. Paris: Gallimard, 1950.

Husserl et la pensée moderne. Actes du deuxième Colloque international de phénoménologie. Edited by H. L. von Breda and J. Taminiaux. The Hague: Nijhoff, 1959.

James, William. *The Principles of Psychology.* New York: Holt, 1890.

Janet, Pierre. *L'automatisme psychologique.* Paris: Alcan, 1889.

————. *Évolution psychologique de la personalité.* Paris: Chahine, 1929.

Journées de Bonneval sur l'Inconscient. Edited by Henry Ey. Paris: Desclée de Brouwer, 1966.

Lacan, Jacques. *Écrits.* Paris: Seuil, 1966.

————. *La Psychanalyse.* Paris, 1961.

Lagache, Daniel. "Conscience et structure." *Évolution psychiatrique* 25(1960), pp. 460–513.

Laplanche, Jean and Pontalis, J.-B. *The Language of Psycho-analysis.* Translated by Donald Nicholson-Smith. London: Hogarth Press, 1973.

Lavelle, Louis. *Les puissances du Moi.* Paris: Flammarion, 1948.

Leme-Lopes, R. Symposium on Consciousness, Rio de Janeiro. *Journal Brasileiro di Psiquiatria,* 1961, pp. 341–412.

Lersch, Philip. *Die Aufbau der Persönlichkeit.* 7th ed. Munich: Barth, 1956.

Lubac, Émile. *Les niveaux de conscience et d'inconscience et leurs communications.* Paris: Alcan, 1929.

————. *Présent-conscient et cycles de durée. Le rôle du corps dans la venue sur le présent conscient.* Paris: Alcan, 1936.

MacIntyre, Alasdair C. *The Unconscious: A Conceptual Analysis.* New York: Humanities Press, 1958.

Madinier, G. *Conscience et mouvement.* Paris: Alcan, 1938.

————. *Conscience et signification.* Paris: Presses Universitaires de France, 1953.

————. *Conscience et amour.* 3rd ed. Paris: Presses Universitaires de France, 1962.

Madison, Peter. *Freud's Concept of Repression and Defense, Its Theoretical and Observational Language.* Minneapolis: University of Minnesota Press, 1961.

Marcel, Gabriel. *Being and Having.* Translated by Katherine Farrer. New York: Harper and Row, 1965.

Merleau-Ponty, Maurice. *Phenomenology of Perception.* Translated by Colin Smith. New York: Humanities Press, 1962.

——. *Signs.* Translated by Richard C. McCleary. Evanston: North-western University Press, 1964.

Minkowski, Eugène. *Lived Time: Phenomenological and Psychopa-thological Studies.* Translated by Nancy Metzel. Evanston: North-western University Press, 1970.

Mounier, Emmanuel. *Traité du charactère.* Paris: Seuil, 1947.

Navratil, Maurice. *Les tendances constitutives de la pensée vivante.* Paris: Presses Universitaires de France, 1954.

Nedoncelle, Maurice. *Le réciprocité des consciences.* Paris: Aubier, 1942.

Neumann, Erich. *The Origins and History of Consciousness.* Trans-lated by R. F. C. Hull. New York: Pantheon, 1954.

Piaget, Jean. *The Construction of Reality in the Child.* Translated by Margaret Cook. New York: Basic Books, 1954.

——. *Introduction à l'épistémologie génétique.* Paris: Presses Uni-versitaires de France, 1950.

——. *The Origins of Intelligence in Children.* Translated by Marga-ret Cook. New York: Basic Books, 1954.

——. *Structuralism.* Translated by Chaninah Maschler. New York: Basic Books, 1970.

Piéron, Henri. *De l'actinie à l'homme; études de psychophysiologie comparée.* Paris: Presses Universitaires de France, 1958–1959.

Pontalis, J.-B. *Après Freud.* Paris: Julliard, 1965.

Pradines, Maurice. *Traité de psychologie.* Paris: Presses Univer-sitaires de France, 1958.

Ricoeur, Paul. *The Philosophy of Will.* Part One. *Freedom and Nature: The Voluntary and the Involuntary.* Translated by Erazim V. Kohak. Evanston: Northwestern University Press, 1966.

Part Two. *Finitude et culpabilité.* Paris: Aubier, 1960.

Part Two. Book One. *Fallible Man.* Translated by Charles Kelbley. Chicago: Regnery, 1965.

——. *Freud and Philosophy: An Essay on Interpretation.* Translated by Denis Savage. New Haven: Yale University Press, 1970.

Rothacker, Erich. *Die Schichten der Persönlichkeit.* Leipzig: Barth, 1938.

Ruyer, Raymond. *Esquisse d'une philosophie de la structure.* Paris: Alcan, 1930.

——. *La conscience et le corps.* Paris: Alcan, 1937.

——. *Philosophie de la valeur.* Paris: Colin, 1938.

——. *La cybernétique et l'origine de l'information.* Paris: Flamma-rion, 1954.

Sartre, Jean-Paul. *The Transcendence of the Ego.* Translated by For-rest Williams and Robert Kirkpatrick. New York: Noonday Press, 1957.

——. *L'imaginaire.* Paris: Gallimard, 1940.

———. *Being and Nothingness.* Translated by Hazel E. Barnes. New York: Philosophical Library, 1956.
Schilder, Paul. *The Image and Appearance of the Human Body: Studies in the Constructive Energies of the Psyche.* New York: International Universities Press, 1950.
———. *Selbstbewusstsein und Persönlichbewusste.* Berlin: Springer, 1914.
Spranger, Edward. *Die Ursichten des Wircklichkeitsbewusstsein,* 1934.
Staub, H. and Tholen, H. *Bewusstseinstörungen.* Symposium de Saint-Moritz. Stuttgart: Thieme, 1961.
Störring, G. E. *Besinnung und Bewusstsein.* Stuttgart: Thieme, 1953.
Teilhard de Chardin, Pierre. *The Phenomenon of Man.* Translated by Bernard Wall. New York: Harper, 1960.
Thomae, Hans. "Das Bewusstseinsproblem in der modernen Psychologie." *Nervenarzt,* 33(1962), p. 477.
Waelhens, Alphonse de. *La philosophie de Martin Heidegger.* Louvain: Institut supérieur de philosophie, 1942; 3rd ed., 1948.
Weizsäcker, Viktor von. *Der Gestaltkreis.* 3rd ed. Stuttgart: Thieme, 1947.
Zutt, J. "Was lernen wir aus den Bewusstseinstörungen über das Bewusstsein." *Nervenarzt,* 33(1962), p. 483.
———. *Auf dem Wege zu einer anthropologischen Psychiatrie.* Heidelberg: Springer, 1963.

NEUROBIOLOGICAL WORKS

General Works on the Brain and Consciousness

Blanc, Claude. "Inconscient, Conscience et Neurobiologie." In *L'Inconscient.* Henri Ey, ed. Paris: Desclée de Brouwer, 1966.
Böring, Edward G. *The Physical Dimensions of Consciousness.* New York: The Century Co., 1933.
Brown, Jason W. *Mind, Brain and Consciousness: The Neuropsychology of Cognition.* New York: Academic Press, 1977.
Chauchard, Paul. *The Brain.* Translated by David Noakes. New York: Grove Press, 1962.
———. *Les mécanismes cérébraux de la prise de conscience.* Paris: Masson, 1956.
Ebbecke. *Des Bewusstsein in entwicklungsgeschichtlicher Betrachtung.* Stuttgart, 1959.
Eccles, Sir John C. *The Neurophysiological Basis of Mind.* Oxford: Clarendon Press, 1953.
———. *Brain Mechanisms and Consciousness.* Oxford: Clarendon Press, 1954.

————. *The Understanding of the Brain.* New York: McGraw, 1973. 2d ed., 1977.

Ey, Henri. "Structure des psychoses aiguës et Déstructuration de la Conscience." In *Études psychiatriques,* Vol. 3. Paris: Desclée de Brouwer, 1954. (See Notes to 1st Preface for complete contents of *Études psychiatriques.*)

————. "Disorders of Consciousness." In *Handbook of Clinical Neurology.* Ed. P. J. Vinken and G. W. Bruyn, 10 vols. Amsterdam and New York: North Holland Publishing Company. Vol. II, pp. 112–136.

————. "Rapport au IVᵉ Congrès mondial de Psychiatrie." Madrid, 1966.

————. Des idées de Hughlings Jackson à un modèle organo-dynamique en Psychiatrie. Toulouse: Privat, 1975.

Globus, Gordon, et al., eds. *Consciousness and the Brain: A Scientific and Philosophical Inquiry.* New York: Plenum, 1976.

Jackson, John Hughlings. *Selected Writings.* New York: Basic Books, 1958.

Kuhlenbeck, Hartwig. *Brain and Consciousness.* New York: Karger, 1957.

————. *Mind and Matter.* New York: Karger, 1961.

Lhermitte, J. *Cerveau et pensée.* Paris, 1951.

Luria, Aleksandr R. *Higher Cortical Functions in Man.* New York: Basic Books, 1966.

Macy Foundation. Symposia on the Problems of Consciousness, 1950–1954.

Piéron, Henri. *De l'actinie à l'homme.* Paris: Presses Universitaires de France, 1958–1959.

Ruyer, Raymond. *La conscience et le corps.* Paris: Alcan, 1937.

Schlesinger, Benno. *Higher Cerebral Functions and Their Clinical Disorders.* New York: Grüne, 1961.

Semon, Richard. *Bewusstsein und Gehirnprozess.* Wiesbaden, 1920.

Vizidi, R., and Bietti, C. *Il problemas della conscienzia in neuropsichiatria.* Pisa, 1966.

Symposia on Higher Nervous Functions

The Physical Basis of Mind. Peter Laslett, ed. Oxford: Blackwell, 1950.

Colloque de Marseille. *Conditionnement et activité E.E.G.* Paris: Masson, 1955.

IᵉʳCongrès des Sciences neurologiques, Brussels, 1957. *Neurologie et Troubles de la conscience.* Paris: Masson, 1957.

The Brain and Human Behavior. Baltimore: Williams and Wilkins, 1958.

Amsterdam Symposium, *Structure and Function of the Cerebral Cortex,* 1959.

The Moscow Colloquium on Electroencephalography of Higher Nervous Activity. Electroencephalography and Clinical Neurophysiology, Supplement 13 (1960).

Symposium Brain Mechanisms and Learning. J. F. Delafresnaye, ed. Springfield, Ill.: Thomas, 1961.

Symposium, Pontifical Academy of Science. *Brain and Conscious Experience.* John C. Eccles, ed. New York: Springer-Verlag, 1966.

Fundamental Works on Sleep and Waking

Kleitman, Nathaniel. *Sleep and Wakefulness.* Chicago: University of Chicago Press, 1939; rev. and enl. ed., 1963.

Dement, William and Kleitman, Nathaniel. "Cyclic Variations in EEG During Sleep." *Electroencephalography and Clinical Neurophysiology,* 9(1957), pp. 673–690.

Henry Ford Symposium, *The Reticular Formation of the Brain.* Boston: Little, Brown, 1958.

Jouvet, M. *Biologie médicale,* 1960, pp. 282–360.

———. *Archives italiennes de Biologie,* 100(1962), pp. 125–206.

Bremer, Frederic. *Archives suisses neur. psych.,* 86(1960), pp. 34–48.

Ciba Foundation Symposium, *The Nature of Sleep.* G. W. W. Wolstenholme and Maeve O'Connor, eds. Boston: Little, Brown and Co., 1960.

Oswald, Ian. *Sleeping and Waking.* New York: Elsevier, 1962.

———. *Le sommeil de nuit normal et pathologique.* (Société E.E.G. de Neurophysiologie française) Paris: Masson, 1965.

Kety, S. S., Evarts, E. V., and Williams, H. *Sleep and Altered States of Consciousness.* New York: Williams, 1967.

Name Index

433

Subject Index

abstract thought, 196–199, 350
accommodation, 238–239, 241
action, and field of consciousness, 110
activation, cortical, 143–145
actuality
   and brain organization, 191–199
   and consciousness, 30–32
   of lived experience, 59–199, 297–299
   in mental disorders, 59–85
affective impressions, 298
affectivity
   and brain, 163
   and consciousness, 10–12, 15
afferent system, 129, 143–148, 156–159
affirmation of the Unconscious, 304–310
agencies, Freudian, 245, 361–364
alienation
   conscious being as disorganization of, 384–388
   and lack of self-consciousness, 337
   of the self, 207–211, 222–225
   use of word, 221n
allocortex, 158–159
alpha rhythm and alpha waves, 167, 173, 175, 189
alteration of the self, 107–211
American Handbook of Psychiatry, 149
Ammon's horn, 156–157, 172, 173
amygdaloid system, 158–161, 171, 186
Anglo-Saxon personology, 258–260
Anglo-Saxon psychology, 234–235, 242
animal sensibility, 8–9, 205, 270, 393–394
anthropology
   contemporary, 24
   existential, 52
   personality theories, 261–266
aphasia, 17, 131–132
apparition, 68–70
arousal, cortical, 166–172, 177, 189, 195
assimilation, 238–239, 241
association centers of brain, 130–132
association nuclei, 150
associationist psychology, 307
attention, 19–20, 40, 87
auditory region of brain, 128
Aufbau der Person, 260
autistic self, 224–225
autochthonous organization, 27–29
autoconstruction of the self, 229–291
   personality theories, 231–266
   structural organization, 267–291

autonomy of the self, 277, 335–337
awakening, 176–182, 194–195
axiology of the self, 279–281

"becoming conscious," 26, 333, 366–379
"becoming unconscious," 369–370
behaviorism
   "molar," 34
   molecular, 235
   negation of self in, 230
being, conscious. *See* conscious being
being and having, 29, 32, 51, 74, 119, 212, 291, 313
Being and Nothingness, 204, 265–266, 345
Being and Time, 52
being-for-itself, 266, 303, 345, 352
being-in-the-world, 53
beliefs, 274, 284
bestowal of sense, 12, 46, 101
Beyond the Pleasure Principle, 244, 247, 316, 318, 324, 326, 376
bioconsciousness, 7–9
biology. *See* neurobiology
biotypologies, 232–233
body
   consciousness' relation to, 49–51
   image in mental disorders, 74–78
   in lived space, 105–106
   and psychical being, 341–342
   Self's relation to, 270–272, 281–282
brain, 122–199
   autonomy, 124
   brainstem, 125, 141–149
   centrencephalic system, 141–163
   cerebral cortex, 126–141
   consciousness' relation to, 193–199
   disorganizations of, 163–199
   in epileptic state, 182–187
   fallacy of "centers" in, 187–188
   and field of consciousness, 187–199
   mathematical-logical structure of, 343
   organization, 123–124, 187–199
   patterning of activity of, 188–191
   rhinencephalon, 154–163
   thalamus, 149–154
   in wakefulness, 163–172
   see also neurobiology
brain lesions, 75, 161–165, 176–182
Brain Mechanisms and Learning, 140
brain pathology, 74

438

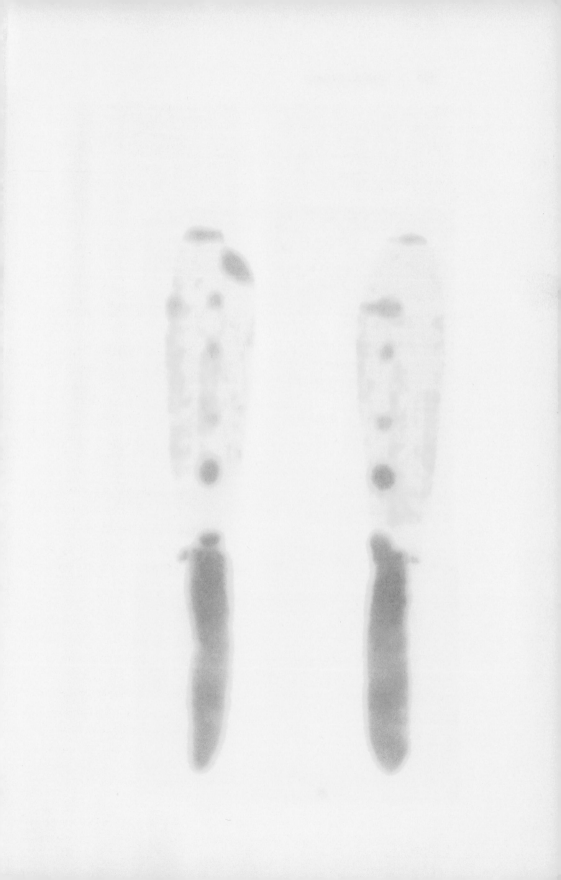

DATE DUE

GAYLORD   PRINTED IN U.S.A.